since 1884

To My Mother and Father

Socialism in Britain since 1884

John Callaghan

Basil Blackwell

British Library Cataloguing in Publication Data

A CIP catalogue record for this book is available from the British Library.

Library of Congress Cataloging in Publication Data

Callaghan, John (John T.)
Socialism in Britain since 1884 / John Callaghan.
p.   cm.
Includes bibliographical references.
ISBN 0–631–16471–5 – ISBN 0–631–16472–3 (pbk.)
1. Socialism–Great Britain–History.   I. Title.
HX241.5.C35   1990
335′.00941–dc20   89–39690
                                                                 CIP

Typeset in 9½/11½ pt Times
by Colset Private Limited, Singapore
Printed in Great Britain by T.J. Press Ltd, Padstow

Contents

Acknowledgements

I would like to thank David Coates, Martin Durham, Sue Martin, Annemarie McMorrow, and an anonymous reader whose help was enlisted by Sean Magee at Blackwell's, for their valuable advice and suggestions. The final text, needless to say, is entirely my own responsibility.

JC

List of Abbreviations

AES	Alternative Economic Strategy
ASE	Amalgamated Society of Engineers
ASRS	Amalgamated Society of Railway Servants
BAIU	British Advocates of Industrial Unionism
BSP	British Socialist Party
CGT	Confederation Générale du Travail
CLP	Constituency Labour Party
CLPD	Campaign for Labour Party Democracy
CND	Campaign for Nuclear Disarmament
COMISCO	Committee for an International Socialist Conference
CP	Communist Party
CPGB	Communist Party of Great Britain
CPSU	Communist Party of the Soviet Union
EEC	European Economic Community
ELAS	National Liberation Army of Greece
ETU	Electricians' Trade Union
GMWU	General and Municipal Workers' Union
GPU	Gosudarstvenoye Politicheskoye Upravleniye (Soviet Secret Police, forerunner of the KGB)
ILP	Independent Labour Party
IMF	International Monetary Fund
IMG	International Marxist Group
IS	International Socialists
IWW	Industrial Workers of the World
LCC	Labour Co-ordinating Committee
LCDTU	Liaison Committee for the Defence of Trade Unions
LPACR	*Labour Party Annual Conference Report*
LRC	Labour Representation Committee
NEB	National Enterprise Board
NEC	National Executive Committee
NGL	National Guilds League
NSSWCM	National Shop Stewards' and Workers' Committee Movement

NUR	National Union of Railwaymen
NUWCM	National Unemployed Workers' Committee Movement
NLF	National Liberation Front (Vietnam)
OECD	Organization for Economic Co-operation and Development
PLP	Parliamentary Labour Party
PCF	Partie Communiste Français
POUM	Partido Obrero de Unificación Marxista
SDF	Social Democratic Federation (previously Democratic Federation)
SDP	Social Democratic Party
SL	Socialist League
SLL	Socialist Labour League
SLP	Socialist Labour Party
STUC	Scottish Trades Union Congress
SWP	Socialist Workers' Party
TGWU	Transport and General Workers' Union
TUC	Trades Union Congress
UDC	Union of Democratic Control
VSC	Vietnam Solidarity Campaign
WFTU	World Federation of Trade Unions
WSF	Workers' Socialist Federation

1

Introduction

The focus of this book is on socialist organizations in Britain since the 1880s; it sets out to examine the versions of socialist ideology which have been promoted, the struggles these organizations have engaged in and the competing strategies and tactics of the movement. No account of socialist ideas and the battle between different conceptions of socialism can ignore the much broader canvas of class and other conflicts within which they are set, through which they are formed and on which they seek to leave their stamp; and it is not my intention to do so here. Nevertheless it is impossible to do justice to all of these aspects of the experience of socialism in Britain in a single volume, even if a suitable polymath could be found to attempt it (which I doubt). Consequently it is necessary to be highly selective. On complex issues such as the impact of the class struggles of 1910–21 on socialist consciousness within the working class, for example, I have relied on the judgement of labour historians who have studied the period in detail, as I have on other questions beyond the scope of my own research. Some important problems have been largely excluded from the discussion altogether, including perhaps the most fundamental of all – the conservatism of the British working class during the period under consideration. I trust nevertheless that the text will make clear that I do not assume a mass following for socialism which was periodically betrayed by corrupt leaders (although it is always possible to find fault with leaders).

Indeed, one reason for focusing on the ideologies and politics of the socialist movement is precisely the recognition of the fact that there was no ready-made mass following for the socialists and if one was to be created the efforts of the socialists themselves could count for a great deal. After all, ideology is an important terrain of political contestation itself as British politics in the 1980s has reminded us. If Gramsci is most often cited by modern Marxists in support of this contention, it should not be taken to mean that Marx or Lenin – both of whom subjected the ideas of other socialists to minute criticism – denied it. Socialists of all descriptions have recognized that political parties do not merely express class and other interests but also seek to shape them; and though they do this in a variety of ways and under definite constraints, as we shall see, ideological struggle is an essential part of the process. Indeed for Gramsci the socialist party needed to be the crucible in which hegemonic values were forged and also the main active element in the construction of intellectual, moral, and political hegemony before a socialist society could be created.[1] By the time socialist organizations were formed in the 1880s the conditions for such an ambitious project in Britain were extremely adverse.

In the first half of the nineteenth century the Chartist Movement emerged as the first class-conscious 'party' of the working class developing a critique of capitalism, albeit in the language of radical democracy rather than socialism, and dangerous revolutionary currents which were defeated in different parts of the country during 1839–40, 1842 and 1848. This was a period in which the British bourgeoisie relied on repression – whether in the form of the New Poor Law of 1834, the Master and Servant Acts, or the use of armed force – to help it create the best conditions for capital accumulation. By the middle of the century a near-perfect labour market had been created for these purposes and a period of capitalist expansion began which lasted until the 1870s. This period of prosperity permitted certain sections of the working class to take advantage of labour shortages while the mass of labourers remained at subsistence level. The minority – such as fitters and turners in engineering and senior minders in cotton spinning – benefited from rising living standards and greater regularity of employment. It seems likely then that the mellowing of class relations in the third quarter of the nineteenth century and the rapid fading of Chartism owed something to the fact that in the face of capitalist expansion the idea took hold that improvements could be extracted from a system which had demonstrated its permanence. A minority of workers were able to bargain over wages and encouraged by experience to believe that it was possible to obtain a fair day's pay for a fair day's work while many others became habituated to the relations of industrial wage labour. Under the circumstances prevailing after 1850 the propertied classes themselves became more optimistic about the prospects for the accommodation of labour. By the mid-1870s trade unions seemed to be on a secure legal footing and the 1867 Reform Act had enfranchised the better-off working men. The idea that reforms could be extracted from the system to deal with particular evils was also given great plausibility by the Ten Hours Act which even Marx hailed as a victory for the political economy of labour. Thus the fundamental objections to capitalism raised by Chartism were largely forgotten as the more able workers turned to self-help and improvement through their unions, co-operatives and friendly societies. By 1867 it was possible for the Liberal Party to represent the interests of these workers with a diluted version of the radicalism of earlier, more tumultous times. Ethnic divisions, following the influx of Irish labour after the famine of 1845, may also have made an independent working-class politics more difficult to achieve. Certainly in the cotton districts, a former stronghold of Chartism, the Tories had established a mass base around the slogan of 'No Popery' by the late 1860s and ethnic divisions helped to attach workers 'more firmly to the framework of bourgeois politics and bourgeois political control'.[2]

Class positions were further obscured in Victorian Britain by the high visibility of landowners in Parliament and the state which gave the appearance of aristocratic rule and enabled the industrial bourgeoisie to represent itself as the champion of the popular forces and the enemy of privilege. Much was made by bourgeois intellectuals of the landlord-parasites 'growing richer, as it were, in their sleep, without working, risking or economising'.[3] It was a useful ideological asset to be able to make moral distinctions in this way between types of wealth and to represent the profits of the industrial capitalists as the earned rather than the unearned increment generated by productive activity that was beneficial to all. Such rhetoric served to obfuscate class relations and helped the Liberal Party to rally working-class support behind it into the twentieth century. In general the Liberal Party, the party of the industrial bourgeoisie, represented itself as the party of progress and the productive classes. The great coalition gathered around it by the 1870s included the champions of political reform, temperance, charitable works, improvement through education, respectability and self-help. Liberal intellectuals developed an interest in the moral and intellectual improvement of the people and the amelioration of their conditions of life. Their 'earnest benevolence' took 'an ostentatiously high-minded and even 'spiritual' approach to the task of elevating and instructing the working classes'.[4] Religion and education were specifically seen as cures for social unrest which was explained in terms of ignorance, immorality and the breakdown of the family.[5]

The 'laws' of political economy were of course the ultimate justification for the *status quo* but even political economy was sanctified by an equally pervasive evangelism. And here, in religion, was another of the cords which bound large sections of the working class to the Liberal Party, the party of Nonconformity, and served to promote individualistic and moralistic explanations of the social world. Though none of these elements of bourgeois ideology could hope to deliver the working class bound and gagged – since there was space within them for the prosecution of the claims of labour – a socialist challenge to the dominant order would have to furnish alternatives to all of them if, as the socialists of the 1880s and 1890s believed, a completely new society was to replace capitalism. It was the discrepancy between the size of this task and the tiny forces prepared to undertake it in the 1870s which accounts for the note of despair in Marx and Engels' comments on the British situation. In 1878 Marx described the working class as 'the tail of the "great Liberal party"', that is of its oppressors the capitalists', and the following year Engels denied that any 'real labour movement in the Contintental sense' existed in Britain. Instead the unions had been 'hopelessly describing a narrow circle of strikes for higher wages and shorter hours not . . . as an expedient or means of propaganda and organization but as the ultimate goal'.[6]

Trade union membership stood at around half a million by the mid-1870s when the unions were put on a legal basis. These members were overwhelmingly concentrated in a handful of industries, especially coal and cotton, in organizations which 'usually rested upon systematic attempts by small groups of relatively privileged workers to defend their status against any encroachments by the mass of the labouring poor'.[7] It was one way of adapting to an economic system whose permanence was no longer seriously questioned. By means of long apprenticeships workers in such industries as engineering, printing and building sought to differentiate themselves from the majority who were subject to ruthless labour markets. In the process these craft unions had become 'impervious to socialism'.[8] Although such unions were capable of waging militant struggles against the employers, many of whom were Liberals, they believed that the 'interests of labour' could best be promoted in the parliamentary arena through the agency of the Liberal Party. In 1874 two trade-union-sponsored MPs were elected to Parliament as Liberals and so inaugurated the Lib-Lab phase of trade union politics which stood as a formidable barrier in the way of both socialism and independent working-class representation for the rest of the century. Of course the 1867 Reform Act enfranchised at best only 30 per cent of adult males in working-class constituencies, and soon after it was introduced electoral costs were massively increased, thus reinforcing the financial power of the bourgeois parties. Nevertheless the unions were also ideologically dependent on the Liberals and the nature of working-class political consciousness generally can be gauged from the fact that the question of social reform dominated none of the general elections during the last thirty years of the century.[9]

The entry of the working class into British politics nevertheless posed a variety of problems for the propertied classes. The extension of the franchise in 1867 and 1884 generated some apprehension and stimulated the concern for the 'condition of the people' which was already present. Somehow, it was felt, the mob had to be cultivated and by the 1880s and 1890s, according to Beatrice Webb, the two great controversies that gave rise to 'perpetual argument' within the ruling class were the problem of mass poverty and the practicability and desirability of political democracy and trade unionism as a means of redressing the grievances of the people.[10] This intellectual ferment did not arise in response to popular agitations; the slum denizens lived in 'brutalised apathy' and the unions were converted to the 'administrative nihilism' of Cobden and Bright. The reformist intelligentsia was moved, in the first place, by ethical considerations. As products, as most of them were, of the world of Victorian evangelism reformist politics was for these people closely related to philanthropy. Charitable foundations proliferated after the onset of the Great Depression and especially in the 1880s when industrial production fell and unemployment became a problem even among the minority of trade unionists. This was the decade when the modern idea of 'unemployment' and 'unemployed' came into common usage and when some of the facts about mass poverty were exposed by social investigators. The growing socialist agitation and occasional riots no doubt also helped to concentrate many minds – especially in London where the large number of casual workers experienced particularly severe distress.

In the last two decades of the century a significant body of opinion within the intelligentsia, impressed by these problems and conscious of the terrible waste involved, moved towards advocacy of greater state intervention. The evangelism of this class helps to explain not just why so many of them were motivated to do something on behalf of the people but also why so few of them defected to the socialist camp. Having been raised with an ethic of service and selflessness and given a sense of mission and solidarity, most of these reformers could satisfy their need for action through charitable works and, when these proved insufficient, by calls for scientific analysis of social problems and appropriate state action. The old individualism may have been in decay but liberalism was able to adapt. John Stuart Mill had already acknowledged, in his *Principles of Political Economy*, which went through successive editions after 1848, that: 'there is scarcely anything really important to the general interest, which it may not be desirable or even necessary that the government should take upon itself, not because private individuals cannot effectually perform it, but because they will not'.[11]

Mill was influenced by the Positivism of Auguste Comte, as well as the utilitarian conviction that an enlightened minority could act in the general interest; and an influential group of English Positivists, led by Frederic Harrison and Edward Beesley, promoted Comte's philosophical system in Britain and thereby helped to fill the gap, felt by many bourgeois intellectuals, which was left by Christianity as it retreated before the advance of Darwinism and its own inability to address the poverty and degradation of the people. The new faith stressed the value of scientific investigation of human societies in helping to dissolve the antagonisms to be found within them. As we shall see, this was a conviction which inspired a whole generation of social reformers in the last quarter of the nineteenth century and motivated the leaders of Fabian socialism.

Social reform was also the surrogate faith which T. H. Green, the Oxford philosopher, offered his followers.[12] Green, who was very influential among the New Liberals, was another social theorist who thought in terms of 'les industriels' against the old landed interests and who was moved to question traditional liberal thought because of the persistence of mass poverty. While Green was never a collectivist and was remarkably uncritical of capitalism as a system, his philosophy was ambiguous enough to appeal to reformers of every kind. His idea of positive freedom – that is, that which tends to promote the individual's self-realization – was read as a justification for state action by those who understood that formal individual liberty could not become a reality unless the means for its attainment were more widely and more equitably distributed. The highest place in Green's moral hierarchy was occupied by the social reformer, which was another reason for his influence

after 1880 when circumstances drove many members of the liberal intelligentsia to seek a new faith in the quest to moralize the masses. This paternalistic moralism, then, was what gave such force to the otherwise imprecise
formula for state action in the thought of Victorian reformers like Green and
Arnold Toynbee: 'they offered in social reform an outlet to the religious
aspirations of their generation through self-sacrifice and philanthrophy.'[13]

The fact that spokesmen for the working class were to be found within the
propertied classes and that the religious sentiments which informed their ideas
found a ready following within the labour movement owes much to the fact
that the classes in Britain were not separated, as on the European continent,
by a great gulf in religious affiliations. The great variety of Nonconformist
sects and free churches had a mass working-class following, especially outside
London, as well as middle-class devotees. To be critical of the Establishment,
the ruling class and the Church of England did not mean, therefore, to be
anti-clerical. Thus it was more common for radical criticisms of the existing
order to be contained within that evangelical social ethic of reformers such as
Green and his followers than for it to break free of this influence. Moral
reform and regeneration was not only the chief concern of the middle-class
missionaries of the Charity Organisation Society and the London Ethical
Society, with their overriding concern to preserve the individual's sense of
responsibility and strengthen his 'character'; it also informed the most
popular variety of socialism – the ethical socialism of the Independent
Labour Party in the 1890s. Instead of class struggle this socialist idiom was
characterized by an emphasis on brotherhood, fraternity, co-operation and
mutual obligation; there was no suggestion of destroying the existing state as
an instrument of class oppression, but rather the same vague idea as contained
in the New Liberalism that the proper function of the state was precisely to
reconcile the clash of opposed interests.

While a powerful critique of the ugliness, squalor and vulgar materialism of
Victorian capitalism was developed – in the writings of critics such as Carlyle
and Ruskin – which converted many intellectuals and workers to socialism,
no great body of the intelligentsia was detached from the ruling class in the
manner expected by Marx and Engels. The middle class, far from dispossess-
ing the aristocracy of its power, contributed to the preservation of its traditional social and political forms. Professional service became for middle-
class morality the equivalent of *noblesse oblige* and the new public schools
provided an appropriate training in this ethic. Yet as the facts of British
inertia in politics and society mounted and evidence of its grave social and
economic problems was brought to light, attempts were made to improve
national efficiency.

Joseph Chamberlain's 'unauthorized' Radical programme, launched in
January 1885, was an attempt to capture the working-class voter and to
galvanize the coalition of causes and special interests which comprised the
Liberal Party around reforms such as manhood suffrage, the end of plural
voting, the direct representation of working men, payment of Members of

Parliament, a smallholdings policy, free elementary education and 'social' taxation. To some extent this was an attempt to transfer into national politics the lessons of Birmingham municipal affairs. As early as the 1860s the Birmingham elite of dissenting Radicals had developed a self-conscious civic gospel which under Chamberlain's mayoralty in the mid-1870s produced a programme of municipal provision of gas, water, street lighting, slum clearance and the construction of libraries, parks and shops.[14] Chamberlain promoted the idea that it was the right of the community to concern itself with communal welfare by owning and controlling local assets and using such resources to improve the working class. Between 1874 and 1880 Chamberlain sought to bring the whole of Radicalism behind this populist ideology. But when the Liberals won the general election in 1880 Gladstone proved that he was just as determined to turn Liberal attention away from the working class and social reform as Chamberlain had been to construct an alliance around these issues. The problem for Liberalism was that the Gladstonian diet of democratic internationalism was quite unable to make the social question go away, and Gladstone's government even disappointed its supporters when the government resorted to coercion in Ireland and the repression of nationalism in Egypt.

Chamberlain's initiative was further proof of the decay of the conventional Liberal apologia for doing nothing about the condition of the people. Bourgeois opinion had tried to persuade itself that just as the wage-earners were helpless to regulate wages, the employers were constrained to act in a predetermined way by the logic of the capitalist system, based as this was on a competitive struggle for maximization of profits; the rich, it was reasoned, would only make the problem of poverty worse if they indulged themselves in bestowing charity upon the poor. Thus Parliament's role was accordingly greatly circumscribed by this reasoning. But by the 1880s a new temper was evident among a significant proportion of educated opinion, impatient of this *a priori* logic and persuaded that real progress could be made once the facts of the situation were fully known. Charles Booth's massive investigation of the *Life and Labour of the People in London* was motivated by these considerations and when the first volume appeared in 1889 it was able to show in impressive detail that 35 per cent of Tower Hamlets' 900,000 residents were in a condition of 'poverty sinking into want'.

Booth's study went against the prevailing idea that the dangerous classes – the criminals, homeless, unemployable and feckless, in short, 'the hordes of barbarians' whom respectable society feared would one day overwhelm it – were not so large as previously supposed. The *Pall Mall Gazette* at first found Booth guilty of making 'too much like a complacent and comforting bourgeois statement of the situation', but as his study unfolded it helped to persuade the middle class that the East End represented a social problem rather than a political threat.[15] The House of Lords Select Committee inquiry on the 'sweating system' between 1888 and 1890 provided another window on working-class conditions, as did the matchgirls' strike at Bryant and May in

1888 which the socialist Annie Besant did much to publicize in the journal *The Link*. Throughout the 1880s the evidence mounted to demonstrate that at the heart of the Empire the imperial race was physically and mentally deformed by the conditions of its existence. Though all middle-class debate was informed by notions of the supposed biological and ecological origins of mass poverty, it nevertheless played some part in strengthening the case for state action to deal with the situation.

Even if the degeneration of the working class was held to derive from life in the slums and the breeding between morally depraved and physically and mentally defective slum-dwellers, society could hardly be content with a policy of *laissez-faire*. The requirements of efficient war-making alone demanded action to improve the health and vitality of the masses, as was graphically revealed during the Boer War when the 'spectre of physical deterioration and racial degeneration' on a large scale was revealed by the numbers of would-be recruits who failed to pass the army's medical test. By that time Fabians, Liberal Imperialists under Lord Rosebery's leadership, and Chamberlain's wing of the Conservative Party seemed set to launch a National Efficiency Party dedicated to promoting collectivist policies designed to stop the economic, social and military rot which they jointly attributed to Gladstonian Liberalism. For as Rosebery put it: 'An Empire such as ours requires as its first condition an imperial race, a race vigorous and industrious and intrepid. In the rookeries and slums which still survive an imperial race cannot be reared.'[16]

The fact that the most sophisticated branch of bourgeois ideology itself – political economy or economic science as it began to be known – could no longer justify the gap between rich and poor naturally strengthened the case of the reformers. In fact economists such as Alfred Marshall had always been prepared to support measures for the redistribution of income and wealth while displaying far less enthusiasm for state ownership of industry or state regulation of wealth production.[17] Nevertheless there were very few defenders of crude *laissez-faire* among the economists, and even Marshall favoured state intervention where community interest conflicted with that of individuals. Others were prepared to go further – notably New Liberals such as J. A. Hobson whose *Problems of Poverty* (1891) was permeated by the language of social efficiency and proposals for the kind of state intervention by which to achieve it. Two years earlier Hobson had achieved a lasting notoriety in established economic circles by arguing that periodic slumps were the result of excessive saving by the rich and insufficient purchasing power on the part of the mass of the poor; once again the failure of the free market was exposed and state action required to correct the maldistribution of incomes.[18] This apparently organic disorder of 'underconsumption' was to be a recurring motif in the critique of capitalism in socialist as well as liberal thought.

These trends towards collectivism in liberal thought are important for a number of reasons, not least because they informed the thinking of many of the leaders of the socialists. The socialist revival did not take place in an increasingly polarized society; it was not the result of a profound rupture with previous modes of thought and organization. Before the creation of the Labour Party the socialists were confined to small, divided groups while the minority of organized workers remained politically wedded to Liberalism. The mass of the working class was outside political activity altogether. These circumstances were more propitious to the New Liberalism than to the emergence of a challenge to the hegemonic order. This is what the Bolshevik Theodore Rothstein drew attention to when he pointed out that:

As against the position of the working class of other countries in similar circumstances, the English proletariat did not find itself isolated but became the centre of attention of bourgeois reformers who quite correctly realised their mission [and] built a moral bridge between them and the capitalist class, enabled them to reorganise upon a new platform, compelled the capitalist class to yield a little to the workers' demands in regard to wages, working hours, and working conditions in general.[19]

This formulation of the question makes the whole process sound conspiratorial, when in fact the strength of the reformist position derived from the absence of a mass following for fundamental change due, in part, to the policy of concessions from above at a time when the wealth and power of the ruling class was still growing. The varieties of socialism which prospered best, under these circumstances, were those which emphasized gradual reforms within the existing political and, wider imperial, system. If we turn now to a more detailed study of the socialists themselves we can examine the reform strategies and programmes they adopted as well as the periodic challenges to this dominant reformism from more radical varieties of socialism.

2

The Marxists

In 1875 Marx's influence in the German socialist movement seemed to become dominant when the German Working-Men's Association, founded by the national state socialist Ferdinand Lassalle, joined the Social Democratic Working-Men's Party led by Marx's disciples Auguste Bebel and Wilhelm Liebknecht. In France the development of a socialist, independent working-class political activity was also begun in earnest in the 1870s. By contrast, socialism in Britain was confined to the foreign refugees' clubs which appeared after the revolutions of 1848 and which received a new lease of life after the collapse of the Paris Commune in 1870. There were some British socialists, of course, survivors of the Owenite and Chartist agitations, some of whom found their way into Marx's International Working Men's Association in the early 1870s, as well as a small Christian Socialist campaign with Charles Kingsley as its best-known protagonist, which fizzled out at about the same time. But the big working-class organizations were remote from these socialist activities. The co-operative movement 'had cut its Socialist connections by the 1860s'[1] and between 1860 and 1880 not a single prominent leader of a trade union called himself a socialist. Nor was there a substantial socialist intelligentsia which could intervene, Leninist fashion, in working-class disputes, injecting socialist consciousness in the process. Britain's relatively liberal institutions seemed to blunt the edge of working-class protest and may help to explain why collective bargaining in particular did not lead to general intransigence and a radical socialist consciousness.[2]

Social criticism in the 1860s and 1870s was best expressed by the agitation for land reform which could draw on a tradition of hostility to landlords and the Ricardian critique of rent. J. S. Mill fashioned a theory of the 'unearned increment' to show how such rents could provide the main source of fiscal revenues and the nationalization of rents was taken up by the Scottish reformer, Patrick E. Dove, who proposed a Single Tax scheme on this basis.[3] The nearest to a socialist organization in Britain by the late 1860s was the short-lived Land and Labour League which was set up by members of the First International to agitate for land nationalization and independent working-class politics, around a programme of compulsory, secular education, a property tax, reductions in the hours of labour, equal electoral rights and payment of Members of Parliament. Land reformers, social reformers and members of the First International also co-operated in the Land Tenure Reform Association which was created, largely under J. S. Mill's influence, in 1870. This restricted itself, however, to advocating the taxation of rents rather than the nationalization of land.

On the eve of the socialist revival the land question reached new heights of political significance when Michael Davitt established the Irish Land League in 1879 and English and Scottish equivalents were created in its wake. In the same year the American land reformer Henry George published *Progress and Poverty*, which he followed with successful lecturing tours of Britain in 1882 and 1884. This particular argument for the single tax on rent must have caught the imagination of social reformers in Britain because the book was a bestseller: 'four-fifths of the socialist leaders of Great Britain in the eighties had passed through the School of Henry George.'[4] By 1880 a sense of crisis and transition in British politics and society was firmly established in many minds searching for answers which organized religion could no longer give them. In his *History of British Socialism* Beer refers to 'stirring years of disquisition and discussion' when ideas were in the same state of flux as Victorian society itself. When it became obvious that Joseph Chamberlain's bid to modernize and radicalize the Liberal Party had failed, as Gladstone returned to power in 1880 determined to keep class out of politics by focusing attention on issues remote from people's lives, many radicals were disoriented. The attempt to get the Liberal Party to champion a welfare state- through educational reform, housing, social services, fair agricultural rents and a measure of land reform – failed to budge the Whig and anti-'constructionist' elements in the party.

When Henry Mayers Hyndman launched the Democratic Federation in 1881 it had no defined programme beyond the hope of stirring the discontent within Radicalism with the object of detaching it from Liberalism. Hyndman had campaigned for an extension of the Empire in whose beneficent mission he firmly believed, and although he was appalled by 'the unscrupulous slaughter of miserable negroes' perpetrated in its name and was alarmed to discover the economic exploitation of India, he was still advocating some kind of Imperial Zollverein by 1879. When, finally, he took his plans for a 'democratic reorganization of the Empire' before Disraeli in 1881 he was advised that Britain 'is a very difficult country to move Mr Hyndman, a very difficult country indeed, and one in which there is more disappointment to be looked for than success.'[5] But for his own robust ego Hyndman's contact with Marx might have been even more deflating. The problem was not that Hyndman wanted a peaceful revolution; Marx showed himself flexible on this question:

If you say that you do not share the views of my party for England I can only reply that that party considers an English revolution not *necessary* but – according to historic precedents – *possible*. If the unavoidable evolution turns into a revolution it would not only be the fault of the ruling classes, but also of the working class. Every pacific concession of the former has been wrung from them by 'pressure from without'. Their action kept pace with that pressure and if the latter has more and more weakened, it is only because the English working class know not how to wield their power and use their liberties, both of which they possess legally.[6]

The trouble arose because Hyndman plagiarized *Capital* in his *England for All* (1881), where the Democratic Federations' programme was rather incongruously joined to an exposition of Marx's theory of surplus value. Engels later explained that 'Hyndman is an ex-conservative and an arrantly chauvinistic but not stupid careerist who behaved pretty shabbily to Marx . . . and for this reason was dropped by us personally.'[7] Thus even as Hyndman prepared to place himself at the head of a workers' party expounding Marxist theories, Marx and Engels disowned him.

Not that the newly-formed Democratic Federation gave any reason to believe that it was either Marxist or proletarian in character. The Federation's programme dwelt on political reforms such as triennial parliaments, payment of MPs, equal electoral districts, abolition of the House of Lords, legislative independence for Ireland and the federal reorganization of the Empire.[8] Hyndman explained that universal suffrage, although attractive, was not enough to bring about the desired social reforms – one had only to look at plutocratic America or Bismarckian Germany or the regime of Napoleon III to see that.[9] Nevertheless the Federation also stood for the nationalization of land and railways, free compulsory education, public housing, and an eight-hour day. In time these measures were to become mere 'palliatives' for Hyndman, and as the list of them grew with each passing year the significance which the Federation attached to them fluctuated according to the whims of the leadership.

However, in the early days of the Federation the dominant issue was Ireland, an issue brought to the fore by Davitt's Irish Land League agitations and the Gladstone government's policy of repression. This was enough to frighten away the first cohort of middle-class supporters and bring Hyndman into contact with Henry George, who was touring the country early in 1882 expounding his ideas on land reform and the Single Tax. Several of those influenced by George – H. H. Champion, Belfort Bax and William Morris among them – were by 1883 members of the Federation, where they were joined by working-class militants such as John Burns and Harry Quelch. In 1883 the second annual conference of the Federation adopted nationalization of the means of production and distribution as its central goal while continuing to demand free school meals, better working-class housing. the eight-hour day, cumulative taxation and the public ownership of railways, banks and land. As *Socialism Made Plain* (1883) pointed out:

Thirty thousand persons own the land of Great Britain . . . A long series of robberies and confiscations has deprived us of the soil which should be ours [but] . . . this is only one and not the worst form of monopoly . . . So long as the means of production either of raw materials or of manufactured goods are the monopoly of a class, so long must the labourers . . . sell themselves for a bare subsistence wage.[10]

To this extent, then, the Federation's long list of immediate reforms were just 'stepping stones' which could be taken towards the ultimate goal of complete common ownership of the means of production; but they might just as easily he skipped over altogether.

The heterogeneous ideological composition of the Democratic Federation made agreement about the organization's strategy and tactics exceedingly unlikely. G. D. H. Cole identifies five schools of thought within it, which included Hyndman and those like him who wanted a British equivalent of the German Social Democratic Party; a group of trade unionists who were less influenced by Marxism and more sympathetic to the unions as vehicles for social change; anarchists such as Joseph Lane and his Labour Emancipation League which was affiliated to the Federation; intellectuals who were learning their socialism as they went along; and, finally, Andreas Scheu's Scottish Land and Labour League which wanted loose affiliation to the Federation in 1884 in opposition to Hyndman's insistence on centralism and discipline.[11] These differences and others that only later emerged soon split the organization, though it is possible that they would have loomed less large had the Federation been able to grow in power and influence.

In fact the Federation was largely confined to London, where it did manage eventually to supplant secularist Radicalism as the chief force among working-class political activists. The labour market in London was as peculiar as the structure of working-class politics in the capital. No more than a sixth of the adult labour force up to the 1890s was involved in factory production, and even this was especially prone to seasonal fluctuations.[12] In London the working-class dissenting tradition was especially feeble. Thus while Non-conformism often provided the link between the working class and the Liberals in the provinces, in London it could not perform this service. Working-class political activists joined radical clubs outside the main Liberal tradition – clubs which preached secularism and republicanism and which stood in the tradition of Tom Paine, Chartism and the Commune. When *The Radical* urged the formation of a new party in 1881 to press for the sort of collective reforms which were anathema to Gladstone, the Democratic Federation was in part created to meet this demand.[13] As we have seen, however, Hyndman failed to hold the Radicals who reorganized as the Metropolitan Radical Federation in 1885–6, although they worked together in 1886–7 in favour of free speech when this was threatened by the suppression of outdoor meetings.

The Radicals themselves exercised little influence over the Liberal government's policy, largely because the low turnout of working-class electors – hampered as they were by effective technical barriers to voting as well as by the social and economic conditions in which they lived – could not compensate for the loss in middle-class support which adoption of demands such as the nationalization of land and the abolition of the House of Lords would entail. This middle-class opinion was to be antagonized by Gladstone's pursuit of Home Rule for Ireland in 1886, and the Liberals suffered the secession of Chamberlain's Liberal Unionists in consequence; the party could not take the risk of further weakening itself by the adoption of the Radicals' demands. Hyndman's fledgeling party, consisting as it did to a large extent of Radicals turning to socialism, was strongly inclined to see Gladstonian Liberalism as the main enemy. Thus the Federation took a dim view of the unions which supported the Liberal Party.

Hyndman's group, given the exceedingly adverse conditions in which it found itself, was for the most part confined, as Engels noted, to the 'young bourgeois intelligentsia', and not many of them at that. Hyndman himself understood the poor prospects the Federation was faced with. In 1883 he observed that

> A few may still be found who are imbued with the teaching of the men of '48; but the mass of Englishmen of the producing class are at present far behind their brethren on the continent of Europe and in America, in all the qualities which can eventually lead to the emancipation of their fellows.[14]

Future generations of socialists would learn to regard the organized working class as the best source of allies or even, in some sense, a vanguard. But in 1880 the unions represented only 4 per cent of the occupied population and operated as an elite, jealously guarding its privileges. Membership had actually fallen in the second half of the 1870s as trade depression took its toll; from 594,000 in 1874 the Trades Union Congress (TUC) first founded in 1868 would claim only 381,000 members in 1880 and it was not until the New Unionism in 1889 that the earlier figure was surpassed. As Hyndman said, the unions were:

> but a small fraction of the total working population. They constitute, in fact, an aristocrary of labour who in view of the bitter struggle now drawing nearer and nearer, cannot be said to be other than a hindrance to that complete organization of the proletariat which alone can obtain for the workers their proper control over their own labour . . . Well off themselves, they too often despise their fellows and consider an underpaid, unskilled labourer as an inferior. It is this which constitutes the danger of Trade Unionism at the present time to the interests of the mass of the workers . . . they prevent any organised attempt being made by the workers as a class to form a definite party of their own . . . but unfortunately use the influence they obtain . . . in aid of this or that section of the capitalist class.[15]

This was an analysis with which Marx and Engels, and virtually the whole of socialist opinion for that matter, concurred.

Similarly, there was nothing controversial about Hyndman's demand that: 'Trade unions . . . must lead to wider and more powerful combinations of the working classes if they are to raise the proletariat of Great Britain from their present degraded state.'[16] But Hyndman also found 'the waste of Trade Union funds on strikes . . . deplorable'.[17] Money used in this way could have been used to finance propaganda for socialism or to fund independent labour MPs. Strikes, in Hyndman's view, were simply futile. Here the Federation invoked Lassalle's notion of an 'iron law of wages' to explain why so long as capitalism existed the working class could do nothing to improve its lot by collective struggle over pay. This argument was used on numerous occasions and over a lengthy period of time in the organization's history. In 1885 it appeared in J. L. Joynes' *The Socialist Catechism*, and it was repeated when Harry Quelch and Belfort Bax updated the pamphlet in 1901 as *The New Catechism of Socialism*. The fact that the Federation persisted with this theory for so long, de spite Marx's devastating critique of Lassalle's economic principles in 1875,[18] may be connected with Hyndman's admiration for the man he approvingly described as 'essentially a national socialist'. But the Federations thinking on this matter was probably also influenced by founder members such as James and Charles Murray, friends of the Chartist Bronterre O'Brien, all of whom took a similarly pessimistic view of the utility of strikes, as well as admirers of Lassalle like Hyndman and John Sketchley.[19] Whatever the causes, the Federation held to this jaundiced attitude towards strikes even when it might profitably have intervened towards the end of the decade when the unskilled and casual workers began to get organized.

Quite naturally for an organization with no more than 500 members by 1884 the Federation – which became the Social Democratic Federation (SDF) in that year – saw itself principally as a propaganda society. But it also sought participation in such democratically-elected bodies as existed, from Parliament itself to the reformed and empowered local authorities after 1888 and the school boards. Hyndman believed that the SDF's 'palliatives' or 'stepping stones' were desirable reforms in themselves which the organization could present to the electors as serious propositions; he even elaborated a theory of municipal socialism proposing that local authorities should assume responsibility for productive business and the provision of wide-ranging social services.[20] But even before the organization's fourth annual conference adopted the name Social Democratic Federation the ideological differences within the group had begun to come to the fore after its failure to seduce the Radical working men's clubs.

These differences were undoubtedly exacerbated by Hyndman's personal authoritarianism and his control of the SDF's journal *Justice*, which was set up in January 1884 with the help of money donated by Edward Carpenter. Initially even William Morris – the 'one acknowledged Great Man' among the socialists of the 1880s – was prepared to show Hyndman the deference which he thought his due. George Bernard Shaw has best captured this aspect of Hyndman's personality, recalling that:

> Had Morris been accompanied by Plato, Aristotle, Gregory the Great, Dante, Thomas Aquinas, Milton and Newton, Hyndman would have taken the chair as their natural leader without the slightest misgiving and before the end of the month would have quarrelled with them all and left himself with no followers but the devoted handful who could not compete with him and to whom he was a sort of god.[21]

This tendency of Hyndman to tolerate no criticism was in itself sufficient to antagonize some of the leading members, especially since these included members of Engels' circle, Eleanor Marx and Edward Aveling in particular, and this group was unfavourably disposed to Hyndman from the start. When Hyndman's patriotic sensibilities were aroused by General Gordon's plight at Khartoum in 1884, the long-standing suspicion of his chauvinistic tendencies was confirmed in these circles. But the SDF was also divided over its attitude to the franchise demonstrations and agitation in which Liberal and Radical working men were involved during the spring and summer. Hyndman, supported by Champion and Burns, wanted to capitalize on this agitation. The question was raised of standing candidates in elections for Parliament. Some members of the group simply opposed the timing of this policy, arguing that the SDF would be made to look ridiculous by crushing defeats. Others like Morris and the anarchists opposed socialist candidatures on principle. Matters came to a head when Andreas Scheu set up the Scottish Land and Labour League in Edinburgh and was met with Hyndman's insistence that the new body should come under the SDF's control and discipline.

   In the end a combination of ideological differences and personal incompatibilities led to a majority of the SDF's executive deciding to leave the organization in December 1884. On 30 December the Socialist League was formed with Morris, Aveling, Eleanor Marx, Bax and Scheu in the leadership. Although Joseph Lane's Labour Emancipation League went its own way, the Socialist League contained a large proportion of anarchists and it was the SDF which emerged from the split a more homogeneous body. Nevertheless Hyndman's defects, as described by Morris, remained:

> Hyndman can accept only one position in such a body as the SDF, that of master . . . [he] has been acting throughout . . . as a politician determined to push his own advantage . . . always on the look out for anything which could advertise the party he is supposed to lead: his aim has been to make the movement seem big; to frighten the powers that be with a turnip bogie . . . all that insane talk of immediate forcible revolution, when we know that the workers in England are not even touched by the movement.[22]

It is true that Hyndman was inclined to use such scare tactics and was talking of 'some fatal national catastrophe' as the catalyst for socialism in 1884;[23] he even predicted that the revolution would come in 1889 – the centenary of the French Revolution. Shortly after the split the SDF collaborated with the Fabians (Hubert Bland, Edith Nesbit and John Hunter Watts were actually members of the Federation as well as Fabians), the Radical clubs and even the Socialist League in a campaign for free speech when the police were instructed to prevent open air meetings in Dod Street, a favourite pitch with socialist speakers. But this unity was to prove short-lived when the SDF stood three candidates in the 1885 general election on the strength of £340 obtained by Champion from the Conservative agent Maltman Barry. It is hard to say which was considered worse – the 'Tory Gold' clearly provided to divide the 'progressive' vote or the fact that the three SDF candidates polled so badly. In Nottingham John Burns received 598 votes but John E. Williams in Hampstead and John Fielding in Kensington were left with a miserable 27 and 32 votes respectively. 'All England is satisfied that we are a paltry handful of blackguards', commented Shaw.[24] The SDF rapidly lost members in the wake of Hyndman's miscalculation (another split briefly produced the Socialist Union) and Morris's earlier charge that the leader of the SDF wanted 'to frighten the powers that be with a turnip bogie' was vindicated; Hyndman had only set out on the Tory Gold tack after approaching Chamberlain – whose agitation for social reform was renewed after the dissolution of Parliament in August 1885 – with a proposal for collaboration backed up with the 'threat' of SDF opposition if this proposal was rejected. The SDF was duly rebuffed and the 'turnip bogie' exposed for what it was. Even the bourgeois press dropped the SDF as it was now impossible to find scare stories associated with it.

The SDF's reputation took a turn for the better in the winter of 1885–6. The years 1884–7 were the worst period of prolonged unemployment until the 1920s. The depression which had begun in the mid-1870s reached its nadir in 1886, prompting the Fair Trade League (1881) to intensify agitation for protectionist policies. In January 1886 a large demonstration took place in Trafalgar Square under these auspices, but the SDF organized a counter-demonstration which Hyndman and Burns addressed with the object of turning attention to anti-capitalist proposals for dealing with the distress. The Federation campaigned for the 'right to work' and demanded state-directed co-operative colonies to be set up on unproductive land. But it also stressed the functional value of unemployment under capitalism and argued that only the complete socialization of industry could adequately deal with it. Burns told the crowd that the House of Commons was composed of 'capitalists who had fattened upon the labour of the working men' and that 'to hang these would be to waste good rope.'[25] When the police finally compelled the SDF to take its demonstration out of the Square, John Burns holding aloft a red flag led the procession down Pall Mall en route to Hyde Park. Along the way a riot ensued when the crowd turned on jeering onlookers, smashing windows in the Reform, Carlton and New University clubs in which they were ensconced. In the immediate aftermath of the riot – which unfavourably impressed Engels, who saw it as the work of the lumpenproletariat – the press once more magnified the threat posed by the SDF and middle class generosity suddenly turned towards the Mansion House Fund for unemployment relief, which soon raised £75,000 after a period of stagnation. Hyndman warned a subsequent demonstration of the unemployed in February to avoid any repetition of the incident; the SDF was now 10,000 strong in London alone and *Justice* was selling 4,000 copies per issue.

When agitation over unemployment died down in 1887, as trade revived, the London Commissioner of Police, Sir Charles Warren, took the opportunity to place a ban on any future demonstrations in Trafalgar Square. The Radicals once again joined with the socialists in objecting to this infringement on free speech. W. T. Stead, the editor of the *Pall Mall Gazette*, set up a Law and Liberty League with the aim of establishing popular control over the Metropolitan Police – an objective that was as remote as ever one hundred years later. On Sunday 13 November socialists and Radicals tried to meet in Trafalgar Square, which was surrounded by troops and police. Some 4,000 constables, 300 mounted police, 300 soldiers of the Grenadier Guards and 350 Life Guards kept 20,000 demonstrators out of the Square, and in the resulting clashes the disciplined and armed minority of police and soldiers made short work of the demonstrators, killing two of them. Only Quelch's Bermondsey branch of the Federation had been properly drilled and these duly broke into the Square and emerged relatively unscathed.

'Bloody Sunday', as it became known, was a traumatic experience for many of those who took part in it. It was as if the event had made them realize what state power meant. But when the ban on meetings was given indefinite extension, something like a genuine united front was formed by the Metropolitan Radical Federation, the Socialist League, the SDF and the Fabians within the short-lived Law and liberty League. On Sunday 20 November 40,000 demonstrators met in Hyde Park while a large crowd gathered around Trafalgar Square. Once again the mounted police repeatedly charged the crowd, on this occasion supported by volunteer special constables. This time a passer-by, Alfred Linnell, was crushed beneath the horses and died of his wounds twelve days later. His funeral cortège was followed by a vast crowd estimated at 120,000 people with socialists such as Morris, Burns and Cunninghame Graham at the head of the procession.

Even SDF members such as Tom Mann, Burns and Champion were now beginning to doubt the value of Hyndman's 'turnip bogie' and the Federation's sectarianism. After the Tory Gold fiasco in 1885 Mann proposed that the SDF should avoid 'such a strong and hostile criticism of the trade union movement . . . and that care should be taken to show that we attached great importance to [it]'.[26] But this only provoked 'severe criticism' from Hyndman and the Federation's annual conference endorsed the old policy. Undeterred Mann proposed that the organization should take seriously its 'palliative' demand for the eight-hour day, even though Burns apparently argued that 'the time has passed for such trivial reforms.'[27] Mann's Battersea branch supported the idea, however, and an Eight-hours League was established in October 1886 with branches in London and Newcastle. At the TUC the previous year T. R. Threlfall had used his presidential address to float the proposal, but to no effect; and even Morris's journal *Commonweal*, as well as *Justice*, ignored Mann's pamphlet on the subject when it was published in June 1886.[28] Nevertheless, the first socialist MP, Cunninghame Graham, supported the idea of legislative reform for the eight-hour day in his maiden speech the following January.

1887 also saw a growing agitation, under Keir Hardie's leadership, in the North for independent working-class representation. This was a time when the SDF had only thirty branches, most of which were in London. Increasingly Mann, Burns and Champion were drawn to the idea of launching a new labour party – especially after Bloody Sunday convinced them of the futility of the physical force rhetoric of the Federation. When their ideas were rejected at the SDF's conference of 1888 and Hyndman reorganized the leadership on a more centralist basis, the advocates of labour candidates went their own way, leaving the Federation and its policy of only supporting candidates who advocated class war. The SDF's quasi-revolutionary attitude only isolated it, however, and by November it was turning back to joint work with the Metropolitan Radical Federation, the London Secular Society and the Fabians in the establishment of a Central Democratic Committee to fight the London School Board elections with demands for compulsory education, free school meals and popular control of state-aided schools. Hyndman even began to see the value of agitation for the eight-hour day.

But the socialists were met with derision when the demand for a statutory eight-hour day was put before the TUC. In 1888 the affiliated organizations were balloted and in a low poll responded by rejecting the proposal by 62,883 to 39,629. Only in the case of the miners was legislation for eight-hours approved at the 1889 TUC. The majority still believed that the measure would simply reduce pay and strengthen Britain's trading rivals, who would be sure to oppose similar reforms themselves. Even at the 1890 TUC arguments against state interference in the hours of labour commanded a considerable following.[29] But by then a momentous change had taken place within the trade union movement.

Some of the older unions reformed themselves in the course of 1888–9; the Miners' Federation of Great Britain was established to replace the defunct Miners' National Union and the Amalgamated Society of Railway Servants was reorganized to produce a more militant organization whose membership tripled in 1889. Havelock Wilson established the National Union of Seamen in 1887 and it was in the wake of a successful strike for wage rises which the union conducted in 1889 that dockers' unions arose in Glasgow and Liverpool. Nobody could have supposed that these wretched casual workers could organize themselves. In 1888 Eleanor Marx described how

The people are starving ... One room especially haunts me.
Room! – cellar, dark, underground – In it a woman lying on some
sacking and a little straw, her breast half eaten away with cancer. She is
naked but for an old red handkerchief over her breast and a bit of old
sail over her legs. By her side a baby of three and other children – four
of them. The oldest just nine years old. The husband tries to 'pick up' a
few pence at the docks – that last refuge of the desperate – and the
children are howling for bread ... We got her to the hospital – for a
long time she would not go because of the 'little 'uns' and now she's
dead. What has become of those children heaven knows. – But that's
only one out of thousands and thousands

Only a perilous margin separated the utterly destitute from those who still saw
themselves as workers:

To go to the docks is enough to drive one mad. The men fight and push
and hustle like beasts – not men – and all earn at best 3d or 4d an hour.
So serious has the struggle become that the 'authorities' have had to
replace certain iron palings with wooden ones – the weaker men got
impaled in the crush! ... You can't help thinking of all this when you've
seen it and been in the midst of it.[30]

These were the workers, the women and children whom even the philanthro-
pists, the bourgeois reformers and Fabian intellectuals were apt to dismiss as
an unfortunate, irremediable social residue – an abyss requiring, perhaps,
'surgical' elimination. And yet by 1889, the dockers were organized.

Already in October 1888 a dock strike at Tilbury had broken out with SDF
involvement. In June 1889 Will Thorne's organization of the gasworkers led
to a successful strike for the eight-hour day which Engels, not usually enthusiastic about developments in the British labour movement, described as 'this
epoch-making event' in the Vienna *Arbeiter-Zeitung*. Ben Tillet, Tom Mann
and John Burns played the leading role in organizing the successful strike
for the 'dockers' tanner' in the summer of 1889, although the socialists
played down their wider politics during the struggle. Engels described the
dockers as

'The most miserable of all the *miserable* of the East End, the broken
down ones of all trades, the lowest stratum above the Lumpenproletariat. That these poor and famished broken down creatures who
bodily fight amongst each other every morning for admission to work,
should organise for resistance, turn out 40–50,000 strong, draw after
them into the strike all and every trade of the East End in any way
connected with shipping, hold out above a week, and terrify the wealthy
and powerful dock companies – that is a revival I am proud to have
lived to see. And all this strike is worked and led by *our* people ... the
Hyndmanites are nowhere in it.'[31]

Indeed, the SDF characterized the trade union work of Thorne, Burns and Mann as a 'lowering of the flag, a departure from active propaganda, a waste of energy'.[32]

The SDF further condemned itself in Engels' eyes by the attitude it adopted at the founding congress of the Second International. In September 1887 the TUC had voted for an international conference to consider the question of eight-hours legislation. In November of the following year a meeting was duly arranged in London at the instigation of the Parliamentary Committee of the TUC and at this meeting it was decided to arrange a full international congress for 1889. But what sort of meeting would it be? Those favouring the formation of a socialist International – especially the SPD, supported by Engels, and the French Marxists led by Jules Guesde – organized one conference while the French 'possibilists' led by Paul Brousse and those who wanted a trade union conference organized another for the same day. Hyndman, always suspicious of German influence, for once lined up with the trade unionists and reformists. Rather than attend a conference which the mighty SDP could dominate and to which his rivals in the Socialist League were bound, Hyndman chose to align himself with the ideologies he was so dismissive of in Britain.[33] Combined with the SDP's attitude to the new unionism this was further evidence that Hyndman was not to be trusted.

The SDF waited until 1897 before its executive began to advocate a more active involvement in the unions, though as we have seen individual members and branches were often involved in trade union struggles much earlier. By contrast Engels started to believe that a real labour movement had begun in Britain in 1889, even though he recognized that it was 'first of all a trade union movement'. But the labour aristocracy seemed to have been swept aside and the demands of the movement had become more far-reaching: not only was there now a majority for a statutory eight-hour day, but a general federation of all the organizations and complete solidarity of the working class also seemed possible. The 'fossilized' men of the old unions, their craft exclusiveness and formalist spirit, was being replaced, thought Engels, by '*one* brotherhood and for a direct struggle against capital'.[34] Against this development, the socialist societies were mere sects. The Fabians preached continued affiliation of the workers to Liberalism even as the workers looked set to press for independence, while the SDF had the distinction 'of being the only party which has contrived to reduce Marxism to a rigid orthodoxy which the workers are not to reach as a result of their class consciousness, but which like an article of faith, is to be forced down their throats at once and without development.'[35]

Hyndman took a consistently negative view of all the popular struggles which took place during his long involvement in socialist politics. Just as he regarded strikes as both futile and wasteful and was unable to see the potentially momentous character of the New Unionism, so he dismissed the feminist agitation of the late 1890s and the syndicalist movement after 1910 as equally remote from socialist principles. Progress was to be measured in this austerely dogmatic view simply by the growth of the SDF and the extent to which others followed the lead it had given. The SDF's Marxism was more of a narrow, scholastic faith in the inevitability of socialism as revealed by certain 'laws' of economic development than a guide to action. The emphasis varied according to Hyndman's latest pronouncement – fluctuating between prophesies of the coming cataclysm and propaganda around the organization's 'palliatives'. Lacking consistency and any conception of the links between these poles of agitation, the SDF contained within its ranks socialists who concentrated exclusively on local issues and others who awaited the coming insurrection.[36] Hyndman also managed to repel leading advocates of both approaches, like Mann and Champion, who wanted consistent work on issues such as the demand for the eight-hour day, and those like Morris who regarded Hyndman as an unscrupulous opportunist who had betrayed socialist principles. The SDF leadership's low opinion of working-class organizations and struggles beyond the control of the SDF was also rationalized in terms of the ignorance and stupidity of the masses and of the need for the workers to reach a social democratic consciousness before any good could come out of their activity. In his autobiographical volume, *The Record of an Adventurous Life* (1911), Hyndman explained that a slave class cannot be freed by the slaves themselves. The leadership, the initiative, the teaching, the organization, must come from those who are born into a different position, and are trained to use their faculties in early life.[37]

The SDF accordingly imagined itself to be a future Committee for Public Safety which would seize the reins of power when 'the day' arrived. Thus it can be argued that the SDF should be understood as an example of the socialism-from-above tradition rather than as an organization which simply suffered from Hyndman's sectarianism.[38] But its chief defect was undoubtedly the whimsical, domineering leadership of Hyndman himself, who found it impossible to collaborate with equals and contrived to combine his own non-socialist views – whether anti-semitic, chauvinist or imperialist – with an insistence that only the SDF represented true socialism.

But what of the Socialist League, which after all contained Marxist opponents of Hyndman and members of Engels' immediate circle – Eleanor Marx and Edward Aveling? From its creation in December 1884 the Socialist League inherited much of the factionalism and ideological heterogeneity of the Democratic Federation, including an anarchist element. Morris shared the antipathy which this anarchist faction felt towards parliamentary reformism, and the whole of the organization – a mere handful rising to at most 700 by the summer of 1886[39] – was committed by its manifesto, *To Socialists* (January 1885), to the view that it had

no function but to educate the people in the principles of Socialism and to organize such as it can get hold of to take their due places, when the crisis shall come which will force action on us . . . to hold out as baits hopes of amelioration of the condition of the workers to be wrung out of the necessities of the rival factions of our privileged rulers is delusive and mischievous.[40]

Thus the League took a dim view of 'palliatives' and had broken away from the SDF partly because Hyndman believed in fighting elections. Morris in particular could not stomach the thought of contesting elections:

> I really feel sickened at the idea of all the intrigue and degradation of concession which would be necessary to us as a parliamentary party, nor do I see any necessity for a revolutionary party doing any 'dirty work' at all, or soiling ourselves with anything that would unfit us for being due citizens of the new order of things.[41]

Morris made the mistake of regarding capitalism as a machine which could be patched-up by reforms and thus made to work more effectively by them. Clearly, if this was the way the system actually worked – increasing its longevity by means of concessions which left its exploitative and repressive character intact – it was no business of revolutionaries to do this job on its behalf. Some Socialist Leaguers were dismissive of the eight-hours agitation precisely on this reasoning. Morris himself argued this in a letter to Joseph Lane in 1887: 'I believe all palliative measures like the eight hours bill to be delusive, and so damaging to the cause if *put forward by socialists as part of socialism.*'[42] Others – especially the Bloomsbury branch of the League where the influence of Engels' circle was dominant – threw themselves wholeheartedly into the struggle for eight-hours and parliamentary reform generally, in the belief that these steps would strengthen the working class and increase its ability to mount further struggles in the future. This faction tried unsuccessfully to change the League's 'policy of abstention' from electoral reformism and after a period of semi-independence left the organization altogether after the fourth annual conference in 1888.

Morris was at the forefront of the argument in favour of 'abstention':

> the Communists believe that it would be a waste of time for the Socialists to expend their energy in furthering reforms which so far from bringing us nearer to Socialism, would rather serve to bolster up the present state of things, and not believing in the efficacy of reforms, they can see no reason for attempting to use Parliament in any way; except perhaps by holding it up as an example to show what a contemptible thing a body can be which poses as the representative of a whole nation and which really represents nothing but the firm determination of the privileged or monopolist class to stick to their principles and monopoly till they are *forced* to relinquish it.[43]

This kind of argument was to exercise a powerful influence thirty years later among the revolutionaries who formed the Communist Party. It took Lenin to persuade them that abstention would simply isolate the Communists and close down an important area of agitation. But Morris's argument and that of the later anti-parliamentary Communists was alert, as Lenin perhaps was not, to the legitimizing role which participation in elections would confer on the very idea of parliamentary representation, which they saw as the job of revolutionaries to expose.

Under Morris's influence guild socialists would later argue that parliamentary representation should be replaced by multiple, functional, representations since the idea that an MP could in any way represent the views of thousands of constituents grouped arbitrarily into territorial units was a complete nonsense. G. D. H. Cole, who did most to develop this critique of parliamentary representation, was also influenced by Morris's stress on the argument that the 'change for the better can only be realised by the efforts of the workers themselves. "By us, not for us", must be their motto,'[44] This was an argument which Morris linked to the policy of abstention:

> the real business of us propagandists is to instil this aim of the workers becoming the masters of their own destinies, their own lives, and this can be effected when a sufficient number of them are convinced of the fact by the establishment of a vast labour organization – the federation according to their crafts, if you will, of all the workmen who have awoke to the fact that they are the slaves of monopoly ... Let them settle e.g. what wages are to be paid by their temporary managers, what number of hours it may be expedient to work; let them arrange for the filling of their military chest, the care of the sick, the unemployed, the dismissed: let them learn also how to administer their own affairs.[45]

Between 1910 and 1921 these arguments would be resurrected when it seemed that the militant rank and file in the unions was actually seeking some form of workers' control of industry preparatory to the establishment of a decentralized form of socialism. But in Morris's own time no such movement existed and Morris's argument with the parliamentary reformers actually drove him into the arms of the anarchists within the Socialist League. The anarchist element within the organization grew in influence partly because the romantic and charismatic figure of Kropotkin was present in London from the spring of 1886 and partly because the judicial murder of the Chicago anarchists on the eve of Bloody Sunday 1887 aroused support for the victims. By 1890 the anarchists had taken control of *Commonweal* and Morris had dropped out of the League's activity.

Henceforward the 120-strong Hammersmith branch would function under Morris's leadership as an independent Socialist Society which nevertheless provided a forum for the whole range of positions within the socialist movement. Morris himself was more consistent in emphasizing the educative dimensions of political and economic struggles and to this extent came closer to the position of Engels. But his enduring legacy consists of writings which brought an open-ended Utopian vision into Marxist socialism. For as he said himself: 'we cannot help guessing at a great deal which we cannot know; and again, this guessing, these hopes, or if you will, these dreams for the future, make many a man a Socialist whom sober reason deduced from science and political economy and the selection of the fittest would not move at all.'[46]

Morris became a socialist as an artist in revolt against the 'eyeless vulgarity', the 'sordid, aimless, ugly confusion' of 'modern civilisation'.[47] Because art was for Morris 'the expression of pleasure in life generally . . . and especially the expression of man's pleasure in the deeds of the present; in his work', it seemed under threat of complete extinction at the hands of capitalism. This was something which Marx had argued in *Capital*:

> Within the capitalist system all methods for raising the social productiveness of labour are brought about at the cost of the individual labourer; all means for the development of production transform themselves into means of domination over, and exploitation of, the producers; they mutilate the labourer into a fragment of a man, degrade him to the level of an appendage of a machine, destroy every remnant of charm in his work and turn it into a hated toil; they estrange him from the intellectual potentialities of the labour-process in the same proportion as science is incorporated in it as an independent power; they distort the conditions under which he works, subject him during the labour process to a despotism more hateful for its meanness; they transform his lifetime into working time and drag his wife and child beneath the wheels of the juggernaut of Capital.[48]

Work had been reduced to an unskilled toil upon which, according to Morris, has been erected a system 'which has made our towns and habitations sordid and hideous, insults to the beauty of the earth which they disfigure . . . The advance of the industrial army . . . is traced, like the advance of other armies, in the ruin of the peace and loveliness of the earth's surface and nature.'[49] Because Morris believed that 'it is workmen only and not pedants who can produce real vigorous art', it followed for him that 'Nothing should be made by man's labour which is not worth making: or which must be made by labour degrading to the makers.'[50] Morris wanted an 'honest society' in which the individual could expect 'a life which will develop his human faculties to the utmost'. Instead capitalism had created an 'age of makeshift' – an age seemingly devoted to the degradation of labour and the production, indeed overproduction, of useless luxuries and debased necessities. Communism, for Morris, was not a society of superabundance in commodities but rather a society in which the capitalist 'complexity of dependence' had been eliminated in favour of 'simple lives . . . and simple pleasures' – the prerequisites in his view of real freedom.[51]

This vision of the new society was given its fullest expression in *News From Nowhere* (1890), in which Morris imagined a community where the 'habit of good fellowship' was firmly established. Communism as depicted here was to be based on principles of co-operative labour, decentralization and the abolition of the old 'machinery of tyranny' that was formerly known as the state.[52] It is clear in this and many of Morris's other writings that communism was the society of the future in which real individual fulfilment could be realized by people in genuine harmony and sympathy with their natural surroundings. But he saw that some form of state socialism was more likely before this goal was reached:

> State socialism does threaten to 'act as master' and take the place of the old masters: acting with benevolent intention indeed, but with conscious artificiality and by means of the employment of obvious force which would be felt everywhere . . . and so at last might even bring on a new revolution which might lead us backward for a while, or might carry us forward into a condition of true Communism according to the ripeness or unripeness of the State Socialist revolution.[53]

Shaw was speaking no more than the truth when he said that 'Morris heartily disliked the Fabians . . . as a species.'[54] For these were the state socialists *par excellence* of their generation and although Morris rejected their creed and thought it impossible of realization as a complete scheme he recognized that 'people have really got their heads turned more or less in their direction'. Occasionally he even feared that the 'Society of Inequality' would survive by virtue of such 'quasi-socialist machinery', by turning the population into what Marx once called 'well-fed instruments of production': 'The workers better treated better organized, helping to govern themselves, but with no more pretence to equality with the rich, nor any more hope for it than they have now.'[55] Until the movement for independent labour representation began to get under way in the 1890s the socialist camp, in Yvonne Kapp's words, comprised 'the anti-Marxist champions of efficiency and the inefficient champions of Marxism'.[56] Faced with this sort of choice Morris was much closer to the SDF, though he never rejoined it. A few months before the foundation of the Independent Labour Party (ILP), Morris was involved in attempts to bring unity to the various socialist organizations. Once the ILP came into existence it was the SDF which used its power to exclude the new party. Although the Federation's policy was officially one of 'benevolent neutrality', *Justice* hit a sectarian note from the outset, declaring that 'outside Social-Democracy there is no basis for a labour party'.[57] The truth is that the SDF also benefited from the socialist upsurge in the North and was able to set up a Lancashire District Council in August 1893 based on a membership of around 2,000 in the north-east of the county, Burnley in particular. The ILP was thus looked upon as a rival. The SDF was also feeling the squeeze in London where a Liberal revival was under way by 1892, thanks in part to the campaigns waged in the *Star* from January 1888.

T. P. O'Connor and H. W. Massingham used the *Star* – which had a circulation of 279,000 by 1889 – to promote a 'war on all privilege' and demand land reform, free education, progressive taxation and a number of reforms specifically tailored to meet the 'labour question'. These issues were raised by the London Liberal and Radical Union in January 1889 in the first elections to the London County Council (LCC), which the Progressives subsequently dominated. With the rise of the new unions independent working-class candidates began to appear on school boards and other elected bodies in London including the Trades Council which set up its own Labour Representation League in November 1891. In March 1892 nine labour men were elected onto the LCC. But neither the SDF nor the Fabians wanted a working-class party. As the new unionism faded, the Liberals recovered the initiative. It was around this time, and shortly before Morris's death, that he apparently told Sidney Webb: 'The world is going your way at present Webb, but it is not the right way in the end.'[58]

Conclusion

While it would be far too simplistic to blame the SDF and the even tinier Socialist League for the failure of Marxism to take root in Britain in the last decades of the nineteenth century, it is arguable that a stronger Marxist presence was feasible within the working-class movement than that actually achieved by these organizations. Eduard Bernstein, the leading exponent of revisionism within the German Social Democratic Party (SDP) at the turn of the century, estimated that 'well over a hundred thousand passed through' the SDF, and these included extremely able agitators and organizers such as Tom Mann, Eleanor Marx, Edward Aveling, John Burns and Will Thorne.[59] Most of these activists – like George Lansbury, Ernest Bevin and Ramsay MacDonald – went on to join the Independent Labour Party (ILP) and the Labour Party itself, towards which the SDF took a sectarian attitude from the start. It can be argued that some of these refugees from the SDF took with them some semblance of a Marxist approach which survived as one of the elements of Labour socialism,[60] but the main body of organized Marxists stood apart – as a later generation, many of them drawn from the SDF's successor, the British Socialist Party, were to do when the Communist Party was formed in 1920. Unlike the Communists, however, the SDF had no clear strategy, and it was equally inconsistent over tactics. Furthermore, Hyndman neglected, rejected, or at best took only an equivocal stance in relation to most of the big movements which might have provided the Marxists an opening to a wider working-class audience.

By 1900, as recalled by T. A. Jackson (then a member of the SDF, later a leading member of the Communist Party), 'there were scores of "unattached" socialists for every one who retained membership of one or other of the sects.'[61] Among the socialists, according to Jackson, there was 'an almost total failure to agree as to what "Socialism" meant in terms of concrete, specific, political practice'.[62] These divisions, however, were not the cause of the socialists' weakness but rather a symptom of it. They may, nevertheless, be relevant to note here because another barrier to the acceptance of the SDF's rather dry, rationalistic, Marxism with its stress on 'the economic factor' was its failure to speak to those workers who looked for a spiritual alternative to organized religion and eventually found it in the ILP's socialism. Only Morris integrated the analytical and the ethical in his Marxist ideology, and the socialists were divided between these different facets of what could have been a unified system. Thus while the SDF's ideology was commonly rejected on the grounds that it made economic self-interest the sole cause of social change, the ethical socialism of the ILP was apt to degenerate into empty rhetoric. The differences between the socialists pale into insignificance by comparison with a host of other factors, however, if we are searching for an explanation of the marginality of the Marxists. In the introduction to this book it was noted that from the second half of the nineteenth century, when the power and wealth of the British ruling class rapidly increased, the two most significant political developments were the growth of working-class associations and the policy of concessions from above, which produced important reforms such as the extension of the franchise and the legalization of the trades unions. Obviously these reforms and the development of working-class self-help organizations which worked within, rather than against, the system, helped to reinforce one another and strengthened the reformist orientation thus established. The existence of diverse working-class organizations such as unions, co-operatives, friendly societies and the like, when taken together with opportunities for many recreational activities, may suggest that there was less scope in Britain for an organization like the SPD which was a rallying point for all sorts of reasons, not just political, and able to provide many of these facilities within itself. The British political system was by any contemporary standards congenial to reformist politics, and unlike the systems of continental Europe had taken major steps by 1875 to withdraw the state from industrial relations. The extension of the franchise also helped to funnel political activity into the parliamentary arena. Thus even among the socialists the vast majority regarded the political system as near-perfect once payment for MPs, abolition of the Lords, and further extensions of the franchise were enacted. There was, then, no widespread alienation from the state as could be found in Germany and Russia, and a relatively rich civil society in which the better-off working class was fully involved. One important aspect of this, as Walter Bagehot had observed in *The English Constitution* (1867), was a system of popular deference which existed thanks to both the 'dignified' (aristocratic-monarchic) and the 'efficient' (Cabinet and Commons) branches of the British state. While Parliament and the emerging democracy helped to establish the conviction that the political system was fair, the monarchy was perceived as standing above politics altogether as the representative of the nation and acting as a guarantor that the legislature would remain impartial between the classes. As Ross McKibbin has argued, 'the ideological predominance of crown, parliament, and nationality inhibited the evolution of the idea of an alternative social system while a libertarian pattern of industrial relations obstructed that sense of fear and resentment which was so characteristic of workers' attitudes on the continent.'[63]

A sense of alienation was also missing from the liberal intelligentsia, as I argued in the introduction to this book. Indeed the term 'intelligentsia' is not really applicable to Victorian intellectuals if we define it, as Tom Nairn does, as 'an intellectual stratum distanced from society and the state; thinkers and writers distanced from and critical of the status quo'.[64] Whereas J. S. Mill had expected the liberal middle class to challenge the powers and privileges of the landlords, virtually the whole of this class was actually reconciled to the aristocracy after 1832. Those of them who developed an interest in social change were able to turn their attention to working-class improvement without this in the least calling into question their loyalty to the political and social system as a whole. Not surprisingly, therefore, few of them found their way to Marxism. Through religion, on the other hand, a proportion of the working class found their way into the company and conventional ethics of the middle class. As we have seen, Nonconformity did not have a strong presence in London, where the SDF was at its strongest, but the capital presented other problems for the Marxists.

A large proportion of the London workforce was engaged in casual labour, self-employment on the streets, and small workshops. Large-scale factory employment hardly existed. This was a population extremely difficult to organize, occupied in activities which hardly encouraged any sense of collectivism or solidarity. These circumstances were more favourable to the 'brutalised apathy' referred to by Beatrice Webb and that 'division of society into innumerable strata' which Engels observed to be connected to a deferential 'respect for [their] superiors and betters'.[65] The crippling poverty in which the bottom half of the working class lived was itself hardly conducive to political activism and these people were also denied the vote. Perhaps when these factors are taken into consideration it is easier to understand why the tiny minority of workers who did break through into the world of books, socialism and political activity often mixed feelings of contempt and pity with anger when they contemplated the mass of workers who could be seen as 'their own worst enemies'. It was all the more frustrating that the organized working class – a little under 12 per cent of male workers in 1901 – were so slow to take up the socialist cause. Even after the reversal of the Osborne Judgement in 1913, when the union membership was required to vote on the question of establishing political funds to finance the Labour Party, an arrangement which the courts had deemed *ultra vires* in 1909, 40 per cent of those who voted were against – and it was not because they wanted Labour to improve its socialist credentials. The SDF's sectarianism was born of these circumstances; if we turn now to Fabianism it will be seen that other socialists wrote the working class out of the socialist script altogether.

3
Fabianism

The motley group of spiritualists, social reformers, and moralists who set up the Fellowship of the New Life in 1883 under the leadership of Thomas Davidson met with the object of promoting 'the cultivation of a perfect character in each and all'. The Fellowship persisted with its work until 1898 but an early breakaway group, formed in 1884 as the Fabian Society, set out to 'reconstruct society' on a material basis on the understanding that its 'general welfare and happiness' was obstructed by the competitive system.[1] Socialism did not appear in the records of the Society until its sixth meeting in 1884 and it was only in the autumn of that year that George Bernard Shaw became a member. Together with Sidney Webb, who joined the Society in 1885, Shaw helped to fashion a distinctive Fabian ideology in the years that followed, and although contributions were made by such intellectuals as Hubert Bland, Annie Besant, Graham Wallas, Sidney Olivier, H. G. Wells and Beatrice Webb, it was the work of Sidney Webb and Shaw which dominated the Society in its first thirty years.

The small and obscure group of middle-class intellectuals which comprised the Society in the years up to 1889 operated as a propaganda and debating association, distributing a number of tracts on socialism and outlining the facts of poverty, waste and inequality generated by capitalism. In these years the Society was not yet completely committed to constitutionalism – a position only finally adopted in 1888 – and contained advocates of anarchism and champions of an independent socialist party such as Hubert Bland. The Fabians were thus divided on important issues and would always consist of socialists with very different views. But it was the publication of *Fabian Essays in Socialism* in 1889 which brought the existence of the Society, whose membership was then about 150, to wider notice and demonstrated the emergence of a distinctive approach to socialism.

The Fabians had already argued that poverty was 'the inevitable outcome of . . . competition for wages' in the Society's first tract *Why Are the Many Poor?*, where 'socialized property' was invoked as the solution. In *Facts for Socialists* (1887) Sidney Webb had compiled a long and detailed array of statistics to demonstrate that poverty resulted from the private appropriation of rents – unearned increments which accrued to property owners of land and capital as well as to individuals whose skills were in short supply. Added together, according to Webb, these three sources of rent appropriated two-thirds of the national income; it followed, therefore, that the restitution to public purpose of this rent would solve the problem of 'poverty and idleness'.[2] Thus on the basis of this reasoning, Shaw's contribution to *Fabian Essays* foresaw a gradual transition to socialism based on the transfer of rent to the State by instalments levied through taxation. The 'gradual extension of the franchise' would help in this matter but it was a central conviction of Fabianism that 'we are already far on the road', as Shaw put it, towards the required solution.[3]

The new marginal economics associated with Stanley Jevons and Alfred Marshall, together with most of the orthodox 'laws' of political economy which they accepted, were never subject to a Fabian critique. Even though the Webbs believed that the politician of the future 'must be before all things a practical economist' they advanced no comprehensive economic theory of their own. If the Webb partnership, as Beatrice noted in 1896, was principally concerned 'to advance economic knowledge, caring more for that than for our own pet ideas', this had little to do with economic theory. Beatrice had concluded, long before the partnership began, that 'abstract economics' was a 'sheer waste of time' and, true to this prejudice, Shaw, in 1896, listed 'Abstract Economics' along with the 'Marriage Question, Religion and Art' as a subject on which the Fabian Society held no distinctive position of its own. Yet after reading Marshall's *Principles of Economics* in 1890 Sidney Webb told Beatrice: 'it will not make an epoch in Economics. Economics still has to be re-made. Who is to do it? Either you must help me to do it; or I must help you'[4]

This paradox can be explained simply enough: the Webbs believed that the truth or falsity of orthodox economic theory could best be demonstrated by studies intended to expose, by detailed historical enquiry, the origins, structure and function, and above all the facts, of evolutionary processes in society which they were convinced were working to produce collectivist arrangements. This helps to explain why they could entertain the thought that their *Industrial Democracy* (1897) could have an effect comparable to Adam Smith's *The Wealth of Nations*, even though their attention to economic theory was minimal. For all practical policy purposes Fabian economics was indistinguishable from those of the marginal utility school. When Shaw was persuaded to abandon Marx it was in order to embrace Jevons's value theory as expounded by Philip Wickstead. So where did the Fabian theory of rent fit into this?

The theory of 'unearned increment' was loosely based on Ricardo, Webb's mentor J. S. Mill and the arguments of Henry George's *Progress and Poverty* (1879). Rent was understood as an income which was the unavoidable result of the special economic advantages, incidental to production and distribution, which was appropriated by almost every social stratum above the level of subsistence wage-earners. General social advances could cause improvements which generated the rents appropriated by individuals. If land values rose in London because of the growth of industry and population was it not the idle landowner who benefited from the increased rents thus generated, even though he had lifted not a finger to bring this increase about? By the same reasoning did not the advance of civilization render some individual skills and capital relatively scarce, thus generating rents of ability and similar surpluses for capital-holders? Clearly if a surplus was being extracted it was not a question of one class exploiting another, as Marx would have it, but of many individuals from diverse social classes taking this tribute from *society*.

Only the political implications of this theory are clear enough: if many incomes contain an unearned increment there is no basis for the politics of class struggle based on a theory of the irreconcilable interests of wage-earners and capitalists. On the contrary a real community of interests could be said to exist. Progressive taxation emerges as an effective instrument of social justice by restoring to the community the surplus which properly belongs to it and which has been taken away by diverse individuals. But in practical terms the Fabian theory of rent was useless. It could not pose as an alternative to orthodox political economy because it did not have its range, being confined to the sole question of income distribution. And yet it approached this one question in such an abstract way that it provided no criteria for distinguishing between the earned and unearned components of factor incomes. Thus it could produce no practical guidance for fiscal policy. If the Fabians attached so much importance to the theory – and Webb was still singing its praises thirty years after the first appearance of *Fabian Essays* – we must suppose that its political implications were prized above all other considerations.

The economic problem was not one of irreconcilable class interests but a social question to be solved by society acting rationally through the state. The theory helped to support the conviction that socialism was merely 'the conscious and explicit assertion of principles of social organization which have been already in great part unconsciously adopted'.[5] In Webb's view, 'No philosopher now looks for anything but the gradual evolution of the new order from the old, without breach of continuity or abrupt change of the entire social tissue at any point during the process.'[6] Clearly this ruled out class struggle as the mechanism for social change. If the Fabians saw the 'irresistible progress of Democracy' as the force behind the progress of socialism it was because they identified every type of state intervention into the social and economic life of the country as so many collectivist responses to the problems of capitalism and believed that 'every increase in the political power of the proletariat will most surely be used by them for their economic and social protection.'[7]

This was in the nature of an 'organic change'; the state was gradually adapting the economic system by means of collectivist measures: new principles of social organization were emerging from the conscious minority of socialists; there was a 'slow turning of the popular mind' to these principles; and political changes were bringing further collectivist impulses directly into the electoral arena. Socialism – 'the economic side of the democratic ideal' – was thus being introduced by men antagonistic to its principles because of the demands of modernity. This was why Webb could cite everything from the issue of dog licences, the maintenance of museums and the registration of hawkers, to the production of guano 'in our Colonies' as evidence of the socialist Zeitgeist acting through Liberal and Tory legislators. No wonder that on reading *Fabian Essays*, Beatrice Potter was struck by 'the delicious positivism of the authors'[8] at a time when she herself was 'falling back for encouragement on a growing faith in the possibility of reorganizing society by the application of the scientific method directed by the religious spirit.'[9]

Webb believed that Comte, Darwin and Spencer – the latter having been 'England's greatest philosopher' in the opinion of Beatrice – had shown that 'history is . . . nothing but constant gradual evolution'.[10] The point had been reached, indeed, where the task was 'not so much to disintegrate or supersede the existing social organizations as to expand them'.[11] The origins of 'Socialistic legislation', in Webb's opinion, could be traced as far back as the 43rd Elizabeth of 1601 and the poor law system then instituted by this Act of Parliament. By 1875 and the Public Health Act of that year it was possible to describe an Act of Parliament as 'wholly Socialist in character' because for Webb this quality merely entailed restrictions upon the free use of private property. Fortunately, according to Webb, 'in no other country are statesmen so ready as in England to carry out political proposals pressed upon them from below', and aided by a Civil Service which is 'generally collectivist' and 'democratic in sympathy' the Liberal Party could be expected to become 'more markedly Socialist in character' with every advance towards democracy.[12]

Equipped with an optimism of Panglossian proportions Webb and his co-thinkers were content to believe that 'English' socialism required no special organization of its own but would proceed by virtue of 'the unconscious permeation of all schools of thought'. The avowed socialists would therefore remain a small educational force 'supplying ideas and principles of social reconstruction to each of the great political parties in turn'.[13] The ultimate objective of those like the Fabians who were already fully conscious of the trajectory of progress was defined by Webb as 'the fundamental idea of a Social organism paramount over and prior to the individuals of each generation'.[14] Indeed, on another occasion Webb specifically drew attention to the Fabian contention that 'the perfect and fitting development of each individual is not necessarily the utmost and highest cultivation of his own personality, but the filling, in the best possible way, of his humble function in the great social machine.'[15]

The idea of a 'great social machine' in which individuals were mere cogs held no terrors for Webb and Shaw. For as the latter observed at the

International Socialist Workers and Trades Union Congress in London in 1896, 'The Socialism advocated by the Fabian Society is State Socialism exclusively.'[16] Well before even male suffrage was established – with some six million men effectively disenfranchised and the Labour Party not yet launched – Shaw told the assembled delegates that 'the opposition which exists in the Continental monarchies between the State and the people does not hamper English Socialists . . . The difficulty in England is not to secure more political power for the people but to persuade them to make any sensible use of the power they already have.'[17] But this 'persuasion' would not extend to the advocacy of any direct forms of democracy. These were opposed 'where their effect would be to place the organized, intelligent, and class conscious Socialist minority at the mercy of the unorganized and apathetic mass of routine toilers'.[18] Thus Fabianism, Shaw argued, 'energetically repudiates' any form of direct democracy: 'Democracy as understood by the Fabian Society means simply the control of the administration by freely elected representatives of the people.'[19] This meant in particular that

> When the House of Commons is freed from the veto of the House of Lords and thrown open to candidates from all classes by an effective system of Payment of Representatives and a more rational method of election, the British parliamentary system will be in the opinion of the Fabian Society a first-rate practical instrument of democratic government.[20]

As on other occasions Shaw made clear that the Fabians' confidence in the British political system extended to the existing bourgeois parties whose policies could be made to work for socialism and democracy by the application of judicious pressure from the socialist minority. The Fabian Society therefore 'does not propose that the practical steps towards Social Democracy should be carried out by itself or by any other specially organized society or party'.[21]

The Fabians saw themselves as 'the Benthamites of this generation' whose utilitarian legislative proposals would affect the conclusions of 'all classes' and induce them to accept new principles under the camouflage of the old party names and ideologies. This being the case they believed that 'the greatest need of the English Socialist Party at this moment is men and women of brains who will deliberately set themselves by serious study to work out the detailed application of Collectivist principles to the actual problems of modern life'.[22] Webb argued that as consciousness of social evolution spread so was it possible for the leaders of society to become deliberate agents in the process of natural selection. It would then be possible for functional adaptation to replace the struggle for existence as the main lever of progress – hence the importance of knowing the correct principles of social action.[23] Socialism represented an organization of society capable of inducing the most efficient performance from its resources; as long as society was run by people with the requisite expertise collectivism was the answer to the problem of international rivalries. In the Fabian view it was this competition between nation states which was replacing the blind conflict between individuals as the principle of natural selection: 'inter-racial competition is really more momentous than the struggle between individuals.'[24]

The Fabians were to prove quick to raise the banner of 'National Efficiency' in their quest to win over the British governing elite to collectivist principles. But this was not the product of mere opportunism; from the Society's earliest days it had felt an undisguised contempt for the working class. Trade unionism was dismissed by Webb in 1890 as of benefit only to the 'aristocrats of labour' which he estimated at no more than 10 per cent of the working class[25] (this may well be the source of Lenin's later calculations). According to Webb, the success of the unions was based on their exclusion of the rest of the proletariat. Not that those excluded inspired any hope or sympathy in the Fabians. As Shaw recalled, 'Our only contribution to the (unemployed) agitation was a report which we printed in 1886 which . . . even hinted at compulsory military service as means of absorbing some of the unskilled unemployed.'[26] And this authoritarian element in Fabian thinking increased as the nineteenth century drew to an end. It was based on a low opinion of the 'average sensual man' and a correspondingly exalted sense of the efficacy of an intellectual aristocracy. Thus a Fabian election manifesto in 1892 complained that 'the average British working man is a political pauper; he will neither do his own political work, nor pay anyone else to do it for him.' In the same year another Fabian tract lamented that the working class was 'so ill-organized, so easily led away by the fine phrases of the political leaders of the upper classes and so deficient in any genuine, practical business-like knowledge of politics and finance'.[27]

The intellectual formation of the leading Fabians ill-equipped them to regard the working class in a more favourable light. Beatrice Webb recalled, for example, that the central article of her father's political faith had been 'a direct denial of democracy'; that she had been reared to regard labour as an abstraction comparable to a mass of gold sovereigns; that she was aware of herself as belonging to a class that gave orders and had 'acquired the marks of the caste' which regarded possession of some form of power over other people as the test of fitness for membership.[28] One of the earliest causes of her repulsion from this order, according to Beatrice, was the apparent debasement of the ruling class as the well-bred and cultivated were replaced by the merely rich. Her distaste for the existing ruling class therefore seems to have been principally based on its unmeritocratic nature.[29]

Not all the Fabians came from such privileged backgrounds as Beatrice – indeed she was very conscious that Sidney was of 'little folk' who strove without difficulty for inconspicuousness.[30] But they shared a similar ideological heritage firmly grounded in Victorian paternalism. The Christian tradition had grown thin and brittle and by the 1870s a different faith was developing out of the legacy of Comte and Darwin and the industry of Herbert Spencer, Frederic Harrison, Francis Galton, T. H. Huxley and

J. Tyndall, who supplied a new religion of science. One of the effects of this evolutionary sociology was that 'man sinks down to comparative insignificance; he is removed in degree but not in kind from the mere animal and vegetable.'[31] At least this was how Beatrice Webb experienced the change. The new science, though clearly bankrupt in choosing the ends of human endeavour, was perceived by its converts as supreme on the question of means. Among the intellectuals with a social conscience an 'almost fanatical faith' in the efficacy of science to solve human problems developed which captured 'the most original and vigorous minds of the 'seventies and 'eighties'. Beatrice Webb described this cult of science as 'by far the most potent ferment at work in the mental environment in which I was reared'.[32] Sidney was also one of its products, and the idea of using science in the service of Comte's religion of humanity inspired many another Fabian intellectual to take on the role of social investigator.

Given the massive social problems generated by late Victorian capitalism and the fact that the governing class of the 1880s and 1890s was 'innately indifferent to the workings of the intellect',[33] this attraction to science can easily be understood. But the irony is that the Fabians sought to convert the system via this self-same governing class. This was surely because, as Beatrice Webb confided to her diary:

> 'we have little faith in the "average sensual man", we do not believe that he can do much more than describe his grievances, we do not think that he can prescribe the remedies. ... We wish to introduce into politics the professional expert – to extend the sphere of government by adding to its enormous advantages of wholesale and compulsory management, the advantage of the most skilled entrepreneur.'[34]

The fact that the Fabians championed municipal socialism, especially in the years 1890–1910, does not alter the clear centralist and bureaucratic thrust of their thinking. They were conscious that local government is after all part of the state, and at a time when it was impossible for socialists to get into Parliament it was expedient to centre Webb's wire-pulling endeavours in a more fruitful field. It was not as if local government presented a focal point for mobilizing working-class opinion in order to forge a socialist consciousness: 'The reforms made between 1835 and 1929 standardized arrangements for local government and eliminated whatever could not be assimilated to businesslike principles.'[35] Far from being centres of self-government, municipalities were absorbed into an expanding positive state as Bentham and J. S. Mill had advocated. Mill had seen the value of using local institutions as a means of inducting the working class into bourgeois politics, a way of socializing them into the norms and values of bourgeois society. Webb stood foursquare in this paternalist tradition. From 1888 the Fabians urged their sympathizers to join Liberal and Radical Associations or, if they preferred it, Conservative Associations or the Co-operative Store. This was what the Progressive majority – full of Fabian ideas, according to Shaw – actually consisted of on the London County Council in 1888.

The *Workers' Political Programme*[36] which the Society published in 1891 differed not at all from 'advanced Liberalism' in its demands for adult suffrage, payment of Members, an eight-hour day, a national system of education, taxes on land and inheritance and progressive income tax. The Fabians' distinctive demand continued to be the proposed tax on the 'unearned increment', especially on land which one pamphlet estimated to have amassed rents worth £16 million per year between 1870 and 1891 in London alone.[37] But since the Society was never able to explain how to identify the unearned component in incomes or elucidate its relationship to risk-taking, saving, and other of the 'functions' ascribed to property owners in orthodox economics, the idea had no policy-making merit whatever. Webb's ire was invariably directed at the 'absolutely unproductive classes'[38] rather than at the capitalists in industry and agriculture and this narrowed considerably even the abstract value of the Fabian fiscal proposals. Even at a time when there was considerable interest in land reform the Fabians regarded its nationalization as a distant prospect.

When the National Liberal Federation adopted the so-called Newcastle Programme in 1891 the Fabians hailed it as proof of the success of the policy of 'permeation'. For the programme wanted free schools, universal male suffrage, payment for Members of Parliament, taxation of land values, ground rents, death duties, mining royalties and the like as well as other Fabian proposals such as shorter parliaments. It was only when Gladstone, the People's William, turned his back on these demands that Webb and Shaw were forced to reappraise the strategy of influencing the existing parties. From February 1893 they advocated an independent force of Labour MPs, concluding that 'the only real difficulty in the way is the apathy of the workers themselves who have not as yet realized the power given them by the Reform Bill of 1884'.[39] When the ILP was formed in 1894 these hopes were encouraged. But though the new party took its philosophy and much of its propaganda from Fabian sources the flirtation with independent labour representation proved brief. In the year the ILP was formed Beatrice Webb recorded the lack of Fabian faith in the 'average sensual man' and was soon back in the old grooves:

> judging from our knowledge of the Labour movement we can expect *no* leader from the working class. Our only hope is in permeating the young middle class man. – (1895)

> The truth is that we and MacDonald are opposed on a radical issue of policy. To bring about the maximum amount of public control in public administration do we want to organize the unthinking persons into Socialist Societies or to make the thinking persons socialistic? We believe in the latter process. – (1896)

> The rank and file of Socialists – especially English Socialists – are unusually silly folk (for the most part feather-headed failures) – (1896)[40]

By 1895 Fabian policy had reverted to type, 'giving to each class, to each person coming under our influence the exact dose of collectivism that they are prepared to assimilate'.[41]

Well before members of the Conservative and Liberal parties took up the cause of national efficiency the Fabians had hammered away at the issue of social and economic decay in relation to Britain's Imperial responsibilities. In *The London Programme* which Sidney Webb wrote for the Progressives in the elections of 1892 the Fabian leader struck a note of fear:

> We dare not neglect the sullen discontent now spreading among its toiling millions. If only for the sake of the rest of the Empire, the London masses must be organized for a campaign against the speculators, vestry jobbers, house farmers, water sharks, market monopolists, ground landlords and other social parasites now feeding upon their helplessness. Metropolitan reform has become a national if not yet an imperial question.'[42]

The Fabians' concern with efficiency naturally caused them to express concern about the under-class of unemployed and casual workers who caused such anxiety among the London bourgeoisie – especially after bouts of rioting. Webb pointed to the 'horde of semi-barbarians' which the individualist system had created and was content to do nothing about.[43] By the middle of the decade another Fabian, Sidney Ball, was intent on affirming the severe standards of socialism by contrast with which the individualist system was tolerant of the wholesale degradation of labour. The socialist policy, he argued, 'favours the strong': 'it is a process of conscious social selection by which the industrial residuum is naturally sifted and made manageable for some kind of restrictive, disciplinary or, it may be "surgical" treatment.'[44] Thus far from pandering to the poor, as some of Socialism's detractors might think, 'the real danger of Collectivism', according to Ball, 'is that it would be as ruthless as Plato in the direction of "social surgery" '.[45]

The Fabians made proposals to weed out and isolate the residuum in the interests of maintaining the physical and mental health of the labouring class and thereby at least preserving national output and performance. The actual breadth of this class of no-hopers was estimated by Webb to be of the same proportion as in 1837 and 'the depth of poverty is as great as it can ever have been'.[46] Between 1892 and 1898 Webb sat on fourteen committees of the London County Council and laboured away at numerous causes including the Technical Education Board. But as early as 1894 Beatrice wondered if all this work on education was not wasted; if it did not in fact amount to putting the cart before the horse. For it seemed clear enough that 'the vastly more important question' could be 'the breeding' of successive generations of people. Collectivism, after all, depended on the characteristics of 'the democracy' which at present was 'left to the chances of the unregulated and haphazard breeding of the slums'. These 'myriads of deficient minds and deformed bodies' could be expected to produce nothing, in Mrs Webb's view, except 'brutality, meanness, and crime'. Unfortunately prudence dictated that this question had to be approached by an attack on the chaos in industry; here *laissez-faire* was already discredited and the collectivist cause could make some headway. Only after progress was made in this area could the Fabians expect to attack anarchy in its 'stronghold' of the family.[47] Meanwhile the more impetuous Shaw never failed to tell his audiences that the breeding of the right sort of person 'is the most important of all questions'.[48]

The Fabian flirtation with eugenics was only one aspect of their positivist commitment to bring science into politics. As Beatrice explained in a letter of 1896:

> I have the fixed idea that if we are to progress quickly and safely *we must apply the scientific method to social questions*. The present politicians of all parties are Quacks – sometimes they hit on the right idea and sometimes they do not . . . Of course, it is a stupendous task to convert politics into a science – it is possible we may only succeed in laying the foundations.[49]

The Fabians depended on the simple proposition that 'facts were facts' and could be recognized by all rational politicians of good faith whatever their ideological allegiances. As Leonard Woolf observed, they applied to society 'methods that had revealed so much about rocks, apes, and earthworms'.[50] Thus with a detachment appropriate to the study of earthworms Webb could declare in 1894: 'It is I think probable that as regards one class of the Unemployed a term of servitude in an educational labour colony on a small scale . . . would be the best . . . means of restoring them to the ranks of productive citizens.'[51] The Webbs believed, as Beatrice acknowledged, that 'human action must be judged by its results in bringing about certain defined ends.'[52] If, therefore, a spell of penal servitude for certain people would help promote the formation of noble character and increased intellectual faculty in the average individual, while of course improving the efficiency of society, then these consequences would fully justify it. Of course armchair architects of the future such as the Webbs were no better placed in reality than other mortals in knowing precisely what the consequences of their proposals could be. But their confidence in 'the facts' obscured this truth: 'If there is one thing I have believed "from the beginning to the end" it is that no progress can be made except on the basis of ascertained fact and carefully thought out suggestion.'[53] The Fabians wanted experts like themselves to moralize and scientize the politicans. It made no difference in this respect whether the party in power was Liberal or Conservative; what mattered was that they were in power and in need of policies to improve the standards of the race, the nation and the Empire. When the Boer War began in October 1899 the Fabian Society held aloof from pronouncing its attitude partly in a spirit of keeping collectivist science out of mere politics, as Shaw had emphasized some years before when he boasted that the Society had: 'no distinctive opinions on the Marriage Question, Religion, Art, abstract Economics, historic Evolution, Currency or any other subject than its own special business of practical Democracy and Socialism.'[54] But this absurd distinction could not be sustained and the majority of the Society took the view that the British Empire had to win the war even before Shaw wrote *Fabianism and Empire* (1900).

Shaw's argument in *Fabianism and Empire* was that the Great Powers necessarily dominated the world and the real question was that they should govern it in the interests of 'civilization'. The main point therefore for the Fabians was that Britain would only live up to its civilizing imperial mission if 'brains and political science' replaced Conservatism and Liberalism. This was an argument appreciated by imperialists in both of the major parties; among the Liberal Imperialists led by Lord Rosebery, who believed in the need for imperial expansion and social reform at home in the interests of national efficiency, and among the Liberal Unionists led by Joseph Chamberlain. It was only when Chamberlain returned from a visit to South Africa in 1903 and made his famous speech for a system of fiscal preferences as a means to imperial unity that the dream of a National Efficiency Party was shattered. Henceforward the imperialists were divided between tariff reformers and free traders, despite the sedulous efforts of the Webbs to bring these disparate forces together in the preceding years: Beatrice had even set up a Co-Efficients Club with the new party in mind. Liberal Imperialists such as Rosebery, R. B. Haldane, Asquith and Grey attended Beatrice's social gatherings along with Balfour and other Conservatives. Of Haldane Beatrice wrote:

> What bound us together as associates was our common faith in a deliberately organized society; our common belief in the application of science to human relations with a view to betterment. Where we differed was in the orientation to political power. Haldane believed more than we did in the existing governing class: in the great personages of Court, Cabinet and City. We stacked our hopes on the organized working class served and guided it is true, by an elite of unassuming experts who would make no claim to superior social status but would content themselves with exercising the power inherent in superior knowledge and longer administrative experience.[55]

Yet neither the Webb correspondence nor Beatrice's diaries evince any interest in the steps that were taken to set up the Labour Representation Committee (LRC) in February 1900. Even though the Fabian Society was represented by Edward Pease at the meeting which established the LRC, the Webbs were more interested in a National Efficiency Party and that meant regroupment within the existing governing class – the one which Beatrice later professed to find so empty-headed. Indeed, Beatrice records the Webb view that at this time a Conservative government was as good for Fabian schemes as a Liberal administration.[56] This was because there were factions within both parties whose minds had been concentrated by Britain's laboured prosecution of the war in South Africa and by the scandal of widespread ill-health which it exposed at home to consider the irony that the 'imperial race' was stunted, congested and decrepit. Sidney Webb therefore supposed that Fabian collectivism – especially measures to maintain a National Minimum Standard of Life – was on the agenda as the politicians asked themselves by what steps then could ensure the rearing of an imperial race equal to the tasks demanded of it.

The Liberal Imperialists and the Fabians showed a 'general attitude towards the Empire as a powerful and self-conscious force', as Beatrice put it, but the potential for agreement covered many subsidiary items:

> In Ireland, for instance, we don't want to abolish the union with England but so to reconstruct the internal government that it will make the bond of union of secondary importance. We do not want to abolish or remodel the House of Lords but to build up precedents for their non-intervention with national expenditure – all collectivism coming under this head. We do not want to disestablish the Church, but to endow science and secular ethics and any other form of intellectual activity that may seem desirable. We don't want to abolish or restrain the development of private enterprise, but, by creating dykes and bulwarks, to control its mischievous effect on the character of the race. We do not want to unfetter the individual from the obligation of citizenship, we want on the contrary to stimulate and constrain him by the unfelt pressure of a better social environment, to become a healthier, nobler and more efficient being.[57]

Sidney blustered that the 'principle of nationality' was 'but Individualism writ large' when it came to movements such as Fenianism and the aspirations of lesser peoples. And yet in the same major essay he dwelt on the shame of 'England' – its inefficiency, the degradation of 'the race' by drunkenness, gambling and slum life. Some eight million destitute persons – one-fifth of the whole population – constituted 'not merely a disgrace but a positive danger to our civilization'.[58] 'What is the use of an Empire', he asked, quoting Asquith, 'if it does not breed and maintain in the truest and fullest sense of the word an Imperial race?' The nations' leaders, according to Webb, had to stop thinking in individuals and start thinking in corporations and communities, then the maximum development of every component of the Empire could proceed apace. The first and most urgent step required was the National Minimum standard of life: 'not merely or even mainly for the comfort of the workers but absolutely for the success of our industry in competition in the world'.[59] How else, Webb asked, could Britain otherwise have an efficient army, state and Imperium? Just as the 1834 Poor Law Amendment Act had once saved the nation from hideous disaster by inventing the workhouse test and thereby preventing the spread of pauperism to the able-bodied, so too could the National Minimum stop the contemporary rot. For, Webb argued, 'it is in the class-rooms of these schools that the future battles of the Empire for commercial prosperity are already being lost' for want of science and technique instilled in the minds of the present generations. German and American standards had already surpassed the expectations of the British. It was time the British acquired 'virility in government' and began the process of lifting the nation up; otherwise, warned Webb, we will not even possess the 'system of scientific fighting' which will settle future wars.[60]

In 1902, the year after Webb put this argument, H. G. Wells published his *Anticipations* of a future scientific and mechanized society which dwelt on the obsolescence of the urban poor, which he described as being composed for the most part of 'criminal, immoral and parasitic' elements engaged in a 'hopeless competition against machinery'.[61] This profoundly authoritarian, racist and elitist book drew the attention of the Webbs who promptly wrote to Wells and drew him into the circle of Co-Efficients. Beatrice described *Anticipations* as a 'remarkable book' which applied the methods of the physical sciences to social problems and commended in particular 'his capacity for seeing the future machinery of government and the relation of classes'.[62] Wells had in fact proposed no solution for the problem of 'the abyss', the vast majority of the manual working class which represented a 'bulky, irremovable excretion, the appearance of these gall-stones of vicious, helpless, and pauper masses'[63], though the necessity for their surgical removal is strongly implied. But he also foresaw the growth of a scientifically literate stratum arising from the reconstructed ranks of the old middle class, and windily dismissed the political system as a useless anachronism – two arguments with which the Webbs could sympathize. His hope and expectation was that 'a really functional social body of engineering, managing men, scientifically trained, and having common ideals and interests, is likely to segregate and disentangle itself from our present confusion of aimless and ill-directed lives.'[64]

In the discussions which followed the publication of Wells's book the Webbs took issue with the idea that the whole manual working class would have to sink deeper and deeper into the morass of misery until it was finally extinguished. They also disagreed with Wells's idealization of the scientifically educated petty bourgeois as the future governor of society. Webb had always championed the role of trained administrators in any future rational society: 'I do not mean the amateur business that is now called government – still less do I mean politics. But all experience shows that men need organizing as much as machines or rather much more (in order) to ensure order, general health and comfort and maximum productivity.'[65]

The trained administrator of the future, explained Webb, will be 'equipped with an Economics or a Sociology which will be as scientific and as respected . . . as Chemistry or Mechanics'.[66] Webb's goal was 'to diminish the sum of huan suffering':

> I am not concerned about this party or that but about getting things done no matter who does them. Elections and parties are quite subordinate – *even trivial* – parts of political action. More is done in England

in politics whilst ignoring elections and parties than by or with them. Nevertheless they too form a part of life which the Socialist cannot ignore.'[67]

This was the real point about the Fabian triumvirates' attitude towards democracy. Wells, as Beatrice noted, 'has hardly realized the function of the representative as a "foolometer" for the expert'.[68] The democratic process was required to legitimize the activities of experts who, as Sidney explained, would set about getting things done 'whilst ignoring elections'.

Popular attachment to such freedoms as pertained under bourgeois rule was also a genuine source of bafflement to Shaw. In 1895 he told an anecdote to illustrate the problem this posed for reformers – a story he repeated almost identically forty years later when offering advice to the Stalinist theorist R. Palme Dutt. According to Shaw,

> In 1888 a Russian subject, giving evidence before the Sweating Inquiry in the House of Lords declared that he left the Russian dominion to work 18 hours in England, *because he is freer here*. Reason is dumb when confronted with a man who exhausted with 13 hours toil will turn to for another five hours for the sake of being free to say that Mr Gladstone is a better man than Lord Salisbury and to read Mill, Spencer and *Reynolds's Newspaper* in the 6 hours left to him to sleep.'

The moral Shaw drew from this was:

> Establish a form of Socialism which shall deprive the people of their sense of personal liberty; and though it double their rations and halve their working hours, they will begin to conspire against it before it is a year old. We only disapprove of monopolists: we *hate* masters.[69]

The truth contained in this story made the Fabian leaders conscious of the need for democratic camouflage rather than enthusiastic advocates of democracy and the extension of democracy. When the hour of the dictators struck, Shaw told Friedrich Adler in 1927 that 'we must get the Socialist movement out of its old democratic grooves', and three days later he claimed that 'We as Socialists have nothing to do with liberty. Our message, like Mussolini's, is one of discipline of service, of ruthless refusal to acknowledge any national right of competence.'[70]

By the 1930s the Webbs had also come round to the support of open dictatorship in the form it took in Stalin's Russia. Although Wells modified his argument to take account of the Webbs' 'samurai' class of administrators when he wrote *A Modern Utopia*, it was he who had the last word, arguing that Shaw and Webb had both shown by the 1930s 'that their trend of mind is all towards such a qualification of crude democracy as . . . I was seeking': 'If Russia has done nothing else for mankind, the experiment of the Communist Party is alone sufficient to justify her revolution and place it upon an altogether higher level than that chaotic emotional release, the first French Revolution.'[71]

Conclusion

The national socialism championed by the Fabian Society was given a theoretical framework that was every bit as deterministic as the most vulgar
Marxism. Socialist politics, in practice, was reduced to the activities of an elite
whose energies were focused on the persuasion of the governing class. The
Fabians believed that the leaders of the bourgeois parties would increasingly
turn to collectivist measures to solve the problems generated by the individualist system as it became clear that this was the route to national and imperial
efficiency. The task of the Fabians was to prod the ruling class in this direction
– a direction towards which historical evolution was already tending.

The main obstacles in this evolutionary process were identified as ignorance
and amateurism rather than antagonistic class interests. The British state was
accordingly regarded as an essentially benign, class-neutral ensemble of institutions which could be put to collectivist work once the right people were in
charge of it. It followed, therefore, that imperial government – which Shaw
admitted could be despotic and bureaucratic – would become 'invincible'
when men of scientific and collectivist intelligence took it over. For just as the
future collectivist state would function in the paternalistic interests of the
average sensual man, the same result would be achieved globally in the territories of the Empire by Britain governing 'in the interests of civilization as a
whole'.[72]

With the proviso that a more intelligent collectivism was required, the
Fabians thus accepted the self-image of the British state; its institutions, both
domestic and imperial, were above class and sectional interest and objects of
general patriotism. In the name of progress or 'civilization' the passive mass,
just like the 'non-adult races',[73] were to be moulded, regulated, perhaps even
surgically removed, as the experts saw fit. Thus in a period of imperialist
expansion, when Tory politicians gave imperialism a prominent place on the
political agenda partly to maintain the working-class Tory vote, the Fabians
did nothing to challenge the dominant imperialist propaganda.[74] In this
respect, as in their conception of the British state generally, they were more
representative of British socialism than the minority of anti-imperialists.

4

Independent Labour
Representation

The achievements of the socialists in the 1880s were considerable. Their organizations managed to maintain journals which effectively propagandized the cause, like *Justice* and *Commonweal*, and which recruited able agitators and organizers of the next generation. These efforts were supplemented by the propaganda work of the Fabian Society and by newspapers associated with particular individuals: Annie Besant's *Our Corner*, Belfort Bax's *To-day*, H. H. Champion's *Common Sense* (*Labour Elector*) and the journals which socialists edited such as the *Link* (Besant) and *Christian Socialist* (Champion). Although the total number of socialists was probably never more than 2,000[1] at any time in the 1880s, the unemployed agitation and the New Unionism brought them to the attention of a very large public and gave a foretaste of what they could do. Had the SDF and the Socialist League (SL) been better disposed to trade unions these results might well have been surpassed.

But it would be wrong to suppose that the Marxists were simply the victims of a bad leadership. Some of Hyndman's personal faults – especially his anti-semitism and jingoism – never left an impression on the SDF and even his and Quelch's hostility to the unions did not prevent the organization's largely autonomous branches from spontaneously involving themselves in trade union work.[2] Nevertheless it is true that Hyndman's domineering style and dogmatic sectarianism estranged most of the talented recruits to the Federation and helped to ensure that it was left behind by the most important developments of the period: the SDF was to remain largely aloof from the movement for independent labour representation when this began to gather pace at the end of the 1880s even though, as also with the New Unionism, members of the party were prominent in the campaign.

The cause of independent working-class representation first became something more than a hypothetical possibility after the Reform Act of 1867. In the same year the London Working Men's Association demanded labour men in Parliament and in 1869 the Labour Representation League was set up with Henry Broadhurst as its secretary to campaign for the registration of working-class voters. But this poorly-financed initiative soon fizzled out and by

1880 there were still only three working-class MPs, including Broadhurst the secretary of the TUC, and all under the Liberal Whip. When the electorate was further extended by another two-thirds in 1884, bringing the number of voters to four million, the working-class vote was tied to the two bourgeois parties. For a time it seemed possible that the Liberals would be best able to adapt to the unfolding democracy. Since his successful time as Mayor of Birmingham, between 1873 and 1876, Joseph Chamberlain had as we have seen put himself at the head of an attempt to galvanize the diaspora of special interests and organizations which comprised Radicalism. On his initiative a National Liberal Federation was formed in 1877 in preparation to drive the Whigs out of the party and promote domestic reforms which would seal an alliance between Radicalism and the working-class electorate.

When Gladstone's government of 1880 divided Radical opinion by its repressive imperialist policies in Ireland, Egypt and the Sudan, and altogether failed in respect of domestic reform, Chamberlain renewed his populist demagogy. The extension of the franchise to the rural working class in 1884 provided an opportunity for more Radical rhetoric against landlordism but Chamberlain was unable to find a convincing urban equivalent for the slogan 'three acres and a cow'. Nevertheless the tone of some of his speeches suggested that some kind of 'urban cow' would have to be found in the interests of preserving capitalism. As he said on one occasion in drawing attention to the contrast between wealthy idlers and impoverished workers:

> If you will go back to the earlier history of our social system you will find that when our social arrangements first began to shape themselves every man was born into the world with natural rights, with a right to a share in the great inheritance of the community; with a right to a part of the land of his birth; but all these rights have passed away. The common rights of ownership have disappeared; some of these have been sold; some of them have been given away by people who had no right to dispose of them; some of them have been lost through apathy and ignorance; some have been destroyed by fraud; and some have been acquired by violence . . . But then I ask what ransoms will property pay for the security which it enjoys? What substitute will it find for the natural rights which have ceased to be recognized? Society is banded together in order to protect itself against the instinct of those of its members who would make very short work of private ownership if they were left alone. That is all very well; but I maintain that society owes to these men something more than tolerance in return for the restriction which it places upon their liberty of action.[3]

The socialists were not taken in by this rhetoric; 'the Radical today', said J. E. Williams of the SDF, 'was the "Artful Dodger" who went up and down the country telling people to take hold of the landlord thief but to let the greater thief, the capitalist, go scot free'.[4] But Hyndman was happy to observe that the logic of Chamberlain's case 'lead(s) inevitably to Socialism'.[5] By 1886

Chamberlain's revolt against Gladstone's Home Rule policy for Ireland led to an irreparable split with the Liberal Party and the would-be social reformer found himself leader of the so-called Liberal Unionists who would henceforth find common cause with the Tories. Though the unions remained loyal to Gladstone the Irish issue, in a Parliament where Parnell's 86 Nationalist MPs held the balance of power, postponed social reform indefinitely. The working-class vote was now more than ever evenly divided between Liberal and Tory. Thus with the Liberals no longer able to pose as the automatic bearers of the 'Labour interest' and with no immediate prospect of social reform from either party the case for an independent labour party was much strengthened.

Engels had first publicly argued for such a party in articles which he wrote for *Labour Standard* between May and August 1881. Within the Socialist League, Aveling, Eleanor Marx and J. L. Mahon represented this viewpoint until the Bloomsbury branch went its own way in 1888 as the Bloomsbury Socialist Society and Mahon seceded with the Labour Emancipation League. The Aveling – Marx group was chiefly occupied with the agitation for a legal eight-hour day while Mahon, together with other militants from the SDF and SL, had helped to build up a North of England Socialist Federation in the course of the great miners' strike of 1887 on the Northumberland coalfield. Although the Federation faded when the strike ended, its published objectives show how far these socialist leaders had departed from the attitudes of Hyndman and Morris:

1. Forming and helping other Socialist bodies to form a National and International Socialist Labour Party.

2. Striving to conquer political power by promoting the election of Socialists to Parliament, local governments, school boards and other administrative bodies.

3. Helping trades unionism, co-operation, and every genuine movement for the good of the workers.

4. Promoting a scheme for the national and international federation of labour.[6]

Within the SDF the most important convert to the cause of independent labour representation was H. H. Champion who, like Hyndman, had come to socialism from Tory radicalism and was to be dogged by this connection for the rest of his life, especially after the 'Tory Gold' scandal of 1885. Champion's military background enabled him to see clearly, after the riots of 1886, that the SDF would either have to take its physical force propaganda seriously or else renounce it altogether. By the August 14 1886 issue of *Justice* Champion was openly arguing that street fighting was a redundant tactic in an age of precision cannon. It now seemed to him that the only useful strategy was one of building a labour representation in Parliament and when the SDF refused to accept this reasoning he dropped out of active involvement and began publication of a monthly journal, *Common Sense*, from which in September 1887 he criticized the SDF as a failure and called for the creation of an independent labour presence in Parliament by means of an alliance of socialists with the existing working-class organizations – principally the unions. This was precisely the position advocated by Engels, and Champion naturally found allies for it inside the Socialist League among Engels' Bloomsbury followers. There was support too within the Fabian Society, though here the influence of Webb and Shaw prevented full collaboration; as we have seen the Fabian leaders were deeply sceptical of the value of any attempts to establish a new labour party.[7]

What Champion was able to do was use the Labour Electoral Committee which the TUC had created in 1886 in the first flush of enthusiasm following the Reform Act of 1884 and see that it did not become dependent upon the Liberals as had its predecessor, the Labour Representation League of 1873. When this Committee was put on a more permanent basis in 1887 as the Labour Electoral Association, Champion tried to take it at its word as 'the Centre of the National Labour Party' and ran its Metropolitan Section with the assistance of sympathizers such as Mann, Burns and Mahon for the purpose of addressing the 'labour interest'. *Common Sense* became *Labour Elector* (1888) and focused attention on such labour issues as the eight-hour day and the appalling working conditions at Brunner's chemical factory in Northwich, while by-elections in the Metropolis were used as an occasion for interrogating the candidates on these matters and threatening to stand independent labour candidates if neither established party proved satisfactory. This policy was put into operation at Dulwich in December 1887 and Deptford in January 1888, where Champion put himself forward until the Liberal candidate made some concessions.

Champion's objective was to create a labour party which would fight for 'the immediate amelioration of the conditions of the [workers'] . . . lives'. Trade unions alone could not secure such improvements because their efficiency was questionable in times of trade depression and they were in any case confined to a tiny minority of workers. Only by parliamentary action could the workers expect to institute such reforms as employer liability for industrial injury and disease, adequate inspection of work premises, decent housing for the poor, public works for the unemployed and a host of other reforms. A legal eight-hour day alone could be expected to engender such benefits as extra employment, more leisure, less competition for jobs and improved quantity and quality of production; compared to the potential of these reforms, trade union action was puny indeed.[8]

The trouble was that the eleven working-class MPs who existed by 1885 could always be expected to put the Liberal cause before the Labour cause. But if independent labour representatives were needed, the franchise, according to Champion, was already sufficiently extended to make getting them feasible and, once obtained, such parliamentary power would prove efficacious.

Champion expressed the view that there was sufficient tolerance, common sense, patience and fairness in all classes in Britain to 'give good grounds for the hope that as our race taught the world the lesson of political liberty so it [would] set it an example in the rapid and peaceful attainment of economic freedom.'[9] There was no doubt in his mind that 'the House now roughly represents the rule of the many' and that 'its decisions cannot be upset by violence, because the big battalions are on its side.'[10]

Champion imagined that truly independent labour MPs would put the demand for an eight-hours bill before every consideration and once their numbers became sufficiently great they would be able 'to wreck one ministry after another until the measure is passed'.[11] Parnell's Irish Nationalist MPs were of course a source of great inspiration to the advocates of a labour party because they showed in practice how an issue could be forced on to the national political agenda once it was represented by a group which held the balance of power and which showed sufficient determination. The election of John Burns on to the first London County Council in January 1889 was taken as further proof of labour's electoral power and the forward march of the labour question was also signalled when the 1 May was adopted in Europe and America in 1890 as a day of international demonstrations in favour of the eight hour day. Champion argued that a labour majority was not required in each or even any of the many constituencies for real electoral progress to be made on this issue. In the first instance it would be enough to simply organize the independent labour vote and use it to influence the constituency results.

Champion himself was quite prepared to advocate protective tariffs if eight-hours legislation endangered the competitiveness of British industry – even though the unions and most of the working class supported free trade.[12] Though there were few followers of Champion's 'Tory socialism', the vigorous group which he gathered around him concurred with Engels in identifying the eight-hours agitation as the 'gateway into a genuine Socialist movement'.[13] If the union leaders were obstacles on this path then, as J. L. Mahon argued, they had to be fought inside the trade union organizations. James Keir Hardie's attack on Henry Broadhurst at the 1887 TUC sought to expose the contradictions involved in the unions' support for the Liberal Party in just this manner. For here was Broadhurst, secretary of the Parliamentary Committee of the TUC for the previous twelve years and a former Under-Secretary of State in the Liberal Government, allegedly supporting a Liberal candidate who employed sweated labour. Two years later Hardie came back to the TUC, this time repeating an accusation of Champion's to the effect that Broadhurst was a shareholder in Brunner's, the chemical company exposed for dangerous working conditions in *Labour Elector*. The more general point, of course, was that the unions were illogically tied to the Liberals for parliamentary purposes while workers were ruthlessly exploited by Liberal employers who fought the unions and opposed reforms in the labour interest. Hardie himself had had to learn this lesson the hard way.[14]

As an advocate of 'advanced Radicalism' and the secretary of the

Lanarkshire miners from 1878 Hardie stressed the values of family life, temperance, thrift and self-help and self-improvement generally. In 1884 he formed a Junior Liberal Association and wrote for a local Radical newspaper. Even after his involvement in strikes on the coalfield in 1879 and 1880 Hardie believed that strong trade unionism would promote concord between capital and labour. By 1883 he was converted to eight-hours legislation, when it became obvious that no amount of self-help could improve pay and working conditions on the coalfield, subject as that was to the influx of unskilled labour from Glasgow and Ireland. Nevertheless since Liberalism, or at least its advanced wing, seemed to be becoming more interventionist as demands for the nationalization of land and free education gained ground within it, Hardie persisted with the belief that collaboration with these elements could advance the cause of labour and so he worked for the Liberals in the general elections of 1885 and 1886.

Even in these years more subversive ideas had penetrated into the mining communities of West Scotland. In the first place it was the Irish and Highland agitations for land reform which opened some minds to new ideas, and after Henry George's lecturing tour of 1884 the Scottish Land Restoration League was set up, while Mahon and Scheu established the Land and Labour League in Edinburgh in an attempt to bring together the demand for land nationalization and the socialist objective of common ownership of the means of production. In the same year a branch of the SDF was created in Glasgow and when its London leadership divided a Socialist League presence was established in Scotland by Mahon and Bruce Glasier. Meanwhile a branch of the Land and Labour League was set up on the Lanarkshire coalfield in 1885 by William Small, who urged the miners to run their own candidate in the general election, the better to press for mining legislation. Both the SDF and the SL organized demonstrations in support of the miners in 1887 when the recently formed Scottish Miners Federation took strike action over pay against the advice of its secretary, Keir Hardie.

While riots accompanied the strike of 1887 Hardie wrote in the *Miner*, which he launched that year, that 'Miners are prepared to render a fair day's work to the employers in return for which they demand a fair day's pay with all the rights of freedom to boot.'[15] This was the pure milk of labourism, but it failed to impress local Liberal opinion which was quite prepared to see the union crushed. It was now that Hardie began to change his ideas, arguing in the *Miner* that poverty, far from being a symptom of the drink problem, would persist until capitalism was abolished. While Hardie demanded state intervention on such matters as industrial arbitration, social insurance and the eight-hour day, the Lib-Lab MPs in Parliament, during the passage of the Coal Mines Regulation Bill in June and July 1887, failed to support the eight-hours demand. Hardie now saw the need for a Labour Party and argued along these lines in the *Miner* from April 1887. Around this time he met Engels and Mann in London and it was under the influence of the group around Champion that he attacked Broadhurst at the TUC in September.

In March 1888 Hardie was selected as the miners' candidate for the Mid-Lanark by-election but was rejected by the local Liberals and was forced to stand as an independent. Hardie's campaign received help from Mann, Mahon, Champion and Cunninghame Graham but was conducted tamely enough – his election leaflets declared that 'a vote for Hardie is a vote for Gladstone'. Though Hardie polled a mere 617 votes out of the 7,000 cast the campaign ultimately derived significance as a step towards the formation of a national labour party. In August Hardie formed the Scottish Labour Party (SLP) while Champion seceded from the Labour Electoral Association in order to use its Metropolitan Section as the nucleus of a 'National Labour Party'. Though the SLP was not committed to socialism the Scottish Land and Labour League dissolved itself into the new organization, which stood for the strategy advocated by Engels – the domination of the labour question over all others for the purpose of welding the widest class solidarity within the proletariat.

When it is remembered that the meagre trade union membership of 549,000 recorded in 1874 fell substantially during the next ten years and was not exceeded until 1889, it becomes clear that the advocates of independent labour had plenty to do. But drawing attention to labour issues could have spectacular results as when the *Labour Elector* and the *Link* exposed atrocious working conditions at Bryant and May during 1888 and helped the largely female workforce to wage their successful strike. This proved to be the beginning of a wave of unrest and trade union organization among the unskilled, as chapter 2 has shown. Eleanor Marx, Mann and Burns helped Will Thorne in the creation of a Gasworkers and General Labourers' Union in 1889 and in the same year Ben Tillett used the services of Mann and Burns in the dockers' strike. Socialists gained substantial prestige from these efforts and the New Unionism also seemed to embody socialist values by extending the principle of trade union organization to everybody and by recognizing the need for political action to achieve lasting benefits for the working class. Socialists now gained a strong representation on the London Trades Council while the 1890 TUC narrowly supported the legal eight-hour day because the miners, engineers and carpenters voted with the new unions.

Mann drew the lesson that trade union organization was a prerequisite for the advance of working class interests and envisaged 'national federations of capitalists and workmen facing and fighting each other in a manner that will make the struggles of the past insignificant by comparison'.[16] It was clearly recognized by those involved in organizing the unskilled workers that unless trade union membership could be extended to embrace the whole mass of unskilled workers any gains made by the organized would be undermined by employers making use of the unorganized. The idea of 'One Big Union' was attractive on this reasoning, but it was a logic which overestimated the potential for such a structure and which underestimated the relative stability of employment and the skill level of workers within particular industries; the unskilled were not as mobile nor as unskilled as some activists supposed.[17] But the New Unionism did promote that class consciousness so keenly awaited by Engels. Mann saw the growth in trade union branches and trades councils as the forum for 'the real educational work on labour questions' and as a source of support for independent political action on councils and in Parliament. The onset of trade depression in the early 1890s, however, badly set back the new unions, which did not fully recover until after the expansion of 1911–14; but at the same time the socialist presence in the older craft unions advanced, to the extent that they represented about one-quarter of the votes at the TUC in the early 1890s.[18]

Champion's *Labour Elector* group broke up in 1890 when the paper was folded. The New Unionism had spotlighted Mann and Burns far more than Champion and these two now went their own way. Burns was elected to the LCC and became more firmly ensconced in the Progressive alliance of Fabian and Radical provenance. The very fact that the LCC had only just been formed provided plenty of scope for reforms over which socialists and Radicals could agree, but undoubtedly detracted from independent labour politics in the capital. The demise of the Champion group was also connected with the fact that Champion's Tory background and connections with Tory agents such as Maltman Barry were a constant reminder of the notorious 'Tory Gold' scandal of 1885. Champion also expounded the idea of an imperial customs union with state-guaranteed minimum wages throughout the Empire, and often used *Labour Elector* to pursue a line more favourable to the Tories than the Liberals. Like Hyndman, he was convinced that Gladstonian Liberalism was more of an enemy to socialism than was Toryism, but this only strengthened the suspicions of those who saw his work as a means of dividing the Liberal vote for the benefit of his Tory friends.

Champion departed for Australia in 1890 but returned in 1891 to resume his campaign for the labour cause. His disdain for the millenarian 'apocalyptic ravings' of the Hyndmanites and his conviction that further constitutional reforms were beside the point were now shared by most of those concerned with independent labour politics. Nor would most socialists demur at the patriotic note in Champion's propaganda which talked of the welfare of the working class as 'of the highest national importance' and promised that 'should grave danger from without threaten our country, the Labour party will hold its hand from its special work until such foreign complications be settled.'[19] The problem with Champion as far as his co-thinkers in labour politics were concerned was that, unlike them, he had no sympathies past or present with Liberalism.

By 1891, however, the centre of gravity of independent labour politics had shifted to the North of England and the London socialists became less important in the immediate struggle. Small groups of socialists had been established in the North for some time; in Sheffield from 1886 Edward Carpenter led a socialist society which he tried hard to keep out of the intrigues of the London organizations; and two years later the SDF still only had 96 members in the whole of Lancashire, distributed in six branches. In 1889 the *Yorkshire*

Factory Times was established with Joseph Burgess, already a pioneer of independent labour representation, as its editor. By 1890 Fabian societies, largely of working-class composition, began (briefly) to appear in the North and Robert Blatchford was using the Radical newspaper, the *Sunday Chronicle*, to espouse the socialist cause. But it was the recession in the woollen industry following the American lurch into protectionism with the McKinley tariff of 1890 which sparked off the most important train of events in the history of labour politics in West Yorkshire.

The New Unionism had already touched the area when the Leeds gas-workers struck in 1890 with the active involvement of the Bradford and Leeds branches of the Socialist League. Engels, who acted, according to Henry Pelling, 'as a sort of revolutionary generalissimo' in this major struggle pre-sented Will Thorne with an inscribed copy of *Capital* for his part in the conflict, such was the importance he attached to the struggle. But when the textile employers tried to reduce wages at the end of 1890 the entire unorganized workforce came out on strike at the Manningham Mills in Bradford, and with the aid of socialists and Burgess's *Yorkshire Factory Times* a Bradford Labour Union was created by the strike leaders which survived the immediate conflict. In November 1891 it fought for two seats on the Bradford Council and asked Tillett and Blatchford to stand in two of the town's parliamentary constituencies. Independence from the bourgeois parties was now emerging as a principle: another Labour Union was set up in the Colne Valley in July 1891 and one in Salford the following month. And when Blatchford launched the *Clarion* in December, another important step was taken in the emergence of an independent labour party.

It will already be evident that this was a local grassroots movement and as such varied from place to place in its immediate causes and ideological con-tent. In West Yorkshire the strike at Manningham Mills became the focus of discontent in part because of the prior agitations of the Socialist League branches in Leeds and Bradford which turned to work within the unions for independent labour representation after 1888.[20] The New Unionism undoubt-edly helped to create a mood more favourable for such work. The struggles of the unskilled in which Socialist Leaguers such as Tom Maguire were involved affected the building trade, tramway workers, dyers' labourers and gas-workers in the area during the year or two before nearly five thousand struck during the five-month dispute at the Manningham Mills. The growth of the New Unionism helped the socialists to reform the trades councils in Halifax, Bradford, Huddersfield, Keighley, Brighouse, Spen Valley, Dewsbury and Batley between 1889 and 1892, turning them into advocates of independent labour. This new generation thus gave a new twist to the idea of working-class self-help which was already so firmly established in the co-operative, trade union and other working-class organizations of the area. Although the activists' understanding of working-class discontent owed much to Marxist analysis and the experience of oppressive Liberal employers and Liberal coun-cils – breaking strikes, opposing the eight-hour day, refusing decent housing and education – the language of revolt in the North drew on Nonconformist traditions. It was an authentic moral revolt against organized religion as well as capitalism which nevertheless employed the ethical language and imagery of Christianity to make its point.

This is one of the reasons why Blatchford's *Clarion* became so important, as we shall see. But nationally the movement was far too fragmented and uneven to enable it to find the resources for a co-ordinated independent labour profile in the general election of 1892. London was generally stony ground; the SDF and the Progressive alliance dominated socialist politics between them and neither were enthusiastic about an independent labour party. It is true that a conference of Fabian societies – mostly working-class in composition – voted for the establishment of such a party in February 1892, but the leading Fabians were more impressed by the conference of the National Liberal Federation which the previous year had adopted a long list of demands in Newcastle designed to attract the working-class vote. This was hailed as proof that permeation was working.

In Scotland Hardie's Scottish Labour Party was divided over its relations with the Liberals and had made no progress since 1888. The *Labour Leader* was in fact absorbed into Champion's *Labour Elector* in 1889 for lack of an independent base. Given these circumstances, no major breakthrough was foreseen for 1892. In the event Hardie won West Ham South and Burns succeeded in Battersea in another straight fight against a Tory. The most significant result was perhaps the 2,749 votes which Ben Tillett attracted in West Bradford – only 600 less than the Liberal victor in a three-cornered contest. This reflected the strength of the Bradford Labour Union and indicated that what had been done in West Yorkshire could happen in the Colne Valley, Swinton, Pendlebury, Manchester, Salford and Newcastle where local organizations for independent labour representation were taking root in 1892. That year Hardie also successfully moved a resolution at the TUC instructing the Parliamentary Committee to prepare a scheme for financing independent labour candidates. It was also at the 1892 TUC that advocates of independent labour representation decided to call a conference of their supporters in Bradford for January 1893. Thus the new party was to be launched in the town where there were already two independent labour councillors.

The SDF rejected a call to assist the new party in every possible way and decided instead, at its conference of August 1892, to assume a position of 'benevolent neutrality'. The Federation had every reason to believe in its own separate future: the growth in socialist activity in the North enabled it to establish a Lancashire District Council with 2,000 members by 1893.[21] It was by no means obvious that it would be eclipsed by the new party. Fabians and SDF members were nevertheless present at the Independent Labour Party's founding conference but the most significant presence was that of young working-class trade unionists. The party's name reflected their wishes and those of socialists like Hardie who saw the need for substantial trade union support if the party was to survive. Hence the argument of Robert Smillie and others who wanted a Socialist Labour Party was rejected, with Tillett weighing in with a tirade against the 'hare-brained chatterers and magpies of Continental revolutionists'.[22] Even J. L. Mahon argued that the party's object was not nationalization of the means of production, as urged by the SDF and many other delegates, but simply 'to secure the separate representation and protection of Labour interests on public bodies'. Yet the committee which prepared the party programme, and which included socialists such as Aveling and Blatchford among its number, included 'the socialist objective' – thus striking a compromise.

Thus the ILP stood from the outset for collective ownership of the means of production as well as labour demands for eight-hours legislation, abolition of overtime and piecework, welfare provision for the sick, disabled, aged, widowed and orphaned, free education from elementary school to university, paid work for the unemployed, and the abolition of child labour for those under fourteen years of age. Shaw also successfully moved that the party should aim for the 'abolition of indirect taxation and taxation to extinction of unearned income'. Later that year ILP members intervened at the TUC to get it to adopt the principle that labour candidates had to support 'collective ownership and control of all the means of production', and in 1894 Hardie successfully moved that the TUC itself should support this objective.[23] But the opponents of socialism fought back by reconstructing TUC standing orders to exclude the trades councils and individuals like Hardie who were neither employed at their trade nor permanent paid officials of the unions. Henceforth voting at the TUC was in proportion to affiliation fees – a measure which strengthened the bloc votes of unions such as those in cotton and coal where the opponents of socialism were strongest. Nevertheless the cause of independent labour was strengthened in Scotland, where the unions were weak and the trades councils relatively strong, when the Scottish TUC was set up in 1897 with trades council involvement. And as sections of the Liberal Party became more interventionist, ILP policies gained more adherents in the older unions. The failures of Gladstone's last administration together with employers' attacks on unions and wages during the recession of the early 1890s also strengthened the ILP case.

In these years the conversion to socialism seems often to have involved all the intense emotions of a religious experience.[24] It often meant a change of friends and lifestyle, with some individuals adopting a Christian asceticism – especially the propertyless, itinerant, proselytizing socialist lecturers who addressed open-air meetings in the language of brotherhood, forgiveness and redemption. It was briefly possible to believe that the promised land was at hand and that such was the force of the socialist message that one only had to spread the word to make converts to it. Thus tactics and policy were not as important as the movement itself and the visions of the socialist future vouchsafed to it. Ideological differences within socialism mattered little to men and women who believed that the most important duty was to bring socialism to those who had not yet heard of it or who only knew what its detractors said of it. Policy, organization, strategy, electoral tactics: these were things that would spring spontaneously out of the conversion of individuals.

No one was more successful in promoting this set of priorities than Robert Blatchford, whose *Clarion* journal was the most popular organ of the socialist press. The main problem as Blatchford saw it was that the state of mind of the working class was still as Carlyle had described it fifty years earlier:

> Thus these poor Manchester manual workers mean only, by fair day's wages for fair day's work, certain coins of money adequate to keep them living – in return for their work, such modicum of food, clothes, and fuel as will enable them to continue their work itself! They as yet clamour for no more; the rest, still inarticulate, cannot shape itself a demand at all and only lies in them as a dumb wish; perhaps only, still more inarticulate, as a dumb, altogether unconscious, want.[25]

It followed, Blatchford never ceased to argue, that the real work for socialism consisted in bringing the socialist case to these people: sharpening their appetites, forming greater expectations, making them articulate. For Blatchford,

> getting men into Parliament is not the chief end of our Party . . . Parliament follows public opinion it does not guide it . . . The great bulk of public opinion is against Socialism . . . while this is so even if we could secure a hundred seats for Socialists those members could do but little . . . for the country would pull them up sharply if they got in advance of the general feeling . . . But get the general feeling in advance of Parliament and it will drag Parliament up to its own level.[26]

Blatchford himself was remarkably successful in converting individuals to socialism. Under the pseudonym of 'Nunquam' he wrote accessible propaganda which was as strong in its moral content as it was weak in economic analysis. But everyone testified to its success. Hyndman, for example, said that: 'in my recent short run into Lancashire from London I found Nunquam's converts in every direction.'[27] Two years later, in 1894, Morris also paid tribute to Blatchford's work and that of the *Clarion*: 'It is difficult to exaggerate the service which has been rendered to the cause by their uncompromising, straightforward, generous and at the same time good-tempered advocacy of Socialism.[28] Morris would have liked Blatchford's emphasis on making socialists and his conviction that 'the object of the Labour Party . . . should be to drive all the Whigs and Tories into one camp and win all the others over to our side and the best means to that end is education.'[29] Since the Tories were 'in the main, unitedly, obstinately and stupidly opposed to us', it followed that only the Liberals stood in the way of the required polarization. Thus the *Clarion* contended that the way forward involved a determined fight to rid the socialist movement of Liberal influences and alliances. Where Hardie ultimately argued for tactical flexibility so that the movement could punish the party which offended the labour interest most, Blatchford believed that this parliamentary orientation was premature and that the first job was the creation of a socialist public opinion.

To that end the Manchester contingent at the ILP's founding conference unsuccessfully tried to get the assembled delegates to adopt their own Fourth Clause which required the membership to abstain in elections where there was no socialist candidate. Shaw said the proposal lacked political intelligence, but such a criticism could cut no ice with Blatchford and those like him who believed that the independence of the socialist movement was everything. There was a strong mood, especially in the first half of the 1890s, which supposed that the growth of socialism was inevitable and a question of advancing enlightenment. As Blatchford said:

> Disband every Socialist organization in Britain and get rid of every prominent writer and speaker in the Socialist movement and I believe the march of Socialism would continue without serious impediment . . . First because Socialism is just and reasonable in itself; and second because Socialism has behind it the strongest sentiment of modern times; the sentiment of human love and mercy.[30]

Blatchford's emphasis, then, was on introducing people to the higher ideals of socialism and exposing the iniquities of capitalism and its defenders.[31] No doubt the success of *Merrie England*, which sold three-quarters of a million copies in 1894, confirmed him in this approach.

In *Merrie England* Blatchford told 'John Smith' that 'no man ever became rich by his own industry' and that profits were made by 'useless encumbrances' called 'middlemen'. The theory of competition was simply 'the most fatuous and bestial' of all 'the many senseless and brutal theories' which tried to justify capitalism. It will be evident that Blatchford's socialism owed little or nothing to Marx; as he said himself, the socialist movement is 'largely the result of the labours of Darwin, Carlyle, Ruskin, Dickens, Thoreau and Walt Whitman':

> It is from these men that the people have caught the message of love and justice, of liberty and peace of culture and simplicity and of holiness and beauty of life. This new religion . . . is something much higher and greater than a wage question, an hours question or a franchise question based though it be upon those things; it is something more than an economic theory, something more even than political or industrial liberty, though it embraces all these. It is a religion of manhood and womanhood, of sweetness and light . . .

> To love each other as brothers and sisters, and to love the earth as mother of us all, that is part of our new religion. Our new religion tears the old dogmas to tatters . . . declares much of that which the economists call 'wealth' to be the same thing as Ruskin calls 'illth'. Our new religion turns its back upon religious symbolisms and ceremonies and display and teaches us that love and mercy and art are the highest

forms of worship. Our new religion claims man back to freedom from commercial and industrial vassalage; tells him that he is as much a piece of Nature as the birds of the air or the lilies of the field; that he no more than they can be healthy or fair, nor in anywise complete, without fresh air and pure water and sunshine and peace; tells him that since he above all his kindred of earth and sea is endowed with spirit so must that spirit be nourished and kept sweet by spiritual sustenance and spiritual effort, else it will inevitably become corrupt and breed disease, contagion; death.[32]

The *Clarion*, with a circulation of over 80,000 by the end of the 1890s, was simply the biggest purveyor of this ethical socialism. But Blatchford's language was the common currency of ILP leaders such as Bruce Glasier and Keir Hardie and other big crowd-pullers of the movement such as Margaret McMillan, Katherine Conway, Enid Stacy and Carolyn Martyn. The blend of utopianism and popular evangelical morality which characterized large sections of the socialist movement in the 1890s also gave rise to the phenomenon of Labour Churches which Blatchford helped the Unitarian minister John Trevor to initiate. The first of these was established in Manchester in 1891 and by 1893 there were twenty-five of them, mostly in Lancashire and Yorkshire, affiliated to the Labour Church Union and organized by the *Labour Prophet*. Since the Labour Churches dispensed with Christianity virtually altogether they functioned chiefly as an expression of the fellowship and solidarity of people whose lives had been changed by socialism and provided an opportunity for them to hear and express their new convictions. When Clarion Clubs increasingly channelled these needs into sporting and other social activities after 1894, the Labour Churches died out after reaching a peak of around fifty organizations.

By the end of 1894 the ILP could claim 400 branches, twice the number with which it had started. But even in this phase of expansion the organization made little or no headway in the slums of the big cities, most rural districts, the South and Midlands and in Wales. The vast majority of the branches were in the small textile towns of Yorkshire and Lancashire with Scotland a long way behind as its third most important stronghold. Up to the 1895 general election the only evidence of the ILP's electoral potential was gained in useful by-election results in Halifax, Attercliffe and Leicester; but the tide of enthusiasm which swept through the movement in these years emboldened it to stand in twenty-eight constituencies when the Liberal government dissolved Parliament. The SDF, which was also growing, put up four candidates of its own. However, when the results came in they revealed that only 44,000 votes had been cast for the thirty-two socialist candidates. All were defeated, including Hardie at West Ham South; all but four of the contests had been three-cornered. Now, the fact that the ILP had made no progress in persuading the unions to support it suggested to the Fabians that their fleeting sympathy for the new party had been misplaced; there was no reason, they concluded, to think that it could do any better than the SDF.

With ILP membership at only 5,000 and falling because of the disillusionment which followed the Tory general election victory, the case for socialist unity and fusion with the SDF was strengthened. Blatchford made himself a leading spokesman of this cause and the SDF, which had also experienced a falling off in membership after the election, could be expected to respond positively. The Federation was claiming 4,500 members in 1894; by 1896 its strength in London – where the ILP was virtually non-existent – was confirmed by its control of the London Trades Council; and it could boast able members such as Will Thorne, George Lansbury and Dan Irving, who had built-up the Burnley branch; even old critics such as Aveling and William Morris had returned to the fold. Indeed, if anything, the SDF seemed to have gained ground at the expense of the ILP after 1895. So when the ILP conference instructed its leaders to open negotiations for fusion with the SDF, against Hardie's wishes, the membership was not deterred by the SDF's initial rejection of the offer. The demand was repeated at the 1896 conference. By then, however, Hardie was supported on the National Administrative Council by Ramsay MacDonald, who joined with other opponents of fusion like Philip Snowden and Bruce Glasier to prolong the negotiations until 1897 before a vote was taken.

Nevertheless, when the referendum of both memberships was conducted it produced a vote of 5,158 for fusion and only 886 against. But the ILP leadership refused to act accordingly on the grounds that only one-third of the party's members had voted. When, finally, another ballot was held in 1898 it was stipulated in advance that fusion would require a three-quarters majority and the issue was effectively killed. It was in fact the ILP not the SDF leadership which feared fusion and recognized that the SDF's militants, with their greater grounding in socialist theory, would be the only beneficiaries. And since the SDF was even less credible with the unions and the electorate than the ILP, fusion would be a step backwards, in this view, for the cause of independent labour representation. The greater popularity of the ILP was evinced by the 400 members it had elected to the councils, school boards and boards of guardians by 1900. But the setback recorded in 1895 seems to have brought about another change within the ILP which also made fusion with the SDF much less likely.

Before the leadership's confidence had been dented Hardie, apparently believing that the membership stood at 50,000, with a large trade union representation, emphasized that it was 'strongly anti-Liberal in feeling': 'The workers are coming to see that Liberalism, not Toryism, is the foe they have most to fear. It keeps them divided, makes them wrangle over non-essentials and prevents the real issues from being seen or grappled with.'[33] This was Blatchford's point, of course, but Hardie went on to explain that the ILP had refused to specify the political reforms which it favoured for fear that 'it would always be possible for the Radical party to point out that it was prepared to go as far as we were politically and that would be a strong argument in favour of some working alliance or agreement with that party.'[34] In fact, according to Hardie, further constitutional reform might simply strengthen the Commons at the expense of the Tory House of Lords when: 'An aristocratic house of Lords is much less to be feared than a bourgeois House of Commons.'[35]

By 1899 Hardie had modified if not completely changed his tune. For now he wrote with Ramsay MacDonald that the problem with the Liberals was their opportunism and lack of 'fixed principles'. While it was still worth pointing out that the Tories had 'no deep-rooted objection to some of the Socialist remedies' proposed by the ILP and that the latter was not chiefly concerned with political reforms, Hardie and MacDonald now stressed that 'The Independent labour party is in the true line of the progressive apostolic succession from the Liberals.'[36] Moreover it was now possible: 'to identify ourselves with those questions of immediate reform upon which Radicals and Socialists are alike agreed with less fear of . . . the party to be swallowed up in the ranks of the shiftless opportunists'.[37] The ILP, it was now asserted, 'has never been adverse to alliances'; after all, 'independence is not isolation'. Well before MacDonald concluded a secret deal with the Liberal Whip Herbert Gladstone to arrange straight fights against the Conservatives in certain constituencies the thought was already being expressed: 'If there is any serious intention to let us alone in a certain number of constituencies an early announcement of what these constituencies are may lead to that harmony which, we are constantly assured, some of our opponents desire.'[38] But before any real headway could be made the ILP leaders knew that some lasting arrangement with the unions was necessary to transform the socialists into a credible electoral force. The Boer War may have helped the ILP leadership to move closer to the Liberals by bringing the anti-war socialists and Radicals together, but a more enduring arrangement between them depended on the ILP finding wealthy backers. It is to these issues that we turn in chapter 5.

Conclusion

Although the New Unionism of 1889–90 was soon in retreat, after the trade boom of those years broke, socialist influence in the unions continued to grow. The New Unionism depended heavily on the organizing talents of socialists such as Tom Mann, John Burns, Eleanor Marx, Will Thorne and Henry Champion and enabled some of them to obtain leading official positions in the new organizations. Thus Mann became the first President of the Dock, Wharf, Riverside and General Workers' Union, while Thorne became General Secretary of the Gasworkers' and General Labourers' Union which also found an official position for Eleanor Marx. Champion's *Labour Elector* for a time acted as the official organ for both of these unions and Champion also helped to found the General Railway Workers' Union for those unskilled workers excluded from the Amalgamated Society of Railway Servants. The expansion of the new unions to the provinces was also aided by the activities of socialists such as those of the Socialist League in the West Riding of Yorkshire.

By the end of the 1890s the membership of the new unions had collapsed and stood at less than one-tenth of the total for all the unions, but socialist influence had spread to the established organizations of labour. The socialist presence at the TUC is one sign of this because it survived the changes in standing orders introduced in 1895 which excluded both delegates from the trades councils and men such as Hardie who were neither union officials nor active workmen. Even as ILP membership fell in the second half of the 1890s, party members exercised an increasing influence in unions such as those of the railway servants, the boot and shoe operatives, the boilermakers, engineers, carpenters and joiners, and even on parts of the coalfield as in Durham and Scotland. In 1896 George Barnes of the ILP was elected Secretary of the engineers and another ILP member, D. C. Cummings, became Secretary of the boilermakers at the end of the decade. ILP-ers were also members of the engineers' executive by 1897 and an ILP man edited the union journal. Clearly this rise to prominence has to be connected to the energy of what was, after all, a small minority of socialist activists who took a militant stand on relations with the employers.

But, as will be discussed in greater detail in the next chapter, the relevance of the socialists increased because the context was one of growing attacks by the employers and the courts on trade union rights. At this point it is worth noting that Lib-Labism, a major barrier to independent labour politics, had not advanced the union cause very far. While the unions grew from 750,000 members in 1888 to just under two million members in 1899 the number of trade union MPs had risen from eight to only eleven in the same period. As Hardie's experience at Mid-Lanark illustrates, however sympathetic the national Liberal leadership might be to the demand for more working class candidates, the local Liberal machine frequently blocked such candidacies and refused to finance them. Lib-Labism succeeded in constituencies where there was not a powerful middle-class bloc to prevent it – as in parts of the coalfield where the working-class vote was concentrated and in London where the working-class Metropolitan Radical Federation held sway.

Socialist agitation for the eight-hour day also helped to discredit Lib-Labism ideologically because this agitation stressed a reform which could apparently tackle unemployment and a host of other problems affecting organized labour much more effectively than any amount of self-help could hope to achieve. Nevertheless, the socialist advance must not be overstated. The ILP, judged as a national party, was a failure. Its most significant influence was in helping to turn trade union members towards the cause of independent labour representation, but this was a process which did not necessarily entail the conversion of the unions to socialism. The alliance between socialism and trade unionism which Hardie wanted would eventually come about, but the socialists would remain a small minority in the new organization. Under such circumstances the inspirational but rather nebulous socialism of the ILP was not best suited to create a radical reforming direction for the trade-union-dominated party.

5

Forming the Labour Party

The 1890s witnessed a number of significant reversals for the trade unions in the courts and ominous developments which threatened to put labour relations in Britain on a footing with those in America. British employers seemed to be learning from their American counterparts, whose well-publicized assaults on organized labour were invoked to explain the successes of industry in the USA. In 1893 a National Free Labour Association had been set up in order to organize blackleg labour in Britain and the following year some members of the Royal Commission of Labour were advocating amendments to the Trade Union Act (1871) with the purpose of establishing the clear legal responsibility of the unions for damages arising out of industrial disputes. Court cases, especially Lyons v. Wilkins (1896, 1899), threatened the right to strike and effective picketing while the employers sought to strengthen themselves with the creation of the Employers' Parliamentary Committee in 1898 for lobbying Parliament. Managerial prerogatives were enforced in a number of industrial disputes during the decade which led to lock-outs in tailoring (1892), the furniture industry (1898) and building (1899). But it was the defeat of the engineers in the great lock-out of 1897–8 which did most to undermine the old confidence in self-help. The engineers were faced with technical changes which threatened the position of skilled workers by the introduction of new machinery and piecework was imposed to boost productivity. By 1897 around 10 per cent of the workforce was unemployed in this industry and steel and shipbuilding were similarly affected. Likewise technical change caused unrest in printing and in the boot and shoe industry. Socialists gained ground in all of these industries and when George Barnes became General Secretary of the Amalgamated Society of Engineers in 1896 he was able to do so on a platform similar to that employed by Tom Mann when he had unsuccessfully campaigned for the same job in 1891 with arguments for independent labour politics. By 1898, after the experience of the lock-out, the ASE was considerably more receptive to the idea of financing its own MP. The Amalgamated Society of Railway Servants arrived at a similar conclusion only months later; here the problem was that the employers would not even recognize the union and the parliamentary arena seemed the best prospect for exercising influence.

By the end of the century the unions had sufficient funds to finance their own MPs and the courts and the employers had given them a reason to do so. Meanwhile the socialists maintained a presence at the TUC and managed to pass a resolution in 1898 calling on the unions to support 'the working class Socialist parties'. That year the ILP also approached the TUC and the Scottish TUC for 'united political action'. In 1899 socialists on the ASRS executive moved a resolution calling for the Parliamentary Committee of the TUC to find 'ways and means of securing the return of an increased number of labour members to the next Parliament'. This was then forwarded to the 1899 TUC where it was moved by an ILP member and passed by the slender margin of 546,000 votes to 434,000. Most of those voting for the resolution remained convinced Liberals but clearly this did not prevent them from reassessing the political situation which had deteriorated so far as organized labour was concerned. The unions needed a certain legal minimum framework in which to operate and it was this which was under threat. This is why representatives of unions with a membership of about 570,000 met with delegates from the three socialist organizations in the Memorial Hall, Farringdon Street, on 27 February 1900 to form the Labour Representation Committee (LRC). The unions represented, despite the fears generated by the employers' offensive, totalled less than half of the membership affiliated to the TUC and this figure was to drop to 353,000 by the end of the year. Conscious of the unions' hostility to socialism, Hardie opposed the SDF's attempt to get the new body to make 'recognition of the class war' its guiding principle and established that the LRC's function was merely to obtain 'a distinct Labour group in Parliament' ready to co-operate with any organization prepared to pursue the labour interest. In fact, as noted in chapter 4, the ILP leadership had begun to talk in terms of working with the Liberals in the late 1890s and on a whole range of issues there was little if any ideological difference between the two parties. Thus the ILP's ethical socialism had no distinctive positions on economic theory, foreign policy, the British Empire or constitutional reform that could set it apart from advanced or even Gladstonian liberalism. So Hardie's opposition to the SDF proposal was not simply an expression of reluctant realism; the ILP opposed the doctrine of class war on principle and shared many ideological positions with the Liberals. Nevertheless mere talk of 'socialism' could still make most trade union leaders nervous and so references to socialism were avoided by the LRC. This did not prevent the minority of socialists in the organization – minus the SDF which withdrew in the summer of 1901 in the interests of doctrinal purity – from playing a leading role within it. Ramsay MacDonald was immediately elected to the post of secretary because no one else with the required organizational talents was available who could afford to take the unpaid vacancy. Socialists would in time also make their presence felt because they had a vision which the trade union leaders lacked and from this vision, though it could be nebulous and sometimes indistinguishable from liberalism, it was possible to shape policies on a whole range of issues on which trade unionism was silent or indifferent. But this would take years to emerge and in 1900 the LRC was conceived as a way of defending trade union interests not as a way of transforming society. In the general election of 1900 the LRC spent a paltry £33 endorsing 15 candidates of whom only two succeeded, Hardie in Merthyr and Richard Bell of the ASRS in Derby. In 1903 Ramsay MacDonald concluded a secret pact with the Liberal Chief Whip, Herbert Gladstone, in order to avoid a repetition of this dismal showing and to ensure that in the next general election the LRC's candidates could fight certain constituencies without having to oppose Liberal candidates and thus harvest the Liberal vote for themselves. But after the election of 1900 it was not obvious that the LRC would last long enough to be able to make electoral pacts with anyone.

It was the House of Lords' decision in July 1901 to uphold an injunction brought against the ASRS in connection with a strike at the Taff Vale Railway Company which turned the tide the LRC's way. This decision made trade union funds vulnerable to legal action for damages and thus rendered strike action extremely perilous from the union's point of view. Trade union affiliation to the LRC rose from 375,000 in February 1901 to 469,000 a year later and to 861,000 by 1903. With the secession of the SDF the number of socialists officially attached to the LRC actually fell during this same period from 23,000 to under 14,000. Thus the ideological balance of forces within the LRC was decisively stacked against any version of socialism. Even at this stage many unions held aloof from the LRC including the miners' federation, the biggest union of them all, which persisted with Lib-Labism until 1909 when it affiliated to the Labour Party (as the LRC became known from 1906). It would seem that this decision was influenced by the fact that by 1909 the Labour Party had demonstrated that it could work in harmony with the Liberals and indeed extract a better electoral deal for working men from them than had been possible for the miners working within the Liberal Party.[1]

The LRC was put on a secure footing after the Taff Vale decision but the organization was in almost every way dependent on the Liberals and liberalism except that trade union funds were available to finance candidates of the new organization. By 1905 there were just five MPs attached to the LRC. Two of these had to be reprimanded for appearing in support of a Liberal by-election candidate in 1904 and another, Richard Bell, was expelled the following year for refusing to sign the LRC constitution; Bell preferred to follow the Liberals instead. Ramsay MacDonald was not then exaggerating when he said of the Labour Party candidates in the 1906 general election that they were 'in almost every instance earnest Liberals who will support a Liberal Government'.[2] Had the local Liberal associations been more enthusiastic about working-class candidates, most of these men would not have felt the need for a Labour Party, particularly after the Trades Disputes Act of 1906 removed the legal disabilities affecting the unions arising from decisions such as Taff Vale.

The 1906 general election gave the Labour Party a real presence in the House of Commons because it returned thirty MPs largely in consequence of the secret deal which MacDonald had concluded with the Liberals in 1903. This allowed Labour to share in the Liberal's resounding success by avoiding three-cornered contests in certain constituencies.

Socialism was not an election issue in 1906 and in the Parliament which followed the Liberals set the pace of domestic reforms with the Labour Party content to follow their lead. The radical agenda was hardly exhausted by such reforms as the National Insurance Act which introduced a contributory scheme for national insurance or the Parliament Act which abolished the House of Lords' veto and introduced payment for MPs; and yet it was Lloyd George who stood out as the leading reformer and MacDonald and Hardie even toyed with the idea of a new Progressive Alliance under his leadership.[3] No doubt the Labour socialists were handicapped by the fact that their Parliamentary contingent was dominated by unadventurous trade unionists, but it is important to recognize the self-imposed reformist limitations of the ILP – the only socialist group committed to the new party.

At its foundation conference the ILP refrained from specifying the political reforms it desired on the grounds that such goals were the common property of all radicals and the distinctive character of the party as the champion of social and economic reforms would be obscured by emphasizing them. Thus when the SDF demonstrated for universal suffrage in 1893 Hardie expressed his regret that it was 'placing itself in line with mere Radicalism'.[4] However, the ILP's apparent concern to distance itself from the Liberal Party did not stop it from seeking alliances with that party at the turn of the century and after 1906, when Labour was virtually stifled by the Liberal embrace, political distinction might have been achieved by vigorously demanding political reforms which the Liberals neglected. In fact the extension of the franchise, the most important of such reforms, was never made into a central issue of working-class politics despite the fact that until 1918 around six million men and the entire female population remained disenfranchised; this ensured that no more than 95 of the 670 Members of Parliament were elected from predominantly working-class constituencies until 1918.[5]

In fact the ILP leaders who came to the fore in the late 1890s – journalist-politicians such as Philip Snowden, Bruce Glasier and Ramsay MacDonald – had no real reforming strategy at all. Their socialism was an amalgam of conventional liberalism and the belief that a new morality of brotherhood was required. The latter essentially depended on a change of heart and was held to represent the interests of all classes. Realizing the kingdom of heaven on Earth, as it was often put, could not be achieved by class struggle or conflict in industry, which the ILP leaders abhorred, but did not readily lend itself to any known mundane strategy. Socialism would arrive by virtue of evolutionary processes operating within a stable political and economic order. Thus when Lloyd George offered some kind of leadership these socialists were readily taken in by his apparent radicalism, even though his tirades against aristocracy and landlordism were only ever intended to achieve a capitalist social peace and national efficiency. The ILP's socialism was itself vague on just these issues. MacDonald, for example, often talked as if the inefficiency of British society was the main economic problem and attributable to the dead weight of aristocracy, rents, and 'caste differences', problems which could be solved by the unity of the 'industrious sections' of the community against the 'idle sections'.[6] Thus, given the close ideological affinity which already existed between the Labour trade union MPs and the Liberal Party, it is not at all surprising that the new party made virtually no impression in Parliament and disappointed the expectations of the socialist rank and file. The Fabians, on the other hand, felt wholly vindicated in their lack of enthusiasm for the Labour Party.

As late as 1910 the Fabians still imagined their future MPs 'enrolling themselves behind Lloyd George and Winston Churchill'.[7] In fact, the Webbs came closest to influencing government policy with their contribution to the reform of the Poor Law which was in the end consigned to a Minority Report, published in 1909. By the time the Liberals' National Insurance scheme had been prepared the spectrum of socialist opposition ranged from those who wanted a non-contributory scheme such as Fred Jowett, George Lansbury and Philip Snowden to those who feared that by subjecting workers to registration and regimentation the proposals would form a step towards state capitalism. As we shall see in chapter 6 this latter view was expressed by syndicalists as well as by writers such as Hilaire Belloc who warned of an approaching 'servile state'. Beatrice Webb was worried, however, by 'the *unconditionality* of all payments under the insurance scheme [which] constitutes a grave defect. The state gets nothing for its money in the way of conduct – it may even encourage malingerers.'[8] It seemed to Mrs Webb that 'this gigantic transfer of property from the haves to the have-nots to be spent by them as they think fit in times of sickness or unemployment' should have been made conditional on 'the obligation to good conduct'.[9]

Engels had hoped that when the Labour Party finally got off the ground the socialist element would be guided by Marxism – though clearly not the dogmatic variant of it propounded by the SDF. In fact the ethical socialism of the ILP was much more influential and so too was Fabianism, which was finally reconciled to the new party ('a poor thing but our own' as Beatrice Webb called it) before the outbreak of the First World War. But since the Fabians had no faith in working-class political initiatives and opposed rank and file movements whenever they raised their head, their activity was self-consciously elitist and confined to shaping the opinions and actions of policy-makers. If we are looking for the socialism which sought to shape the Labour membership directly we have to examine the ideology of the ILP which until 1918 virtually monopolized the recruitment and organization of individual converts to the party.

Something of the character of the ILP's approach to socialism is contained in Fenner Brockway's account of a local branch gathering in 1907: 'On

Sunday nights a meeting was conducted rather on the lines of the Labour Church Movement – we had a small voluntary orchestra, sang Labour songs and the speeches were mostly Socialist evangelism, emotional in denunciation of injustice, visionary in their anticipation of a new society.'[10] The strength of this approach lay in its inspirational quality, so evident in the 1890s and in campaigns such as that of Victor Grayson in the Colne Valley in 1906 which was conducted 'like a religious revival' and without reference to specific political problems.[11] Its great weakness was its non-analytical character. In the hands of Hardie, Glasier, Snowden and MacDonald socialism was a vague protest against injustice; it was 'not only right', according to Glasier, 'but good and beautiful . . . the only system of society in which mankind can attain to true freedom and true human grace and dignity.'[12] It was pitched at such a level of abstract emotionalism that Glasier, for one, never felt the need to revise or supplement his views because, as the *Manchester Guardian* said in 1920 in a review of *The Religion of Socialism*, his ideas 'have never in the main passed beyond a nebulous and inchoate form to which the changes of time, events and opinions can make little difference'.[13] Typically, Marxism was rejected by socialists of this ilk as an ideology which based everything on crude materialistic motives. Glasier never bothered to analyse Marxist theory and other currents of socialism – syndicalism, guild socialism, the workers' control idea – came on to the scene without causing him the least intellectual concern. What mattered was the rightness of socialism and the change of heart which he believed the protest against capitalism adumbrated. From this lofty position one could wash one's hands of the 'fratricidal strife and unabashed dictatorship of [the] Russian and German Revolutions' which were merely 'glorying in the socialist name' after 1917, just as one could look down upon 'the selfish and inconsiderate strike outbreaks and boycotts of the working class'.[14] What mattered was 'the growth of a nation-wide, yea, a world-wide conscience and activity, not merely against open, brutal violence and plunder, but for the permanent elimination of the covert and more subtle, and often more inhuman forms of callousness and greed, and above all for the extinction of the causes, the poisoned streams of social wrong'.[15]

This was the appeal which Hardie's speeches also invariably sought to utilize. Was it, he asked his audience at Pendlebury in 1898, 'pleasing to God . . . and his kingdom on Earth that in England 4 millions were living below the poverty line and never had enough food and clothing?'[16] It was surely not. But when Hardie came to set out the socialist case his argument was similarly metaphysical: 'There must be some principle of beauty and perfection in the Universe towards which all creation is reaching out and seeking to attain . . . the socialist . . . is the human agent consciously co-operating with that great principle of growth and development which for lack of a better term we call the Divine Life and assisting it to find higher and fuller expression in the human race.'[17]

The problems this moralistic thinking could cause and obscure can be illustrated by considering Snowden's argument about the nature of imperialism.

By 1921, when *Labour and the New World* was published, even democratic liberals were insisting on the right of nations of self-determination; the American President Woodrow Wilson had done much to publicize this issue in attempting to mould the post-war settlement. Snowden was prepared to argue that capitalism bred imperialism and militarism and led to annexations and major conflicts like the Great War. However, the ILP leader thought that there were 'inexorable limits to the right of self-determination'. Just as the exclusion of particular races in South Africa 'cannot be maintained on moral grounds or in world interests', neither could 'China . . . deprive the rest of the world of access to her material resources. By no moral right may the ownership and control of the natural and material resources of a territory be regarded as the absolute monopoly of the people who happen to be settled there . . .'[18]

Thus, on these utterly obscurantist grounds Snowden concludes by supporting 'the policy of the "open door" '[19] or, in other words, the policy which the capitalist powers occasionally championed in their pursuit of imperialism. Socialism in these hands, then, was little more than a word used to express approval for good things and a yearning for better things to come. The Snowden example is particularly relevant since, until he became Chancellor of the Exchequer in 1929, when he adhered to rigidly orthodox economic policies, the moral fog in his speeches and writings had always obscured this fidelity to the *status quo*.

More than any of the other ILP leaders it was Ramsay MacDonald who exercised the biggest influence on the Labour Party's strategy and tactics. MacDonald demonstrated rather more interest than Snowden in foreign affairs and actually became Foreign Secretary as well as Prime Minister. But the reader of his *Labour and the Empire* (1907) searches the book in vain for any idea of how socialism and foreign policy might be related. In common with other democrats MacDonald advanced the case for indirect rule over the colonies, but the rest of his argument was vague and equivocal. Somehow, for example, India would be allowed autonomy in settling its own affairs while continuing to remain within the Empire – national independence did not even enter the argument. It could not be imagined from this that MacDonald believed socialism to be a 'scientific inquiry for the study of society' which could be 'as much detached from politics as . . . Darwinism.'[20]

In fact MacDonald's socialism bore as much resemblance to science as alchemy. It stood for 'economic chivalry' or a 'moralizing' of the system by means of political power (that is, forming a government) which MacDonald saw as the arm of social progress. A 'change of heart' was the key thing for MacDonald; economic analysis came a poor second. Thus after announcing that 'Labour's quarrel with capitalism is not in the sphere of production but in the sphere of distribution',[21] MacDonald proceeds to denounce the growth of trusts which 'reduce competition to a minimum' and produce a class that supplies capital but takes no further part in production. This class is then described as a 'burden on the community'[22] although, some pages later,

MacDonald emphasizes that 'capital, capitalist and capitalism are three absolutely distinct things' and that 'the Socialist objects to capitalism.'[23] Undeterred by these contradictions the argument alerts the reader to the 'present development of industry' which 'is to organize capital and create interests which threaten to dominate our political and civic existence by putting the life of the State under the control of a few commercial syndicates.'[24] Thus, it seems that capitalists, against whom socialists have no objection (though they became a burden on the community), have reorganized the sphere of production, with which Labour has no quarrel, in such a way that 'the life of the State' is at risk – which is more the pity because political power is for socialists the arm of social progress. Fortunately, MacDonald concludes that: 'this pure evolution of capitalism has not been manifested so much here as in America, mainly because we have a social history which mingles with and colours the pure industrial stream of tendency.'[25]

Let us leave 'the pure industrial stream of tendency' and the rest of MacDonald's economic mysticism and turn to his conception of socialist politics. Here MacDonald's intentions, at any rate, are clearer: 'Socialism is no class movement. Socialism is a movement of opinion, not an organization or status. It is not the rule of the working class; it is the organization of the community.'[26] The class war was for MacDonald 'nothing but a grandiloquent and aggressive figure of speech.'[27] Socialism was to emerge as a process of gradual enlightenment and therefore:

> The socialist appeal . . . is to all who believe in social evolution, who agree that the problem society has now to solve is that the distribution of wealth, who trust in democracy, who regard the State not as an aspect of individuality and who are groping onwards with the co-operative faith guiding them.[28]

If 'socialism marks the growth of society, not the uprising of a class', as MacDonald said it did, it followed that this was an organic process and as such the new community of interests which socialism represented was built into it. Socialists were merely those in possession of an advanced scientific insight into this evolutionary process. The socialist theorists 'assume that society is fulfilling its part in evolving the more efficient forms of the future . . . Thus the whole of society, its organization, its institutions, its activities is brought within the sway of natural law . . .'[29] The socialist method, according to MacDonald, is the Darwinian method which 'proceeds from facts, classification, causal analysis, the where and whither of society'. Nevertheless, he was much more interested himself in the metaphysical expression of the socialist case and rarely stooped to consider specific solutions to particular problems.

But since the state was for MacDonald 'the organized political personality of a sovereign people – the organization of a community for making its common will effectual by political methods'[30] – he was, as an aspiring leader, concerned with statecraft. Nothing could be more important for one who

believed that individual and state were organically related 'because the perfect
individual is a necessary element in the perfect humanity which is the final
achievement of society and to serve which is therefore the function of the
State'.[31] Leaving aside this highly dubious perfectionism, it is interesting that
MacDonald argued as if the state in Britain had already reached something
close to perfection which unruly individuals always threatened to ruin. Thus
he is almost Burkean in his celebration of the British political system:

> The working of the representative system combines the opposing
> tendencies, and as the centripetal and centrifugal forces in the universe
> harnessed together, produce that motion by which the suns are kept in
> their places and the relations of the universe remain in their fixed order,
> so the art of government consists in uniting the opposing motives and
> mental attractions of the citizens so that an orderly and steady advance
> may be possible.[32]

Decoded, this seems to mean that it is the job of government to pace and
present reforms in such a way as to carry the whole of society with the reforms
in question. This role is jeopardized unless a good portion of the people are
deferential towards their governors: 'We hardly appreciate how delicately
adjusted is the whole system of government. Remove it from the trust and the
deference of the people, make it common and unclean and it begins to crumble
to dust.'[33] Thus, on such grounds MacDonald finds that 'to degrade in the
imagination of the people even a bad House of Commons is a crime – a most
heinous crime for socialists'.[34] This is the sin of socialists such as Victor
Grayson – MacDonald was not yet troubled by syndicalists and Leninists –
who refused to observe parliamentary conventions. It is on such reasoning
that MacDonald opposed unsettling constitutional reforms such as the referendum and changes in the electoral system.

It is scarcely surprising that the Labour Party should have been wholly out
of sympathy with the wave of militancy which threatened to engulf Britain in
the years between 1910 and the outbreak of the First World War. This was a
period of irresolution, dissension and decline in the fortunes of the parliamentary group which, still tied to the Liberals by the electoral pact which
preceded the 1906 general election, lost 6 of its 42 seats in by-elections between
1911 and 1914 and performed extremely badly in the Commons. The high
point of the party's parliamentary interventions was probably the Unemployed Workmen's Bill which MacDonald introduced for propaganda purposes in July 1907, demanding the right to work and requiring that the local
authorities be responsible for providing work or adequate maintenance. Yet
the Liberal government's reforming zeal quickly evaporated after 1911 – the
very time when Labour seemed at its most ineffective. Thus while syndicalists
and suffragettes organized militant action the Labour Party was unable and
unwilling to champion their grievances. Andrew Bonar Law's Conservatives,
on the other hand, openly threatened to defy the constitution and use physical
force if the Liberals went ahead with their plans for Home Rule for Ireland.

In preparing their unemployment bill the Labour leadership drew on Fabian arguments developed from the work of the statistician, A. L. Bowley. These arguments are worthy of notice because they attempted to formulate a counter-cyclical public works policy even though unemployment was still primarily viewed as a problem of casual labour. The Webbs' basic idea was that the government should retain a proportion of its normal appropriations for the purpose of financing public works when unemployment rose above 4 per cent. This would not constitute an 'artificial' demand for labour – the bugbear of economists, which the Webbs shared – but merely an adjustment in the timing of ordinary demand. Moreover the scheme would hire workers with the requisite skills and pay them the going rates. It would, therefore, not seek to employ the unemployed indiscriminately, but only those with talents which were actually required. Thus the plan would avoid 'artificial' employment and the typically charitable character of previous public works schemes which normally employed poorly paid workers on meaningless tasks. The scheme would also be cheap, according to the Webbs, and required no radical change in existing economic, social or political arrangements. Although these plans came to nothing they are as near as the Labour Party ever got to a practical policy for unemployment before its conversion to Keynesianism in the 1940s. For although the unions were certainly interested in tackling unemployment, their devotion to economic orthodoxy and free collective bargaining was much stronger.

Labour was still very much dependent on the uncertain loyalties of the unions. When the Trade Union Act of 1913 obliged the unions to hold ballots on the payment of political funds to the Labour Party around 40 per cent of the membership of the nine largest unions were opposed to the use of union money for the support of independent Labour candidates. This figure might well have been higher had Labour pursued real independence from the Liberals, since such independence would have entailed many occasions when the Tories benefited from a divided progressive vote. The unions were also becoming more bureaucratic. The number of full-time officers had for some time been increasing more rapidly than the membership. More large branches and districts were creating full-time secretaryships and more national executives were appointing additional 'organizers'. In the first decade of the century only 10 per cent of union funds was spent on strikes, lockouts and victimization benefits, whereas 25 per cent was devoted to administration and the rest was dispensed in friendly benefits and unemployment benefit.[35] Of course these developments could be invoked by militants to suggest that the unions were becoming too conservative; the syndicalists made just this point after 1910. But the strike wave in the period after 1910 helped to strengthen support for Labour within the union ranks and Lloyd George shrewdly observed that the party's parliamentary leaders were 'the best policemen for the Syndicalist'.[36]

The Labour Party was something of an enigma to the socialist organizations of the Second International, many of whom doubted that it could be described as in any way socialist. The SDF did what it could to exclude the Labour Party from the International Socialist Bureau, though without success. Lenin intervened in the debate over this issue in 1908 to support Labour's involvement on the grounds that though

> the British trade unions, insular, aristocratic, selfish and hostile to Socialism which have produced a number of outright traitors to the working class who have sold themselves to the bourgeoisie for ministerial posts (like the scoundrel John Burns) have nevertheless begun *moving towards* Socialism awkwardly, inconsistently in zig-zag fashion, but still moving towards socialism.[37]

But this was not how Lenin's future supporters in Britain saw the matter. Quite apart from Hyndman and the SDF, which by now was sectarian towards the Labour Party almost by tradition, the Socialist Labour Party (SLP), based chiefly in Scotland, took the view – which it borrowed from the American Marxists Daniel de Leon and Eugene Debs – that the trade union and Labour leaders were mere 'stool pigeons' of capitalism.[38] The SLP was formed in 1903 when the Scottish divisional council of the SDF broke away with around 80 of the area's 200 members. Since 1902 this group had been publishing *The Socialist* and while Hyndman sought unity with socialists such as Blatchford, Robert Smillie and Hardie, the dissidents around this newspaper denounced them all as social imperialists and parliamentary opportunists. When the SLP was formed it gravitated towards industrial trade unionism and the creation of rank and file organizations which would break the hold of trade union officialdom and combat the craft prejudices which held the unions back from class consciousness. Thus, contrary to the SDF, the SLP gave priority to its agitations within the unions which it foresaw as the administrative power of a future socialist society. During the war militants from the SLP became prominent in the Clyde Workers Committee and the shop steward movement.

Disaffection with the Labour Party's performance in Parliament led to renewed calls for a regrouping of socialists and in 1910 Victor Grayson named Hyndman, Blatchford and Hardie as the leaders who could bring this about. There was in fact sufficient interest in this idea to bring about a Socialist Unity Conference in 1911 composed of the SDF, some branches of the ILP, the Clarion Clubs and a variety of local socialist societies. Many of the latter had been formed by working-class Marxists associated with the journal *Plebs* which had been founded in 1908 by students at Ruskin College, Oxford, before they broke away to set up the Central Labour College the following year. Together the groups at the Unity Conference launched the British Socialist Party (BSP), but within a year the new organization was losing members rapidly as unresolved doctrinal differences rose to the surface. Many of the ILP groups which joined the BSP were strongly opposed to state socialist measures such as welfare reforms and nationalization, which they saw as measures of state capitalism. They were strongly supportive of revolutionary industrial methods as canvassed by the syndicalists and industrial unionists. On both counts they clashed with the Hyndman–Quelch faction and left the new organization in droves. Even if the figures are inflated, it is significant that from 40,000 claimed in 1912 the membership slumped to 13,500 in 1914. Nevertheless, there is no evidence that disillusioned BSP members returned to the ILP, since the latter's own membership fell by 25 per cent between 1909 and 1914.

Another looming problem and source of division was the danger of war, which socialists had been warning against since the 1890s. The majority of socialists in all the organizations took an internationalist view and supported the position adopted by the Second International in 1907 which promised to end hostilities by co-ordinated working class action leading to the overthrow of capitalism. But Hyndman and Blatchford were known as notorious chauvinists well before 1914. Blatchford had taken a pro-British stance during the Boer War and began to advocate faster rearmament against Germany in a series of articles published by the reactionary *Daily Mail* from the end of 1909. His chief concern was that 'Germany is deliberately preparing to destroy the British Empire' which would constitute 'a blow to civilization throughout the world'.[39] By comparison with this threat, Blatchford believed that it was 'sheer criminal lunacy to waste time and strength chasing such political bubbles' as constitutional reform, the so-called 'People's Budget' and so on. The Germans could only obtain their own empire by depriving the British of theirs – something which Blatchford saw as a self-evident disaster. Hyndman took a similar view at the founding conference of the BSP but was out-voted by the internationalists.

Socialist internationalism lasted until within days of the war's start. Demonstrations of international solidarity took place in all of the European capitals and Hardie and Arthur Henderson spoke against the war in Trafalgar Square on the Sunday before it started. By the following Sunday, however, Henderson declared it a war of national defence which must be supported. MacDonald, having pleaded for neutrality on 3 August, resigned as chairman of the party two days later when Labour agreed to support war credits; Henderson took his position as party leader. Hardie, Jowett, Richardson and Snowden also opposed the war, as did a good proportion of the ILP membership – as many as four-fifths according to Fenner Brockway, considerably less according to recent local studies.[40] What is clear is that only a tiny minority of those who opposed the war did so for pacifist reasons – Brockway himself, Bruce Glasier and Clifford Allen were the most prominent.

Brockway helped to organize the socialist pacifists in the No Conscription Fellowship which was set up in November 1914. By 1916 the number of conscientious objectors of all persuasions, however, amounted to only 16,500. But the war also offended the principles of some Liberal Radicals who claimed that it was chiefly the result of secret diplomacy. This was the argument which Jowett, MacDonald, Hardie and Snowden adopted and which the Union of Democratic Control (UDC) was created to champion in August

1914. Its chief exponents were the Liberals Norman Angell, Philip Morrell, Arthur Ponsonby, Charles Trevelyan and E. D. Morel. In practice, association with the UDC's line did not prevent the expression of patriotic sentiments and though individuals like MacDonald gained notoriety during the conflict and considerable prestige after it for taking an anti-war stance there was nothing so clear-cut about their attitudes. Jowett, Hardie and MacDonald all believed that since the war had started it was necessary to go through with it.

A revolutionary defeatist attitude was confined to the Socialist Labour Party, which asserted that its attitude 'is neither pro-German nor pro-British but anti-capitalist and all that it stands for in every country of the world. The capitalist class of all nations are our real enemies and it is against them that we direct all our attacks.'[41] The SLP was still an organization of only eight branches and perhaps 100 members but as we shall see in chapter 6 the war created conditions which enabled its militants to become prominent in labour disputes. The BSP, on the other hand, was divided. Hyndman and the unequivocally pro-war lobby were expelled in April 1916 and went on to create a short-lived National Socialist Party while retaining control of *Justice*. The majority of the BSP expressed a clear anti-war position in *The Call*, which was established in February 1916 to rally the internationalists within the organization, while Hyndman collaborated with pro-war trade union leaders – including Ben Tillett – in the Socialist National Defence Committee. Most of the Fabians, Sidney Webb and Shaw included, took the same patriotic line as the trade unions, but relations between the pro-war majority of the Labour Party – represented in the Cabinet by Arthur Henderson – and the equivocators such as MacDonald were good enough to enable them to work together in the War Emergency Workers' National Committee where the Labour Party clarified its attitude to the social problems arising out of the war. War-weariness by 1917 enabled the two factions to adopt a foreign policy informed by the arguments of the UDC and by the 1920s, of course, this liberal-pacifist sentiment and support for the League of Nations were extremely strong attitudes within the party.[42]

The war also hastened the decline of the Liberal Party by causing the split of 1916 between Lloyd George and Herbert Asquith, from which it never recovered. The conflict forced the Labour Party to find a programme equal to the problems the war would leave in its wake and created the opportunity for Sidney Webb to leave a permanent mark on the party's future. Webb helped Arthur Henderson to write a new constitution for the party during 1917 and a manifesto, *Labour and the New Social Order*, with which to fight the general election in 1918. Thus in the context of world war, revolution in Russia, and the growth of new statements of socialism at home, the Labour Party adopted the socialist objective in its 1918 constitution:

> To secure for the producers by hand and by brain the full fruits of their industry and the most equitable distribution thereof that may be possible upon the basis of the common ownership of the means of

production, and the best obtainable system of popular administration and control of each industry and service.

This careful formula was written with an eye on the guild socialist, the shop steward, and the revolutionary discontent which was beginning to affect socialist opinion. But *Labour and the New Social Order* was restricted to Fabian demands such as a National Minimum, the elimination of waste and inefficiency, and the common ownership of land, coal, transport and electricity – industries which the War Cabinet had been running in the 'national interest' since 1916 and which could now be placed permanently upon this basis. These were eminently reasonable demands, as were the other policies in the manifesto such as the commitment to free collective bargaining, the use of 'surplus wealth' for expenditures in the common interest (education, health, research etc.) and the call for redistributive taxes on inheritance and capital.

But the new constitution did not signal the wholesale conversion of the unions to socialism. Many of the policies in the 1918 manifesto were old favourites with particular unions but the real purpose of the new constitution was organizational. Henceforward the ILP's monopoly of individual recruitment was to be broken because the Labour Party would set up parties of its own in every constituency. An enlarged party executive would now be dominated more than ever before by the unions. Thus the weight of the socialist ILP was actually reduced under the new arrangements because the party managers 'had to reckon with the danger that if the Socialist representation were maintained there might be a Trade Union secession to form a separate Trade Union Party'.[43] The increased power of the unions was the price Henderson and Webb paid to induce them to support the new constitution and provide the increased affiliation fees without which a genuinely national party could not be sustained. The 1918 constitution transformed the Labour Party into a centralized, nationally cohesive organization where before there had been a loose federation of affiliated bodies; it did not transform it into a socialist party. On the contrary, unless the trade unions could themselves be transformed the new arrangements virtually guaranteed the permanent subordination of the Labour socialists.

Conclusion

When the 'labour alliance' which Hardie had fought for finally came into existence it was an alliance of trade unions concerned to safeguard the legal minimum requirements of free collective bargaining, but otherwise loyal to many central features of Liberal Party ideology, with a socialist minority led by individuals whose own beliefs owed much to liberalism. It is not surprising, then, that the performance of the Labour Party's small contingent in Parliament, which was content to follow the Liberal lead, disappointed many socialists who began to look to other forces for social change – whether from industrial militancy, socialist regroupment, or different kinds of socialism (which will be considered in chapter 6). But when this widespread disquiet led to a vote against Hardie, Snowden, MacDonald and Glasier at the ILP's conference of 1909 the 'big four' called the assembled delegates' bluff by resigning. The immediate response was a virtually unanimous call for these leaders to resume their places at the head of the organization. The ILP had just been given a lesson on the paramountcy of the parliamentary leadership, its refusal to support extra-parliamentary political struggle, and the absence of an alternative leadership.

And yet the growth of socialism in the British working class in the years between 1900 and 1918 had much more to do with the mass industrial unrest which the Labour leaders disapproved of and the impact of events over which they exercised no influence (the World War, the division of the old Liberal Party, the October Revolution) than to their parliamentary performance. These events nevertheless strengthened Labour rather than the socialist dissidents who, like the ILP radicals in 1909, did not have mass support for an alternative socialist strategy. Thus most of the leaders whose beliefs had been formed by Lib-Labism, Radicalism and ethical socialism took the party into the post-war era. They were now armed with a shopping list of reforms, written by Sidney Webb, which the war years had done so much to render respectable and moderate. The Labour Party itself was from 1918 also ostensibly committed to socialism, though the socialist membership had even less power to make policy than had been the case before the war began.

The beliefs held in common by the trade union and socialist leaders of the Labour Party centred on a critique of the unjust distribution of national wealth which was to be rectified by redistributory policies. The capitalist system was not to be overthrown or even fundamentally restructured but reformed so that the baneful influences within it could be removed. Typically rentiers, middlemen and landlords – in short a host of 'parasites' – were identified as the main culprits at one end of the scale and poverty at the other. The Labour leadership was confident that parliamentary action supplemented by free collective bargaining would suffice to address these issues, though the leading socialists emphasized the first of these approaches and were at best ambivalent about the utility and desirability of strikes. The trade union leaders themselves also disapproved of industrial militancy if it was an expression of uncontrolled rank and file movements, but as representatives of the industrial 'wing' of the party they were ultimately more sympathetic to the demands of this arm of the movement.

Both sides of the leadership were deeply reverential towards the British state and the national interest as conventionally defined. Even reforms such as the extension of the franchise and the abolition of the House of Lords were far from priorities and, of course, there was hardly a trace of republican sentiment at any level of the Labour Party. Naturally, if the British state was conceived as a neutral, essentially benign instrument which could be put to the task of civilizing British society, it followed that the peoples of the Empire could hope for no better servant of their own interests. Thus the party leadership, which had demonstrated virtually no interest in foreign policy except when it was forced on their attention by war, was composed of imperialists and patriots who espoused a less aggressive, more democratic programme for the maintenance of British interests abroad than their Conservative counterparts, much as sections of the Liberal Party had done before them.

Unlike the Liberals, however, Labour was formed to protect and promote the economic and social interests of the organized working class. For such a party other matters – international, political and constitutional – were much less of a priority than they had been for 'advanced' Liberalism. Thus Labour began the inter-war period led by men still very much in the Lib-Lab mould – men who were overwhelmingly concerned with the material interests of the working class but unsure of how to advance and protect them. A more militant-sounding generation of socialists would soon enter the fray but, as we shall see, not until the first Labour government had been and gone did they turn their minds to the question of the reforms by which socialism could be brought about in Britain.

6

The Democratic Challenge:
Syndicalism and Guild Socialism

By 1910 there were 2.6 million trade union members in Britain, more than in any other country except Germany. Trade union membership was concentrated in particular industries such as mining and cotton and was higher among skilled male manual workers than in any other group.[1] Strikes were much more frequent after 1910, but it was largely because of unrest among coalminers, dockers, cotton weavers and transport workers that 70 million days were lost between 1911 and 1914. This unrest was perceived by some commentators as a symptom of the deeper social malaise which had also produced a militant suffragette movement and the threat of civil war over the future of Ireland.[2] Contemporary opinion was also alarmed by the appearance of syndicalism within the unions.

By 1910 there were three small centres of agitation which can be loosely described as syndicalist. The Socialist Labour Party, already mentioned in chapter 4, attempted to build industrial unionism alongside the existing organizations which were, of course, divided along craft and sectionalist lines. The SLP was mainly centred on the Clyde, while in South Wales similar ideas were associated with the educational work of the Plebs League. After breaking away from Ruskin the Plebs established the rival Central Labour College devoted to the development of working-class education, which also stood for industrial unionism but rejected the 'dual unionism' of the SLP in favour of working within the existing organizations. This was also the position of the Industrial Syndicalist Education League which Tom Mann launched in Manchester in September 1910.

What all three organizations had in common was a disdain for socialist strategies which depended on political action and a correspondingly high opinion of the potential of trade union power – once properly organized and led – for the transformation of capitalism and the administration of a future socialist society. These ideas had dominated the French Confédération Générale du Travail (CGT) in its first twenty years after 1895. In America the exclusive craft unionism preached by the American Federation of Labour was opposed by the industrial unionism promoted by Daniel De Leon's Socialist

Labour Party which helped to found the Industrial Workers of the World in 1905. Tom Mann was inspired by the CGT and IWW when he set up the Industrial Syndicalist Education League and the journal *Industrial Syndicalist* (1910). This was the start of what Pribićević has called a vigorous, nation-wide syndicalist campaign, calling for industrial unity, an aggressive industrial policy and the establishment of a new society in which not only the industries of the country but the whole social life would be controlled by the unions'.[3] For just three years or so syndicalism seemed to flourish and respectable opinion was alarmed; the Labour Party and the officials of many unions repudiated it as an irresponsible subversion of society.

Yet Mann's purpose was simply to educate trade unionists on the need for industrial unions which prosecute the class struggle. To that end he launched an amalgamation movement seeking to build one union in each industry. Unofficial rank and file movements sprang up which embraced this goal in mining, railways, engineering and the transport industry. In the autumn of 1911 a journal called the *Syndicalist Railwayman* appeared and at the 1912 conference of the ASRS the majority of delegates resolved to obtain workers' control of the industry by means of industrial action. Although the unions' officials were initially opposed to this militancy, the syndicalist agitation contributed to the creation of the National Union of Railwaymen (NUR) out of the old ASRS and four other railway unions in 1913; during the next five years the NUR was to be one of the strongest supporters of the idea of joint control – between government and union – in the management of the industry.

The *Syndicalist Railwayman* began its life with the argument that the emancipation of the working class could not be advanced by mere nationalization as the ILP suggested. The same argument was put by the Unofficial Reform Committee (led by such men as Noah Ablett, W. H. Mainwaring and Will Hay) of the South Wales Miners' Federation in *The Miners' Next Step* (1912). Indeed it argued that nationalization would actually worsen the miners' position because it represented the last refuge of the employers in their struggle to preserve their capital. It

> simply makes a National Trust, with all the forces of Government behind it, whose one concern will be to see that the industry is run in such a way as to pay the interest on the bonds with which the coalowners are paid out and to extract as much more profit as possible.[4]

What was required instead, according to this argument, was some kind of 'industrial democracy'. But again, these ideas were opposed by the union leadership until they were converted to the idea of joint control, partly under the influence of guild socialist ideas, at the end of the First World War. By 1919 the miners were able to propose to the Sankey Commission a detailed scheme for power-sharing in the industry between government and the unions. Undoubtedly the linkage which existed between advocacy of industrial democracy and rank and file criticism of the trade union leaders was one reason why the latter were easily alienated from the idea of workers' control. But it should be remembered that convinced socialists and syndicalists were only a divided minority, and more typical trade union opinion was devoted to free collective bargaining backed up by social reform under the auspices of the existing state. Indeed, many trade unionists still believed that progress could best be achieved by pressurizing the Liberal Party and pointed to the Liberal reforms of 1906–10 as proof of the efficacy of that organization.

With the exception of the tiny SLP all the socialist groups believed that socialism would be achieved only by the capture of political power. That depended, according to the conventional wisdom, on building a large socialist party which could use state power to lay the cornerstone of socialism in the form of public ownership. It was commonly argued that if only the socialists were as united as trade unionists the job would be done much more easily. In their own way the syndicalists challenged this assumption as much as they challenged all the other aspects of the majority socialist strategy. For as James Connolly pointed out, the workers 'are most hopelessly divided on the industrial field and . . . their division and confusion on the political field are the direct result'.[5] It was therefore the central proposition of Connolly's SLP that recognition of the need for concerted common action of all workers against the capitalists in the industrial battle must precede the realization of this consciousness on the political front. This was the rationale for industrial unionism. As far as Connolly was concerned, those who fought for the creation of industrial unionism not only solved the problems of day-to-day class struggle but were 'at the same time preparing the framework of the society of the future'.[6] For Ireland's greatest Marxist regarded the existing political institutions as 'simply the coercive forces of capitalist society' – a proposition later to be associated with Lenin.

However, Connolly's critique of the elected components of the modern state maintained that such representation as was achieved was entirely inappropriate to the needs of a modern industrial society. Instead of representation based on 'an indiscriminate mass of residents within given districts', the SLP wanted the administration of affairs in the hands of representatives of the various industries elected by industrial unions and therefore based on a functional expertise born of experience. In Connolly's view,

> It will be seen that this conception of Socialism destroys at one blow all
> the fears of a bureaucratic state ruling and ordering the lives of every
> individual from above . . . it blends the fullest democratic control with
> the most absolute expert supervision . . . the political, territorial, state
> of capitalist society will have no place or function under Socialism.'[7]

The SLP established the British Advocates of Industrial Unionism (BAIU) in February 1906 in order to propagate these ideas and lay the basis for a British equivalent of the IWW. In 1909 the BAIU was reorganized as the Industrial Workers of Great Britain and its tactics shifted from educational work to the recruitment of all industrial unionists in opposition to trade union officialdom. The SLP's role in all of this was to disseminate the ideas of De Leon and Eugene Debs until enough workers were convinced and the SLP could form a majority government. Its first act on so doing would be to help the unions lock out the employers and, when this was accomplished, the old state could be dissolved. There was no evidence in any of this that the SLP had any conception of the complexity of industrial management or of how a socialist society might be run. Thus from this quarter there was never any elaboration of the idea of workers' control.

Dissatisfaction with the dominant statist conception of socialism was not, however, confined to the syndicalist groups. In 1912 a similar critique was presented as 'guild socialism', articulated by middle-class intellectuals who believed that future power in society could be shared between consumers represented by the state and producers organized in industrial unions supporting a parallel set of political institutions.[8] The guild socialists began to expound these ideas in the pages of A. R. Orage's *The New Age*, which published a series of articles by S. G. Hobson outlining the new strategy in 1912.[9] Instead of the general strike envisaged by syndicalists, the guild socialists imagined the transformation of society proceeding from the gradual encroachment on managerial prerogatives by the unions. In emphasizing that the future socialist society would be characterized by industrial democracy and the restoration of the dignity of labour, Hobson drew on the work of William Morris and to a lesser extent on Ruskin who had proposed in *Fors Clavigera* (1871–84) that the unions should reconstitute themselves as self-governing guilds. A more immediate influence on Hobson may also have been A. J. Penty's *Restoration of the Guild System* (1906).

Penty was an architect and a follower of William Morris who resigned from the Fabian Society in 1902 in revolt against the crude utilitariansism which he detected in its policies. But his counter-proposals amounted to a return to the small-scale agricultural and stationary economy of the Middle Ages in which hand production would dominate and craftsmen would ensure the maintenance of quality. In Penty's analysis, the chief problems of modern capitalism stemmed from the degradation of work caused by machine production, the division of labour and a society dominated by consumer, rather than producer, interests. The unreality of his proposals for dealing with these problems may help to explain why Penty's *Restoration of the Guild System* rapidly sank into oblivion.

Certainly there were other thinkers concerned with some, if not all, of the issues which Penty raised. The recent growth of the state, for example, had prompted a challenge to the complacent assumption that state socialism was compatible with increased democracy and freedom. Of course in England, where any extension of the state was equated with the reduction of individual liberty, and where state intervention was in fact less developed than in other capitalist societies, such a reaction was always likely to come from socialism's detractors. What is significant, however, is that suspicion of Fabian and ILP socialism was growing among socialists to the extent that critics from outside the socialist camp could influence thinking within it.

Hilaire Belloc had written on the subject of the 'servile state' as early as May 1908 in the pages of the *New Age*, though his book of that title was not published until 1912. Belloc argued that the growth of state intervention to stabilize the capitalist system would continue to the point where employers would be required by law to act in the workers' welfare. This in turn, he reasoned, would require legal regulation of workers' lives: the Liberal's National Insurance legislation was, he believed, a step in this direction. The prospect which Belloc foresaw – workers reduced in status to the level of well-fed instruments of production – chimed with the syndicalist critique of Labour socialism. Both believed that mainstream socialism would only hasten this process.

These ideas probably influenced the guild socialists, who were concerned to recreate society upon the basis of a pluralist power structure in which producers and consumers would be organized at all levels from the local to the national. In this concern the guild socialists could also draw on the academic work of F. W. Maitland, the legal historian, and J. N. Figgis, the historian and churchman. Between them Maitland and Figgis challenged the notion that the state was the exclusive repository of popular sovereignty by arguing that the many groups which existed in society were often older than the state and certainly logically prior to it. These groups should be given the same legal status as individuals and regarded as sources of authority since they represented some aspects of the popular will. Certainly the philosophical pluralism developed in works such as Figgis's *Churches in the Modern State* (1913) emphatically denied that the state had any right to pose as an omnicompetent authority.

The New Age had initially sympathized with syndicalism but by 1912 Orage was persuaded that it could only reduce society into a thousand sectionalisms. Hobson's guild socialist scheme for a partnership between the unions and the state was thereafter promoted as a socially responsible alternative to it. Although the syndicalist agitation fizzled out in 1913, almost as quickly as it had appeared, industrial unionism did not. Indeed the credibility of guild socialism was derived in large measure from the fact that the demand for workers' control was kept alive within the trade union movement until the early 1920s. When war came in 1914 it created peculiar conditions of labour, particularly in the engineering industry. Full employment was sustained by the insatiable demand for munitions and strengthened the bargaining power of the workers at the very time when patriotism demanded no-strike agreements. By the Treasury Agreement and the Munitions of War Act of 1915 the unions agreed that in the interests of war efficiency it was necessary to suspend free collective bargaining and submit to compulsory arbitration in order to settle industrial disputes. At the same time the workforce in engineering was to be increased by the rapid induction of unskilled, mostly female, labour. Clearly this 'dilution threatened the privileges of skilled workers who were expected to submit to speed-up and restrictions on their job mobility at the same time. As essential workers, however, they were to be exempt from military service and were promised that these exceptional circumstances would not be abused by the employers who would gracefully return to the *status quo ante* once the war was over.

Here then was a combustible package of measures which almost immediately rendered the national trade union officials superfluous while forcing shop stewards in engineering to become vigilant guardians of the Agreement in the localities. This became apparent when the Clyde Workers' Committee emerged in 1915 at the head of a strike caused by the refusal of the employers to honour an overdue pay rise. Further strikes followed – on the Clyde again in 1916, in Sheffield towards the end of that year, in Barrow in March of 1917 and then a great engineering strike in May involving 250,000 workers. In all these disputes the grievances of the workforce were articulated through locally elected committees of shop stewards. On the Clyde all the leading members of the Workers' Committee were members of the SLP with the exceptions of William Gallacher (BSP) and David Kirkwood (ILP). Naturally the SLP wanted the committee to concentrate on agitation for a new industrial union in engineering, while in England members of the Amalgamation Committee Movement played a similar role. From 1916 the journal *Solidarity* waged the same campaign in London and the following year J. T. Murphy, secretary of the Sheffield committee, used its pages to expound the principles of the workers' committee movement.

Murphy argued that a permanent tension existed between the interests of the rank and file and those of the officials in the existing unions. Trade union officialdom was subject to different pressures and a different rhythm of life which were conducive to bureaucracy. He also acknowledged that the passivity of ordinary trade unionists reinforced these tendencies and that a proper fighting trade unionism required structures of participatory democracy. A minimum condition, for Murphy, was that the whole membership should be balloted before important decisions were taken by the national trade union leaders: 'The more responsibility rests upon every member of an organization the greater is the tendency for thought to be more general, and the more truly will elected officials be able to reflect the thoughts and feelings of the members of various organizations.'[10] An advocate of workers' control like Murphy obviously could not accept the conventional assumption that the national leadership was the best judge of the workers' interests. As a socialist Murphy was against all kinds of elitism including those based on craft divisions and sex prejudice, which weakened the trade union movement: 'Content to treat women as subjects instead of equals, men are now faced with problems not to their liking.'[11] If employers could now undermine trade unionism and the position occupied by skilled men by introducing cheaper unorganized female labour, this could be regarded as having much to do with the sex prejudices of male trade unionists. But Murphy's chief purpose in writing *The Workers' Committee* (1917) – which sold 150,000 copies – was to sketch an outline of how workers could be organized on the basis of a participatory democracy.

Starting from the workship committee, Murphy described a national structure of elected committees which would represent the workers by industry and as a class:

> Working in the existing organizations, investing the rank and file with responsibility at every stage and in every crisis; seeking to alter the constitution of every organization from within to meet the demands of the age; working always from the bottom upwards – we can see the rank and file of the workshops through the workshop committees dealing with the questions of the workshops, the rank and file of the firms tackling the questions of the plant as a whole through the plant committee, the industrial questions through the industrial committees, the working class questions through the working class organization – the workers' committee. The more such activity grows the more will the old organizations be modified, until, whether by easy stages or by a general move at a given time, we can fuse our forces into the structure which will have already grown.
>
> So to work with a will from within your organization, shouldering responsibility, liberating ideas, discarding prejudices, extending your organizations in every direction until we merge into the great industrial union of the working class.[12]

Clearly this grandiose scheme envisaged the rank and file movement in engineering spreading to all the other great industries and producing a system of administration fit to run society. By the time Murphy's pamphlet was published the shop stewards in engineering had already made two unsuccessful attempts to form a national organization in their own industry; the second of these attempts was aborted when the conference dealing with the issue in May 1917 in Manchester learned of the outbreak of another engineering strike which spread from Rochdale to Sheffield, the Midlands, Leeds and Liverpool. A real beginning for the National Shop Stewards' and Workers' Committee Movement (NSSWCM) had to wait until the following August. It was then that a National Administrative Council was formed, but it was given only administrative functions and its very name reflected the suspicion of its most influential figures of any kind of centralist leadership. Ironically, the appearance of soviets in Russia – which the NSSWCM enthusiastically welcomed – 'also retarded all efforts to secure a centralized leadership and strengthened them in the "rank and file" philosophy of *The Miners' Next Step*.'[13]

In fact the NSSWCM was confined to engineering, though contacts were made with rank and file movements in mining and railways in 1918. The movement was weakened in some areas by a rapid return to pre-war industrial practices in early 1919 and large-scale victimization of shop stewards. In Merseyside and London, however, the movement was consolidated and in Scotland it was reinforced by the emergence of a miners' reform movement. The October Revolution began to influence all its thinkings by 1919 and the idea that workers' control could be introduced before the seizure of state power was discredited among the revolutionaries in the leadership such as J. T. Murphy, Arthur MacManus and Willie Gallacher. The national conference of 1920 hailed the soviets as a model of working-class self-government but was sufficiently ignorant of the real nature of these councils as to confuse them with the workers' committees in Britain. Not until 1921 did the shop stewards' movement adopt a constitution and seek to organize all rank and file movements in industry. But it was still negative about its relationship with socialist parties until, after petitioning for membership of the Communist International, its leaders were persuaded by Lenin to help form the British Communist Party. But by then the rapidly worsening economic situation in Britain had begun to undermine the rank and file organizations on which the shop stewards' movement was based.

Guild socialism suffered a similar fate as a practical movement. A National Guilds League (NGL) had been formed in 1915 after the secession of 500 members of the Fabian Society when these dissidents failed to convert it to the new ideas. The NGL was conceived as an educational body and it was not until 1920 that guild socialism achieved a major trade union presence when a National Building Guild briefly flourished in the post-war property boom. For a while the Building Guild was able to take advantage of the availability of credit and the high demand for houses to provide quality homes at reasonable prices, but when conditions changed it was faced with insolvency and was wound up in 1923. Nevertheless by then there was a considerable body of guild socialist thought and the ideas of participatory democracy had been strengthened in the Labour movement. Even *Labour and the New Social Order* (1918) – drafted by Sidney Webb – had been obliged to refer to the need for a 'steadily increasing participation of the organized workers'.

No one had done more to promote industrial democracy in these years than G. D. H. Cole, who spent the war years as a researcher and adviser to the ASE. Cole had first put the case for 'functional democracy' in 1913. Drawing on the work of Rousseau and William Morris, he came to the conclusion that the character of socialism would be determined by just those issues which the Fabians ignored: the present wage system and capitalist relations of production. Under capitalism industry was ruled autocratically and Cole reasoned that this concentration of economic power enabled the capitalists to exercise a disproportionate influence over the state, which was shaped by the interplay of economic forces over which it exercised little real control. It followed that any serious attempt to change the nature of the state must also change the dictatorial rule of the capitalists in industry.[14]

Nevertheless, Cole, like the pluralist Harold Laski, was persuaded that the state was 'nothing more or less than the political machinery of government in a community'.[15] Both of them believed that while the priorities of economic power holders set the limits on what a Tory or Liberal government could do, a socialist government disdainful of such vested interests could help to abolish capitalism. In fact Cole and Laski thought that the advance of political democracy in Britain had greatly modified the state so that it was already something more than the mere expression of property interests.[16] But according to this argument, if the working class was already able to exert pressure on the state, further progress towards the realization of the state's 'true purpose' – the representation of general rather than sectional interests – depended on the complete elimination of capitalism. Until then the state's claim to be representative was simply absurd in Cole's view. Society was increasingly comprised of voluntary associations which actually represented different facets of the citizen's interests and yet, Cole argued, the state claimed a monopoly of popular sovereignty. The danger (and the syndicalists and Marxists were also arguing this) was that the fiction of the representative state would be used to justify its encroachment on civil society. State capitalism would thus arise on the destruction of such group and individual liberties as existed. For Cole, capitalist democracy was especially vulnerable to this danger because it restricted participation to the ballot box and an arena called 'politics'.[17]

The guild socialist solution as set out in the Storrington Document of 1915 envisaged the abolition of capitalism by means of the combined activities of industrial unions pursuing workers' control and a parliamentary majority of socialists enacting nationalization of the key industries.[18] The strength of this strategy seemed to lie in its recognition of the significance of economic power and of civil society as the source of that pluralism which alone could reconcile collectivism with democracy and individual liberty. It also seemed realistic. Cole believed, and recent developments seemed to support him, that the unions were objectively impelled to challenge managerial prerogatives because even the routine preoccupations of labourism were permanently imperilled if they did not. It was also tempting to believe that a latent communal spirit was being awakened and could be harnessed once the reorganization of industry was set in motion.[19]

For Cole, a strategy such as this gave practical application to Marx's insight that the emancipation of the working class must be the act of the working class itself. The gradual encroachment on capitalist power in industry by the trade unions was a way of bringing the ends and means of socialism into close correspondence. A socialism based on participatory democracy, in this view, could not come into existence unless socialists adopted a strategy which would enchance working-class self-government even as the new society emerged out of the old. Clearly for a time this would involve workers' participation in the management of capitalism, but Cole believed that such a 'common responsibility' would merely sharpen the appetite for more workers' power rather than lead to integration and co-option. The consciousness of the workers as a class with interests incompatible with those of capitalism would develop only through a prolonged school of management within the system in which the workers would develop the skills and experience necessary for a truly democratic socialism.

The guild socialist blueprint for the new society was less persuasive that its critique of the *status quo*, being based on the idea that a federation of trade union organizations representing the producers would share power with a parallel pyramid of consumers' organizations. To save this system from bureaucratic sclerosis Cole had to assume an extremely active and well-informed citizenry. But his optimism on this score proceeded from the assumption that the prolonged struggle for socialism would have created a new socialist man and woman – organized, knowledgeable and endowed with political judgement. And the strength of guild socialism lay in its challenge to those reformists who had written off the 'average sensuous man' and ended up preaching a technocratic collectivism devoid of democratic and cultural objectives.

Advocates of participatory democracy were in truth a small minority within European socialism. But with the emergence of soviets in Russia in 1917 this minority received a powerful stimulus which soon divided the movement for workers' control in Britain, as Cole later reflected, into 'out-and-out revolutionaries, most of whom passed into the Communist Party of Great Britain ... and the idealists of workers' control who were ... only left-wing reformists'.[20] Guild socialism thus lost supporters to the Communist movement because Leninism seemed to represent a genuine workers democracy, but it was the prolonged industrial depression of the inter-war years which eliminated a strong workers' control faction within the unions. However, as the centre, after 1920, of working-class militancy, the Communist Party must take some of the blame for this decline. Leninism changed the radical socialist catechism. Henceforward the focus of Marxist activity was party building for the purpose of smashing the bourgeois state, crudely understood as 'bodies of armed men'. Meanwhile socialism rapidly came to mean the system of power in the USSR which, it was noted, was perfectly compatible with the survival and extension of the most barbarous practices developed in capitalist industry. Now it was possible for British Marxists to argue that as long as the Bolshevik party-state existed these 'superficially capitalist' industrial forms were of no consequence.[21]

The British Communist leaders – J. R. Campbell, Arthur MacManus, Willie Gallacher and J. T. Murphy from the shop stewards' movement, William Mellor, R. Page Arnot and R. P. Dutt from guild socialism – had travelled a long way, ideologically speaking. They were now prepared to regard workers' control as something which made sense only in the form of the collective class-control of the proletarian dictatorship. They accepted on Lenin's authority that there was no meaningful distinction between the proletarian dictatorship and the dictatorship of the revolutionary (Bolshevik) party. In addition to these authoritarian aspects of the Leninist ideology, Cole noted shortly after the October Revolution that a marked preference for centralism, large-scale organization and power also characterized the Bolshevik approach and were sought after by them as intrinsic to socialism. All this was far removed from the desire to end industrial autocracy, wage slavery and centralism which had animated the syndicalists, industrial unionists and guild socialists in Britain.

The workers' control idea survived into the 1930s despite these adversities, though it was inevitable that the twenty-year depression should turn attention to the question of what the state could do to deal with the mounting agenda of necessary reforms. In these circumstances there were not many socialists who insisted on the linkage between genuine socialist reforms and changes in popular values brought about by a self-reliant, self-determining socialist movement. This was, however, the basis of R. H. Tawney's Christian socialism, which argued that socialist values could only be constructed through widespread participation, devolved power and economic equality. In Tawney's view the existing democractic arrangements were in any case unstable so long as they tried to coexist with social oligarchy and the class system.[22] Democracy in these circumstances was always vulnerable to the magnates of industry and finance whose interests might clash with it.

Since 1918 Tawney had justified industrial democracy on the grounds of civil liberty, economic efficiency and social harmony.[23] In these early years he had supposed that the guild socialist strategy of trade union encroachment combined with state action would bring about workers' participation. By 1921 Tawney was arguing that the elimination of the capitalist from the 'highly organized trades' would demand state intervention, but he was careful to observe that nationalization was not an end in itself and should not be allowed to impinge on experiments in self-government.[24] The object of nationalization in this view was not to establish the state management of industry but to release latent forces of professional pride by providing for as much rank and file power as was needed to generate a sense of social responsibility. Tawney realized that this could not be produced simply by an Act of Parliament but required a prior enlargement of trade union powers and responsibilities which, to be genuine, had to be the work of the unions themselves.[25]

In the catastrophic 1930s, with mass unemployment, fascism and war the main socialist preoccupations, such ideas were bound to be eclipsed. Tawney's ethical socialism, in particular, looked especially naive since his chosen instrument of reform, the Labour Party, was far removed from the sort of politics which could have breathed life into these ideas. The trade unions were led by unadventurous, ideologically conservative men such as Ernest Bevin and Walter Citrine. It was all the more necessary, then, to examine the relations of power, the class and institutional obstructions, which stood in the way of those socialist values which Tawney emphasized.

Conclusion

The spontaneous revolts of the low paid during 1911, at a time when only one-fifth of the workforce was affected by collective bargaining but after years of falling real wages, provided the immediate context in which movements of rank-and-file opinion could be receptive to the ideas of syndicalists like Tom Mann. But these ideas had developed in some measure because of the apparent 'treachery or incompetence of the politicians of the Labour Party', as *The Syndicalist* put it, and the conviction that trade union official-dom was no longer representative of the organized workers.[26] Labour's apparent submersion in the Liberal Party in Parliament persuaded militants that the electoral route to socialism was a dead end and that real power lay with the general strike which would signify 'the actual Social and Industrial Revolution'.[27] To that end *The Syndicalist* preached solidarity and direct action (including sabotage) and regularly carried advertisements for the 'King' air rifle over the legend 'learn to shoot straight'. The government was sufficiently worried by all this to prosecute Mann and four of his comrades in 1912 under the Incitement to Mutiny Act of 1797 – the first time this legislation had been invoked since 1804. The immediate effect of the trial, however, was to boost circulation of *The Syndicalist* to 20,000.

Although the syndicalist agitation soon receded, the peculiar labour conditions created by the war kept alive unofficial movements of the trade union rank and file as well as the suspicion that union officials were becoming increasingly incorporated into the state apparatus. In fact the state had become involved in the arbitration of industrial disputes as early as the Conciliation Act of 1896, which had been used on 365 occasions by 1909. The appointment of trade union officials to government administrative posts started even earlier, in 1886, when John Burnett (the General Secretary of the ASE) became Labour Correspondent to the Board of Trade. In the years that followed many union leaders followed this path and even more acquired part-time advisory or mediatory positions. By 1911 when the National Insurance Act was passed, providing a state subsidy to unions for the operation of the unemployment insurance scheme, there were real fears that this signalled the transformation of the unions into agencies of the state. The war seemed to hasten this process as union leaders not only agreed to oppose strikes but were drawn into the National Advisory Committee to help police the control of labour.

By 1918 and the end of the war this was no longer possible, but full employment, which lasted until the end of 1920, helped to maintain the unofficial movement within the unions and Bonar law commented that 'the trade union organization was the only thing between us and anarchy'.[28] In fact the Cabinet was by then accustomed to regular intelligence reports on the internal situation and ready to imprison strike leaders, as it had in 1916 in dealing with the Clyde workers and was to do again in 1919 in connection with the Glasgow strike. When the police took industrial action in 1919 the army was brought in to deal with unrest in Liverpool and Birkenhead and the Police Act was hurriedly passed to prevent this happening again. In the same year Lloyd George prepared a contingeny plan for dealing with any future general strike, though this was not needed until 1926.

The leaders of the ILP and the Labour Party had no sympathy with the industrial militants and many socialists – Philip Snowden and Bruce Glasier in particular – were deeply hostile to strikes *per se*. Yet these struggles helped to create a stronger socialist current within the unions and the experience of repression – as on the Cambrian coalfield in South Wales in 1910 and during the dock dispute of 1911 – did much to alienate working-class opinion from the Liberals. Trade union membership also rose from 2½ million in 1910 to over 4 million in 1914 and on to a peak of 8¼ million by 1920. An observer like Tawney saw in all of this social conflict evidence of collective moral disorder but also proof that a formative experience in working-class politics was taking place.[29] This revolt against wage slavery, he argued, would shift the central concern of reformers from the issue of wealth distribution to the question of the control of industry. In fact the struggles of 1910–14 and those during and immediately after war contributed to the growth of an anti-capitalist left within the Labour Party and the broader movement of which it is part. Although the strength of the unions collapsed with the onset of industrial slump in the years that followed, at least two more aspects of this experience endured: socialists would no longer regard the unions as mere defensive organizations but would look upon them as potential instruments for wielding state power, while the state would seek to use the unions as managers of discontent.

7

The Impact of the Bolshevik Revolution

The euphoria which greeted the news of the Tsar's downfall in March 1917 was not confined to socialist circles in Britain. It was immediately supposed that the new situation would strengthen the struggle of the Entente against Germany and thus the Labour and trade union leaders who supported the war effort joined Liberal and even Conservative opinion in applauding the new Provisional government in Petrograd. As Beatrice Webb noted in her diary, it was now more plausible to represent the conflict as 'democracy at war with autocracy', though by May she was also obliged to observe that British reactionaries were already 'alarmed at the revolutionary tendencies in the United Kingdom and in the Empire, heightened by the Russian revolution'.[1]

Although *The Times* reported that 'something like a parliamentary government' was now in control of Russia and every shade of opinion in Britain saw the revolution as a triumph for liberalism, the minority of anti-war journals – *Labour Leader*, *The Call*, *The Socialist*, *The Woman's Dreadnought* and *The Herald* – hoped that it would bring peace nearer and looked with interest at the activities of the Petrograd Soviet. The Soviet had already abolished military hierarchy in the armed forces and demanded 'a peace without annexations and indemnities', while a minority of 'Maximalists' (the Bolsheviks), according to the British press, were campaigning to take Russia out of the war immediately. The leaders of the Labour Party had welcomed the revolution with a telegram, however, in which they declared it a step towards victory over Germany. In May Arthur Henderson went to Russia as a representative of the war cabinet and put the British case. But he came back persuaded that the Russians would only stay in the war if the Labour Party accepted their peace programme and participated in a conference of all socialist parties which was to meet at Stockholm. The conference never took place but this did not prevent the war cabinet from forcing Henderson's resignation. Henderson was replaced by G. N. Barnes, a former leader of the Labour Party, and the other Labour ministers remained in office; 'Uncle Arthur' may have been kept waiting on the doormat while the other cabinet members decided his fate but organized labour was still behind the war effort.

Nevertheless the departure of Henderson was the beginning of the end for Lib-Labism and the emergence of labour as a national party.

The anti-war element within the Labour Party had been slightly strengthened in 1916 when the British Socialist Party (BSP) affiliated and proceeded to form the United Socialist Council with the ILP in April as a step towards unity. It was this body which organized the Leeds Convention in June 1917 to hail the March Revolution. Around 1,200 delegates representing every shade of opinion in the labour movement resolved at this gathering to set up soviets in Britain 'at once in every town, urban, and rural district'.[2] It will be instantly recognized that few if any of these delegates really understood what the soviets were. The Convention temporarily swept Marxist, pacifist and trade unionist together but produced no lasting effects. It was an outburst of euphoria, but as Beatrice Webb said at the time: 'To read the speeches one would think that they shared the thoughts and feelings of the Petrograd extremists. But who can imagine MacDonald or the Andersons or even the Snowdens leading a revolution of the Russian type – even if there existed the material for such a revolution in the British working class.'[3]

Only the small Marxist groups such as the BSP after the departure of Hyndman, the SLP and Sylvia Pankhurst's Workers' Socialist Federation (WSF) were wholly behind the Bolsheviks, though the ILPs anti-war stance made many in that organization also receptive to 'Maximalist' opinion. Elsewhere in the labour movement the Soviet and the Bolsheviks were blamed for the collapse of the Russian front. Indeed the 'collapse of Russia' by early October 1917 moved at least one British socialist to hope that faith in the 'cant of anarchic rebellion' would thereby be destroyed and Britain's own syndicalists discredited.[4] In fact, of course, these hopes were fulfilled in ways Beatrice Webb could never have imagined.

When news of the Bolshevik seizure of power arrived it was confidently held that the new regime would not survive more than a few weeks. But on the Marxist Left there was jubilation. Even the prodigious quantities of disinformation poured forth from the news media could not disguise the fact that the new government intended to bring Russia out of the war, had exposed the secret protocol which laid bare the imperialist war purposes of the Entente and had declared the right of nations to self-determination. British socialists also celebrated Bolshevik reforms in housing, land ownership and the length of the working day.[5] The SLP proclaimed itself the 'British Bolsheviks' while the BSP rejoiced that 'genuine socialists' held power in Petrograd. 'The expected has happened', announced *The Call* on 15 November 1917; but in reality the socialist revolution had been a complete surprise and those who rallied to it had no idea how it would develop.

Even in Liberal and Labourist circles the Bolshevik reforms and open diplomacy were admired, but among these observers there was also a very deep misgiving. As the chairman of the Labour conference said in January 1918: 'everything must be done to prevent the Russians from making a separate peace . . . [and to] help them to a fuller understanding of our position.'[6]

By the spring it became clear that 'everything' *was* being done – Russia was invaded and ultimately fourteen nations joined in the attack with Britain (from 2 August 1918) and France among them. Only the ILP and the revolutionary Left immediately condemned British intervention and from these elements a Hands Off Russia agitation had been started as early as November 1917, though a national committee by this name was not formed until early in 1919. The Labour and trade union leaders took the view that as long as the European war lasted they were obliged to support Lloyd George's aggression against Bolshevism as a *fait accompli*, and Arthur Henderson put this argument to the second Inter-Allied Conference of Labour and Socialist parties when this met in London in September 1918. Earlier in the year the question of armed intervention had been discussed by Labour's Advisory Committee on International Questions chaired by Sidney Webb. But the committee was divided and abstained, though with more interventionist members (Webb himself, Rex Leeper and R. C. K. Ensor) than those against (H. N. Brailsford).

Maxim Litvinov had used the pages of *The Herald* and other papers of the labour movement to put the Bolshevik case, and when he addressed delegates to the Labour conference in January 1918 he warned that soviet democracy was imperilled by the rapid advance of the German army. Nevertheless the official Labour view deplored the Treaty of Brest-Litovsk which the Bolsheviks were forced to conclude in March precisely to save these soviets even at the price of national humiliation. In June 1918 a second Labour conference was entertained by Kerensky who assured the assembled delegates – to some booing but also to a chorus of 'For he's a jolly good fellow' – that Brest-Litovsk was the work of fanatics and German agents who had destroyed democracy and installed a 'police terrorism' preparatory to 'hurling Russia into the abyss of annihilation'.[7] The Labour delegation to the Inter-Allied Conference in September supported Kerensky's argument that 'if the Treaty of Brest-Litovsk stands it would confirm the collapse of the Russian Revolution.'[8] Not until the armistice of 11 November 1918 was it possible to mobilize the British working class against the anti-Bolshevik machinations of Lloyd George and Winston Churchill.

Trotsky had expected an end to the civil peace in Britain and a growth in pro-Soviet sentiment when the electoral truce was terminated in June 1918.[9] But not until the election campaign in December did Labour demand an end to intervention against a barrage of propaganda which tried to portray the party as the dupe if not the agent of Bolshevism. In the event Lloyd George was able to exploit a last wave of popular chauvinism while Labour increased its MPs from 39 to 59 – all but one of whom had been put forward by a trade union. All the prominent ILP members were defeated and, with only two exceptions, the Parliamentary Labour Party was entirely composed of ex-trade union officials.

On the few occasions that these men raised the issue of the war against Bolshevism they did so by observing that while they were sure that the new regime was worse than Tsardom, the Russians really ought to be left to their own affairs. This was not a very compelling argument to men like Lloyd George and Winston Churchill who feared, as the Prime Minister put it, that 'the whole existing order . . . is questioned by the masses of population from one end of Europe to the other' and this was a situation, he believed, which 'Bolshevik imperialism' would exploit.[10] In any case there was the Empire to consider and Britain's rulers saw its Asian territories under immediate threat from the Bolshevik menace.

In Britain revolutionaries like John Maclean also took the view that the issue of Bolshevik Russia's survival would be decided within months rather than years. Since February 1918 Maclean had been Consul for Soviet Affairs in Scotland. By the beginning of 1919 he was arguing that there was only one way 'to save Russia' and that was 'by developing the Revolution in Britain' before the end of the year.[11] Saving Russia was also the sole preoccupation of the Hands Off Russia Committee which demanded the immediate withdrawal of the British troops, the raising of the blockade, the resumption of diplomatic relations and recognition of the Bolshevik government. It is significant that the Committee avoided any commitment to the view that the Bolshevik regime was a workers' state; had there been a strong feeling of class solidarity with the new state the militants in the forefront of the campaign would surely have stressed its socialist and working-class credentials. As it was, the working class was in the main untouched by the Soviet struggle for survival.[12] Under these circumstances the best sentiment which could be tapped by the opponents of intervention was war weariness and fear of military escalation. Meanwhile the Right of the labour movement – as represented by men such as J. R. Clynes and J. H. Thomas – urged Parliament to lift the blockade as the best way to *defeat* Bolshevism.

MacDonald and Snowden had urged recognition of the Bolshevik government almost from the moment it had been formed. As socialists they were sensitive to the new regime's appeal in socialist circles. Nevertheless MacDonald worked hard to delegitimize the Bolsheviks' socialist credentials and never wavered in his insistence on the irrelevance of Bolshevism and the Russian experience for Britain. Indeed a majority of the leaders of European socialism had arrived at the same views which were given expression in Branting's resolution endorsed by a meeting in Berne in January 1919 where steps were taken to create a regular International Labour and Socialist Conference. The Labour contingent, led by MacDonald, supported the argument that 'A revolution that does not establish liberty is not a revolution towards socialism and is not a revolution which socialists ought to make themselves responsible or allow the outside bourgeois reaction to impose the responsibility for upon them.'[13] As we have seen, MacDonald always took the view that socialism had to emerge organically, though his predilection for evolutionary change had not prevented him from joining the celebrations when the Tsar's government collapsed in March 1917. But on that occasion, of course, it was believed in London that the new government, though created by force, was akin to the one at Westminster.

One of the problems with Bolshevism, from MacDonald's angle, was that it would be used as a stick with which to beat British Labour by the party's Tory and Liberal opponents. There was also the question of the Bolsheviks' intense antipathy towards all shades of reformist socialism. The Menshevik opponents of the new regime inside Russia were the main source of social democratic analysis of the Soviet state and Bolshevik repression of Menshevism provided European socialists with, as it were, a preview, of how they stood in relation to their own 'Bolsheviks'. In Britain Lenin's supporters were mainly to be found in the ILP, the SLP and the BSP – the three largest socialist organizations with perhaps a combined strength of 35,000. In these organizations there was a conviction that Bolshevism, as Robert Williams put it, 'is simply Socialism with the supreme courage of its convictions'.[14] That being so, these militants were inclined to support the argument articulated at the Berne conference by the defeated minority opposed to MacDonald and Hjalmar Branting that 'even the act of questioning the legitimacy of a government that the capitalist classes of all countries are gunning for with implacable hatred would serve the purposes of those governments who dream of annihilating by economic blockade and military intervention that which we call Bolshevism'.[15]

A certain polarization of views on Bolshevism had hardened, then, by 1919. It was reflected in the fact that the report of the Executive which was put before the Labour conference in June of that year omitted any reference to the war of intervention and thus accurately conveyed the PLP's virtual indifference on this issue at a time when the party's head office was receiving a flood of resolutions proposing industrial action to defeat the government's Soviet policy. The threat of direct action, which was conveyed to the government by a formal deputation representing both wings of the movement after a joint conference of the TUC and the Labour Party in April, may well have been enough, however, to influence the timing of Churchill's announcement of the withdrawal of British troops. Only a month after the stormy debate on this issue in June the government made clear its intentions; after all the brief post-war boom was not yet over and the militant shop stewards' movement was still intact. The cabinet was told to expect a 'Bolshevist rising' in Glasgow sometime in the year and such was the hysteria in some quarters that the 'universal epidemic' of Bolshevism was detected even in a local strike for the 40 hour week which the *Glasgow Herald* perceived as 'the first step towards this squalid terrorism'.[16]

The threat of another war reappeared within months of Churchill's peace announcement when bankrupt, famine-stricken Poland attacked the Soviet Union in the spring of 1920 just as the Red Army was beginning to get on top of the situation in the civil war. French and British connivance was unmistakable and the clamour for direct action intensified particularly as there were portents by the summer of a renewed attempt to involve the British army directly. On the day in May, however, when the newspapers announced that the Polish army had captured Kiev, London dockers refused to load the *Jolly George*, which they believed was bound for Poland with a cargo of weapons. The popular mood was undoubtedly shifting Leftwards. In April the ILP had voted for immediate disaffiliation from the Second International and in June a motion to the same effect was defeated at the Labour conference by only 1,010,000 votes to 516,000, with half the delegates abstaining. The unions had never been stronger or more militant and anti-war feeling – which peaked in the 1930s – was already on an upward course.

It was in this situation that *The Times* alluded to the imminence of war in the first week of August 1920 and Arthur Henderson notified every local Labour organization of this 'menacing possibility' and called on them to demonstrate the following Sunday. On Monday 9 August the TUC and the Labour Party issued a statement which warned that 'the whole industrial power of the organized workers will be used to defeat this war.'[17] The great demonstrations which had already taken place served notice that this was no idle threat and on 13 August a Council of Action was formed empowered to call a general strike in the event of a declaration of war against Russia. Many years later Churchill, who was always leader of the war party, admitted that Lloyd George was 'constrained' to advise the Polish government to accept the Russian peace terms.[18] Whether the threat of political strikes had succeeded or not we may never know, but two days after the Council of Action was formed the Red Army advance through Poland was stopped outside Warsaw and the crisis was effectively over.

The Labour Party and the unions continued to call for recognition of the Bolshevik government and MacDonald even made this an election issue in December 1923, but the most telling argument in the movement's propaganda was that trade with Russia would ease Britain's growing unemployment problems. Among the socialists in Britain, however, many were moved by the sheer romance of a revolution which in spite of seven years of war had made massive humanitarian strides in education, health, sex equality, labour laws and much else besides. But perhaps above all else it was the vision of direct democracy as represented by the soviets which inspired the Bolsheviks' British sympathizers. For as George Lansbury told a packed Albert Hall at the end of February 1920: 'You have been told that Russia is in the grip of a gang of despots. The fact is that Lenin and his supporters have no individual power other than that delegated to them by the Soviets.'[19] Lansbury was among the first of many British visitors to the USSR who came back persuaded that it was governed by the workers themselves acting through a pyramid of soviets.

Other more critical accounts of the Bolshevik state were available – certainly from the time that the British Labour delegation published its remarkably balanced report in 1920. This noted, among other things, that the soviets were dominated by the ubiquitous control of the Communist Party and that the trade unions and the co-operatives had become 'a definite part of the State machinery'.[20] However, by 1920 most of the militants who had been excited by the soviets since the start of the revolution knew nothing about their construction and functioning. British proponents of workers' control took the soviets to be whatever they themselves had fought for and, as J. T. Murphy recalled many years later, 'we were so overwhelmed with the fact of the revolution that we were at times inclined to justify everything.'[21] What was important to founders of the British Communist Party like Harry Pollitt, who was to become its longest-serving General Secretary, was 'that lads like me had whacked the bosses and the landlords . . . These were the lads and lasses I must support through thick and thin . . . for me these same people could never do nor ever can do, any wrong against the working class.'[22]

For an energetic and courageous minority these were the sentiments inspired by the Bolshevik revolution. Under Lenin's direct influence Marxists from the BSP, SLP and WSF together with some former guild socialists, shop stewards, and members of the Plebs League began protracted unity talks which created the British Communist Party during 1920 and 1921. In other words the Communist Party of Great Britain (CPGB) emerged from the fusion of small groups whose total membership was no more than 2,000 by 1920. The Bolsheviks certainly had active sympathizers elsewhere – a vote for immediate affiliation to the Comintern received substantial support in the ILP in April 1920 – but there was no great split in the ranks of the Labour Party and even the ILP lost few of its members to the Third International. The new organization was led by working-class men who had already rejected the reformist strategy and much of the socialist vision to be found in the Labour Party and the ILP in favour of revolution and direct democracy. In fact they had been unable themselves to greatly advance the discussion of how their preferred alternative was to be achieved and this, no doubt, helps to explain why their demand for workers' control 'was subsumed into the theory of the struggle for soviet power and the notion of a strategy of encroaching control co-ordinated by a massive and tightly organized industrial union was finally abandoned'.[23] But a great deal was lost in the process of this conversion, as we shall see.

Membership of the Third (Communist) International which Lenin founded in Moscow in 1919 was dependent on acceptance of the Leninist canon as contained in the Twenty-One Conditions of Membership adopted by the Second Congress in 1920. The stated purpose of the twenty-one conditions was to bar organizations which had not already become Communist. But the only way of knowing who these groups were was whether or not they showed unconditional acceptance of the conditions.[24] The conditions were therefore designed to keep mere sympathizers out of the organization and to force splits in other working-class associations. The faithful who passed through this net were then subject to a thorough induction process which lasted many years. J. T. Murphy later described (without criticism) the pupil-teacher relationship between the foreign Communists and the Bolsheviks as it operated at the second Comintern congress in 1920: 'The whole Congress and especially its commissions were schools in which we immature Socialists were being drilled into a theoretical understanding of Marxism as propounded by Lenin,

Trotsky, Zinoviev, Bucharin and Radek.'[25]

With the tremendous prestige of the October Revolution behind them and a leader as skilled as Lenin, the Bolsheviks wholly dominated the new International and provided every aspect of its ideological *raison d'être*. Revolutionary politics, in this view, proceeded from an understanding of the character of the imperialist epoch which the world had entered in the 1890s. The emergence of monopoly capitalism, which Marx had predicted, was connected by Lenin to a decline in the rate of profit in the technologically advanced countries and a growth in capital exports as the monopolies searched for a higher rate of return on their investments. Thus a struggle to divide and re-divide the world was now a feature of the system and so, therefore, was war as the major powers collided in their haste to acquire colonies. The monopoly capitalist system was inherently unstable in Lenin's view because it bred wars, dragged the colonial peoples towards a modern nationalist consciousness, and depended on the more or less precarious super-profits which it extorted abroad rather than on the development of the productive forces at home. Nevertheless, insofar as monopoly capitalism succeeded in this foreign plunder it was able, according to Lenin, to buy off a layer of the proletariat with higher wages. This corrupt minority – perhaps 10 per cent of the working class – therefore had a vested interest in the survival of imperialism and formed the core support of the reformist trade unions and socialist parties which had 'betrayed' the cause in 1914 by supporting their own ruling class in the imperialist war.[26]

The two most important lessons which the early Communist International drew from this analysis were that: first, the reformist trade unions and socialist or labour parties were appendages of the bourgeois state inside the workers' movement. They were therefore enemies against whom an unremitting struggle had to be waged. Second the bourgeois state, however democratic in form, was merely the dictatorship of monopoly or finance capital (the terms were synonymous for Lenin). Real democracy, according to the Comintern, consisted exclusively in soviet or council democracy. When critics of the regime pointed out that the soviets were in fact controlled from above by the Bolsheviks and that the dictatorship in Russia was of Lenin's party and not the proletariat, both Lenin and Trotsky affirmed the identity of their party with the class it was supposed to represent. Thus to distinguish between the two, it was argued, only testified to the confusion in the minds of the Bolsheviks' critics.[27]

The thing that really mattered, then, was the conquest of power by the revolutionary party. This was the real criterion of progress towards socialism, according to the Communists. For years the main currents in British socialism, such as Fabianism and leading influences within the ILP, had argued that the progress of socialism could be measured by the growth of the collectivist state. Their opponents had criticized this formalism and drawn attention to the need for major democratic reforms if state capitalism were to be avoided. Leninism now made this debate seem redundant. It was argued that the essential problems today are political struggles – the struggles of rival national states and the class struggle for control of the State . . . The question of where ultimate power resides is the important thing and not the mere superficial forms of industrial administration . . . However far in response to economic expediency the forms of industrial administration in Russia may be modified to a superficial resemblance to capitalist forms (for example scientific management, bonus wage-payments, credit and currency systems etc) Russia will remain separated by a great gulf from the capitalist world, so long as supreme power rests with the working class.[28]

By reasoning in this way the leaders of British Communism – many of them former revolutionary shop stewards, industrial unionists and guild socialists – lost sight of the arguments to which they themselves had called attention in the war years: a class which is oppressed by 'wage slavery' is in no sense 'in power'; representation through a single, centralized organization is a fiction.

But Leninism turned British Marxism into a doctrine of action around the construction of a mass Communist Party. Whereas they had once held faith in a 'materialist conception of history', promising socialism by virtue of economic collapse but presented in a language dependent on biological metaphors which betrayed the fatalist and evolutionary bias within, Marxists in Britain now embraced a technology of revolutionary action. The electic and abstruse philosophical works of Dietzgen and Haeckel were displaced by lucid political works which dwelt on strategy and tactics. It was a changeover reflected in changed attitudes to Marxism within the Labour Party; where once it had been regarded as a doctrine with its uses, if also its fallacies, it was now perceived as a pernicious threat which needed to be frozen out.[29] But if Leninism injected new life into British revolutionaries it did so at the cost of a further narrowing of Marxism along the route indicated by Engels. Without ideological rivals within the Comintern, the Bolsheviks presented their doctrines as definitive truths requiring no further elaboration. Leninism soon became a pseudo-science of tactics whose significance depended on the alleged propensity of imperialism to produce revolutionary crises.

In Britain the immediate and lasting problem was how the CPGB would negotiate the massive obstacles represented by the unions and the Labour Party. The close organizational links which existed between these wings of the working-class movement suggested from the beginning that the tiny revolutionary groups would have to find some sort of united-front relationship with them if the Communists were to avoid total isolation. Whereas the Comintern was launched as an open rival to the Second International, the tactic of splitting the social democratic parties which it pursued in Germany, Italy and elsewhere had no impact in Britain. Lenin urged the CPGB to affiliate to the Labour Party, believing it to be a federal organization tolerant even of its open enemies. Unlike the continental social democratic parties, moreover, the

Labour Party was bound by a unique structural link to the trade unions. In Bolshevik calculations there could be no mass radicalization of the British working-class which did not express itself through the most powerful trade union movement in the world and therefore through the Labour Party, since most of the big battalions of organized labour were affiliated to it. Against considerable resistance from within British Communism, Lenin succeeded in persuading its leaders that affiliation would enable the CPGB more effectively to support the Labour leaders, in the way a rope supports a hanged man.

Communists were expected to find common cause with the Labour Left – especially the local rank and file – while maintaining a ceaseless polemic against the party's leaders and strategy. They were expected to walk the tactical tightrope on one side of which lay conciliation and the deviation of 'right opportunism' and on the other 'ultra-leftism' resulting from sectarianism. In fact these errors could only be identified retrospectively by the Bolshevik leadership of the Comintern. There was no independent criterion available to enable the British Communists to exercise independent judgement in this matter. The Bolsheviks' characterization of the Labour Party was no help to them since it invited both errors; it was described as a 'thoroughly bourgeois party' but also as 'the political organization of the trade unions'.[30] It is not surprising, therefore, that the united front tactic was not understood in the CPGB.

The first application for Communist affiliation to the Labour Party provocatively dwelt on the differences between the two organizations, pointing out that the CPGB believed in the dictatorship of the proletariat, soviet democracy and membership of the Comintern. When it was rejected the CPGB adopted a triumphant tone: 'so be it; it is your funeral not ours.' The Labour conference of 1921, however, was moved to take the offensive in this ideological battle and denounced the armed suppression of the Georgian Menshevik government by the Bolsheviks, calling for free elections supervised by international socialist and communist parties. The party executive also took the opportunity to observe that

> attempts made by Moscow to control national organizations not only in general Socialist policy but in the details of their own national work must prevent every such organization with any self respect and any sense of national freedom from putting itself under such a yoke.[31]

The following year, as death sentences hung over forty-seven Socialist Revolutionaries, the Labour conference supported a motion condemning the severity of Bolshevik justice while Communist delegates argued that the prisoners were guilty of terrorism and deserved their fate.

The Labour leaders figured in Communist demonology as the 'most dangerous enemies' confronting the revolutionary movement, while the trade union leaders were denounced for their 'damnable treachery' which had allegedly surfaced on every occasion since the armistice when the rank and file looked ready for action.[32] J. T. Murphy eventually came to the conclusion that the ferocity of the CPGB's polemics had been counterproductive and had actually 'strengthened the hands of the reactionary and conservative elements within the Labour movement'.[33] Certainly the CPGB functioned as a purely oppositional force for most of the time, but until the end of 1924 it contained conciliatory elements as well.

The formation of the first, minority Labour government under Ramsay MacDonald's leadership after the general election of December 1923, for example, was greeted in the British Communist press as a step forward in its own right, and the CPGB's leading theoretician, R. Palme Dutt, even looked forward to some solid achievements from the first 'workers' government'.[34] Yet Labour had presented itself to the electorate as 'the best bulwark against violent upheaval and class wars' – the very things the CPGB believed inevitable.[35] It is little wonder that the CPGB was admonished by the Comintern for displaying 'Right tendencies' and 'grave mistakes' in its application of the united front. It had to be reminded that the Labour government was a mere soap bubble on the froth of the cauldron of chronic imperial crisis.[36] In fact, as Zinoviev, the President of the Comintern, now insisted, Britain was 'ripe' for a mass Communist Party and objective circumstances were making the CPGB 'the most important section of the Communist International at present.'[37]

Britain was in the first phase of the inter-war slump when the Comintern raised these expectations. Between 1921 and 1933, 400,000 jobs were eliminated in mining, 150,000 in textiles, 250,000 in steel and 200,000 in shipbuilding. Undoubtedly the Communists expected that such a contraction would provoke revolutionary struggles and as early as October 1920 the CPGB took the initiative in organizing the unemployed and launched the National Unemployed Workers' Committee Movement (NUWCM) in April 1921. Neither the TUC nor the Labour Party were interested in 'direct action' over unemployment and both did their best to isolate the NUWCM, especially after the General Strike in 1926.[38] But it was in the unions and among the employed where the CPGB failed to make the expected impression.

The 1920s were years of bitter conflict in industry but union membership had already begun to fall dramatically when the decade opened. From 8,253,000 in 1920 the trade unions shrank to just over 5 million in 1926 and then, after the General Strike, to below 5 million until the end of the 1930s. The Comintern did not accept that the unions and the working class generally were faced with the prospect of largely defensive struggles. In 1921 it had established a British Bureau of the Red International of Labour Unions (Profintern) charged with turning the unions into instruments of revolutionary struggle. Then in 1923 the CPGB was encouraged to create a Minority Movement which would organize the united front in the unions. Its counterpart in the Labour Party – the National Left Wing Movement, which was launched at the end of 1925 – succeeded for a time in creating a large milieu for Communist and Left Labour views; in 1926 the *Sunday Worker* which acted as the organ of the united front claimed a circulation of 85,000. But the Minority Movement only took root in the mining industry.

Conclusion

The British labour movement survived both the war of 1914–18 and the October Revolution without experiencing the bitter and massive splits which affected the working class on the European continent. Thus when the CPGB was formed it represented the fusion of small quasi-revolutionary groups orchestrated from abroad rather than a significant section of the Labour and trade union movement. This is the best evidence that the periodic upsurges in militancy since the late 1880s, though they helped to promote socialist politics in the working class, did not represent the degree of estrangement from the political system and reformism which was required for the creation of a strong revolutionary current in Britain. Thus the revolutionary strategy represented by Lenin was a non-starter in Britain though the founders of the CPGB could not have known this in 1920. Leninism did provide the Marxists with a coherent analysis of modern capitalism, tactical and organizational intelligence which their predecessors lacked, and membership of a world movement which could claim the only socialist success to its credit.

These factors explain why the Communists exercised an influence out of all proportion to their numbers and why their Labour and trade union opponents went to considerable lengths to purge them from the movement. But in the end numbers count and it was possible for the Labour leadership to rebuff every Communist overture for joint action, let alone affiliation to the Labour Party itself, because the CPGB was a negligible force electorally and could do nothing to hurt the mass party where it really counted. Similarly it was possible to purge the constituency Labour Parties of Communists because at no time in the inter-war period was there a co-ordinated movement of radical opinion within the Labour ranks, despite the CPGB's efforts to create one, that was big enough to defy and challenge the leadership. Had the General Strike of 1926 resulted in a more favourable outcome for the strikers it is possible that the Left would have been greatly strengthened *vis-à-vis* the right of the movement and things could have been different. In fact the CPGB was unable, despite heroic efforts, to build up a membership of more than 10,000 until the late 1930s, by which time the party was severely handicapped by the advent of Stalinism.

8

Labour in Power?

The struggle to establish a mass Communist Party in Britain was fought and lost inside the trade union movement which the Third International identified, along with the factory, as the principal site for party building. As early as 1922 the *Report on Organization* drafted by R. Palme Dutt sought to Bolshevize the party by reconstructing it on the basis of factory cells so numerous that its ultimate target would make 'the whole present membership of our Party not . . . more than sufficient to constitute a single good district'.[1] With this aim in view, 'The purpose of the Party's work in the trade unions is to transform them into mass organizations of the revolutionary struggle under the leadership of the Party.'[2] The Communist nucleus, according to the Report,

> will endeavour to weaken the position of reactionary officials and leaders by pressing issues which will force them to take up an unpopular stand; it will aim at pushing the rules to their limit and so expose their unwieldy character, and work for their alteration; it will work for the election of accredited Communist candidates as officials and delegates to conferences.[3]

There was continuity in some of these aims with the work of the SLP and the militant shop stewards, of course, but the new ingredient was central control and co-ordination of all these activities by the Communist Party which would subordinate every consideration to the all-important task of building the party.

The leadership of the trade unions certainly left much to be desired, as was shown in the defeats inflicted on the best organized group of workers – the miners. In January 1919 the Miners' Federation demanded a package of measures including nationalization of the industry and proved by ballot that it was prepared to call a national strike to enforce its demands. Its partners in the Triple Alliance (formed in 1914 with the railwaymen and transport workers) meanwhile formulated their own demands separately. But the miners' strike notices were suspended when the government set up a Royal

Commission under Sir John Sankey, pledged to investigate the union's claim
and implement the inquiry's findings. When the Sankey Commission duly
reported in June it recommended the nationalization of the coal industry, but
the government did nothing until the third week in August. Neither the Miners' Federation nor the Parliamentary Labour Party made much of an effort
to sustain the impetus that had been evident in January, and when Lloyd
George announced the government's rejection of the Sankey Report the
union was beaten.

In April 1921 the miners were let down by their colleagues in the Triple
Alliance when the concerted action promised by the Transport Workers'
Federation and the National Union of Railwayment was called off at the last
minute. 'Black Friday' was seen as a betrayal, but already the growth in
unemployment was helping to make the general circumstances unfavourable
to strike action. Communists continued to keep faith in revolutionary trade
unionism because they believed the worsening economic circumstances would
trigger a growth in class consciousness.

When the General Council of the TUC was formed in September 1921 in
place of the old Parliamentary Committee, its thirty-two members included a
sizeable Left which was further strengthened when some figures on the Right
of the movement were returned to Parliament in 1922, as Labour increased its
representation from 75 to 142 MPs. The Communist united front now sought
to draw in men such as A. A. Purcell, Alonso Swales, Ben Turner and George
Hicks on the General Council, together with the Labour Party Left, which
was now made to appear stronger than ever following the return of the Red
Clydesiders to Parliament in 1922.

After the general election of December 1923, when a minority Labour
Government was about to be formed for the first time, the CPGB took a
remarkably conciliatory line. R. Palme Dutt saw 'the approaching menace of
a Labour Government' as proof that Britain was being brought into line with
the radical currents agitating Europe as a whole. This seemed to represent an
'unknown, dangerous, and even revolutionary factor', from the bourgeois
standpoint, even though, as Dutt observed, Labour 'still follows its traditional policy of clinging close to Liberal lines'.[4] Thus in the belief that
Labour's imminent assumption of power marked an objective step forward,
Dutt argued that 'the first need of all of us at the present moment, whatever
our criticisms and distrusts, is to unite in support of a Workers' Government
and its supremacy first and foremost.'[5] This attitude was to bring a stinging
rebuke from the Comintern which referred to the 'reformist epidemic' in the
CPGB, but it is interesting to note that a good deal of Dutt's enthusiasm for
the incoming Labour government was connected to the perception that it
would mean an enormous shake-up in British foreign policy. Apart from
Labour's intention to recognize the Soviet government, the party had been
virtually unanimous in the period since 1919 in denouncing the Treaty of
Versailles as a robbers' settlement based on the plunder of Germany, which
was condemned under the infamous 'war-guilt' clause. Versailles was also

held to have violated President Wilson's 'Fourteen Points' in respect of the self-determination of nations, and many critics thought that it was likely to bring about another war in Europe. Labour thus stood for revision of the Treaty, opposition to French militarism, and the inclusion of Germany and the Soviet Union in the League of Nations. These views were championed by former Liberals and members of the UDC such as Arthur Ponsonby, Charles Trevelyan and E. D. Morel, who were among about seventy prominent individuals who shifted to Labour from the old parties between 1918 and 1922 because they saw it as the best vehicle for the promotion of such ideas. Indeed these former Liberals became the party's leading spokesmen on foreign affairs in the House of Commons despite the fact that their conversion to Labour involved 'no sudden revelation of the cogency of socialism, no rejection of past credo'.[6]

E. D. Morel's passionate espousal of the UDC's case gave rise to an interesting episode in 1920 which deserves mention here. When the French army, including detachments of Morroccan troops, occupied a number of German cities in April 1920 Morel wrote an article in George Lansbury's *Daily Herald*, then at the height of its powers, in which he talked about France 'thrusting her black savages into the heart of Germany'. The 'barely restrainable beastiality of the black troops' had led, according to Morel, to many rapes which 'for well-known physiological reasons' nearly always results in injury or even death for the white women.[7] This crude racism was given credibility by the *Daily Herald* which alone among the British newspapers drew special attention to the 'race' of the French troops. Lansbury expressed the hope that his readers would ponder over Morel's account of the 'sexual outrages' in particular, and Morel's equally racist follow-up pamphlet, which was presented to every delegate at the 1920 TUC, was reviewed favourably by the ILP. Resolutions on this matter from ILP, trade union, and Labour Party branches were all concerned with the 'dangerous and degrading practice' of using black troops in Europe. The *Daily Herald's* racism generated little criticism (although there was some, notably from Norman Leys), and this episode suggests that even on the Left of the movement, which was generally more concerned with anti-imperialism than elsewhere in British politics, racist attitudes persisted. Thus while the defenders of Empire often justified British rule on paternalistic grounds, it was possible for men like Morel, with a record of anti-imperialism, to share in such attitudes while seeking to protect the black man from the ravages of capitalism.

The backwardness of the British Left on the colonial issue was also revealed at the second congress of the Comintern where the British members of the Commission on the National and Colonial question balked at the suggestion that they should organize revolutionary movements in the colonies. The British Marxists knew full well that the issue of imperialism was essentially marginal to organized labour, while there were those in the movement – J. R. Clynes and J. H. Thomas, for instance – who believed that the Empire was essential to the interests of British workers. The cotton unions had even advocated the conscious deindustrialization of colonial territories which threatened their interests.[8] But even mere indifference to the British colonies could rest on racist attitudes which the CPGB was obliged to combat. During the First World War Tom Quelch, a leading member of the BSP, was taken to task by Chicherin, a Bolshevik then resident in Britain, for the note of racist alarm which Quelch struck when black labourers, or 'jolly coons' as he preferred to call them, were used as strikebreakers. On this occasion too, the 'starved' sexual appetites of these men was invoked as a threat to English women.[9] By 1925, when the British Communists were free from such attitudes, the CPGB was engaged in systematic colonial work and did its best through its agents in India and Egypt to assist in the creation of anti-imperialist movements, work that was also carried out under the auspices of the League Against Imperialism which the Comintern launched in 1927.

The Labour Party's *Memorandum on War Aims*, (1918) had talked of a need for the 'frank abandonment of every form of Imperialism' and the annual conference of that year declared its intention to give India dominion status. But Labour's conservatism on such issues was revealed closer to home in relation to the issue of Ireland. By 1913 the party belatedly adopted Gladstone's policy of Home Rule which fell somewhat short of Irish independence and assumed the maintenance of the unity of the Imperial Parliament. The Easter Rising of 1916 had no place in these plans and was condemned by Labour's annual conference, and as late as 1919 party policy rejected any settlement leading to an Irish republic. By 1920 both the ILP and the Labour Party had declared in favour of a united Ireland, though the latter demonstrated no unanimity on the issue and could still not countenance a republican settlement. Thereafter it preserved a discreet silence on the subject which could easily be dismissed as a distraction from more compelling issues of domestic social and economic reform.[10] There was nothing in any of this to suggest that more distant peoples living under the British flag, many of them regarded as 'non-adult races' unfit for self-government, would fare any better from a Labour government.

MacDonald formed his government of 1924 with no less than nine members of the UDC in the Cabinet. But there were no plans to begin the process of revising the Treaty of Versailles, which was becoming to be seen as a force for European stability. On the contrary, MacDonald championed the Dawes Plan which the Americans formulated to help Germany pay reparations without altering the total amount of German war debt. It was soon apparent that MacDonald's foreign policy was little different to that of the Conservative Party. J. H. Thomas, a self-avowed imperialist, was put in charge of the Colonial Office; Sidney Olivier, a former colonial governor, was sent to the India Office; Lord Chelmsford was given the Admiralty though he did not belong to the Labour Party and had defended the Amritsar Massacre of 1919 in which at least 1580 unarmed demonstrators had been killed or wounded by British troops in India; and General Thomson, another establishment figure, was put in charge of the Air Force. These appointments did nothing to encourage the nationalist forces in India. Indeed MacDonald told the Indian nationalist leaders, who were all strict adherents of constitutionalism, that 'no party in Britain will be cowed by threats of force'. MacDonald's intention in forming this first Labour government had been to demonstrate Labour's fitness to govern and this apparently meant strict observance of given arrangements. Thus Labour's only distinctive policy, the Capital Levy, a device for taxing large capital holders for the purpose of paying off the National Debt, an idea which Labour borrowed from the ex-Liberal Sydney Arnold who joined the party in 1922, was promptly dropped upon taking office.

By May 1924 R. Palme Dutt had so changed his tune over the Labour government that he was describing 'MacDonaldism' as 'the greatest enemy of the working class at the present stage'.[11] Certainly MacDonald proved in 1924, as he did again in 1929–31, that the British Establishment had nothing to fear from Labour governments which were remarkably orthodox in both foreign and domestic policy. In fact, where these governments were not orthodox they seemed to be devoid of ideas, a fact which prompted the ILP Left to formulate specific policies where Labour was so lamentably silent. In relation to the Empire, leading Leftists such as George Lansbury and John Wheatley now argued that Labour should seek to transform the area under British protection into a commonwealth based on socialist principles which, in contrast to the competitive, bellicose world of capitalism, would represent a new co-operative idea of international relationships. According to Lansbury, 'There is no reason for breaking up the British Empire any more than there is a reason for smashing our own national institutions. Our duty is to transform the British Empire of Domination into a Commonwealth of free nations, including within this Commonwealth those people who themselves desire to join with us.'[12]

Wheatley came to similar conclusions, because he was concerned to do something about unemployment, which he diagnosed as in part the effect of competition in a world in which many foreign and colonial workers lived at a standard of life much lower than their British counterparts who were consequently driven out of employment. Given that the Empire was an established fact, some Clydeside radicals now reasoned that it was incumbent on socialists to turn it into 'a bloc against world capitalism'.[13] In the summer of 1925 this kind of reasoning led some of the Clyde group to vote in favour of Imperial protection in the House of Commons and R. Palme Dutt concluded for the Communists that 'when it comes to policy and expression they are as much the slaves of the "nation" and the "Empire" and the rest of the cant as any.'[14]

The failure of the first MacDonald government in 1924, which achieved virtually nothing of value to socialists, strengthened the conviction of the revolutionaries and their allies that the real power of the working class could only be expressed through industrial struggle. MacDonald's performance also did much to embitter relations between the Left and Right of the labour movement. The Labour government had fulfilled its election promise to recognize the Bolshevik government – although real enthusiasm and commitment on this issue was displayed by the ex-Liberals in the government rather than the Labour men. But MacDonald's extreme timidity in all matters concerning Communists prevented him from ratifying the trade treaties with Russia which his government had promised and contributed to his administration's early demise and electoral defeat. The Liberals and the Conservatives exploited MacDonald's indecisiveness in the prosecution of the Communist J. R. Campbell – who was charged with incitement to mutiny by the Attorney General – and similarly made the most of the so-called Zinoviev Letter during the 1924 election campaign, thanks in part to the failure of MacDonald to denounce it as a forgery.

Meanwhile Communists were banned from individual membership of the Labour Party and from adoption as Labour candidates, with MacDonald thundering against the CPGB's 'pettifogging conspiracy, secret associations, backstair wirepulling, mischievous stirring up of strife [that] are neither in method nor in ideal the Socialism that has built up our Labour Party'.[15] In fact the CPGB turned to quasi-clandestine activities within the Labour Party increasingly after 1924. But the unions remained its main field of activity – all the more so because the Communists held that the first Labour government had demonstrated the impotence of reformism. They correctly analysed the return to the gold standard in 1925 as a sign that the economic crisis would be 'solved' by wage cuts and the decline of working-class living standards. The coalowners were among the first employers to announce the necessity of these measures, but the miners, supported by the General Council, threatened to resist by strike action. On Friday 31 July – 'Red Friday' – the Prime Minister, Stanley Baldwin, averted the strike by making available a subsidy to maintain wages and by promising an inquiry into means for improving the productive efficiency of the industry. This reprieve was to last nine months but before it was over a pretext was found for imprisoning the Communist leaders. During these nine months the government and the employers took a range of other measures to prepare for the inevitable conflict, in sharp contrast to the General Council which did nothing. Thus, when on 3 May 1926 the country was pitched into a nine-day general strike, it was entered with extreme reluctance on the TUC side. Support for the strike was still growing when the General Council called it off without securing either the agreement of the miners themselves or any guarantees that the strikers would not be victimized when they returned to work. This dramatic capitulation testified to the success of the Baldwin cabinet in defining the strike as a challenge to the constitution, for this was never the intention of the moderates of the General Council who were frankly appalled at the prospect of the strike achieving a radical momentum of its own. It may also have entered their heads that any favourable resolution of the strike would strengthen the Left in the unions, with whom they had been in increasingly bitter conflict throughout the 1920s.[16]

The defeat of the General Strike was in fact followed by a wave of victimization and a collapse in trade union membership. The miners were left to their own devices with the result that the power of the union was broken after a six-month-long struggle. Although the Communist Party increased its membership to over 10,000 and made considerable headway on the coalfields, its relations with the trade union and Labour Left were at their worst since the party had been formed. For it now rounded viciously on its former allies such as A. J. Cook and, under pressure from the Comintern, admitted to 'Right tendencies' in its application of the united front. The Communist International insisted that 'the masses' were now moving faster and further to the left than the CPGB's erstwhile friends such as James Maxton and the Clydesiders. Even before the end of 1926 it announced that the final struggle between the Labour Party and British Communism was on the immediate agenda.[17] By the end of 1927 the CPGB would be denouncing the 'sham Lefts' like Cook and Maxton as 'social fascists'.

Throughout the 1920s Communist theoreticians had predicted the imminent decline of the Labour Party and had reasoned that its leaders would evolve away from socialism as it became clear that their reformist ideas could be put to no good use in an epoch of capitalist decline.[18] Yet these were years in which the party grew electorally as well as in membership, while socialists within the organization developed the ideas with which Labour was increasingly associated. The blows struck against trade union radicalism also turned the minds of many former guild socialists to the question of how the Labour Party could use the state to make socialist reforms. It now seemed to Laski and Cole and Tawney that in the new circumstances the state simply had to be the main vehicle for social reform.

Of course the Webbs were never in any doubt about this, and though they made several concessions (mainly verbal) to the guild socialist critique of state socialism their blueprint for the future socialist society, published in 1920, was, as Margaret Cole said, a 'bureaucratic nightmare'.[19] Although they now argued that the growth in executive power was merely the most important of a host of factors making for less democracy than was desirable, they still believed that the great thing about democratic arrangements in the British political system was their 'psychological influence in obtaining general acquiesence', a benefit that was derived from the 'consciousness of consent'.[20] But their main concern was to increase governmental efficiency by proposing a reform that would create two parliaments – one concerned with 'what is strictly political', the other to be concerned with 'the control of social and industrial administration'. It was an idea, adapted from guild socialist discussions, which would turn up again later in Winston Churchill's Romanes Lecture of 1930.[21] But in the Webb's scheme the 'Social Parliament' would be concerned with the administration of the major industries and services through multiple tiers of committees.

It has been pointed out that the implied revolutionary change in the Webbs' proposals was 'to be put through from no motive except tidiness and a problematic efficiency'.[22] This was testimony to their continued belief that power

holders would give up their privileges if exposed to sufficient rational and
moral exhortation. Similarly the Webbs conjured away conflicts of interest in
their system by arguing that the question of who gives the orders will become
'largely meaningless'. It would make no material difference, they argued,
who had power in a society where the 'searchlight of published knowledge'
will enable decisions to arise by 'common consent'. Experts would provide
'accurately ascertained and authoritatively reported facts' but would 'have no
power of command and no right to insist on [their] suggestions being
adopted'.[23] Thus once these 'disinterested and independent' individuals presented their evidence the truth would become self-evident, according to the
Webbs, under the glare of publicity. It is difficult to say whether this reasoning was merely naive or evidence of Bertrand Russell's charge that the Webbs
'regarded it as the function of a statesman to bamboozle or terrorise the
populace'.[24]

It was reasoning that was in any case repeated in *The Decay of Capitalist
Civilization* when this appeared in 1923.[25] Here it was acknowledged that the
Webbs' 'professional brain-workers' emerged historically 'as the hirelings of
the governing class' and 'naturally serve the proprietors of the instruments of
production'. Such people, therefore, 'are almost inevitably retained consciously or unconsciously in the maintenance and defence of the existing
social order in which the private ownership of the means of production is the
cornerstone'.[26] Nevertheless according to the Webbs the professionals and
experts in society were beginning to rebel against the nepotism, the privileges
and the mental constraints which the system encouraged. Meanwhile the
profit motive was losing its usefulness since it had only ever been (in its
Victorian heydey), 'the world's substitute for qualities which did not at that
time exist for self-discipline, for professional technique, for scientific knowledge, for public service, for the spirit of the association, for common honesty
itself.'[27] In the Webbs' view these were qualities which now existed in abundance among the growing 'intellectual proletariat'. It was only a matter of
time before this '*nouvelle couche sociale*' would find in socialism 'the dignity
and security of a public service'. This was the development which 'makes
possible an alternative system of industrial organization'.[28]

This was a conviction to be found in the writings of many Labour socialists
in the 1920s. R. H. Tawney's vision of socialism, for example, was far more
democratic than that of the Webbs and he understood that a social revolution
could never happen unless the labour movement embodied anti-capitalist
values; for 'An appeal to principles is the condition of any reconstruction of
society because social institutions are the visible expression of the scale of
moral values which rules the minds of individuals and it is impossible to alter
institutions without altering that valuation.'[29] Tawney analysed the rise of
capitalism in relation to generations of moral change involving the rise of the
motive of personal gain at the expense of the idea that the significance and
measure of institutions and practices was the common end to which they were
related.[30] But his optimism that this process could be reversed derived from

the conviction that the growth of the professions signalled the rise of social responsibility and the exclusion of 'speculative profit' from the motives of a growing proportion of the intellectual workforce.[31]

G. D. H. Cole and Harold Laski also made much of this purported retreat of 'functionless property' before the advance of salaried managers, technicians and other scientific workers. Cole argued for an enlarged definition of the proletariat to account for these new intermediate groups and maintained that their social power was sufficient to make or break the socialist movement.[32] Indeed he argued that it was the absence of this layer from Russia which explained the peculiarity of the Bolshevik road to power and which rendered that strategy inapplicable in Britain.[33] He also reasoned that the scientific demands being made on this new 'salariat' made them more receptive to the socialist critique of the waste, disorder and irrationality of capitalism.[34] Even in the catastrophic 1930s when Cole and Laski shifted to the Marxist Left, echoes of their earlier optimism concerning the encroachment of democratic principles on capitalist oligarchy could still be found in their work; indeed even in the year of Hitler's accession to power Laski could claim that 'whatever . . . be the forms of the modern state, the character of its society is increasingly democratic.'[35]

The difference in Cole's and Laski's thought as the 1920s progressed concerned the place of the state and the working class in the transition to socialism. Laski, for example, had expressed concern in 1920 that the growth of state power in the first two decades of the century threatened to destroy democracy. But he also professed confidence in the future of democracy because of the growth of voluntary associations.[36] These ideas had made Laski an enemy of that 'rigid collectivism' which saw the answer to a well-ordered community in the transfer of industry to government. Instead he believed in the necessity for an extension of democracy to industry in order to destroy the plutocratic tendencies of modern industrial societies.[37] Indeed he expressed the conviction that 'the ultimate object of labour activity is democratic self-government in industry.'[38] Like Cole and Tawney he was deeply impressed by the apparent revolt in sections of British industry, arguing that 'it was in the workshop and factory that the new ideas were being forged'. It was here that Laski detected a movement for participatory democracy concerned with the 'vastest problems of the age' – from the sheer scale of contemporary life to the dehumanization of work represented by Taylorism and the narrow pursuit of efficiency which fetishizes centralization. All these issues had their source in the corruption of the state by the industrial autocracy of the capitalists, since:

> The State . . . is in reality the reflexion of what the dominant group or class in a community believes to be politically good . . . and it is reasonably clear that political good is today for the most part defined in economic terms. It mirrors within itself, that is to say, the economic structure of society.[39]

By the mid-1920s Laski and Cole were compelled to acknowledge the demise of the democratic movement in the trade unions. Laski now changed his mind on the importance of industrial democracy; from having enthusiastically supported the most sweeping changes in the structure of power in industry he was now an advocate of parliamentary control over the boards of nationalized industries. Workers' participation was reduced from a fundamental 'directive' role in Laski's socialized industry to the part of a mere works committee which makes suggestions and discusses grievances.[40] Meanwhile Laski was so enamoured of the alleged growth in functional associations – despite the obvious setbacks encountered by trade unionism between 1920 and 1925 – that he had come to the startling conclusion that 'the sovereign state becomes . . . little more than a machine from registering decisions arrived at elsewhere.'[41] All his former fears concerning the Servile State were now dispelled and nationalization of industry without workers' control no longer worried him.

While the Leninists predicted the growth of authoritarianism Laski announced that in Western Europe 'democratic government has become a commonplace beyond discussion.'[42] He continued to insist on the corrupting influence of the big property owners but was now confident that Parliament had the power to deal with these magnates without trampling on the liberties of other citizens. By 1927 Laski was trying to reconcile a Marxist analysis of British society with faith in the exceptionalism of the British state.[43] That is to say, he accepted that economic power rested with the capitalists and could determine state policy but hoped that a Labour government acting constitutionally would be able to use the British constitution to introduce socialism. Around the same time Cole was also converted to the idea that the state – which he had earlier castigated as the agent of capitalist interests – would now provide measures of reform advantageous to the working class. This was more than simply recognition of the weak condition of organized labour at the very time when the agenda of reforms was rapidly growing; Cole's confidence in the efficacy of state action by 1929 was connected with the appearance of Keynesian economics. Certainly he was now a convert to the theory that a distributionist fiscal policy could enable the state to indirectly determine industrial policy.[44]

Disappointment with the first MacDonald government acted as a spur to drive reformist socialists to find measures which would enable the next Labour administration to take definite steps towards socialism. Within the ILP John Wheatley, whose Housing Act had been one of the few successes of the first Labour government, built upon the underconsumptionist theories of J. A. Hobson to help fashion the programme *Socialism in Our Time* (1926). This document drew attention to the lack of 'effective demand' consequent upon the maldistribution of incomes and wealth in a capitalist economy. Wheatley and his colleagues reasoned that a redistribution policy could secure a 'living wage' – a statutory national minimum – if it was supported by social policies such as a family allowance system. By raising living standards these measures would help to generate employment, as well as tackle poverty, because employers would be faced with a rising demand for goods. The ILP programme also demanded the nationalization of certain key areas of the economy – land and the financial institutions were among them – as part of the same package of reforms designed to undermine capitalism and introduce socialism. But the Communist Party denounced Wheatley's reasoning as 'socialism by kind permission' and even before the end of 1926 it had written off the ILP as 'the Left-wing party of the bourgeoisie'.[45] It was therefore contemptuous of the campaign to win the Labour Party over to the ILP's thinking which A. J. Cook and James Maxton spearheaded in 1928 with the so-called Cook–Maxton manifesto.

The Communists' contention that the ILP proposals could only result in a managed capitalism derived some credibility from socialist thinking going back to the First World War when Bukharin and Lenin pointed to the emergence of a more organized system. Even before the war the emergence of trusts and monopolies had alerted some socialists to the dangers of state capitalism. But the growth of state controls after 1914 had made an 'indispensable contribution to the winning of the war', while doing nothing to expropriate the capitalists, and a number of administrators – including William Beveridge, Arthur Salter, Josiah Stamp and Hubert Llewellyn Smith – 'came to feel that these operations could with advantage be continued in time of peace'.[46] Certainly in the 1920s men such as these were advocating collectivist measures to deal with the economic crisis. This was also a period which saw the emergence of ICI (1926), Unilever (1927), Vickers Armstrong (1927) and the Distillers Company, by process of industrial concentration. Many of the leading capitalists were well-known spokesmen for the benefits of 'rationalization' and the idea of ordered industries and markets was taken up by some of the modernist Tories in works such as *Industry and the State* (1927), by Robert Boothby and Harold Macmillan, which sought salvation for the British economy in the growth of industrial amalgamation assisted by state action.

The war experience, particularly in the form of the German Economic Council, influenced the penchant for an 'Economic General Staff' in these circles. Although 'planning' really came into vogue in the 1930s, the idea of its compatibility with free enterprise was already established among the avant-garde in the 1920s. Of course on the Right it was comforting to believe in technocratic solutions to economic distress as an alternative to the class conflict which especially characterized the period up to 1926. But the ILP intent was just the opposite – to persuade the Labour Party of the inevitability of this class conflict. It was a message that was never likely to be heeded, for as G. D. H. Cole observed the mood among socialists was such that they were 'not encouraged by the growing difficulties of capitalism: they are frightened by them'.[47] The slump had created problems for which socialists had no answers – except the Communist call to revolution which nobody took seriously.

What was the point of nationalizing 'sick industries', asked Cole; this had never been part of the socialist project. Plans for the restoration of capitalist viability were more relevant. Similarly, in this view any real solution for unemployment requires 'the reorganization of our internal economic life', since the traditional demand for the 'Right to Work' means nothing more in the new conditions than 'the useless employment of redundant labour'. Cole therefore proposed the setting up of a National Investment Board able to assist private firms and to create new ones. It would be empowered to encroach on corporate power by appointing its own directors. Cole, the erstwhile anti-statist, now believed that: 'for the regeneration of industrial society it is necessary to secure a great increase in the economic powers and functions of the State.'[48] To ensure that socialism is built on the foundations of the most up-to-date capitalism, socialists must use the state to insist on the creation of industrial combines and, where this is resisted, nationalization. Cole also realized that the workers' control envisaged in 1920 would not be appropriate to such massive enterprises and that work would remain for most people an irksome task devoid of intrinsic interest. All this pointed to a bigger role than he had previously envisaged for 'the expert'.

This new-found faith in the efficacy of experts was also connected to Cole's conviction in 1929 that the policy of private industry could be controlled by the state without entailing direct administration of the industries concerned. Fiscal measures, state-owned banking, the National Investment Board and commissions of appointed experts would suffice. Together these would provide the control 'necessary to ensure that each important industry and enterprise falls into its proper place, and performs its appointed service in the general economic scheme'. It is interesting that Cole, who stood well to the Left of the Labour Party leadership, could not now identify a single industry which it was desirable to 'nationalise quite in the old way'. This was true even of the coal industry where the growth of vertical integration had pushed the owners to acquire interests quite remote from mining. Cole assumed that such developments had happened because they paid, because they were efficient. It was no business of the socialist state to break up efficient units 'which stand for the last word in the evolution of modern industrial technique', but nor was there any logic, according to Cole, in nationalizing a huge mass of enterprises unrelated to mining simply because some socialists want state ownership of the coal industry.[49] If one objects to private profit, he argued, this can best be dealt with by taxation, especially through death duties.

Cole's proposals added up to a form of state monopoly capitalism which was receiving support across a wide spectrum of ideologies. The same urge to transcend class conflict in the name of that efficient organization of Britain's declining industries informed the presidential address at the 1927 TUC. Walter Citrine and George Hicks produced the statement which sought 'effective machinery of joint consultation between the representative organizations entitled to speak for industry as a whole'. Sir Alfred Mond of ICI responded to this initiative and briefly the TUC met with capitalists from some of Britain's largest firms in the so-called Mond–Turner talks. Industrial decay and mass unemployment, together with the declining powers of organized labour, formed the context in which reformist socialists turned to technocratic solutions to the crisis. Thus a certain deference towards 'science' (where this is equated with the perceived precision of the physical sciences) and a corresponding denigration of politics as a source of confusion and inefficiency was reinforced in socialist thought. Such beliefs were already strongly entrenched among the first Fabians, who always believed that problems were somehow obvious and presented themselves to the disinterested analyst independent of political argument, but these beliefs now surfaced in the thought of their successors such as Laski and Cole. Common to all these modernizers, from Cole to Harold Macmillan, was a gross underestimation of the radical political changes which were required if an integrated programme for industrial regeneration was ever to be implemented by the British state, dominated as that was by commercial and financial interests.

When Labour emerged with 288 seats, as against 260 for the Tories, after the general election of 1929, MacDonald was able to form his second minority government. Unemployment figured prominently in the election campaign, with Lloyd George proposing a range of public works and infrastructural investments as the best means of overcoming the 'intractable million'. J. M. Keynes, who had helped to write the Liberal manifesto, *We Can Conquer Unemployment*, observed that the scheme's political opponents were convinced that there were mysterious and unintelligible reasons of high finance and economic theory to prove that it was impossible: 'Abra would rise, cadabra would fall.'[50] And there is no doubt that MacDonald and the Labour Chancellor, Philip Snowden, together with J. H. Thomas who was made Minister for Employment, suffered from a deep faith in the shibboleths of economic orthodoxy: free trade, the gold standard and balanced budgets. But their rejection of Lloyd George's 'flashy futilities' was as much to do with their political conservatism, which took the given institutional arrangements within the British state for granted and saw any attack on them as unconstitutional.

MacDonald even fell back on the old imperialist expedient of emigration as a cure for unemployment in the King's Speech which opened the 1929 Parliament. In the debate which followed he expressed the hope that Parliament could conduct itself as a Council of State above the faction and conflict of its predecessors. This was not merely a plea for the suppression of the usual partisan motives – Lloyd George had already made it clear that the Liberals would support Labour if MacDonald boldly tackled unemployment but was effectively rebuffed. The unity MacDonald sought was one which would upset as little as possible of the institutional and ideological orthodoxy of the day. The Labour Prime Minister 'freely confessed to being mystified by the problems of finance',[51] but this does little to explain why his government adamantly stuck by an economic dogma which penalized the people his government had been elected to represent.

The Labour leaders had no programme for the transition to their self-avowed socialist goal. This may be connected to their metaphysical belief in the 'inevitability of gradualness', as Skidelsky suggests.[52] Their paralysis in the face of growing unemployment after the Wall Street Crash, however, has probably more to do with the conundrum of how they could introduce recognizably socialist measures in parliamentary instalments while preserving the institutions of British capitalism. For their enemies were invariably identified as the 'functionless rich', the 'parasites' and 'coupon clippers' – capitalists who served a function were by strong implication fully justified in the Labour governments scheme of things. MacDonald and his co-thinkers did not need Cole to tell them that there was no point in nationalizing bankrupt industries and that the successful industrial conglomerates represented the highest form of capitalist technique which should be respectfully left alone. And in matters concerning the British state the Labour leaders were even more reverential. It is difficult, therefore, to imagine how MacDonald could be expected to challenge the Treasury and the City of London – to take obvious examples – when these institutions were so intimately connected to the 'national interest' and the imperial interests that were bound up with it. No wonder Snowden told the 1929 Labour conference that the control of credit and currency had to be kept free from political influences – the whole intricate business depended on an expertise beside which Parliament was hopelessly incompetent. There was no question, then, of doubting the utility of these institutions or of the necessity of their autonomy.

The socialism of MacDonald and Snowden was thus reduced to the pious hope that one day people would rise above sordid money matters and learn a higher morality; but these were just economic possibilities for their grandchildren. When Oswald Mosley – then a junior Minister in the government – presented the Cabinet with a programme for dealing with unemployment the Treasury pronounced his scheme a constitutional issue and the Cabinet duly threw it out. For Mosley was proposing measures very similar to those contained in the Liberal election manifesto, but combined with an institutional shake-up which would remove the initiative in policy-making from civil servants and demote the Treasury. He also wanted the reorganization of banking along German industrial-banking lines and the introduction of state direction and planning in industry. MacDonald rejected this memorandum in May 1930. He also ignored proposals from his own Economic Advisory Council which would have seen the introduction of tariffs, import controls and state-directed investment. In the same year the Macmillan Committee on Finance and Industry argued for 'conscious and deliberate management' of the economy and a 'definite national policy' to be imposed on the state and the financial institutions. But it was the advice of the May Committee on National Expenditure which MacDonald actually followed.

This advice restated the ruling orthodoxy that Britain had to maintain the gold standard and the pre-war exchange rate of £1⅔$4.86. Orthodoxy also insisted on balanced budgets, with revenue surpluses used to pay off bits of the National Debt. This view also insisted that state expenditure on public works would merely draw off labour and capital from 'normal industry' and so add not at all to the volume of employment; it would merely 'crowd out' private business activity. Trapped in this logic and by MacDonald's passive constitutionalism, the government ultimately disintegrated when a sizeable minority of Cabinet members refused to finance an American loan by cuts in public expenditure and dole. MacDonald, Snowden and Thomas, putting the national interest as defined by the Conservatives before any other consideration, joined with them to pose as a party of national unity in the general election of 1931. The Labour Party – like most governing parties unable to deal with an economic crisis – was subjected to a crushing defeat with less than fifty MPs returned to Parliament. MacDonald now headed a National Government composed almost entirely of Conservatives and, with business confidence restored, proceeded to do the impossible – take Britain off the gold standard and introduce tariffs.

Conclusion

The Communists expected that the experience of Labour government would demonstrate the impotence of the reformist strategy, in the context of capitalist decline, and cause substantial sections of the working class to move to the Left in search of more radical solutions to the crisis. In fact the CPGB's analysis of reformism, and the Leninist theory upon which it was based, emphasized the role of corrupt leaders and bourgeois propaganda in explaining support for the parliamentary road to socialism and massively underestimated popular attachment to the democratic rights and freedoms which Communist literature dismissed as mere sham and confidence trick. Given this miscalculation it is easy to understand why the CPGB expected that loyalty to the system would evaporate once Labour proved incapable of extracting improvements in living standards from it. The long economic crisis of the inter-war years, however, caused a massive slump in trade union membership which helped to extinguish the combative rank and file movements of the preceding period. In the areas of greatest unemployment poverty and disorganization also weakened the working class. It is difficult to know how far the defeat of the General Strike demoralized those who took part in it but it certainly ended a period of bitter conflict in industry during which the Left increased its influence in the unions. After the strike the Left was more acrimoniously divided than ever before and moderates such as Walter Citrine and Ernest Bevin became the dominating figures on the General Council. These leaders sought to increase trade union influence through conciliation in industry, as in the Mond-Turner talks, and the return of a Labour government; in both respects the CPGB was seen by them as a mischievous, disruptive influence.

In 1927 the Baldwin government took its revenge on the strikers by passing the Trades Disputes Act which banned sympathy strikes and made the unions' financial support for the Labour Party more difficult to obtain. By the end of the year the CPGB was turning to an ultra-Leftist position which condemned it to complete isolation and a rapidly falling membership. The failure of the first, very brief Labour government did not produce the radical change in working-class opinion which the CPGB had predicted. But it did cause the ILP to examine the kinds of reforms which the next Labour government could champion; in a sense, therefore, this is the period when reformism, understood as a strategy aimed at the transformation of capitalism by successive instalments of systematically related changes, began at last to be considered in the light of the dissatisfaction which was felt in the MacDonald-Snowden leadership still apparently stuck in a Lib-Lab mould. It was clear, at least to the Left of the Labour Party, that ethical socialism could supply no solutions to unemployment and Fabian gradualism, which had always assumed the eventual conversion of the ruling class to collectivism, was irrelevant for purposes of governing a country in crisis. Thus, after 1924, reformism, far from being in retreat, was just beginning to be considered as the Left began to ask about the kind of measures which could enable a Labour government to take the first steps towards socialism.

At first the ILP proposed, in *The Living Wage* (1926), a programme of state action to increase effective demand in the economy by boosting working-class incomes. These proposals subsequently evolved into an emphasis on class struggle and wholesale socialization of industry which the Labour leadership rejected. Instead Labour fought the 1929 election with all the old commonplaces of ethical socialism and gradualism intact, although leading intellectuals within the party, such as Laski and Cole, had already become firm advocates of a state-directed economic recovery. Thus while the party leadership was completely bereft of ideas for tackling unemployment, former advocates of guild socialism and members of the ILP began to advocate a more regulated and organized capitalism, by means of state initiatives, for purposes of national efficiency. Only by making capitalism more efficient, it was reasoned, would it be possible to improve working-class living standards and introduce socialist proposals. Hence, under the influence of Hobson and to a lesser extent J. M. Keynes, radicals in the Labour Party became champions of capitalist rationalization and even argued that the Empire could be reorganized for socialism. In fact during Labour's second term of office Britain and its Empire were governed in the old way, except that the scale of repression in India increased dramatically as did the level of unemployment at home.

The depth of feeling of betrayal which followed the demise of the second MacDonald government can be understood when account is taken of how far the party had changed since 1914. For although the beliefs of many in the leadership were clearly rooted in the pre-war past, the succession of industrial struggles generated between 1910 and 1926 and the massive increase in trade union strength between 1910 and 1920, together with the experience of the war itself, helped to produce a different temper within the working class and a break with the Liberal Party. It has been pointed out that this was the period when the Co-operative Commonwealth stood as the utopia of most Labour activists and the first three decades of the century witnessed the greatest period of growth of Co-operation as a social and political movement.[53] After 1918, indeed, Labour moved closer than ever before to the organization of 'the total environment of its active members in a way reminiscent of the pre-1914 German Social democratic Party', with its own theatre groups, Sunday Schools, alternatives to the Boy Scouts, its own press, and so on.[54]

Clearly these developments were evidence of a labour culture different from that existing before 1914 and this was also the period in which the 'socialist generation', as Max Beer called it, began to make its mark on the Parliamentary Party and Labour thought. But the rank-and-file activists felt a tremendous loyalty to the Labour Party, as is demonstrated in local studies which show how the constituency parties followed the advice of the party centre in shunning contact with the Communists or in abstaining from concerted involvement in the General Strike, except as trade unionists.[55] There was not a little deference felt towards the leaders of the party and by all accounts MacDonald and Snowden were the most revered and loved of Labour's representatives. Thus the shock of their 'betrayal' was all the greater.

9

The 1930s

The demise of the second Labour government in 1931 disturbed the party's faith in 'the inevitability of gradualness', as Sidney Webb had termed it, and shifted the party to the Left. By 1933 something like 30 million people were unemployed in the capitalist world. Labour's slogan in the 1931 election had been 'we must plan or perish', but the truth is that the leaders of the party only began to think about planning in any detail after the election was lost. While the Left of the party saw the events leading to MacDonald's 'betrayal' in 1931 as an indication of the constitutional obstructions which a socialist government might face in the future, leaders of the party such as Henderson were more concerned to question the ILP's faith in Parliament. In the 1931 election the nineteen candidates of the ILP were refused endorsement by the Labour Party Executive because of their refusal to sign a pledge, which was put before candidates for the first time, that they would obey the Standing Orders of the PLP requiring them, among other things, to not vote against its decisions.[1]

In fact the ILP was rapidly moving to the conclusion that even *Socialism in Our Time* was insufficiently radical to deal with the capitalist crisis. Fenner Brockway, James Maxton and F. W. Jowett urged the party to disaffiliate from the Labour Party so that it could better pursue a revolutionary policy. Among the rank and file a Revolutionary Policy Committee was formed by Jack Gaster and Dr C. K. Cullen to urge the ILP to work with the Communist International. In 1932 these forces succeeded in severing the ILP's links with Labour and the organization embarked on an independent course which was to bring it a declining and faction-ridden membership and many zigzags in policy which we will examine later. Meanwhile the opponents of disaffiliation, led by Frank Wise, created the Socialist League in 1932 for the purpose of pursuing a socialist policy within the Labour Party.

But even the loyal Labour Left asked if socialism could come by constitutional methods now that MacDonald's surrender to international finance had, in Stafford Cripps's words, provided 'the clearest demonstration of the power of capitalism to overthrow a properly elected Government by extra-Parliamentary means'.[2] The fact that the Socialist League opted to stay in the

Labour Party in order to convert it to real socialist measures meant of course that in the last analysis its leaders such as Cripps believed in the efficacy of its parliamentary strategy. They believed that as long as a large majority of socialist MPs was elected on the basis of clearly defined socialist measures the legitimation which this victory would confer on a Labour government would suffice to see socialism introduced by Act of Parliament. All that was required were certain organizational changes within the party which would enable it to keep control of the Labour Cabinet and Prime Minister. It would then be possible to enact an Emergency Powers Bill on the first day of the new Parliament and proceed to make sweeping changes in British society. In this Labour Left scenario – which still had its adherents as recently as the 1980s – little change was envisaged in the British system of government. Apart from certain procedural changes to speed up the work of the Commons and the expedient of swamping the House of Lords with instantly created Labour peers, even those doubtful of the constitutional road on the Labour Left saw no need for constitutional innovation; their main worry about parliamentary socialism was whether the capitalists would allow it to survive.

After Hitler's assumption of power in January 1933 and the systematic destruction of German democracy in the eight months which followed this was, of course, a matter of urgent consideration. Harold Laski probed the question of the compatibility of capitalism and democracy more than anyone else on the Labour Left and arrived at essentially Leninist conclusions. He reasoned that parliamentary democracy had arisen when capitalism had been an expanding, competitive and optimistic system. It had worked best when its dominant political parties had shared fundamental values as the Tories and Liberals had done in the two-party system before 1914. Since then, according to Laski's argument, monopoly or finance capitalism had entered an epochal crisis and was faced with a socialist challenge which was objectively so fundamental in scope that the old parliamentary tolerance, compromise and give-and-take, grounded as these had been on a basic consensus, were now in jeopardy. For socialists, Laski reasoned, the lesson of fascism was that the class antagonisms endemic in capitalism and greatly accentuated during economic crises could be settled only by force. Democracy had co-existed with industrial oligarchy during a phase of capitalist growth, but the capitalists would rather extinguish democracy than see it turned against their own interests. Yet the economic crisis placed just such a popular resolution of the slump on the political agenda. This was why Laski concluded that 'it is clear that fascism . . . is simply the expedient adopted by capitalism in distress to defeat the democratic political foundation with which it could be successfully linked in its period of creative expansion.'[3] Democracy was everywhere in retreat, according to this analysis, because the capitalists were compelled to adopt authoritarianism to quash the increasingly insubordinate working-class movements and to prepare for imperialist wars.[4] The stark choice which Laski put before his readers was between socialism and fascism. But despite his conviction that the Marxist theory of the state 'holds the field' Laski continued to argue that it was the duty of the labour movement to use constitutional methods until such time as its enemies forced it to turn to coercion.

After 1933 the influence of Marxism could be seen in the ILP, the Socialist League, the Fabian Society, the *New Statesman*, the Left Book Club, *Tribune* (from the moment Cripps established it in 1937) and in the agitations for Left unity which the CPGB spearheaded from 1935. But the spread of fascism and the growing danger of another world war did not lead every socialist to see the relationship between capitalism and democracy in the way Laski depicted it. The young Hugh Gaitskell, for example, happened to be in Vienna in February 1934 when the Dollfuss clerical-fascist government turned the artillery against the socialist working-class areas, killing or wounding 6,500 workers and destroying their military and political power. Soon after these events Gaitskell reflected that he had 'learnt as never before to value the freedom of British political institutions.'[5] By the end of the decade Evan Durbin was able to cast these sentiments into a theory of 'democratic socialism'.

Durbin and Gaitskell, together with Douglas Jay, helped to rationalize the extreme timidity which characterized Labour politics in the 1930s. For far from concluding with Laski and the Left that democracy needed massive reinforcement and extension, the party's young economists narrowed their vision and urged restraint so as not to upset the precarious balance which made it possible at all. Democracy for Durbin was simply 'the ability of the people to choose a government'. The state was nothing more than an expression of the beliefs of those holding governmental power and 'the nature of the decisions taken by the government will depend upon the character of the persons forming it.' So as to leave the reader in no doubt, Durbin argues that 'democracy is the epiphenomenon of a certain emotional balance in the individuals composing a nation.'[6] Now this had definite consequences. It meant that democracy was possible 'only if party strife is strictly limited in method and scope'. For purposes of illustration Durbin invoked the experience of the second Labour government whose main problem he perceived as 'a breakdown of financial confidence' for which it was itself responsible. Thus the MacDonald government was found guilty of stretching party strife to the limit.

For similar reasons Durbin saw 'uncompromising party programmes' and even proportional representation as factors which can weaken strong democratic government. Socialist strategy, in Durbin's view, had to take account of the delicate calibration of liberal democracy. This meant among other things that 'the battles upon which the future of democracy depend must be fought within and not between the parties contending for power.'[7] Well before the post-1945 Cold War, then, Durbin concluded that Labour's contribution to democratic stability involved making 'the extremist minority on the Left of the Labour Party' subject to 'continuous defeat'.[8] This is what the leadership had endeavoured to do for years, of course. But while these sentiments had been expressed in diaries and in private, Durbin's public honesty was rare indeed and indicates quite a different temper in this generation of the Labour

Right. These people, seemingly, were not afraid to acknowledge that, while the activists had their uses, they were too often 'highly partisan and doctrinally orthodox' – qualities which Durbin thought inimical to democracy. After the war, of course, such reasoning became a hallmark of Cold War propaganda and participatory democracy was denounced as the harbinger of totalitarian mass societies.

Durbin anticipates other elements of Cold War liberalism in his reduction of political behaviour and institutions to affective conditioning and its irrational and subliminal dimensions in particular:

> macroscopic institutions of government and property, party and revolution . . . dissolve into a thousand fragments of personal ambition and patriotism, of secret love and hatred, unconscious purpose and need . . . Systems of thought can then be traced to secret emotional roots and great institutions, rich in dignity, to the primitive fears of childhood and the jungle.[9]

Such thoughts were clearly inspired by the ranks of jackbooted Nazis and the files of robotic Communists which haunt the pages of Durbin's book. Between them these monsters served to drive away any thought that capitalism itself was the jungle which socialists were concerned to eliminate.

On the other hand, Durbin became almost Panglossian in his optimism once the discussion turned to an examination of British capitalism. The growth in state powers in the existing 'socialized' sector is pronounced 'revolutionary' and a programme of limited nationalization will in the future transfer such power to the state that it would be possible to 'reduce general unemployment to zero and to maintain it there indefinitely'.[10] All that was needed was 'a technically competent House of Commons' prepared to influence credit expansion and the rate of saving and to use unbalanced budgets 'if necessary'. This is a striking conclusion to reach after nearly twenty years in which there were never less than one million people unemployed in Britain. It is all the more interesting because Durbin managed for many years to combine membership of the Labour Party with adherence to the economic ideology associated with Friedrich von Hayek and Lionel Robbins. Even in 1940 he lamented the 'ossification of the labour market' and the 'loss of plasticity of wage rates and of mobility' associated with the growth of the trade unions. According to Durbin, 'There can be little doubt that the increase in the average level of unemployment in Great Britain through all phases of the Trade Cycle in the last fifteen years is largely due to the rigidity of money wages'.[11] These idea were clearly part of the old Treasury orthodoxy; that they survived alongside more recent beliefs in the power of 'unbalanced budgets' and even 'central control' rested in a 'Supreme Economic Authority' is testimony to the flux in socialist economic thinking after 1931.

The apparent success of the first Five-Year Plan which Stalin launched in 1928 greatly impressed many British socialists. After all, the capitalist world was in crisis and Britain's peculiar economic problems had been apparent since 1920 without calling forth a bold government policy for industrial reconstruction. The USSR could seem 'a simple country of progress in a crisis-stricken world'.[12] British Communists were quick to see the propaganda value of this perception. Hardly a day passed without the *Daily Worker* reporting wage increases, price reductions, new output achievements and the glorious holiday entitlements of the Soviet worker. On the plane of theory the success of the plan was held to vindicate the centralism of the Soviet political system.[13] It even made the one-party dictatorship an essential requirement of socialism, for, as Maurice Dobb explained, otherwise 'one could hardly see how uniformity let alone continuity of executive policy could be maintained with legislative-executive unity.'[14] In other words a system which fuses executive and legislative powers in a single institution has no scope for an official opposition party or parties. For the Communists Lenin had provided a convincing justification for the fusion of executive and legislative powers. It therefore remained simply to be pointed out that

> It is precisely in securing a degree of uniformity and expertness which would otherwise be lacking in the Soviet system that the Communist Party has its unique role. As the ruling party in the Soviets it guides and initiates legislation; at the same time it fills the role in the executive of a trained and disciplined body of administrators. Ultimately all decisions as to policy are taken by the Party (as indeed happens in any Party system) and no rival party organisation is allowed.[15]

There was no room in this system for an opposition because any rival party would in effect be a rival state.

Many socialists in the Labour Party reasoned along similar lines. In one Fabian study of Stalin's Russia the system was described as 'more truly democratic than the parliamentary system of this and other professedly democratic countries'[16] – even though the author, H. L. Beales, acknowledged the existence of a 'ubiquitous and all-powerful' GPU, the demise of the soviets during the civil war and the monopoly power of the leadership of the Communist Party of the Soviet Union (CPSU). But none of this is allowed to count against the system because it 'would not be true to suggest that there is a divergence of interest between the proletarian masses and Stalin and his comrades of the Politbureau who exercise power on their behalf.'[17] Fabian visitors to the Soviet Union in the 1930s habitually translated Russian reality into the comforting categories of thought which they had developed in England.

This habit had the effect that the Communists were depicted as 'an organised vocation' imbued with all the selflessness, expertise and public spirit which Sidney Webb had once sought in the British professions and the civil service.[18] Beales was reminded when he encountered the CPSU of 'the public school spirit without the debilitating attributes of class'. Of course it is possible to find plenty of evidence which suggests that some of these visitors were misled by their Soviet hosts – G. R. Mitchison's portrait of a 'typical' Russian factory is a case in point[19] – but the striking thing about many of these accounts of the USSR is not so much the gullibility of their authors as the fact that they were aware of the system's tyrannical side and found it excusable, even laudable. Dictatorship was seen as the necessary form of government for a society which aimed at classlessness and was engaged in building the future.[20] George Bernard Shaw had been saying this since the early 1920s, but it was not until the Five-Year Plan that he was joined by Sidney and Beatrice Webb even though they admitted that 'the sum of human suffering involved is beyond all computation.'[21]

The Webbs were undoubtedly attracted by the bureaucratic order which they perceived to be at the heart of Stalinism. They were relieved to find that the factories were run with 'the same kind of managerial discipline' as their British counterparts and that foolish notions such as workers' control had long since been dispensed with. It was a vindication of their own work to find a whole society being run by experts. Another Fabian, Barbara Wootton, concluded from her own study of planning that detailed knowledge was its most important prerequisite, coupled with high standards of administrative competence and integrity. This meant that experts were required to draw up the plan and something like Gosplan, the central planning agency in the USSR, was needed to see that it was properly executed. Wootton's analysis displayed a technocratic contempt for politics as well as all the *naïveté* of one who regarded planning as a purely technical problem:

> Now we may immediately disabuse ourselves of the common belief that the appointment of such a body would imply the destruction of ordinary political freedoms or the substitution of dictatorship for democracy. The business of the Planning Commission would be to determine what factories should be built, what pits closed, what wages paid in this and that trade and what prices charged for such and such goods . . . To propose . . . to bring them under review by a central planning authority is in no way to suggest the abolition or curtailment of political liberties since these matters have never been within the purview of any political Government at all: certainly they have never been made the subject of any kind of democratic control . . . At worst it would substitute one arbitrary authority (that of a publicly constituted body) for another (that of a soverign captain of industry).[22]

Wootton did not even consider the possibility that decisions such as the ones she cites are quite as much political issues as technical matters susceptible to the deliberations of experts. For the same reason she envisaged no new organs of democracy to contend with the increased power of the state which such centralized planning would inevitably entail. And if the Planning Commission usurped some of the functions performed by Parliament, Wootton was inclined to regard this as a positive boon:

> And here surely encroachment has a great deal to commend it, for it is generally agreed that democratically elected Parliaments have proved themselves quite incapable of dealing with all the economic

technicalities in which they have been entangled in recent years. There is no part of their job which Parliaments do worse than their economic work and no department of affairs in which the theory of democratic control is further removed from actual practice; and no wonder when one considers on the one hand the amount of detailed technical knowledge that constructive economic planning demands, and on the other the means by which members seek and gain election ... So ... this pathetic inability of amateur Ministers and Members of Parliament to handle extremely complex technical questions ... agitates every school of political reformer ... The satisfactory course surely is to recognise once and for all that economic administration is a job for experts and to hand it over to them. Detailed democratic control of economic affairs is at best a hopeless morass and at worse (and more commonly) a hypocritical pretence.[23]

For Wootton, then, the problem could be reduced to 'how to find the right bosses'; it would be 'the Russian system modified to suit a democratic political structure'.[24]

The Communist Party did little to challenge this bureaucratic conception of planning – it was, after all, supposed to represent Soviet reality. It is true that the CPGB warned that such proposals as were contained in the Liberal Yellow Book in 1927 or in Labour's *Immediate Programme* (1937), or as promoted by business interests such as the Next Five Years Group, would only lead to a stronger, better organized state capitalism; even the party's 'scientists and technicians' argued this. But the Communist alternative – 'the problem of class power must be solved as a pre-requisite of any social planning' – was not as radical as it sounded because it meant merely the coming to power of the omnipotent vanguard party.[25] Once this Communist truism was asserted, party publicists could dwell with real enthusiasm on 'the explosive and revolutionary nature of science' and on the apparent elevation of the scientist in the Soviet scheme of things. Capitalism by contrast was depicted as holding science back and excluding the scientist from his rightful place in government and administration; it made him 'the servant and not the master of production'.[26] With the exception of Lancelot Hogben, who was opposed to Stalinism, the leading Marxist scientists in Britain glorified the Five-Year Plan as proof of the identity of science and socialism without concerning themselves in the least with the authoritarian nature of the experience. J. D. Bernal, for example, even saw the Stakhanov movement as 'impressive proof of the possibility of workers taking a leading part in transforming the processes of industry',[27] when what it really represented was a massive increase in the intensity of work which provoked sporadic popular violence against its practitioners.[28]

While acknowledging that scientific technologies can be oppressive, Bernal, Joseph Needham and J. B. S. Haldane clung to the party orthodoxy which declared this an experience confined to class societies – thus excluding the Soviet Union. Once this formality was dispensed with their emphasis was on the progressive role of a reified 'science'. According to Bernal, 'science conscious of its purpose can in the long run become a major force in social change. Because of the powers which it holds in reserve, it can ultimately dominate the other (economic and political) forces.' Not for the first time it was asserted that 'the advancement of science and socialism mutually pre-supposed one another' because

> Science implies a unified and co-ordinated and above all conscious control of the whole of social life; it abolishes or provides the possibility of abolishing the dependence of man on the material world. Henceforth society is subject to the limitation it imposes on itself . . . The socialised, integrated scientific world organisation is coming.'[29]

Something called 'Science' emerges in the thirty-odd books which Bernal, Needham and Haldane wrote between 1931 and 1945 as the chief agent of social change and the model for social organization as well as the panacea for social ills. Their books perhaps best illustrate that Enlightenment optimism in human progress by virtue of applied reason which so many socialists in the 1930s thought they had discovered in the Soviet Union.

Confidence in the efficacy of a 'Supreme Economic Council' was not con-fined to the new Saint Simonians, however. It touched nearly all socialist thinking in the 1930s, including that of Labour leaders such as Clement Attlee, Hugh Dalton and the younger Labour economists Durbin, Gaitskell and Jay. But their planning proposals always fell short of a basic restructuring of the financial system in Britain even though the City of London was enfeebled by the world recession and therefore at its most vulnerable. Few of those who participated in the debate about Labour's economic policy after 1931 recognized the need for such an institutional shake-up if the party's avowed priorities – industrial restructuring informed by socialist values – were to be achieved.

Most of the party's economic thinking was done under the the the auspices of the New Fabian Research Bureau (1931), the TUC Economic Committee (1932) and a number of National Executive Committee (NEC) sub-commit-tees created for this purpose in 1931. The most important of these was the sub-committee dealing with finance and trade chaired by Hugh Dalton who 'virtually wrote Labour's economic and financial policy in the early 1930s'.[30] Nothing that these various committees recommended was likely to become party policy unless it first won the approval of the National Council of Labour – the reorganized National Joint Council – which was established in 1934 with a built-in TUC majority. This meant that Ernest Bevin and Walter Citrine were able to steer Labour policy in conjunction with the parliamentary Right of the party. The coterie of economists grouped around Dalton was in any case steeped in the neo-classical orthodoxy which looked on Alfred Marshall's work as the last word in theory and economic 'science'; indeed Dalton, Durbin and Gaitskell actually taught this in the universities, and as a lecturer at the London School of Economics Dalton was quite unable to challenge the dominant Robbins–Hayek case for free markets. Nevertheless, as we have already observed, a case for government intervention in the economy could be constructed from marginal utility theory. And after a visit to the Soviet Union Dalton was converted to the idea of physical control planning which he equated with a centralist 'elite corps of super-directors'.[31] No sophisticated economic theory was required to convince socialists in the Fabian tradition that experts wielding state power could cut through the random chaos of the self-regulating market and impose order, efficiency and progress – as Stalin had done in Russia.

There was, however, no commitment to a wholesale reorganization of the state and its relationship to the financial and commercial sectors of the economy in order to make planning work. Dalton's *Practical Socialism for Britain* (1935) seemed to argue that industrial reorganization could be injected into the existing arrangements and the *Economist* remarked on the similarity of his arguments with those of the Next Five Years Group whose primary purpose, it will be recalled, was to revitalize British capitalism. Obviously Soviet-style planning required such fundamental changes in the relationship of the state to the economy that Labour's passive constitutionalism could not be expected to take it on board. Until the second half of the 1930s Durbin, Dalton and Gaitskell were even persuaded that Keynes's ideas for reflating the economy were 'fiscally irresponsible', and as another indication of their conservatism it is worth noting that there was a conviction among Labour's centre-Right economists that the fiscal burden was already so great that any programme designed to increase the scope and quality of social policy by this means threatened to destroy private investment.[32] Physical control planning was no real alternative as far as Gaitskell, Durbin and Jay were concerned because they agreed with the argument that the price mechanism was the only efficient and accurate form of economic calculation and resource allocation.

The Left of the party took a more robust view. In the wake of the 1931 crisis, hostility to the financial institutions was riding high in the Labour Party and it was possible for Frank Wise successfully to move an amendment at the annual conference of 1932 calling for nationalization of the joint-stock banks. Indeed Cole's New Fabian Research Bureau – which Dalton ignored as a base for policy – argued that if the state was to control the *direction* (as well as the volume) of investment it was necessary to take over 'the main financial institutions' as well. Dalton's committee on finance and trade quashed such proposals on the grounds that the threat to nationalize insurance would create electoral disadvantages while the proposal to take over the joint-stock banks was superfluous to requirements.[33] Instead the party leadership proposed that nationalization of the Bank of England and the creation of a National Investment Board would suffice. It was reasoned that the export of capital, the direction of investment and the policies of institutions which had always neglected long-term industrial investment would be controlled indirectly by the investment policy of the proposed National Investment

Board.[34] It is noteworthy here to observe that a common Labour assumption, more marked on the Right than the Left of the party, was that the nationalization of an institution was sufficient to change its character. Thus the proposal to nationalize the Bank of England did not involve specific recommendations to change its mode of operation or its relationship to the government or the type of policy it would pursue; it was assumed that all these things would be accomplished by the mere fact of nationalization. Even when a leftist like Frank Wise advocated nationalization of the private banks he did not propose to change their 'short term credit and deposit operations'; nor did he propose to alter the specific weight of the City – after all, as he pointed out, the London financial institutions allowed Britain to 'influence the course of events, both financial and political, in other countries'.[35]

There was already, then, a strong disposition on the part of most participants in the debate over Labour's economic policy to leave most things alone even before the party leaders were converted to Keynesianism. It is true that talk of centralized planning continued throughout the war years, but by the late 1930s references to the 'Supreme Economic Authority' already meant little more than a bureau charged with the provision of statistical information, economic forecasting, analysis and calculation as far as the Labour Right was concerned. On the Left Cole was adamant that the rationalization of private capital plus state banking would not be enough to achieve socialist goals because monopoly interests would retain the power to sabotage them; only substantial state ownership of industry could remedy this defect.[36] But once Keynes was understood to have shown how full employment could be achieved by the indirect controls afforded by monetary and fiscal adjustments, the initiative lay with the Right of the party because the leadership of both wings of the movement, industrial and political, had never been keen to upset the institutional *status quo*. Douglas Jay's *The Socialist Case* (1936) played an important part in this by showing how Keynesianism could help to achieve socialist goals with the minimum of fuss, and

> Gradually, even hesitantly, this argument became part of official Labour Party doctrine. Before the end of the decade and unknown to the vast majority of its own members the Labour Party had quietly adopted an expansionist approach to economic policy that was at least semi-Keynesian.[37]

By and large the Labour membership was loyal to the leadership and inclined to show deference to the parliamentary party. This is why, despite Communist efforts to drive a wedge between Labour's grassroots and its national leadership, there was no wholesale revolt in protest against the latter's feeble opposition to the National Government. On the contrary the Executive was able to disaffiliate constituency labour parties which fostered links with the CPGB – twenty-seven were dealt with this way between 1926 and 1929 and dozens more were threatened with similar action.[38] From March 1928, when the CPGB adopted the notorious 'Class against Class' line (foisted on it by the Comintern), there followed a period of intense sectarianism which saw the destruction of all those bridges to the Labour rank and file which the CPGB had laboriously constructed around the Minority Movement and the National Left Wing Movement. Communist membership now fell from 9,000 at the beginning of 1927 to 2,555 in November 1930.[39] Most of the Communist membership now consisted of the unemployed and the only field of Communist influence was the National Unemployed Workers' Committee Movement which, under the dynamic leadership of Wal Hannington, managed to organize tens of thousands of the jobless for direct action on this and related issues. Its members swore 'never to cease from active strife until capitalism is abolished', and after the introduction of the Means Test in 1931 this strife became more embittered than ever, often ending in violence.[40]

Throughout these struggles the Labour Party and the TUC stayed aloof and boycotted each of the four national Hunger Marches organized by the NUWCM in the 1930s. The NUWCM was denounced as a Communist front despite the fact that its membership was many times higher than that of the CPGB. In 1933 the Labour Party published a pamphlet, *The Communist Solar System*, which named a number of organizations that the constituency activists were warned to keep clear of. But the refusal of the Labour establishment to support the Jarrow Hunger March in 1936, which was organized by the town council, shows that Communist participation is not a complete answer to the question of why Labour boycotted these demonstrations. The fact is that the party leadership was loath to support any extra-parliamentary action, however tokenistic. The Communists simply made this easier to apply by vilifying the Labour Left as 'social fascists'.

When real fascists took power in Germany in January 1933, the *Daily Worker* saw 'an extreme intensification of the class contradictions in Germany . . . open Fascism is a brutal declaration of terror upon the working class. The intensification of the crisis and the increasing resistance of the revolutionary masses has compelled the bourgeoisie to show its real dictatorial face.'[41] Though the Comintern described its German policy as 'completely correct', the Communists began to move away from the sectarian 'Third Period' policy because Hitler's victory generated a powerful feeling for unity against fascism in the European working class and compelled the Soviet Union to protect itself by means of 'collective security' with the 'bourgeois democracies'. Stalin could hardly continue to call socialists 'social fascists' when he was now prepared to find allies in any party if it was opposed to the Hitler state. In Britain the mood for unity was apparent in the fifth national Hunger March of 1934, which received considerable assistance from trades councils and Constituency Labour Parties in defiance of the official ban on collaboration with the Communists. Within a year of the Nazi success the ILP pledged itself to the unity of all working-class organizations committed to the struggle against fascism. Around the same time, however, the Trotskyists concluded that the Comintern was beyond redemption and called for the creation of a Fourth International, thereby insisting that this was the only body capable of providing the necessary leadership for socialism.[42] Just as the activists in all working-class organizations felt the need for unity, then, the tiny groups of Trotskyists demanded new splits and from June 1933 Trotsky advised his British followers to work to that end inside the ILP.[43]

In the electoral calculations of the Labour and trade union establishment there was nothing to be had from unity with the fast-dwindling, faction-ridden membership of the ILP, let alone from conjunction with the Communists. But considerable numbers of the Labour rank and file believed otherwise and when the CPGB proposed united action around specific issues in March 1933 it sought to strengthen the pro-affiliation lobby within the unions and the constituencies. Recognizing that these sympathies had recently grown, the National Joint Council was moved to issue the manifesto *Democracy versus Dictatorship* which argued that fascism and communism were equally bad and existed in almost symbiotic relationship to one another as fears generated by one extreme stimulated the growth of the other.[44] This drew a scathing response from R. Palme Dutt who shredded Labour's democratic credentials by reviewing its governmental record in relation to the Empire; from this he concluded that all of its democratic calculations were based on the precept (to quote Orwell) of 'not counting niggers'.[45] Dutt was never better than when engaged in exposing hypocrisy in the Labour Party and the CPGB was close enough to the ultra-leftism of the previous period for him to announce that Labour's rejection of the unity call placed it in a united front with fascism. The list of proscribed organizations which was circulated to all the Labour constituency organizations simply got longer as the leadership added the Relief Committee for Victims of German Fascism to the League Against Imperialism, the NUWCM and many others. Thus in 1933, faced with mass unemployment, the rise of fascism and their own parliamentary impotence, the Labour and trade union leaders urged their membership to refrain from setting up 'special organisations for any political or industrial purposes'.[46]

This was tantamount to an attempt to demobilize the Labour activists and could not wholly succeed, given the catastrophic circumstances which then affected the whole of Europe. Nor could the attempt to anathematize the Communists wholly succeed when Labour and trade union officials were themselves almost routinely invoking the success of Soviet planning and the need for collective security against fascism. Thus two of the biggest issues which preoccupied the Communists in the 1930s found ready support at the highest levels of the labour movement. This simply did not square with the argument that the Communists were no better than the fascists. Communist influence grew in spite of attacks such as the TUC's 'Black Circular' of October 1934 which forbade trades councils to accept Communists as delegates. While there was no general revolt against Labour's timid leadership, many constituency organizations worked openly alongside the Communists. But the Communists themselves set limits to left unity by their vanguardist pretensions which soon made 'day-to-day' collaboration with the ILP impossible. By Easter 1934 the pro-Comintern feeling which had caused the ILP only a year previously to 'ascertain by what way the Independent Labour Party may assist in the work of the Communist International' was quashed. In the course of those twelve months the ILP had learned that nothing less than the complete absorption of the organization into the Communist Party would satisfy the Comintern leadership; for, as Harry Pollitt explained, two parties claiming to be the revolutionary party of the working class was an obvious absurdity.

In chapter 8 it was pointed out that after the defeat of the General Strike the General Council was increasingly geared towards collaboration with both government and employers. Bevin and Citrine thus strove to eliminate dangerous rank-and-file movements in the unions which could undermine their authority as part of their attempt to create a responsible trade unionism which could have a say in top-level policy-making. The weakness of the trade union Left after 1926 aided this process although it was necessary even in these circumstances for the General Council to oppose grassroots movements among miners, transport workers and engineers when these developed in the 1930s. Through the National Council for Labour the TUC leadership was able to play a major part in obstructing and opposing the Left in the Labour Party as well. Indeed MacDonald's 'betrayal' of the movement and the decimation of the Parliamentary Labour Party in the 1931 election, which under George Lansbury's leadership presented a feeble spectacle, served to strengthen the TUC's authority at the highest levels of the party. By the end of the decade the TUC's authority with the government had so increased that Bevin was able to boast that it had 'now virtually become an integral part of the state and its views and voice upon every subject, international and domestic, heard and heeded'.[47]

The nature of the TUC's influence can be gauged from its collaboration with the Colonial Office. Beginning in 1934, the Colonial Office was faced with a rising tide of working class unrest in colonies such as Northern Rhodesia, the West Indies, East Africa and Ceylon. This unrest was frequently associated, in the absence of settled trade union movements, with rank-and-file labour organizations led by militants who linked bread-and-butter demands to nationalist aspirations. It occurred to the Colonial Office that the General Council of the TUC, speaking as it were with the authentic voice of labour, could be of assistance in helping to transform these potentially revolutionary forces into respectable managers of discontent; but in 1938, of its own initiative, the TUC 'offered to sort out those colonial unions that were not in the "right hands", as Citrine put it, from those that could be trusted to follow constitutional ways'.[48] Continuous collaboration between the TUC and the Colonial Office on such matters did not become routine until 1940 but from the 1930s, according to Peter Weiler, 'the TUC approached colonial labour with the same assumptions as the Colonial Office', that is with the intention of discouraging radical movements which threatened the integrity of the Empire.[49]

Labour's reputation for enlightenment on colonial issues stemmed from its ability to pose as the champion of improved conditions and more progressive ways of administering the Empire rather than a consistent anti-imperialism, though individuals like Fenner Brockway honestly took up this cause and the annual conference was capable of voting for full self-government and self-determination for India as early as 1927. But this was an area where rhetoric and reality were often widest apart. On international questions generally Labour talked of the need for 'world planning, world action, and world control in economic and financial matters'.[50] These rather nebulous goals existed alongside a very real suspicion of capitalist governments and international finance after 1931 which served to strengthen the pacifism and anti-militarism among the party membership. Annual conference repeatedly voted for large reductions in armaments expenditures while demanding a policy of collective security through the League of Nations (which the Soviet Union joined in 1934). The rise of the dictators and the growing threat of another European war eventually exposed the contradictions in this policy although the ILP, whose membership shrank from 16,773 in 1931 to just over 4,000 in 1935, persisted with the argument that a war with Nazi Germany would only amount to another inter-imperialist conflict.

The Communists began to change their tone only after the Seventh Congress of the Comintern reoriented the whole movement in 1935 towards the People's Front policy pioneered by the French Communist Party (PCF) and championed by G. Dimitrov in Moscow. Henceforward the Communists were enjoined to seek the widest possible alliance of anti-fascist parties and the election of governments based on this coalition. Their own sectarianism had seen the Comintern's membership fall by over 25 per cent since 1928 and 43 of the 67 communist parties were 'practically destroyed' by fascism by 1935.[51] Even Palme Dutt could see that a change of line was required without having to be told so by the leaders of the CPSU. In October 1933 he wrote to Harry Pollitt observing that the idea that bourgeois democracy was simply a sham was now 'out of date.'[52] Fascism was belatedly teaching the Communists that 'bourgeois democracy' had been created with the blood, as Dimitrov put it, of the workers and that the working class 'will naturally fight with all its strength to retain bourgeois democratic liberties'.[53] Social democracy was now characterized as a coalition which contained genuine anti-fascist elements, normally on its Left wing – the wing formerly denounced by the Communists as especially insidious. It is little wonder that the People's Front was dismissed as a Trojan Horse by the *Daily Herald* and as a mere tactical ploy by Friedrich Adler, the Secretary of the Labour and Socialist International. Many of the delegates to the Seventh Congress took a similar view of it. But the *New Statesman* announced that the Communists were human after all and capable of learning from experience, while the *Manchester Guardian* stressed that there was 'something much more evil' than Communism in Europe.[54]

This evil had already destroyed the socialist and communist parties of Italy,

Germany and Austria. In France the fascist leagues had attempted to seize power in 1934 and in the same year an uprising on the Asturias coalfield in Spain was savagely repressed. By 1936 and the emergence of a Popular Front government in France led by Leon Blum it seemed to many British socialists that the French had found a formula to stop fascism. The opening of the civil war in Spain in July invested this conviction with renewed urgency. By January 1937, when the ILP, the CPGB and the Socialist League launched a Unity Campaign, an estimated one-fifth of Labour's 90,000 members in London were involved in the pro-unity lobby.[55] But within days of the launching of the Unity Campaign – which *Tribune* promoted from its first issue – the Labour Party disaffiliated the Socialist League. In May 1937 the League decided to dissolve itself so that its members could stay in the party and campaign for unity – a decision which some in the ILP opposed and which they believed had come about after pressure from Pollitt and the Communist Party, who were interested in preserving the lobby for CPGB affiliation and not averse to the liquidation of a potential rival.[56] Over a thousand organizations, including the Fabian Society and the Miners' Federation, had already supported CPGB affiliation at Labour's conference in 1936 and the Communists claimed that 57 of the 62 constituency Labour parties had worked with them in the London County Council elections of the same year.[57] Communist membership trebled between 1935 and 1939 to 17,539, but the party's influence was clearly much bigger. Weekend sales of the *Daily Worker* could reach 200,000 while Communist pamphlet sales topped the million mark.[58]

But perhaps the best indication of Communist influence was the Left Book Club which Victor Gollancz established in March 1936. This very quickly accumulated 57,000 members and an estimated readership for each of its titles of a quarter of a million.[59] It has been described as 'the most active and largest body in Britain working for a Popular Front', but Julian Symons has rightly stressed that 'in practice the Left Book Club's chief function was to serve as a propaganda machine for Communism.'[60] The Club would never touch a book by Trotsky and rejected George Orwell's *Homage to Catalonia* – an experience which left him convinced that the Communists practically controlled literature in Britain during the four years or so before September 1939. *Tribune* and the *New Statesman* always gave the Communists the benefit of the doubt (when they could not actually support them) in this period and many literary journals were dominated by fellow-travellers such as W. H. Auden and his circle of friends. About a third of the Left Book Club's publications were actually written by Communists and the rest were selected by two advocates of the Popular Front, Gollancz himself and Laski, together with John Strachey who called himself a Communist though he never carried a party card. By May 1938 the Club had created a thousand local discussion groups which were able to distribute some of its pamphlets in their millions. Its monthly journal, *Left News*, was distributed free to all members and its first year's run in particular carried a large number of eulogies of all things Soviet, including several eloquent vindications of the Moscow Trials.

Strachey was in no doubt that Bukharin, Trotsky, Zinoviev and the other defendents were guilty of the fantastic charges that were brought against them. He argued that 'the whole future of humanity was dependent on their detention and execution.[61] Kingsley Martin's *New Statesman* struggled to understand the Moscow 'frame-ups', as the Commission headed by John Dewey called them in September 1937, but finally concluded that the integrity of observers such as D. N. Pritt – a barrister whose opinions invariably reflected official Soviet policy – was 'beyond question'. If these people said that the trials were authentic, Martin reasoned that they must have been; and after visiting Trotsky in Mexico – the Trotsky accused by Moscow of working with the Nazis to overthrow the Soviet government – Martin returned 'rather less inclined to scout the possibility of Trotsky's complicity than I had been before, because his judgement appeared to me so unstable and therefore the possibility of his embarking on a crazy plot more credible'.[62] Even Francis Williams, editor of the *Daily Herald* which was not taken in by the 'confessions' of the accused, lamented that 'it is the enemies of the Soviet Union who were delighted, its friends who are dismayed by the new terror.'[63]

But in Second International circles there was a greater preparedness for the Moscow Trials, if only because leaders of the organization had been exposing Bolshevik violence against other socialists since the first days of the October Revolution. Friedrich Adler had denounced the 'witch trials' of 1931 when so-called Mensheviks were in the dock; there was no need to revise the essentials of his argument in 1936, 1937 or 1938. The ILP too, because of the influence which Trotsky's arguments exerted within it, was able to develop a critique of the Comintern, the Soviet state and the new terror against Stalin's political opponents. It also opposed the Popular Front on the grounds that it encouraged class collaboration with Liberals and other anti-fascist 'progressives'. For the same reason it could not stomach the idea of an alliance between the USSR and the imperialist governments of Britain and France. From the ILP awkward questions were asked about the Communist line in the Spanish Civil War and in particular the repression of the Partido Obrero de Unificación Marxista (POUM) and the anarchists which Orwell witnessed in Barcelona in May 1937. Elsewhere on the Left – among fellow-travellers, Labour Leftists, supporters of *Tribune*, the *New Statesman*, the Left Book Club and the Popular Front – socialists were riding for a fall. They had all given the Soviet Union the benefit of many doubts concerning the authoritarian nature of the regime because of its apparent readiness to fight the Nazis. Should anything disturb this little 'deal' a great many people were in danger of rediscovering their consciences.

Conclusion

It is clear that the debacle of 1931 changed the temper of debates within the Labour Party and shifted the socialist argument to the Left. This is evinced (paradoxically) by the secession of the ILP, the formation of the Socialist League, the demands for planning, the doubts expressed about the efficacy of parliamentarism and the growth of Communist influence among the intellectuals. The world capitalist economic crisis, contrasted with the apparent successes of planning in the USSR, the rise of fascism and the prospect of another world war all added to the sense of urgency which activists now felt, in the wake of MacDonald's desertion.

The trade union and party leadership, however, never wavered in their opposition to demands for extra-parliamentary campaigns even though the much reduced contingent of Labour MPs in the Commons had no prospect of influencing the so-called National government. Similarly the trade union leadership had no time for rank and file movements in the industrial wing of the movement, or among the unemployed, which were perceived as an obstacle to greater influence with the government. Of course any contact with the CPGB was shunned, but even where there was no question of Communist 'front' activity Labour witheld official recognition from protest marches such as that organized by the town council of Jarrow. While fascism prompted many socialists to question the compatibility of capitalism and democracy the leaders of the Labour movement equated fascism with Soviet communism and held that they equally imperilled British democracy. Events like the Moscow Trials helped to reinforce the hostility towards communism which was already ingrained in men such as Bevin and Citrine. But the real point is that neither the trade union nor the political 'wings' of the movement ever lost their faith in British political institutions and so they remained true to their original project of seeking to exercise influence within them.

The fact that the doubters, such as Cripps, Laski, Cole and the Socialist League, also believed ultimately in the reliability and utility of the existing constitutional arrangements should caution us against overstating the extent of the radicalism after 1931. It is also worth pointing out that much of the CPGB's enhanced credibility in this period derived from its association with the Soviet Union, which was widely perceived as a beacon of economic progress and a firm enemy of fascism; the CPGB's friends and fellow-travellers were not necessarily converts to Leninism and the party itself moved to a non-Leninist position after 1935. When all the rhetoric is cast aside the apparent lurch to the left after 1931 resulted in few tangible changes. There was certainly a widespread belief in the need for planning – a belief which was not confined to the labour movement – and even people associated with the Right of the party, such as Durbin, Gaitskell, Dalton and Bevin saw the necessity at some unspecified future point for state control of some industrial activity – but prior to the Second World War Labour's actual programmatic commitments in this area, were very limited. *Labour's Immediate Programme* (1937) only envisaged public ownership of the mines, electricity, gas and the railways. Gone was the talk of taking over the joint stock banks, the land and large sections of manufacturing industry. Gone also, in the same year, was Labour's opposition to the National government's rearmament programme. Labour's immediate goals were much the same as in 1918.

10

The Second World War

The signing of a non-aggression pact on 22 August 1939 between the Soviet Union and Nazi Germany was itself enough to disillusion many socialists and Communists alike. For years past Popular Front agitations had been based on the assumption that Stalin was the only certain ally in the struggle against fascism, though from the sidelines Trotsky had insisted time and time again on the falsity of this hope: now, it appeared, the USSR was prepared to stand aside from that struggle. Of course the Pact could be justified as an expedient forced on Stalin by the capitulation of Chamberlain and Daladier at Munich in 1938; if the French and the British would stop at nothing in the appeasement of Hitler – as long as his armies were moving eastwards – the Russians, it was reasoned, were compelled to buy time in which to prepare for the inevitable onslaught. The secret protocol of the Pact which made provision for the partition of Poland was of course not yet known, but even without this knowledge the *realpolitik* embodied in the Hitler–Stalin accord sickened some former supporters of the Popular Front.

Tribune's response to the Pact, however, was to declare 'Soviet Peace Move Exposes Chamberlain'.[1] The paper's fellow-travelling editor, E. Y. Hartshorn, continued to get things wrong until the Soviet invasion of Finland on 30 November. On the very day that the Nazis invaded Poland, for example, *Tribune* announced that 'Russia has not given Hitler a free hand'. The day afterwards, 2 September, the CPGB published a manifesto repeating the argument of the past five years that in association with the USSR, Britain and France should wage a war to defend democracy against fascism. Both the *Daily Worker* and *Tribune* argued that the war had to be fought on two fronts – against Hitler, but also at home against the appeasers, crypto-fascists and plutocrats who could not be trusted to wage the anti-fascist struggle effectively and who would certainly stand in the way of the required social renovation in Britain. While a small number of Trotskyists and ILP members characterized the war as an imperialist conflict and championed a revolutionary defeatist policy, the Labour Left and the Communists argued that an imperialist outcome could be avoided because the anti-fascist nature of the war would unleash democratic forces in Britain which would clear out the old gang and transform British society itself. Orwell came to very similar conclusions in *The Lion and the Unicorn* (1941), where he predicted the emergence, for the first time, of a 'specifically *English* Socialist movement' from the fusion of the patriotic and radical impulses which the war had set in motion.

On 14 September – three days before the Soviet invasion of Poland – the first Soviet radio broadcast since the war began announced that the conflict was 'imperialist and predatory on both sides'.[2] The day after this broadcast R. Palme Dutt asked the CPGB's Political Bureau to re-examine the party line, though it was not until the Central Committee meeting of 24 September that the revision was made after the return from Moscow of the party's representative, Dave Springhall, armed with the authority of Dimitrov and Stalin.

Pollitt and J. R. Campbell initially refused to accept the new position, but by November public self-criticisms had appeared from both of them and Pollitt was no longer General Secretary of the party. On 7 October the CPGB issued a new manifesto which said:

> This war is a fight between imperialist powers over profits, colonies, and world domination . . . The leaders of the Labour Party and the Trade Union movement have sided fully with the Government of Chamberlain and Churchill and are attempting to get the working class movement to support their imperialist war aims.[3]

The Communist Party now demanded peace negotiations and even claimed that, having annexed Western Poland, Hitler now wanted peace.

While the Russian invasion of Poland had been widely defended – even by Churchill – the Soviet attack on Finland at the end of November 1939 caused outrage in Britain. The Communists justified this attack as a defensive manoeuvre of a piece with the annexations of Poland and the Baltic states. This was an argument which had carried weight with the *New Statesman* when it was used in connection with Poland – 'Brest-Litovsk Revenged', it had declared – but which it now renounced. The attack on Finland, declared Kingsley Martin, 'compels us to rank [Stalin's] dictatorship with that of the other totalitarian regimes . . . he has a contempt for all arguments except that of superior force.[4] Martin now blamed the October Revolution for the emergence of National Socialism while continuing to insist on the fundamentally progressive character of the Soviet system. This sort of contradictory logic was very common in Left analyses of the USSR. Orwell, for example, rightly claimed that 'the sin of nearly all left-wingers from 1933 onward is that they have wanted to be anti-Fascist without being anti-totalitarian.' But during the war he also argued that 'the USSR cannot altogether escape its past and retains enough of the original ideas of the Revolution to make it a more hopeful phenomenon than Nazi Germany.'[5] Only a few years before writing *Nineteen-Eighty Four* he went so far as to agree with Laski that the Soviet Union was 'the real dynamo of the socialist movement', while criticizing him for saying nothing about 'purges, liquidations, the dictatorship of a minority, the suppression of criticism and so forth'.[6] Even determined opponents of the 'Soviet myth' then could continue to believe that the USSR was 'the real dynamo of the socialist movement'.

In a similar contradictory vein Kingsley Martin argued in December 1939 that: 'By the inexorable laws of its dialectic Bolshevism brought into being its antithesis National Socialism. Today the question being asked is whether the ugly thing that now reigns from Vladivostock to Cologne is turning into the inevitable synthesis, National-Bolshevism.'[7] But this was a conclusion the editor of the *New Statesman* wanted to resist, because:

> While condemning the attack on Finland we should not forget that the achievements of the Russian Revolution are not transitory. That workers shall not be exploited; that education shall be the key to freedom and power for all; that the great resources of the modern world shall be planned under public authority for a happier future – these and other basic conceptions took root and blossomed in the USSR and the strength of their hold in the minds of men and women everywhere is due in large measure to the Bolsheviks. These achievements and ideals are not transitory.[8]

John Strachey was one of the few who supported the CPGB's abrupt change of line, arguing in December 1939 that once the Nazi – Soviet Pact came into existence the British Government realized that Hitler's next assault would be on the Empire and that this was the only reason why Chamberlain dropped his policy of appeasement. Hence, he reasoned, this was why 'we' characterize the war as imperialist:

> It is a war between capitalist Empires waged in order to decide which of them should dominate a large part of the world . . . The way out lies through the struggle of the people of Britain, France and Germany and the people of every other Imperialist power against their own governments.[9]

Victor Gollancz could not accept this logic because in common with the vast majority of British Socialists he believed that there were real differences between democracy and fascism (the Popular Front had been saying so for years) which made the former worth defending. But like Kingsley Martin, Gollancz continued to stress the lasting gains of the October Revolution which made the USSR a progressive force in the world despite its unjustifiable attack on Finland. Now, however, he could see that the abolition of capitalism, though still the *sine qua non* of a 'completely free society', 'would not necessarily produce a good society'. And whereas he had previously justified the system of unfreedom under Stalin as somehow the price that had to be paid for the USSR's objective strides towards human liberation, he now wanted to emphasize that 'Of all the "goods" of which humanity is capable there is not one so basic and so final as the free and independent mind: and if once the ideal of intellectual freedom passes into contempt the race is doomed.'[10]

Gollancz undoubtedly had in mind the blatant absence of the 'free and independent mind' in the Communist Party. The change from the Chamberlain government to Churchill's coalition Cabinet in May 1940 did nothing to alter the Communist line, which continued to insist that the government's real policy was anti-Soviet and designed to impose a fascist government on Britain in the cause of imperialist expansion.[11] After all, it was reasoned, 'Britain declared war not Germany. Attempts were made to end the war but the Soviet-German peace overtures were rejected by Britain. All through these months the British and French Governments have had the power to end the war. They have chosen to extend it.'[12] R. Palme Dutt took up this theme at an open air meeting in Hyde Park in April 1940 where he told the crowd that the extension of the war to Scandinavia was a 'crime' whose main responsibility 'must be placed with Chamberlain, Reynaud, Attlee and Blum'.[13] In May Dunkirk had to be evacuated and in June France fell to the Nazis. Suddenly the CPGB dropped its calls for peace with Hitler and referred to 'the appalling catastrophe that has befallen the French people'. Its emphasis was now on the need for a workers' government that would arm the people; while behind the scenes Willie Gallacher, Communist MP for East Fife, pleaded for passports so that his comrades could intercede with Stalin – presumably to change the line.[14]

But with the fall of France the CPGB's opposition to the war effort came to be seen in an altogether more sinister light. Gollancz now claimed that the French Communists had 'objectively assisted in the worst betrayal of the working class in modern history'.[15] Strachey, who had now broken with his former friends, was moved to denounce the Communists for weakening the will to resist of the French workers.[16] Such criticisms were in fact more accurate in expressing the sense of danger that now prevailed in Britain than in describing the situation in France, but they certainly helped to isolate the CPGB more than ever and to harden its attitude. By the autumn of 1940 its propaganda dwelt once again on the imperialist character of the war. At the end of September 1940 the *Daily Worker* called for a People's Convention to be held on 12 January 1941 to rally support for its oppositional stance. Already it had organized a conference on 'Labour and the War' at which 878 delegates claiming to represent 340,000 people debated the CPGB's analysis. The party had also mobilized its dwindling band of supporters to fight a number of by-elections on an anti-war ticket. These activities intensified around the People's Convention and the Home Secretary, Herbert Morrison, banned both the *Daily Worker* and *The Week* in December 1940. When the Convention met the following month 2,234 delegates were present, claiming to represent over a million people. Among them were representatives of Indian nationalism such as Indira Nehru and well-known fellow travellers such as Paul Robeson.

As we have seen, prominent Leftists had continued to keep faith in the

Soviet Union even after the partition of Poland. But this should not be allowed to obscure the fact that the Labour leaders were not so indulgent: from the moment the Hitler–Stalin Pact became known they were loud in their denunciation of the Soviet system. Citrine and Bevin, for example, were inclined to equate the Nazi and Soviet regimes, while the *Daily Herald* saw 'naked territorial gain as the motive for the Pact'. Hugh Dalton described the Russians as 'double-crossers by nature'[17] and by the time of the war against Finland the *Daily Herald* declared: 'Now finally Stalin's Russia sacrifices all claim to the affection and respect of the world-wide working class movement which Lenin's Soviet Russia had as a right . . . The Soviet Union is dead, Stalin's new imperialist Russia takes its place.'[18] But among socialists the belief persisted that despite all the manifold defects in the Soviet system something valuable and progressive remained. Even those with the most sophisticated appreciation of how the Soviet system actually worked, such as the Trotskyists and those influenced by them like the ILP, believed that the foundations of the regime were progressive and were accordingly wary to avoid lining up with those who would destroy this socialist base.

It is estimated that by 1938, 8 million people inhabited the *gulag*; perhaps 12 million people died in the Soviet Union as victims of Stalin's dictatorship between 1936 and 1950, together with a further 3½ million who were destroyed in the forced collectivization programme. Real evidence concerning the enormity of the dictatorship's crimes reached the outside world through Trotskyist and Menshevik channels. During the war a number of important testimonies were published in English including Anton Ciliga's *The Russian Enigma* (1940); Walter Krivitsky's *I Was Stalin's Agent* (1940); Louis Fischer's *Men and Power* (1941); Alexander Barmine's *One Who Survived* (1945); and parts of Victor Serge's *Memoirs of a Revolutionary* which appeared in English translation in *Politics*, June 1944–June 1945 (though the full story was not available until 1963). After the war D. J. Dallin and B. I. Nicolaevsky wrote *Forced Labour in the Soviet Union* (1948); Margarette Buber-Neumann published *Under Two Dictators* (1949); and there was Freda Utley's *Lost Illusion* (1949). Before long many more socialists were ready to write of the 'god that failed' as the Cold War sucked numerous ex-Communists out of the Left wing altogether. But this was for the future. Once the USSR entered the war the belief that it was objectively progressive was powerfully reinforced, even in circles which never forgot or forgave the 1939 perfidy of the British Communists.

When the news of Operation Barbarossa reached Britain on 22 June 1941 the CPGB did not have to be told that it was once again necessary to change the party line. The Communists henceforward were the most fervid supporters of the war effort and became associated with the drive for greater productivity in industry as well as the campaign for a second front in Western Europe. But the party was also the champion of shopfloor grievances and in the context of the official industrial truce and approval of Britain's Soviet ally the CPGB was able to increase its membership to an all-time peak of 55,000 by

1944. In certain factories the Communists achieved for the first time the sort of profile which the Comintern had envisaged in 1919. For example, the CPGB branch at Metro-Vickers at Trafford Park in Manchester was 500 strong, and similar branches existed in other engineering establishments.[19] It is perhaps then not so astonishing that within a year of Russia's entry into the war the CPGB was a plausible candidate for affiliation to the Labour Party in the eyes of tens of thousands of Labour activists.

The war was a radicalizing experience for British society. The Left naturally expected and encouraged this process. Orwell, for example, looked forward to 'Red militias billeted in the Ritz' and in June 1940 called for the arming of the people not just in order to defend the country against the Nazis but also because he shared the conviction expressed in much of the old Popular Front propaganda that a successful war effort required a social revolution. But the extent of the radicalism generated by the war remains a matter of dispute. The surveys conducted by Home Intelligence in 1942 concluded that public opinion had moved under the impetus received from the military successes of the Soviet Union and was characterized by a revulsion against any return to pre-war conditions and opposition to vested interests.[20] Gallup Poll evidence also shows a shift in political attitudes after 1942. In the years 1940–2, according to Paul Addison, 'the main force of radicalizing propaganda was certainly not the official Labour apparatus, but the leftish intelligentsia.'[21] An early example of such literature was *Guilty Men* (1940), which the future Labour leader Michael Foot had a hand in writing. This dwelt on the disastrous policy of the Chamberlain government and indicted the Tory establishment. At a time when reading and listening to radio broadcasts – where Left opinion was also more conspicuous than ever before – were on the increase, it sold nearly a quarter of a million copies.

There was no Tory equivalent of the popular radical literature of these years and, under the unique circumstances pertaining, Leftish ideas also found their way into the Army Bureau of Current Affairs. The war was, after all, an anti-fascist struggle and as such it set an ideological agenda congenial to the Left. Angus Calder has characterized it as the 'People's War': 'So the people surged forward to fight their own war, forcing their masters into retreat . . . The war was fought with the willing brains and hearts of the most vigorous elements in the community, the educated, the skilled, the bold, the active, the young, who worked more and more consciously towards a transformed post-war world.'[22] In this view the war 'set off a ferment of participatory democracy' which was ultimately defeated by the old forces of reaction. But even if we accept this verdict it has to be remembered that the rough and ready egalitarianism of wartime conditions and the expectations of social justice for the future which they nourished had to contend against a deeply conservative society. It is significant that a party preaching these principles, Common Wealth, made such spectacular progress in by-elections, and that the unions and even the CPGB greatly increased their numbers, but public opinion seems to have been 'following in the footsteps of Wells of Lloyd

George' rather then Lenin'.[23] This is suggested, for example, by popular enthusiasm for the Beveridge Report in 1942 which proposed an all-in social security scheme quite in keeping with the needs of a more progressive capitalism. Gallup Polls on the eve of the 1945 election continued to reflect this popular demand for social reform and showed that the people's priorities were housing, employment and social security. Thus the war generated a demand for reforms which Liberals such as Beveridge and Keynes could meet.

The war provided an opportunity for an influx of such radical intellectuals into the British state, and Whitehall for the first time was peopled by Keynesians and quasi-Keynesians such as Gaitskell, Jay and Durbin. Beveridge's *Full Employment in a Free Society* (1944), which adopted Keynes's proposal for a National Investment Board and talked of the socialization of demand rather than production, was the most radical document produced by the Keynesian Left (Joan Robinson, Barbara Wootton, Nicholas Kaldor, E. F. Schumacher and Frank Pakenham helped Beveridge prepare it). The report argued for public expenditure programmes on housing, roads, schools, increased social security and progressive and redistributive taxation. Even so, it was presented as having 'by-passed the socialist-capitalist controversy'[24] and had to compete with the *White Paper on Employment Policy* (1944) which specifically disowned budget deficit financing. Under Hugh Dalton's guidance Labour prepared its own *Full Employment and Financial Policy* (1944), which mixed Keynesian ideas with physical control planning. Here, as in other areas of Labour policy, 'the most immediate influence' on the party was Whitehall, though as Pimlott points out this was Whitehall 'in an imperial and reformist mood'.[25]

'The Gentleman in Whitehall is usually right', concluded Douglas Jay after the war,[26] and this attitude expresses well the technocratic approach which allowed Labour's Keynesians to feel comfortable with the mandarinate and believe that together they could manage Britain's future. The state was of course 'rediscovered' during the war as the centre of enormous power and the repository of the national interest. But there were many on the Left who objected to the Labour leadership's easy assimilation to these institutions of power and to the assumptions they held. As early as April 1942 Laski was complaining that 'in return for a handful of social reforms, some of them fundamental in character, we are inviting the vested interests of this country to strengthen their hold upon state-power . . . I suggest that on all fundamental matters we do the giving and the Tories do the taking.'[27]

But the gap between socialist expectations and the actual conduct and thinking of the Labour members of the government was nowhere bigger than in the area of international relations as these were being prepared for the post-war world. In 1937 Attlee had argued (in one of the Left Book Club's most unpopular publications, incidentally) that a Labour government could believe in the successful administration of capitalism no more than it could believe in the foreign policy of a 'Capitalist Government': it was simply 'impossible for a Socialist Government to pursue a foreign policy that is at variance with its principles'.[28] In fact even at his most radical Attlee, in common with Herbert Morrison, Dalton, Bevin and the rest of the party leadership, was unable to envisage a foreign policy which did not presuppose a continuing imperial role for Britain and a lasting Great Power status. Nor did these socialists fashion an alternative conception of the national interest to the one which the Foreign Office stood for.

However, this was obscured by pro-Soviet rhetoric for as long as the war lasted. The chairman of the 1942 annual conference, for example, referred to Labour's 'consistent' policy towards Russia since 1919, which amounted to the idea that: 'Together the Soviet Union and ourselves can play a great part in not only establishing peace on a permanent footing but shaping that better world which we both desire'.[29] When the Comintern was dissolved, the following year, the party was once more faced with a sustained campaign for Communist affiliation which lost by 1,951,000 to 712,000 votes when the proposition was put before conference. In mobilizing against this campaign the Labour leadership lost no opportunity to expose the CPGB's *Record of Hypocrisy and Treachery to the Workers of Europe*, as one pamphlet was called. Nevertheless in the conference debate on CPGB affiliation Morrison was careful to distinguish between types of Communist. For the CPGB was, he claimed, 'a very different and very much less responsible body than the Communist Party of the Soviet Union'.[30] Former supporters of the Popular Front such as Laski and Cole now agreed with Morrison's appraisal of the CPGB. But they also took up and elaborated on the common theme of how 'Left would talk to Left' in the post-war world.

Few socialists during the war could imagine a future Labour government constructing socialism in Britain without the close friendship and co-operation of the Soviet Union. After the USSR entered the war this sentiment was to be found in *Tribune*, the *New Statesman* and even the *Daily Herald*; it was expressed by the patriotic Labour Left as well as the handful of fellow-travellers in the party; old ILP members such as Fenner Brockway and Emrys Hughes, together with mavericks such as Konni Zilliacus, subscribed to the same view: some form of working alliance with the USSR was a basic precondition for the achievement of socialism in Britain. Cole raised the issue as early as 1941 and reasoned that 'we must take our stand, fundamentally, on the real achievements of the Russian Revolution.'[31] The USSR was 'by virtue of its basic economic and cultural institutions a Socialist country and therefore necessarily the principal rallying point for the forces of Socialism throughout the world'.[32] One could acknowledge the horrors of the regime, according to Cole, without its affecting this basic issue; there was 'the terrible disregard of suffering' in the forced collectivization of agriculture; the persecution of dissent as treason; the GPU whose activities had inspired the Gestapo; the degeneration of Russian Marxism into pure dogma – all this and more could be conceded but did not affect Russia's socialist credentials. For Cole and many other socialists, the tyrannical side of Stalin's regime was explicable by reference to the legacy of Russian barbarism working in the context of foreign encirclement and aggression. It did not negate 'the essential economic institutions of Socialism' which 'have been not merely maintained but immensely strengthened'.[33] There was no question in Cole's mind of the emergence of a new class of exploiters in Russia because major steps had already been set in train to strengthen Russian democracy in the future, steps such as collectivism in agriculture, the introduction of planning and the development of education. Together these forces were creating an urban, educated, proletariat on an immense scale and nothing could prevent it from bursting out of the cage of Stalin's dictatorship.

One thing was certain for many socialists: the rest of the world was capitalist and, as Cole pointed out, in its strongest heartland – the USA – 'it is true that this system and this structure are almost unchallenged':

In these circumstances there is a natural tendency for adherents of British capitalism to seek reinforcement for their own position by the closest possible links between Britain and the United States. The more closely they can link the economy of this country to that of America and the more they can bring America in as a partner not only in the war but also in the tasks of post-war settlement, the larger appears the chance both of the war being won under capitalism and of the peace taking shape as a restoration of capitalist power in Britain and, perhaps, on the continent as well.[34]

The alternative had to be co-operation with the USSR, which because of its socialist base was for Cole, 'necessarily the principle rallying point for the forces of Socialism throughout the world'.[35] It was absurd in this view to suppose that socialism could be the basis of the post-war settlement without Soviet assistance. Moreover the American and British ruling classes would conspire to extinguish European socialism if socialists allowed their differences with Communism 'to become – with whatever excuse – the foundation of a profound antagonism and [so] commit the movements to which they belong, to mere sterility ... We socialists are not so strong or so assured of victory even when Hitler had gone down to defeat that we can refuse to work together.'[36]

As the war drew nearer its end the Labour Left began to think more about these issues. Laski, who could rarely resist ruining a good argument by exaggeration, thought that it was 'impossible to doubt that the spectacle of Russian heroism in the two years of the struggle against Hitlerism has convinced the common man, all over the world, that there was a magic in the Revolution of 1917 somehow adaptable to his own concerns.'[37] He now believed that 'the civilized tradition can be rebuilt [only] upon that which the idea of the Russian Revolution is founded', and that seemed to be a new spirituality, a 'religion of service', of 'strength in adversity'. These were the qualities of the Bolshevik elite which have 'created the conviction that to work for the common good of humanity, to take even a small step towards freeing it from its chains, is infinitely worthwhile.'[38] Even when due allowance was taken of the barbaric elements of the Russian experiment, Laski asserted that 'the solemn truth remains that in the Soviet Union since the October Revolution more men and women have had the opportunity of self-fulfilment than anywhere else in the world.'[39]

Within a couple of years Laski would be denouncing the British Communists as an 'organized conspiracy' under orders from Moscow and bent on a 'strategy of strangulation' of rival workers' organizations. But although he argued that 'democratic socialists' should have no truck with 'authoritarian socialism', he also persisted with other nicer distinctions which could not be sustained in the circumstances of the developing Cold War. Thus, he reasoned,

> Socialists can understand a straightforward negotiation with the Russian Communist Party which seeks a genuine entente between the Russia of the great Revolution and the Socialist parties of the Western world [but] Western Socialists are so convinced that the Communist Parties outside Russia act without moral scruples, intrigue without any sense of shame, are utterly careless of truth, sacrifice without any hesitation the means they use to the ends they serve, that they reject organic unity with them.[40]

Laski did not see that if all of this were true and Moscow, moreover, was at the centre of it, a 'genuine entente' with Russia was impossible. He had himself provided arguments that would soon be used to anathematize the Soviet Union as a singularly evil force in world politics.

Most of the Left accepted Laski's characterization of the Communist Party while insisting as he did that a *modus vivendi* with the USSR was the precondition for a strong post-war European Left. The *New Statesman* believed that this was possible as well as necessary because

> There is reason to believe that the USSR is not anxious to occupy Germany and that Stalin has the same war aim for all the states of Eastern and Central Europe. Russia wants "Popular Front" governments friendly to Russia and capable of entering into economic and political arrangements with their neighbours.[41]

Nye Bevan expressed a similar sentiment shortly afterwards in the pages of *Tribune*:

> It is quite natural and inevitable that Russia should influence preponderantly the life of nations immediately on her borders and that she should seek to prevent them from combinations that may be aimed at her. That is the price we have to pay for the bitter recent past.[42]

A similar argument was to be seen regularly in *The Times* under E. H. Carr's editorship. Kingsley Martin even believed that a Popular Front with the USSR and the liberated countries of Europe – which the whole Left envisaged moving towards socialism – would take the form of a 'common policy of economic welfare with integrated transport and social services for the whole continent'.[43]

The USA, on the other hand, was perceived by virtually the whole of the Left in the labour movement as an expansionary imperialism. By the end of the war it was clear that the USA had emerged immensely strengthened with global ambitions which, as Laski noted in 1946, were manifested in its interference in the politics of Greece, Turkey, China, Japan and Iran as well as Germany and Italy.[44] Michael Foot depicted Wall Street as 'arrogant, self-confident, merciless, capitalism', and *Reynolds News* believed that President Truman had made 'clear beyond any shadow of doubt that the men who rule America are determined to go to any length to stop the development of Socialism and to open up the world as a vast colonial area for American capitalism'.[45]

There was, however, another imperialism much closer to home. Before the war Britain had acquired an Empire which covered one-fifth of the world. It was governed by methods which gave substance to the Communist claim that bourgeois democracy was a hollow sham; or, as Orwell claimed it stood on the backs of 'six hundred million disenfranchised human beings'.[46] Well before the end of the war British policy-makers realized that Britain had been so weakened by the military effort – it had cost a quarter of the nation's wealth by 1945 – that it could not expect to resume its former world role without receiving considerable assistance from the USA, the only power which the war actually enhanced:

By 1945 American production had reached levels that were scarely believable . . . forty five per cent of the world's arms and nearly fifty per cent of the world's goods. Two-thirds of all the ships afloat were American built.[47]

By contrast the USSR was a picture of devastation; an estimated 20 million dead; 25 million homeless; 31,850 factories destroyed; 65,000 kilometres of railway track ripped up; widespread famine and agricultural production only half of its pre-war level.[48] The situation was so bad that:

Material damage inflicted upon Soviet cities, factories and agriculture appeared practically beyond repair by the end of the war. Fully 1,700 cities and towns were devastated and seventy per cent of the country's industrial installations demolished.[49]

It is inconceivable that British policy-makers were unaware of the contrast between the war-torn Soviet system and the buoyant American economy. Had the socialists been conscious of the true dimensions of these differentials, however, it is equally difficult to believe that they could have regarded the USSR as a viable ally in the construction of socialism across the European continent.

The Labour members of Churchill's coalition Cabinet had a much better idea of what was going on, and indeed were adamant that the government's foreign policy was, in Bevin's words, 'a combined effort'.[50] While the war raged the government took steps to defend Britain's imperial interests even if this meant interference in the politics of countries which though not part of the Empire bore some strategic relationship to it. Even before the Allies invaded Italy, for example, the terms of the fascist surrender were calculated in London and Washington to exclude the Italian Communists and socialists even though these were the backbone of the partisan units which had liberated Northern Italy.[51]

At the end of 1944 a more spectacular example of this policy was provided by British military intervention in Greece, where the success of the National Liberation Army (ELAS) in driving out the Nazis looked set to introduce a government composed of Communists and socialists since the Left dominated ELAS.

But a Communist–socialist government in Greece might endanger British interests in the Middle East where Britain was the dominant imperialist power. In 1939 it had been in military occupation of Cyprus, Egypt, Sudan, Iraq, Jordon and Palestine, and possessed the lion's share of the oil. If Britain were to resume its accustomed dominance in that part of the world Greece could not be allowed to lurch to the Left. So in December 1944 British forces intervened on the pretext of preventing a Communist *coup*. In fact it was:

> an intervention to crush the whole Greek Resistance in order to restore the semi-colonial dependence of the past, an intervention carefully prepared at both the diplomatic and the military levels by Churchill since the summer of 1943.

> The intervention in Greece was part of a British policy for re-establishing the Empire and for the safeguarding of its communications together with the erection of an anti-communist bastion against the Soviet Union. In the framework of this policy the Mediterranean and more especially Greece in its important strategic position played a central role.[52]

With the Labour leaders and Stalin collaborating in this policy the odds were stacked heavily against the European Left. Far from nurturing ambitions for a continental socialism, Soviet policy was concerned to establish a stable buffer zone on its Western frontiers. Stalin agreed to observe Churchill's scheme for dividing Europe into spheres of influence to secure that end and no doubt recognized the value of the precedent when the British army occupied Athens. As for the Labour Party, it needs to be emphasized that it was an active element in shaping the government's foreign policy. Dalton's *The International Post-war Settlement*, drafted in June 1943 in response to an NEC request for a positive foreign policy, recognized that preservation of the Empire in the form of the Commonwealth was a precondition for the retention of Britain's Great Power status.[53] The substance of his proposals was approved by the 1944 annual conference of the party even though the Left was outraged by the invasion of Greece.

At the beginning of 1945 the *New Statesman* lamented that the government was 'Still Shooting Our Friends', but few realized that this was a policy with which the Labour members of the Cabinet wholly concurred. By the time of the general election in July talk of a 'socialist foreign policy' was heard in many constituencies again, but during the campaign Attlee had accompanied Churchill to the summit conference at Potsdam and had taken the opportunity publicly to assert this support for 'unity on foreign policy'. Laski had warned Attlee that he should regard himself as no more than an observer at Potsdam and not be bound by any decisions taken there. But this only earned the chairman of the NEC a stern rebuke and the remark that 'a period of silence on your part would be welcome'. Events were to prove that those like Laski who believed in the possibility of a socialist foreign policy were an unstable minority in a movement overwhelmingly preoccupied with domestic reform.

Conclusion

There was nothing in Labour's pre-war record to suggest that when put to the test its vague talk of a socialist foreign policy would amount to anything; the evidence of the MacDonald governments pointed the other way – Labour took the same view of the national interest as the Tories. Even before the experience of 1929–31 it was possible for a foreign observer of the party to see clearly its 'close affinity . . . with the traditions of national culture'.[54] The economic and political crisis of 1931 increased the volume of Left rhetoric but did nothing to seriously disturb this relationship, while entry into the Churchill coalition, with its emotional posture of 'exalted patriotism', did much to reinforce it during the war.[55]

The prevailing pro-Soviet mood obscured this truth for a time and even after Bevin emphasized that the Labour members of the coalition had played a full part in the Government's decision to invade Greece in December 1944 the Labour Left continued to think of this act of aggression as Churchill's policy. The party leader's long involvement in the War Cabinet obviously served to strengthen their patriotic sentiments and drew them tighter in the net of pragmatism and conventional assumptions concerning problems of government and administration, but they did not start from a radical base in the first place. Thus it would appear that whatever else was in doubt by 1945 – the extent of Labour's future reforming programme should it gain office, the degree of popular support for radical change, the solvency of the country, its relationship with the USA and the Soviet Union – nobody in the party leadership questioned Britain's Great Power status and the maintenance of the Empire on which it was based.

Clearly if the entire party leadership expected Britain to resume its global, imperial role once the war was over the problem of managing this gigantic enterprise would go a long way in determining Labour's foreign allies and

friends as well as setting limits on the extent of its domestic reform programme. Disturbing influences in the international arena such as nationalist
movements, the spread of communism and other radical forces, would necessarily alarm the party policy-makers if such forces affected Britain's over-
extended sphere of influence. Men like Bevin, Attlee, Morrison and Dalton
had always been staunch anti-Communists anyway, as their dealings with the
CPGB illustrate; and as early as January 1942, according to one detailed
study of the period, Bevin and Attlee 'had emphatically demonstrated their
basic distrust of Soviet ambitions in Eastern Europe'.[56] Buoyed up by popular, pro-Soviet sentiments, much of the Left nevertheless wanted to believe
that a Labour government could work with the USSR to strengthen socialism
throughout Europe. Soviet policy, however, was guided by its own security
interests and since these could not be guaranteed to coincide with socialist
internationalism such a compact was never a realistic possibility, even had the
Labour leadership desired it.

On domestic policy a consensus emerged during the way years over the need
to maintain full employment and create a welfare state. Differences
remained, of course, over the extent and duration of state intervention, but
already by 1937 Labour's reform programme had jettisoned the more radical
public ownership proposals adopted in reaction to the trauma of 1931. Advocates of economic planning could be found in all the political parties and on
both sides of industry before the war began, but 'middle opinion' on this
subject amounted to a belief in a limited publicly owned sector and the provision of statistical information by the state to indicate certain desirable economic targets to the private sector. The war itself required massive state
intervention, notably in the form of physical controls, and enabled advocates
of planning and Keynesianism to enter government and administration. By
1944 Attlee was able to talk as if the old Fabian strategy of permeation had
worked and the governing elite had actually been won over to socialism, or at
least to a major step in that direction: 'I have now witnessed the acceptance by
all the leading politicians in the country of the conception of the utilisation of
abundance . . . It colours all our discussions on home economic policy. There
follows from this the doctrine of employment . . .'.[57] Given such a perception
of consensus it is easier to understand why Labour left the established power
structures in British society undisturbed after 1945.

11

Welfare and Cold War

English Socialism's 'blissful dawn', as Michael Foot described Labour's land-slide victory in the 1945 general election,[1] was anticipated by only a minority of socialists including Nye Bevan, and, less conspicuously, the tiny Revolutionary Communist Party in which Britain's Trotskyists were now organized. The CPGB was so enamoured of the 'progressive unity' embodied in the wartime alliance of the Big Three that it looked forward to a continuation of the coalition at home. In April 1945 R. Palme Dutt had warned that 'it would be dangerously unrealistic for the labour movement and progressive opinion to dismiss idly and without consideration the need for a National Government in the transition years following victory in Europe.'[2] Dutt's opinion invariably reflected the Moscow line and so this argument is significant both as an expression of the wider Communist policy in Europe as well as an indication of a local pessimism concerning the prospects for an independent Labour victory. In fact when the war ended Communists used their powerful influence in countries such as Italy and France to promote 'national unity' and there is evidence that where they pursued revolutionary objectives – as in Yugoslavia, China and Greece – they did so contrary to Stalin's policy.[3]

The drift of the CPGB's thinking in Britain can also be gauged from Harry Pollitt's *Looking Ahead* which was published in 1947. For the first time British Communists specifically repudiated the idea that the October Revolution was the model for socialist transition and asserted that: 'The progress of democratic and Socialist forces throughout the world has opened up new possibilities of transition to Socialism by other paths than those followed by the Russian Revolution. The path . . . is necessarily different for each country.'[4] In particular, Pollitt, in common with other European Communist leaders, argued that it was 'possible to see how the people will move towards Socialism without further revolution'. He added, however, the novel observation that this could be achieved 'without the dictatorship of the proletariat'.[5] The French Communist Party had to wait until the 1970s before they could dispense with this formula and then only after an acrimonious row which the CPGB had been able to avoid altogether. Pollitt's thoughts had not yet crystallized into a new programme – that had to wait until 1951 when *The British Road to Socialism* was published – but there is no doubt that the Popular Front idea was very much in Communist minds as the war ended and in Communist practice on the European continent when the first post-war governments were formed. All this helps to explain the CPGB's enthusiasm for the Churchill coalition. The shock which was felt by many on the Left when Labour actually won the 1945 election also suggests that there had been widespread pessimism about Labour's chances of gaining power independently and this may have entered calculations about the wisdom of breaking free from the Conservatives. When the decision was taken, however, leading Left-wingers in the party were enthusiastic about the coming struggle.

Bevan described the general election as 'a real struggle for power . . . between Big Business and the People'[6], but although the Left of the Labour Party campaigned as if the election would settle the question of who was to control the wealth of the country and in whose interests, the campaign overall has been described as 'a quiet contest, perhaps the most tranquil of the century'.[7] The result, however, was undoubtedly dramatic with Labour winning 393 seats out of a total of 640 based on 47.8 per cent of the vote against a Conservative share of 39.8 per cent. For the first time the Labour Party had won the parliamentary majority which its supporters envisaged as the beginning of the socialist reconstruction of Britain. Central to this project was the idea of public ownership of industry.

Organized labour's nationalization proposals can be traced back to the 1880s, as has been shown. By 1900 the Miners' Federation had committed itself to a policy of 'the mines for the miners' while still supporting the Liberal Party. In 1906 the Labour Party and the TUC adopted the goal of nationalization of mines and railways, but the purpose and method of public ownership, as well as its extent, remained unclear throughout the 1920s, and as late as 1929 it was possible for Labour to fight a general election campaign without public ownership proposals. Meanwhile socialist thinkers like R. H. Tawney had already learned to regard nationalization as a means to socialist ends such as equality and not an end in itself. The theorists had also stressed the variety of forms which public ownership could take ranging from co-operatives, municipal undertakings, the purchase of shares in private firms by the state, and arrangements which would secure varying measures of workers' control and participation. When planning came into vogue in the 1930s public ownership acquired an added dimension and under pressure from Soviet experience and the crisis in private enterprise the Labour Party evolved its *Immediate Programme* (1937), which outlined a list of industries and services to be brought under state control.

During the 1930s Dalton, Attlee and Morrison were among those who talked about public ownership as if it was the end of socialism. In *Practical Socialism For Britain* Dalton argued that 'the degree to which any particular society was socialist [is] broadly measured by how far its economic life was socialised.'[8] Similar arguments were put by Morrison in *Socialism and*

Transport (1933) and by Attlee in *The Labour Party in Perspective* (1937). The influence of Stalin's Russia at this time has already been discussed, but it is worth noting that even a moderate such as Dalton could refer to the Soviet Union as a 'living example of a Planned Socialist Economy'.[9] This was the ideological context in which Morrison's bureaucratic conception of public ownership came to be embraced by the Labour Party. As Minister of Transport in MacDonald's second government Morrison had championed a bill which intended to create a public authority to run London transport by a Board of Managers. This scheme excluded trade union representation, let alone the more radical visions of workers' participation. Though Morrison's bill was never enacted a similar measure was carried by the National Government in 1933, the same year in which Morrison argued that this form of nationalization should be a paradigm for all future public ownership schemes. In 1944 the TUC General Council confirmed its acceptance of this argument in its *Interim Report on Reconstruction* and even Leftists such as Laski and Cole embraced the model in the absence of trade union pressure for workers' control.

By the time *Let Us Face the Future* (1945) was adopted, however, the list of industries which had been considered ripe for nationalization in 1937 had shrunk. Thus the party campaigned on a programme which made no mention of manufacturing and which excluded land, joint-stock banking, machine tools and cotton-spinning, all of which had figured before the war as objects of nationalization. In fact the younger economists in the party – above all Jay, Durbin and Gaitskell – had been concerned to downplay 'socialization', as it was commonly termed, even in the 1930s.[10] And although the Executive's Reconstruction Committee had recommended the nationalization of gas, electricity, coal and transport during the war no specific nationalization proposals (except for the Bank of England) were put before the party when it debated economic policy at its annual conference in December 1944. It seems evident that the party leaders could envisage the reconstruction of Britain's war-torn economy without giving detailed attention to the public ownership issue. The 1944 conference nevertheless carried a composite resolution moved by Ian Mikardo which called for public ownership of all forms of banking, transport, fuel and power as well as land, building and heavy industry. It became clear, however, when *Let Us Face the Future* was debated the following year, that the case for nationalization was to be confined to certain basic industries which could be held to have 'failed the nation'. In posing public ownership in strictly technical and utilitarian terms rather than presenting it as an element in a much broader socialist case against private enterprise, the party leaders signalled their doubts and also gave hostages to fortune. Henceforward Labour's opponents could dwell on the inefficiency of the nationalized industries as measured in profit and loss as proof of the undesirability of public ownership *per se*. The bureaucratic form of nationalization was unpopular well before the end of the government's life, moreover, though Attlee himself seems not to have seen the connection between this and the failure of state ownership to inspire public service ideals, which he later described as his biggest disappointment. How could the workers be expected 'to respond to the philosophy of public ownership' when it was articulated in such a statist and managerialist form?[11]

Planning was another area of economic policy associated with the Labour Party in which there was more sentiment than coherent thinking and commitment. Labour's nationalization proposals were not originally conceived as aids to planning but rather as extensions of democracy. By the 1920s planning was associated with attempts to organize capitalism and did not figure as a central feature of socialist ideology in Britain until after 1931. Soviet experience above all else influenced the Labour Left and even the party leaders to regard the extension of the state in the name of industrial efficiency, output and growth as a desirable objective. The experience of a war economy in which physical control planning was widespread might be expected to have reinforced these technocratic proclivities. If so, it raises the issue of why planning did not feature in either the party's programme or in its six years of office after 1945. After all, Labour inherited an economy in dire straits.

Although the first meeting of the United Nations described war damage in the UK as negligible, the war effort cost Britain £1,118,000,000 in foreign assets and accumulated debts of £2,723,000,000. In total Britain lost a quarter of its wealth in fighting the war. Right from the outset, moreover, the USA exploited these circumstances to ensure more favourable trading and military arrangements for itself. One of the conditions of Lend-Lease in February 1942 had been the 'elimination of all forms of discriminatory treatment in international commerce' – a measure intended to undermine the Empire as a protected trading bloc.[12] The Americans used their superior bargaining position to obtain military bases from Britain even before the USA itself entered the war. No sooner had the war against Japan ended than President Truman abruptly terminated Lend-lease – thus giving another demonstration of what the special relationship really meant. This forced the Labour government to negotiate a loan of $3.75 billion in the winter of 1945.

Those who imagined that the 'special relationship' might enable Britain to secure a gift from the USA – or at the very least an interest-free loan – were rudely disappointed. Not only was the loan payable at 2 per cent interest, but the Americans also swept Keynes's objections aside and insisted on the need for sterling convertibility and their intolerance of any discriminatory import quotas against US goods. Meanwhile American firms had used the war to encroach on British markets in South America and the Middle East. The Middle East was of particular concern since Britain had always used its imperial hegemony in the area to monopolize the oil reserves. By 1946, however, the American oil companies, with government backing, were able to break off their pre-war production and marketing arrangements with Britain. The US share of Middle Eastern oil output had already increased during the war from 16 to 31 per cent; by 1953 it stood at 60 per cent.

The vast American economy – which was producing three quarters of the

world's manufactured goods by 1945 – needed free trade if it was to secure
the growth in international trade essential to the attainment of full employment and prosperity at home. American policy-makers necessarily took a dim
view of the British Empire and were alarmed by those who imagined a sterling
area extended to include Africa, the Middle East and Western Europe as well
as the Dominions, for this bloc could be self-sufficient and protectionist.[13]
Instead the US loan negotiators expected the UK to ratify the 1944 Bretton
Woods agreements for an International Monetary Fund and a World Bank
before the end of 1945. These institutions were part of an American plan,
which included the General Agreement on Tariffs and Trade (GATT) ratified
in the spring of 1947, for an open-access world economy. Within the Labour
Cabinet, Shinwell and Bevan protested that the conditions attached to the
American loan were designed to break up the Sterling Area and were, in
Shinwell's words, 'incompatible with the successful operation of a planned
economy in this country and would ruin our export trade'.[14] But these were
only token protests. Britain was in no position to resist these terms and no one
seriously contemplated defying American policy by opting for autarky.

Where the Labour government was successful, as we shall see, was in
helping to persuade the US government that the survival of the British Empire
– Commonwealth was vital to its own interests. And it solved the balance of
payments crisis which inexorably followed the return to sterling convert-
ability by encouraging a massive increase in exports coupled with greater
austerity at home. There is no doubting the appalling economic circumstances
which Labour had to contend with during its six years in office. Nevertheless,
most comparable economies were temporarily in even worse condition and
this is no doubt why it was possible to increase British exports by 1949 to a
level more than 150 per cent above that of 1938. But despite the fact that the
war had brutally exposed the deficiencies of British manufacturing – by 1941
Britain was totally dependent on America for over twenty types of advanced
machine tool, for example[15] there was no plan produced during Labour's term
of office which even addressed this problem.

This deficiency may have been connected to the perception – which was
challenged by not one significant figure in public life – that, far from being
weak, Britain remained a Great Power, indeed one of the Big Three. It was the
Empire – Commonwealth which sustained this illusion. But after an initial
turn to the Left following MacDonald's defection in 1931, Labour's planning
aspirations had been in retreat in any case. Banking (except for the Bank of
England) and machine tools had been dropped from the nationalization
agenda by the time *Labour's Immediate Programme* was published in 1937.
And the scope of nationalization narrowed so did its rationale. By 1945 the
Fabian preoccupation with 'efficiency' was the principle invoked to justify
public ownership and the corporate model associated with Morrison seemed
best suited to achieve it. Thus the measures of public control actually taken
were essentially technical and institutional: not only were relations within the
nationalized industries left the same, but so was their *modus operandi*. There

was to be no reorientation, for example, of the financial system, through the nationalized Bank of England. All the talk concerning a National Investment Bank – which was originally mobilized to show that there was no need to nationalize the joint-stock banks – simply evaporated. The nebulous reference in *Let Us Face the Future* to the need for a 'plan from the ground up' resulted in nothing more than retention of the war controls which even the Tories saw as necessary for dealing with shortages and controlling personal consumption. These achieved some control over prices, as intended, but that is all.[16]

Finance and economic planning, insofar as the latter existed at all, occupied separate compartments in Chancellor Dalton's mind. It was thus possible for Tory planners such as Robert Boothby to berate Labour for evading the need for investment controls. But the drift of the government was to reduce the level of economic control after 1947 – a process which culminated in Harold Wilson's 'bonfire of controls' in November 1948. When the Conservatives returned to government in 1951 they were obliged to increase these controls, so successful had Labour been in dispensing with them. The Labour government had directed planning to strictly short-term objectives such as improving the balance of payments. As Andrew Shonfield later argued, once 'the pressure of particular shortages was removed so the overall view of national economic objectives was discarded'.[17] At no time in the 1930s, however, had the party conceived of planning as anything more than a corrective to the market.[18] The role of the state in Labour's policy pronouncements was correspondingly confined to a vague utilitarianism. The party never elaborated plans for industrial reconstruction, not even in the name of national efficiency. With the growth in influence of Labour's Keynesians it was all the easier for the leadership to believe that its economic objectives could be achieved without the need for national plans.

The war had seen a great deal of planning, however, in specific areas of social policy. The sheer inefficiency from a national angle of ill-health, poverty and unemployment was graphically revealed. Deficiencies were exposed in existing arrangements for health care, education, the alleviation of poverty, the provision and quality of housing and so on. Beveridge denounced want as 'a needless scandal' and assumed that a comprehensive system of social insurance would be predicated on full employment, family allowances and a universal health scheme. By 1944 a Government White Paper on *A National Health Service* was preparing 'a comprehensive cover for health provided for all people alike', but it was left to the Labour government to implement the scheme with only slight modifications. Bevan introduced the National Health Service Bill in 1946, but his battle to see the system accepted by the doctors continued up to and beyond the 'appointed day' in July 1948 when the service began. More than any other measures the new health system seemed to embody values which challenged and undermined the capitalist principles of profit and 'effective demand'. With Bevan steering the health service in against obstructions from vested interests and in the face of accusations of profligacy the Labour Left were all the more disposed to regard the new Welfare State as 'the envy of the civilized World' and a large step taken towards socialism. Even now it seems remarkable that these reforms were introduced at a time of appalling economic problems and it is testimony to the character and strength of the war-generated radicalism that they were taken at all.

Probably the worst year for the government was 1947. It was a year of sterling crises, balance of payments problems and shortages in almost every basic resource. Already the government was running out of ideas and inspiration. In May Richard Crossman, Michael Foot and Ian Mikardo published *Keep Left*, which urged the government to extend nationalization to 'embrace every industry' which either exercised 'a hold over our national economy' – chemicals and insurance were cited as examples – 'or which cannot be made efficient in private hands', such as iron and steel, cars and electrical components.[19] The authors saw the nationalization of steel, about which there were considerable doubts in the Cabinet, as proof of the government's resolve 'not to be content with half-measures in the renovation of British industry'. Thus the *Tribune* Left was inclined to see nationalization as the high road to economic renewal, which (in the case of steel) 'will incidentally [sic] involve a challenge to the citadel of capitalist power in this country'.[20]

Keep Left paid tribute to the Labour government's achievements, which it saw as a first step towards socialism, but argued that much sterner measures were required if it was to survive the economic crises and sustain its reforms. A Ministry of Economic Affairs was required to plan the economy; the 'Battle of Production' was of heroic dimensions and had to be fought with sweeping powers over the deployment of labour, the allocation of raw materials and the control of what was to be produced; distributed profits were to be taxed at punitive rates. The pamphlet also referred to a 'wholehearted extension of industrial democracy', but Crossman and his co-authors thought that this could be achieved by joint production committees, compulsorily introduced by Act of Parliament into all but the smallest establishments, which would function as conveyors of 'decisions reached by the Government in top-level consultation with the Federation of British Industries and the Trades Union Congress'.[21]

These corporatist proposals were part of a larger conception of planning which had few active supporters in the government. But they also reflect more widespread centralist and bureaucratic dispositions in the government. Within the parliamentary party there was no real discontent with the government's domestic programme. Foreign relations were a different matter, however, though even here strong dissent was never broad enough to seriously trouble the government's majority. And yet the foreign policy which Bevin pursued was indistinguishable from Churchill's and the Conservatives occasionally took the trouble to tell him so across the floor of the House of Commons. It was a policy which took as axiomatic Britain's Great Power status (indeed Bevin was deluded enough to think that of the Big Three,

Britain was the biggest). Accordingly British influence was to be preserved in
Greece and the eastern Mediterranean, in the Middle East, in Africa and Asia.
Thus while the American army demobilized so rapidly that by the beginning
of 1947 it had shrunk from 8 to 1 million men, the British, though faced with
acute labour shortages at home, maintained a somewhat greater force
throughout the Empire and its associated spheres of influence. Britain's military establishment represented 18.7 per cent of available manpower, while
defence expenditure was 18.8 per cent of National Income; the comparable
figures for the USA were 10 and 10.6 per cent respectively.[22] From the
moment the last shots of the Second World War were fired, indeed even
before the anti-fascist struggle had finished, the British army was already
engaged in another war. In Greece and Vietnam and Malaya, Communists
were prominent in the national liberation movements which the British army
was trying to repress. In fact nationalist sentiments had been aroused
throughout Asia by the World War and were bound to challenge the old
colonial powers. *Keep Left* wondered how British imperialism could be sustained in the face of Britain's obvious bankruptcy, and answered its own
question by suggesting that attempts were being made to manipulate American fears of Russian aggression in order to bolster up the British Empire.[23]

This, according to Crossman, Foot and Mikardo, was the meaning of
Churchill's Fulton speech:

> he believes that America can be persuaded to assist Britain with loans
> and to provide most of the capital for the reconstruction of Western
> Europe and for the development of such valuable resources as the oil of
> the Middle East.[24]

American policy-makers were already committed to this view, *Keep Left*
claimed, but had yet to persuade the American electorate to tolerate a continuation of the war. Communism was an actual threat to the *status quo* in
Greece, China, Indonesia. Vietnam and Malaya. It was a potential problem in
France and Italy, which emerged from the war with discredited elites and mass
Communist parties. But in all these cases Communist influence derived from
local factors and represented the aspirations of a sizeable proportion of the
people. For communism to be seen as a bogey by small-town America it had to
be represented as synonymous with the alleged expansionist ambitions of the
Stalin regime.

Well before Russian coercion in Eastern Europe could provide evidence to
support this analysis of Soviet strategy – the statisation of the economies
under Red Army occupation and the formation of the Cominform in 1947
were of this order – Bevin's policy was firmly anti-Communist and pro-
American. Right from August 1945 the Labour government sought to promote a special relationship with the USA. It has been argued that

> The British people might have wanted to turn inwards but the newly-
> elected Labour government fought to sustain Britain's role as a world

power and despite the economic difficulties, to ensure that it was the pax Americana that replaced the pax Britannia and not a world dominated by Russian communism.[25]

As early as May 1944 the American Joint Chiefs of Staff predicted that the British Empire would not have the strength to withstand the threat posed by communism and after the war advocated 'all feasible political, economic and if necessary military support' to maintain Britain as the principal power in Western Europe.[26]

There were, however, other voices in the USA. There was pressure for rapid demobilization once the war was over; for example, in the summer of 1945 US troops staged mass demonstrations in Germany and Italy demanding to be sent home immediately. Neither Congress nor American public opinion was initially prepared to finance a huge military establishment into the indefinite future. There was even confident speculation that America did not need such huge forces now that the country possessed a monopoly of nuclear weapons.[27] In addition, as has already been noted, some American policy-makers saw the British Empire as an obstacle to their grand design of an open global economy. But none of this signalled a possible retreat into isolationism. The British Foreign Office was perfectly aware of American expansionism and had been on the receiving end of it from the moment war began. But Britain's insolvency forced it to enlist American help in securing the survival of the Empire – Commonwealth. The USA was the only possible candidate for this role, if only because the end of the war 'found the United States occupying, controlling or exerting strong influence in four of the five major industrial areas of the world'.[28] Only the Soviet Union operated outside the American orbit.

America was the dominant power in East Asia and its Pacific approaches, but as Bevin's biographer Alan Bullock points out, 'Southern and South East Asia were a different story.' Here was the heart of European colonialism where Japanese victories in the earlier phase of the war had helped to undermine the myth of European infallibility and stimulate national liberation movements. In this region, 'the one course that was not discussed was for Britain to withdraw from Asia altogether and make no effort to reoccupy the countries she had previously ruled.'[29] On India alone was there a fairly clear Labour commitment to withdraw, although even here the motive and intention, as Attlee told Cripps in 1942, was that a self-governing India would be 'saved for the British Empire'.[30] For Attlee and Bevin, Indian independence within the Commonwealth was compatible with the preservation of London as the directing centre of a force whose resources would be at Britain's disposal in times of crisis and even in peacetime so far as the South Asian possessions were concerned. It was also envisaged that India would remain in the Sterling Area and the Ottawa system of preferential tariffs. In the event the actual settlement with India was rather different, of course, because of Britain's feeble negotiating position. Even so, as late as the summer of 1948

Bevin was complaining that General Wavell's 'Breakdown Plan' for withdrawal from India was 'defeatist', and the Foreign Secretary asked Attlee to
abandon the policy. In reply the Labour Prime Minister was forced to ask
Bevin if he was 'prepared to take a strong hand in India' and 'put in enough
troops to enforce our rule' – policies which would 'go back on pledges that
have been given by Governments of every political colour'.[31] Bevin was forced
to back down but it is highly instructive that he could seriously contemplate
enforcing a different settlement on India in the face of American support
for independence and Britain's chronic manpower shortages and financial
insolvency.

However, Labour's 'almost fanatical promotion of the Commonwealth',
as D. K. Fieldhouse calls it, was based on the perception that 'the Empire and
Commonwealth seemed essential to the survival of Britain and to her position
as a world power.'[32] This was indeed Attlee's 'primary policy objective':

> the whole approach to the future of Palestine, Egypt, the Italian posses-
> sions in North and North-East Africa, British East Africa and territo-
> ries in South and South East Asia was based on the assumption that
> Britain must have sufficient strategic bases and committed allies to
> enable her to maintain her role East of Suez in competition with Russian
> and America.[33]

Yet this was a country, it will be recalled, which had been bankrupted by the
war. The institutions of imperialism were expected, however, to benefit
Britain materially; Bevin even told the House of Commons that the standard
of living of British workers depended on their survival. Certainly the Sterling
Area had been used during the war to deprive net dollar earners such as the
Gold Coast and Malaya of this purchasing power so that Britain could use the
dollar surpluses to buy American arms and goods; in exchange for these
scarce dollars the countries concerned were credited with sterling balances
which they could not use. This was simply a device to facilitate compulsory
lending to Britain at low interest rates. The expectation that such imperialist
devices would survive the war was more than vindicated: 'The basic fact is
that between 1945 and 1951 Britain exploited those dependencies that were
politically unable to defend their own interests in more ways and with
more serious consequences that at any time since overseas colonies were
established.'[34]

The Sterling Area survived America's early attempt to destroy it when full
convertibility had to be abandoned in 1947. Britain was able to continue to
control colonial trade by means of licensing and by rationing shipping space.
The principal colonial exports were absorbed by Britain which as a
monopsonist was able to fix prices in London. A system of marketing boards
within the colonies was established to enforce this monopsony. The same
countries, however, were starved of investment capital; while the colonies
received £40 million in one way or another from Britain, 'they were forced to
lend or tie up in London about £250 M.'[35] Although many of these countries

were creditors in relation to Britain they were not allowed many of the goods they needed because the government needed dollars and could only get them by exporting to the USA:

> Few things did more to discredit Britain in colonial eyes and it is now a commonplace that much of the political unrest in West Africa that led ultimately to the growth of nationalist parties stemmed from nothing more fundamental than a prolonged shortage of consumer goods coupled with a price inflation that reflected this artificial shortage.[36]

In short, the Labour government used the colonies to protect Britain from the full cost of post-war reconstruction. This was social imperialism as classically defined. No wonder Transport House appointed a Colonial Assistant to its International Department in 1949 whose task was to help with the increasing number of students coming from the colonies and 'to prevent these potential national leaders from falling into the hands of the Communist Party'.[37]

Nationalism was the main threat to the Empire–Commonwealth but when communism and nationalism came together they were capable of upsetting more than just the colonial *status quo*. Nothing could be more detrimental to the American goal of international 'free trade' than the economic autarky which held sway in Moscow and which the nationalist movements might seek to emulate. Here was a powerful reason for the USA to see the utility of helping to keep Britain and its colonial possessions afloat. Events in Eastern Europe helped to make the Soviet threat more tangible even though Western governments were well informed as to the extent of the devastation experienced by the Russians during the war. Though it was never credible to depict Soviet behaviour in Eastern Europe as proof of a master plan for Communist domination, the CP monopoly was achieved by 'a succession of manoeuvres, strategems and tricks which in the end fell into the pattern of a revolution but which in themselves were petty and wicked'.[38] George Kennan, who helped to construct US policy after the war, later claimed that 'the image of a Stalinist Russia poised and yearning to attack the West and deterred only by our possession of atomic weapons was largely a question of the Western imagination.'[39] But this is disingenuous; Labour Britain conspired with Truman's America to create that image: 'Moves to consolidate Soviet power in Eastern Europe instead of being seen just as power politics as usual were presented as the retreat of democracy and the advance of communism; seen in these terms there could be no certainty as to where the advance would stop.'[40]

It was noticed during the loan negotiations which the British were forced to conduct with the Americans at the end of 1945 that anti-British talk was apt to abate in Washington as fear and suspicion of the Russians grew. Churchill's Fulton speech in March 1946 helped this process along nicely, for by the summer 'speaker after speaker in the House of Representatives announced his support for the loan as a measure connected with the problem of combating the spread of Soviet ideology.'[41] The British were well placed, given their global possessions, to keep the Americans on their toes on this matter. Faced with Communist insurgency in Malaya, for example, Bevin's friend and co-thinker Anthony Eden, Churchill's future successor as leader of the Conservative Party, told the House of Commons in September 1947:

> What we are faced with is a determined Communist attempt to seize power, an attempt which is integrated with the Communist insurrection in Burma and with Communist activities across the border in Siam. It is all of a pattern . . . and has as its objective the overthrow of law and order throughout South Eastern Asia . . . and as a result the complete disruption of the economy of that area.'[42]

Ironically Eden's Parliamentary Private Secretary, Sir Oliver Harvey, complained during the war that no one except Eden would stand up to Churchill's anti-communism in Cabinet, 'not even the Labour Ministers who are as prejudiced as the PM against the Soviets because of their hatred and fear of the Communists at home'.[43] As we have seen, the CPGB certainly used the popularity of the Grand Alliance for the purpose of a renewed campaign for affiliation to the Labour Party, and Pelling tells us that as late as the annual conference of 1946 'Ministers had been principally worried about the possibility of the massive card vote of the unions committing the party to accept the affiliation of the Communist Party.'[44]

This was yet more Scotch mist as it transpired; the Communists had few supporters outside the AEU, NUR and Fire Brigades Union. But the trade union anti-Communists – led by Bevin himself of course – were ready to take the offensive. While Bevin treated the USSR as if it was a truculent and disobedient section of the Transport and General Workers' Union (TGWU), his allies in the TUC did what they could to rally union support behind his anti-Communist foreign policy. Citrine, for example, led the commission of inquiry concerned with atrocities in Greece and his report – which focused one-sidedly on stories implicating ELAS – 'played a major part in turning around so much of press opinion and reassuring it of the ultimate benevolence of British purposes in Greece'.[45] Citrine also resisted the creation in 1945 of a World Federation of Trade Unions which included the Soviet 'unions'. By 1947 the WFTU was under attack at the TUC as a Communist front as the British trade union leadership drew closer to the American Federation of Labour which was engaged in well-financed attempts to split the unions along ideological lines in Europe and Latin America.[46] Increasingly the price of anti-communism, as the Left predicted during the war, was alignment with reaction and even as the British unions began to purge themselves of Communists, the American Congress was engaged in passing anti-trade union legislation in the form of the Hartley and Taft Bills.

Tribune at first took the view that Communist bahaviour in Eastern Europe, although often atrocious, was no more atrocious than British behaviour in Greece, and rightly suspected a *quid pro quo* arrangement and the division of Europe into spheres of influence.[47] By 1947 *Keep Left* predicted that the USA would seek a system of forward defences against Russia, especially in Japan, Britain, Greece (where US forces replaced the impecunious British), Turkey and the Middle East. Collective security against Communism would inevitably mean American 'dollar loans to prop-up anti-Communist regimes around her frontiers'. It assumed 'an unbridgeable gulf between Western and Eastern Powers' and 'ruin for Europe divided into rival spheres of influence'. The Russians, in this view, would go on the defensive until their own scientists produced enough atomic bombs to redress the balance of military power and then the danger of a third world war would loom. Real democracy would perish in any case, 'squeezed out between the rival blocs', and in the cause of anti-communism Britain would end up supporting odious regimes, whether 'in Spain or in Northern Ireland, in the southern states of America or in the Union of South Africa'. (In fact when South Africa adopted apartheid in 1948 it declared itself in 'complete agreement' with Labour's foreign objectives and was allowed to remain in the Commonwealth.) Greece also proved *Keep Left's* argument that 'totalitarian methods are not the monopoly of Communists': 'By accepting the American lead in a world alliance against Russia we shall merely ensure that every small people has to choose between the bleak alternatives of anti-Communism and Communism. We shall sharpen the conflict instead of leading it . . .'[48]

This had been a consistent refrain on the Left since the war years; Crossman even moved an amendment to the King's Speech in 1945 hoping that the government would 'provide a democratic and constructive Socialist alternative to an otherwise inevitable conflict between American Capitalism and Soviet Communism'. While Bevin talked of the dangers of a return to US isolationism the Left confidently referred to 'the beginning of that policy of economic world domination' which the Americans were ready to use 'unscrupulously in [their] bargaining for free access to all world markets'.[49] The British Left in these years was inclined, however, to downplay the extent to which the Labour government itself was actively pursuing an imperialist and anti-Communist policy and tended instead to blame Churchill, Bevin and the Americans. *Keep Left* ludicrously invoked the government's crisis management in India, Indonesia, Burma and Malaya to illustrate the positive side of its policy. But at least it recognized that 'Britain's financial supremacy has gone for good' and that the country was 'no longer defensible in a major war'. From these insights it deduced the need to recognize that 'we British have become Europeans whose prosperity and security depend on that of the rest of Europe.' The Empire was 'a strategic anachronism' and proper defence now depended on a European Security Pact, withdrawal from the Middle East, international agreements on arms inspections and renunciation of the manufacture and use of nuclear weapons.[50]

Keep Left's analysis was undoubtedly informed by President Truman's pledge, delivered in March 1947, to contain communism and defend 'democracy'. The Labour leadership, however, responded warmly to the Truman Doctrine, for it signalled the long-sought-after American involvement in British plans for defending the *status quo*. The editors of *Reynolds News* on the other hand saw that Truman had made 'clear beyond any shadow of doubt that the men who rule America are determined to go to any length to stop the development of Socialism and to open up the world as a vast colonial area for American capitalism'.[51] Crossman and Foot took the same view, with the latter describing America's anti-Red frenzy as 'a roaring hymn of hate towards all things Russian'.[52] But within weeks of the publication of *Keep Left, Tribune* was won over to Truman's scheme of things by the announcement of the American plan to rescue the European economy. Foot described the Marshall Plan, which was first floated on 5 June 1947, as an 'offer of a fresh start ... in the work of bringing sustenance to the hunger-stricken peoples of this tragic post-war epoch' and declared that 'if the Russians ... contract out, then they alone will be the architects of a divided Europe.' While a tiny minority of socialists, such as Fenner Brockway and Konni Zilliacus, saw the European Recovery Plan as inextricably connected to American interests and designed to exclude the USSR, Foot used *Tribune* to enthuse that it meant that 'the rebuilding of Europe' could now take place 'with American aid but along socialist lines'.[53]

Most of the Labour Left simply looked on Marshall Aid as the means for financing Labour's domestic programme and dropped their critique of the Bevin – Truman policy. *Tribune* now projected Truman as a progressive force in world politics hampered by reactionary and isolationist elements in Congress. His anti-Communist rhetoric was now described as a mere device to overcome the 'self-interest, political indifference, misinterpretation and ignorance' within Congress which would otherwise stand in the way of a humane policy – the Marshall Plan.[54] On 2 August 1947 the USSR rejected Marshall Aid and the following October launched the Cominform. From then until the early 1950s there was little to choose between *Tribune* and the Labour leadership concerning the nature of the Soviet Union and communism.

The Communists attacked Marshall Aid on the grounds that its 'military and political purpose ... is to weld Western Europe into a war bloc'. They also referred to 'the Marshall Standard of Life' and argued that the American scheme would increase the exploitation of British workers.[55] Now was the time for industrial militancy to resist this onslaught, according to CP propaganda. Communist opposition to Marshall Aid – which was hailed as the saviour of the British economy by most of the Labour Party and trade unions – was an excuse to intensify the anti-Communist campaign in the unions. Communists were now seen behind every grievance in British industry just as Bevin detected them in every attempt to disturb the international *status quo*.[56] This practice soon made it routine to identify criticism of Labour policy as Communist, Communist-inspired, or playing into the hands of the Communists. *Tribune* itself used this type of 'argument' when its editor-in-chief Michael Foot backed Truman against Wallace in the 1948 Presidential elections, explaining that the latter was a dupe of the Communists. In Britain Communists were forcibly removed from elected positions in some of the unions – nine were ejected from the TGWU's thirty-four strong executive council, for example – as well as the TUC General Council.

When Bevin launched the idea of a 'Western Union' on 22 January 1948 in a Commons speech employing terms virtually identical to those contained in Churchill's 'iron curtain' peroration, *Tribune*, forgetting all its earlier predictions of a two-camp world, concluded that: 'Thanks to the Marshall Plan and the possibilities of a Western Union there is still a chance . . . that Britain can pursue a policy which offers something more than a mere negative containment of Soviet expansion and an eventual military showdown in alliance with America.'[57] When this policy led to the formation of NATO in 1949 *Tribune* welcomed the pact. The intervening months had witnessed increased tension in relations with the USSR as Stalin consolidated the Russian dominance of Eastern Europe. *Tribune* went along with the conventional wisdom of Anglo-American policy-makers in seeing the Prague *coup* of February 1948 as another step in the systematic encroachment of Soviet totalitarianism on democracy. It warned that the Communists 'cannot be appeased by any number of concessions'[58] and denounced critics of British and American policy like Zilliacus for 'ludicrous distortions of [its] true character', despite the fact that these criticisms were identical to the arguments promoted by *Keep Left*.[59] Under the dramatic heading *The New Apocalypse* the editors invoked Heinrich Heine's prophecy to the effect that 'the future smells of Russian leather, blood, godlessness and many whippings' to explain why Eastern Europe 'is besieged by doubts and fears. It trembles before the spectacle of Russian power and is inhibited from action by the strength of internal Fifth Columns.'[60]

Although *Tribune* occasionally argued that democratic socialism was the only effective barrier to communism there was no disguising the fact that it saw the future in terms of an alignment between democratic socialism and such 'enlightened democrats' as Truman. Russia, on the other hand, was perceived as the main threat of war for which the only antidote was an emphatic assertion of the West's 'will to resist'[61] Under the impact of the Communist offensive against socialists in Eastern Europe during 1948 *Tribune* even applauded the Italian voters who, when faced with a choice between 'a Communist dictatorship or a clericalist-dominated Coalition with little or no idea of the radical measures needed to rebuild the country', chose the latter.[62]

With *Tribune's* critical faculties in such poor condition the Left's alternative foreign policy necessarily lost such coherence as it originally possessed. The Prague *coup* finally destroyed the remnants of wartime faith in the Popular Front which lingered on in the minds of its most fervent supporters such as Kingsley Martin. Only Zilliacus continued to believe in the necessity for a Popular Front if socialism was to be built in Europe, but the pages of *Tribune* and the *New Statesman* were closed to him. This was a pity, because although he was naive about the Soviet Union's interest in such an arrangement he never pretended (as *Tribune* did) that Marshall Aid could be accepted without also accepting the lead of American foreign policy. And it was certainly arguable that Russian policy in Eastern Europe made a 'third force' in world affairs more, not less, necessary if a bipolar freeze in international relations was to be avoided, since as *Keep Left* had argued: 'The way to make it certain that democratic Socialism can never be achieved in Eastern Europe is to superimpose on the class struggle the struggle of the Great Powers – the Anglo-Americans supporting the Right and Russia the Left.'[63] While it is true that the nature and composition of this 'third force' varied from one Left faction to another, the Attlee government never gave the idea serious consideration because it was fastened to the Empire–Commonwealth alternative. In practice this meant subordinating British policy to that of the USA. Ironically, Crossman and Foot effectively reached the same conclusion when they argued that NATO was as near to the third force idea as it was possible to get in the Cold War era.[64]

If the greater proportion of the Labour Left was harnessed to the Cold War by the end of 1947, even though they had done so much to predict and warn against it, this position was reached in part because their own illusions in Russia had been so high. Undoubtedly the Soviet-inspired offensive against East European Socialists and the memory of the Communist 'betrayal of the Left' in September 1939 turned socialists like Michael Foot into rabid anti-Communists in the last few years of the 1940s. Those with a better understanding of Stalin's Russia–Fenner Brockway, G. D. H. Cole and Emrys Hughes's *Glasgow Forward* are good examples – questioned the wisdom of accepting Marshall Aid without embracing either Atlanticism or Stalinism. But the divisions on the Left were also between those whose patriotism encouraged them to think of British Social Democracy as especially fitted to build socialism and those, of whom Konni Zilliacus is the best example, who were genuine internationalists. The former, grouped around *Tribune*, changed their attitude to the USA when, having belatedly realized the grim economic condition of Britain, they came to see Marshall Aid as necessary for the survival of Labour's reform programme. This is why critics of Marshall Aid, even when they employed arguments which *Tribune* had itself championed before June 1947, were anathematized as Communist-inspired wreckers. Needless to say, the task of promoting clear thinking about Labour's foreign policy was made harder by the fact that the Communists – whose critique of the European Recovery Programme was full of insight – were incapable of critical thought about the Soviet Union. This subservience had won the CPGB many determined enemies and general suspicion of anything associated with it. It was thus all the easier to discredit critics of Labour's policy as agents of Moscow.

When the Korean War began *Tribune* fulminated against Soviet Russia as a new Nazi Germany employing the same sinister techniques. These included an active fifth column which in Britain had allegedly infiltrated the unions, the universities, scientific research and other activities and institutions. *Tribune* found more evidence of Communist bad faith in the CPGB's 'Outlaw the Bomb' campaign which was motivated, it said, by knowledge of 'the overwhelming preponderance of Soviet land forces'. The editors even found time to question the wisdom of any demand for nuclear disarmament in the light of the purported aggressive expansionism of the USSR and the lessons of Appeasement. Finally they warned their readers to beware of anti-Americanism because, 'Like Nazi Germany so Soviet Russia sees in the power of the United States the greatest obstacle in the way to world domination. Hence the concentration of political warfare attacks against alleged United States' plans to rule the globe.'[65] The *Tribune* Left was soon to discover the consequences of such thinking. The defence budget of the UK already stood at £700 million or 7.5 per cent of National Income when the Korean War began in June 1950. Under pressure from the USA the Cabinet agreed to raise expenditure to £1,800 million for the year and to £3,600 million over the next three years. Soon after Gaitskell replaced Cripps as Chancellor in October 1950 the Americans asked for Britain's contribution to rise to £6,000 million over the three year period. They finally settled for £4,700 million, but even this lower figure represented a disastrous 14 per cent of national income.

The only way this could be financed was by incursions on domestic expenditures including the introduction of charges on the provision of spectacles and dentures. Three Ministers resigned over this issue – Nye Bevan, Harold Wilson and John Freeman – on the grounds that the proposed Budget was unrealistic and (a point emphasized by Bevan) destructive of the principles on which the government's health service had been erected. At this point the *Tribune* Left changed its views on foreign policy, since it became clear once again that the Welfare State was endangered by it. Just as Britain's perceived moral leadership of European socialism had required the sustenance of Marshall Aid, it was now endangered by the very American policy which the Left had learned to support in order to obtain that aid in the first place. By July 1951 the *Tribune* pamphlet *One Way Only* was arguing that the Soviet threat was grossly exaggerated and that the massive resources devoted to meeting it could be better spent on supporting the social revolution in the colonies which it described as 'the dominant fact of the twentieth century'. But this was a forlorn hope. The government had been bereft of progressive policies and ideas since 1947. Its majority was slashed to a mere five seats in February 1950 although the Labour vote substantially increased. When Labour returned to the polls in October 1951 it gained the highest ever vote in a British general election – almost 14 million, which represented nearly 50 per cent of the votes cast – but it lost the election due to the vagaries of the British electoral system. The party was divided and disorientated; the question to be decided was what did Labour stand for now that the goals of 1900 had been realized.

Conclusion

The policies pursued by the Attlee governments show the influence of forces operating on the party from the outside as well as evidence of internal pressures. The domestic programme of reforms really represented long-standing Labour aspirations which can be traced back to the origins of the party. In this sense the achievements of 1945–51 signify the end of a particular road rather than the first step in the construction of socialism, as the Left of the party believed. Furthermore, nothing that Labour introduced under Attlee had not already been advocated by non-socialists, especially Liberals but also Conservatives. Apart from the immediate impact of Beveridge, Keynes and R. A. Butler it is valid to trace a certain 'middle opinion', as Arthur Marwick has done, back to the inter-war years in search of the sources of the 1945 settlement.[66] But it took the war to create the mass radical pressure which brought these ideas into focus and Labour into power. Socialists undoubtedly contributed to this radicalization but the Labour machine itself was inactive for as long as the party leaders belonged to the coalition.

Attempts from within the party to shift policy to the Left ultimately had less impact than these essentially external forces. Pre-war conference majorities for the nationalization of joint stock banking and machine tools were soon dropped and the pressure for a more radical foreign policy had no discernible effect on the Labour Cabinet. Similarly Labour lost the chance to introduce comprehensive education, even though it was party policy, because ministers paid no heed to internal pressure groups like the National Association of Labour Teachers but preferred existing ministry policy instead.[67]

Apart from pressures for change, the war was also a source of conservative influences. Britain emerged on the victors side and patriotic sentiment could look with pride on institutions which had apparently served the country well. This applies to the institutions of government which unlike their European counterparts had survived the war intact and did not figure to any serious extent in Labour's reforms despite pre-war promises, for example, to devolve power from Westminster to Scotland and Wales. It also applies to the strong perception of Britain as a world power ready to resume its accustomed role at the head of an Empire. Only modest changes were envisaged in Britain's relationship with its colonies; the independence granted to India is only a partial exception since the sub-continent was ungovernable, and though Britain lacked the resources to retain power in the old way Labour ministers did their best to create a settlement that would be economically and politically beneficial to Britain. Although all sections of the party loudly proclaimed Labour's abandonment of imperialism – 'capitalist exploitation' was dead according to Morrison – the dependent territories were exploited as never before. Africa was to be the new Eldorado and nearly every minister – Bevin, Cripps, Wilson, Strachey, Creech Jones, Attlee and Morrison included – talked of the urgent need for its 'development'.[68] The Tribune Left, utilizing the old 'Empire Socialism' rationale of the 1920s, joined in this enthusiastic chorus.[69] Communism was an obvious threat to this imperial revival and the preservation of Britain's global possessions could not but have coloured the government's attitude to the Soviet Union. This is not to diminish the negative effect which the Soviet Union's often brutal policy in Eastern Europe had on the Labour Left; it is simply to point out that in order to preserve as much of the Empire as possible at a time when Britain itself was unable to mobilize the required resources, the Labour government was obliged to turn towards the USA the moment the war was over, and the task of enlisting American support was made that much easier once the alleged expansionist aims of the Russians were established. After June 1947 and the announcement of the Marshall Aid programme, most of the Tribune Left was converted to Bevin's policy; indeed *Tribune* regularly offered its own advice on the need to 'stand firm' in the colonies against 'communist bandits'.[70]

Labour's attachment to the Empire led the Government to hold aloof from and occasionally pour scorn on attempts to involve Britain in a united Europe. Arguments about the need to protect the achievements of British socialism from the dangers of European reactionaries appeared alongside appeals to the natural ties between Britain and its 'kith and kin' in the Dominions. But if the British Establishment survived intact after Labour's six years in office it is surely connected to the Government's complete unwillingness to disturb any of the power relations which had long characterized the British state. Imperialism gained a new lease of life and Britain joined the world's strongest capitalist power as junior partner in the 'special relationship'. At home the institutions of government were left unmolested and the new institutions, such as the nationalized industries, instantly fell under the control of the old elite.

12

Revisionism

In the struggle to determine the future purpose of the Labour Party, which commenced around the time of its electoral defeat in 1951, the Centre Right of the party held the initiative. For it was this faction which enjoyed the support of most of the trade union block votes in all alliance around anti-communism, support for the Atlantic Alliance, and the mixed economy consensus which congealed as the full employment boom got underway in the 1950s. But if the theoreticians of the mixed economy around Hugh Gaitskell and Anthony Crosland – soon to be called revisionists – derived much of their strength from the belief that the Attlee governments had radically changed the character of the system, they were greatly helped by the fact that the Left around Bevan took a similar view. For the Bevanites also believed that Labour had effected a revolution or its first major step by the legislative reforms of 1945–51. The *Tribune* Left pointed to the undermining of market values promoted by the Welfare State which supplied goods and services according to need and without reference to price or the ability to pay. A new morality had been advanced, or so it was argued, but the job could not be finished unless the public sector in industry was greatly extended.

The first problem with this argument was the fact that the existing nationalized sector was already generating public complaints before the Attlee governments left office and there was little support for a second instalment. Even on the Left the advocates of socialization were careful to distance themselves from the type of state-run industry which already existed, which was widely regarded as bureaucratic and based on conventional commercial and managerial principles. The most favoured antidote to the problem of bureaucracy was some measure of workers' control but throughout the 1950s this was little more than a totem routinely invoked by both the Left and Right of the party. A second major obstacle to another wave of nationalization was the fact that the party and trade union elite had been won over to Keynesian ideas while the Left was unable to fashion a socialist alternative based on the fragments available.

Cole had argued for the need for a new socialist economics for some time and restated this conviction in 1950 in opposition to the 'Keynesian Liberalism with frills' which he said now passed for socialism in the Labour leadership.[1] The subject of socialist economics, according to Cole, was not state economic management but

> the good life as affected by the entire process of production and consumption of goods and services. Its *pluses* are the goods and services made available for consumption *and* the satisfactions derived from the work of producing them: its *minuses* are the damages inflicted on natural beauty and amenity in the course of production, the using up of irreplaceable natural resources or of resources which cost effort to replace *and* the dissatisfactions arising out of dull or irksome labour or an excess of labour . . .'[2]

This made economics a branch of moral theory, but as Cole observed it was better to be 'an untidy social moralist than leave out half of the relevant factors in order to achieve a speciously scientific conclusion'. The Keynesians, in this quest to turn economics into a pure technique like dentistry, rejected this approach. But they also overlooked the insights of socialist economics.

The debates over economic policy in the 1930s had shown that state control over aggregate investment, for example, was not enough if socialists also wanted to affect the direction of investment. For this more direct controls were required that the fiscal and monetary measures advocated by the Keynesians. Similarly it was not enough to manipulate aggregate demand if the object of the exercise was full employment without inflation. Here the Keynesians ignored the source of slumps in periodic crises of over-production rather than deficient demand. Only if the state is also an investor and owner on a considerable scale, according to Cole, would it be possible to sustain full employment without generating inflation. If the public sector is dwarfed by the private economy, moreover, it is not in control of the conditions of its existence and will inevitably reproduce capitalist norms. Cole recognized, however, that Keynes had provided socialists like Gaitskell and Jay with a theory which bridged their political commitments to the Labour Party and their intellectual commitments to 'economic science'. For here was a justification for more state intervention which could be reconciled with the individualist assumptions of liberalism.

Thus what eventually became acceptable within the fold of economic orthodoxy and mainstream Labour politics were those Keynesian ideas that could most easily be assimilated into classical economics. The 'euthanasia of the *rentier*', for example, which Keynes referred to in the *General Theory* was not to be accomplished by the socialization of investment as socialists like Cole insisted but by indirectly increasing the stock of capital to the point where *rentier* income could be eliminated. Assuming both a limited demand for capital and that basic needs were near to fulfilment it would be feasible to imagine a point where the marginal efficiency of capital would be very low.

However, the Labour Keynesians were also advocates of ceaseless and rapid economic growth – but here was the source of an explosive increase in perceived or relative needs. The affluent society, which was soon to become an article of faith with the revisionists, is a society in which conspicuous consumption is encouraged and generalized and thus persistent capital shortages are guaranteed. It is a society in which the elimination of relative poverty is impossible and a world of endemic scarcity tailored to the needs of capital inevitable. An enormous fiscal burden is levied on the wage and salary earners to maintain the public sector and achieve full employment. Keynesianism comes to mean a system of fiscal incentives, spending concessions, state grants and other inducements designed to entice private investors. Fiscal and spending policies are evaluated on the basis of their impact on these investors rather than on the basis of equity.

Much of this was said by socialist critics of Keynesianism when the controversy first opened. But their own preferences were often devoid of the sort of humanist content which Cole tried to champion. Ian Mikardo's *Labour's Second Term* (1948), for example, argued that the next Labour government should nationalize banks, insurance, industrial assurance, shipbuilding, shipping, aircraft and aero engines, motor vehicles (excluding luxury and sports cars), margarine, flour, sugar, bricks, shoe machinery, cement and some specialized chemicals. Only cursory attention was given to democratic issues in relation to this swollen state. When Cole convened a series of meetings to examine future policy in detail in the summer of 1949, the deficiencies of nationalization were openly conceded by the Left though this did not prevent them from advocating public ownership of the commanding heights and a centrally planned and controlled economy. Socialists like Mikardo and Bevan wanted more democratic control inside the public sector and were saying so before the cause of 'participation' was taken up by the revisionists, but they were at best perfunctory as to how this would be achieved. As Cole's policy workshops progressed through to the Autumn of 1950 this Left initiative was largely transformed into a statement of the 'new thinking' associated with Gaitskell and Crosland. It was published without Cole's participation as *New Fabian Essays* (1952).

It was here that Crosland argued that 'capitalism is undergoing a metamorphosis into a quite different system and . . . is rendering academic most of the traditional socialist analysis.'[3] Marxists had 'absurdly underrated the socioeconomic consequences of continued political democracy' which in Crosland's view had enabled powerful anti-capitalist parties and trade unions to arise and influence the capitalist parties themselves in a collectivist direction. Two world war had aided this process by demonstrating the necessity for planning and the experience of prolonged capitalist crises had compelled the system's defenders to find ways of eliminating the trade cycle. The old competitive capitalism was in Crosland's assessment morally weakened and intellectually discredited. It had in any case undergone a process of change partly stimulated by the forces mentioned above but also generated from within as the growth of firms led to the dominance of joint-stock companies. In these companies control had passed to professional managers while ownership was typically dispersed in the hands of countless shareholders. The old-style capitalist who both owned and controlled the firm was a thing of the past, and with control now in the hands of modern managers the propertied class was left functionless – and 'so the power slips away.'[4]

Marx himself had commented on the organizational changes in capitalist firms consequent upon the arrival of the joint-stock company, but it was the American ex-Trotskyist James Burnham who argued in the light of the fascist and Stalinist dictatorship of the 1930s that the world was headed for managerialism rather than socialism or any other 'ism'.[5] Though few shared Burnham's belief in the coming of a bureaucratic, state-managed era in which the old ideologies were rendered obsolete aspects of this thesis were very influential in the Labour Party in the 1940s and early 1950s.[6] Crosland, for example, accepted the argument that a greatly increased state power would work together with the managers of giant corporations. Both were allegedly interested in achieving a planned, stable order and together would 'dominate the economic life of the country'. Thus 'the absolute autonomy of economic life' disappears and 'this one change alone would justify the statement that the capitalist era has now passed into history.'[7] By 1951, therefore, 'Britain had in all essentials ceased to be a capitalist country.' In its place was what Crosland called statism, 'because the most fundamental change from capitalism is the change from laissez-faire to state control'.[8]

Already 'statism' was characterized, according to Crosland, by 'more equality', thanks to the growth of the state's welfare functions. Now that Britain possessed 'the Keynesian techniques' and a government 'with the will to spend its way out of depression', 'a recurrence of chronic mass unemployment is most unlikely.' The ideological shift which Crosland claimed to detect in the move from rights of property to the duties of the state in providing economic security after 1945 meant that 'no right-wing party could now survive a year in office if it permitted the figures of unemployment which were previously quite normal.'[9] In Crosland's view there was now such effective control over the level of employment that the consequent gain in stability and output made the economy 'if not immune from at least much less vulnerable to the strains and stresses inherent in any industrial society'.[10] And with professional managers holding the reins of corporate power the profit motive had receded as the dominating motive of private firms. Like the state bureaucrats, these were above all interested in a planned, predictable future. Everywhere capitalism was being superseded by different forms of managerialism. In Britain it was a benign statism that was now dominant; but in other less fortunate countries a 'dictatorial managerial society' or a 'bureau-technocracy' or 'pluto-technocracy' beckoned. Even the USA, Crosland reported, was changing towards statism. The New Deal had left the USA a 'permanent legacy' in the form of an 'enormous growth of trade union strength', which had shifted the balance of power away from business interests. Economic success and twenty years of reforms since the Roosevelt era began had 'cured the worse abuses of the system'. Unfortunately the 'communist attack' had enabled capitalism to rally support, but even so the problems it once generated in the form of mass unemployment were a thing of the past, according to Crosland, because of 'anti-depression policy' and 'the effects of rearmament [which] will . . . be on balance beneficial'.[11]

Statism, however, was not socialism and Crosland argued that the distinctive contribution of the latter was to promote equality so that human fellowship could grow as the class system was eliminated. But the equality which Crosland stressed in 1952 was that which would dissolve pernicious distinctions that prevent social mixing on equal terms – what we might term snobbery. Thus he mentioned 'equality of status' and the need for 'equality of entry' or meritocracy in the professions and industry. Crosland laid especial stress on the *feeling* of inequality as the characteristic problem of the British class system which caused so many problems in industrial relations. This is why he was able to invoke the USA as a more equal society which Britain would do well to emulate, mentioning in particular its less rigid class stratification, its relatively egalitarian system of education and its 'high degree of equal opportunity in industry'.

It is clear that the Labour and trade union leadership in these years made a concerted and conscious effort to whitewash the USA and present it as a beacon of progress and enlightenment in the world. In the same volume of Fabian essays John Strachey wanted the USA 'to join with us as the senior partner in a joint endeavour of unprecedented magnitude to develop the underdeveloped continents', warning that if it did not these regions would 'pass into the Russian orbit'.[12] Denis Healey's discourse on 'power politics' asserted that 'strategically Britain needs America even more than American needs Britain.' Indeed, 'Anglo-American unity is . . . a condition of Britain's survival.'[13] Needless to say, Healey's main reason for thinking this was the threat posed by the USSR – 'a totalitarian regime which believes itself destined to rule the world'.[14] Those who purported to share this phobia – the entire Gaitskellite contingent included – were not much disposed to check the anti-democratic tendencies within their own 'statism' even though they all seemingly believed, as Healey put it, that this was the century of the managerial revolution. Of the contributors to *New Fabian Essays*, only Richard Crossman argued that 'the enemy of human freedom is the managerial society and the central coercive power which goes with it', and that 'The main task of socialism today is to prevent the concentration of power in the hands of *either* industrial management *or* the state bureaucracy – in brief to distribute responsibility and so to enlarge freedom of choice.' But then Crossman also recognized that the Labour leaders 'profoundly distrust active democracy'.[15] While Crossman suggested that the main danger to democracy came from the state, it was more typical of the Bevanite Left to give equal emphasis to the vested interests of private firms and hope that nationalization with workers' participation would solve both problems.

However, every faction in the party believed that the experience of 1945–51 had proved conclusively that capitalism could be reformed, contrary to the 'pessimism' of the 1930s. In support of this conviction any member of the parliamentary party in 1952 would cite, as Tawney did, the great strides made against poverty as shown in Rowntree's research recording a massive fall in the numbers of people affected from 31 per cent of the country in 1936 to 3 per cent in 1950. Such a Labour MP would argue that a major redistribution of income had taken place in favour of the working class and that 'the two most massive pillars of indefensible inequalities', as Tawney described education and inherited wealth, had been greatly eroded.[16] Indeed, it seemed in the light of these advances that nationalization had acquired 'a mystical halo' to many on the Bevanite Left, particularly as 'the danger of a top-heavy bureaucracy and remote control' in these public corporations was real to all concerned. The clash between those who wanted further instalments of public ownership and those who did not produced the absurd proposal in the 1950 programme to take over sugar and cement. Nothing could have better pronounced nationalization irrelevant to the needs of planning, social justice, equality, power and individual interests. It was necessary for a new statement of the rationale for common ownership and the way in which an enlarged state sector could be made compatible with democracy.

Bevan attempted to confront these issues in 1952 in his *In Place of Fear* with the statement that: 'The issue . . . in a capitalist democracy resolves itself into this: either poverty will use democracy to win the struggle against property or property in fear of poverty will destroy democracy.'[17] This was to repeat, of course, the argument which Laski formulated after the Nazis took power in Germany, when the economic crisis sharpened the class struggle at the very time when reforms were a distant prospect. It seemed then that where capitalist democracy was in crisis, democracy could survive only by abolishing capitalism: otherwise the defenders of property would stifle democracy. Although Bevan believed that parliamentary democracy was 'a sword pointed at the heart of property power', he also described Parliament itself as a 'social shock absorber placed between privilege and the pressure of popular discontent', 'an elaborate conspiracy to prevent the real clash of opinion which exists outside from finding an appropriate echo within its walls'.[18] Nevertheless Bevan proposed to use Parliament to deliver the fatal blows to capitalism, since otherwise: 'Private property in the main source of production and distribution endangers political liberty for it leaves Parliament with responsibility and property with power.'[19] In this view public ownership is the essential first step to socialism because it shifts power to the public sector and reduces the danger of the state being manipulated by private vested interests. It makes available direct instruments of economic planning and does away with the need for 'bribes and inducements' which are otherwise necessary to affect the behaviour of economic agents. But Bevan had no answer to the charge that the state itself becomes a danger to freedom when it controls as much of the economy as he proposed. All that he could say was that effective democratic control of the state requires better facilities for MPs and – apropos the boards of nationalized industries – that it was not proper for MPs to defer to non-elected persons. But these comments could not answer the charge that the Bevanite utopia would create a bureaucratic nightmare.

Bevan was much more successful in showing the deficiencies of the Keynesian conventional wisdom which was fast gaining support in both of the major parties. It was, he said, foolish to preach 'consolidation' like Morrison and expect the existing public and private sectors to sit side by side in perfect harmony when in fact both would be subject to strains generated by the other. It was necessary drastically to alter the power relations of public and private property so that the former would dominate the 'mixed economy'. Only then would it be possible to keep taxation and inflation under control and enjoy the benefits of planning. To those who complained of bureaucracy Bevan pointed to the bureaucracy which results when the state attempts to control private business indirectly – controls which grew apace even under the Conservatives. These Keynesian methods would also transform parliamentary action into 'the handmaiden of private economic activity' which would 'provide it with a stimulant when it looked like flagging'. The dependency on fiscal controls was foolish in a society in which some could avoid taxation and others had no choice but to pay it. As state responsibilities grew, argued Bevan, so would taxation and its 'harsh impact on individual plans and ambitions'. Political debate could be reduced to the issue of a penny on or off the income tax and the curse of inflation would be 'ever threatening'. As for equality, there were definite limits in Bevan's view as to how far it could be approached using redistributive taxation; death duties, for example, were easily evaded and 'as a device for financing expanding social services' fiscal policy was decidedly limited.[20]

Between 1949 and 1953 the public ownership issue was treated as a division between long and short shopping lists as promoted by the Labour Left and Right respectively. The 1950 manifesto, *Labour and the New Society*, had asserted that public ownership made industry directly accountable to the people and so represented the most democratic as well as the most effective form of public control, but as already demonstrated this lacked conviction when it came to specific proposals. The emphasis was on state influence of investment and industrial location policies since the argument that control did not depend on ownership was already a favourite with the party leadership. Thereafter the Bevanites fought to extend the list and managed to move a resolution at the 1955 annual conference demanding 'that all policies shall have a Socialist content'. The Left proceeded to argue for nationalization of 'all banking and credit facilities' as well as iron and steel, textiles, engineering, shipbuilding, chemicals and building – all with workers' control and without compensation to the owners. This proposal was seconded by Walton CLP, already a Trotskyist stronghold and soon to become the base for the Revolutionary Socialist League, the forerunner of Militant, but with the caveat that the motion 'did not go far enough'. Ralph Miliband, speaking in the same debate, doubted the utility of a list but argued for 'a clear reaffirmation that we stand by the Constitution of our Party'. In his view this put the party 'unequivocally behind the social ownership and control of the means of production, distribution and exchange': 'We have nothing to be ashamed of in our record in that regard and we know that if we abandon that we abandon that which makes us a Party of the future.'[21] But others in the debate felt the need, in view of the party's defeat in the 1955 general election, for a new statement of 'the basic principles of socialism'. It is indicative of the Left's preoccupation with the defence of public ownership in domestic policy that such a restatement never appeared from that quarter. Instead it was the Gaitskellite faction which took the initiative through the publication of Crosland's *The Future of Socialism* (1956). Aided by the acknowledged defects of 'actually existing' nationalization and the absence of anything other than nebulous proposals to improve on it, the revisionists were able to construct a new socialist agenda.

The passage of time had hardly dented Crosland's complacency. Following a routine refutation of Marx intended to show the irrelevance of traditional socialist analyses in the context of a post-capitalist Britain, *The Future of Socialism* outlined the by now familiar managerialist-statist thesis which Crosland first proposed in 1952. It was now possible Crosland argued for the state to 'exert any influence it likes on income-distribution' – with the clear implication that it will actually obtain the distribution it prefers. The national shift to the Left to which Crosland referred in 1952 was now pronounced 'permament'.[22] Full employment had allegedly strengthened the trade unions and weakened the business sector; the latter had in any case become more responsive to collectivist goals set by the state for, as we have seen, Crosland believed that technocratic managers sharing the same *weltenschauung* as the central bureaucracy had displaced the old-time capitalist obsessed with profit maximization. This was, he claimed, one of the main reasons why in the modern collectivist consensus trade unions had more power under Conservative governments than private business had under Labour.[23] The war years and the Attlee governments had between them apparently made great strides in the elimination of poverty, in the growth of wages as a percentage of national income, the diminution of unearned income at one end of the scale and low pay at the other. Full employment was of all the benefits obtained in this period the least vulnerable to political reaction.[24] While conceding that assurance about planning had receded 'in the face both of our limited knowledge of how the economic system works and of the number and heterogeneity of the variables to be taken into account', Crosland was confident that 'We stand, in Britain, on the threshold of mass abundance.'[25]

Crosland's confidence was based on the belief that it was possible to manage the mixed economy in such a way as to produce sustained growth. Whatever the problems he recognized in detailed planning, he was certain that 'the Keynesian techniques', as he called them in 1952, were efficacious in respect of major factors such as full employment and growth. Indeed, Crosland's belief that a smooth transition was taking place to a more meritocratic and just society had much more to do with his view of the state as a potent and benign force for progress than with his views on changes in the class structure or the organization of industry. With the arrival of Keynesianism the old Fabian conviction concerning the collectivist consciousness of the professional middle class became a settled prejudice and the state was seen as the centre of the web which give it social coherence. Socialism had ceased to be a myth because it had become party of reality. But in making this transition, according to Crosland, it had fulfilled some of its earliest goals – or was on the brink of so doing. As a protest against material poverty and capitalist inefficiency socialism had no future, since in Crosland's view these problems were nearly overcome. But in one major regard there was much left to achieve before post-capitalism could be changed into socialism, and that was the achievement of the 'classless society'.

If the supreme goal of socialism was equality, understood as the precondition for genuine liberty and democracy, the question to be settled was the nature of this equality and the relationship to it of other ends and means associated with the movement. For the Gaitskellites nationalization was only ever intended as a means in the achievement of social justice (social equality), for as Gaitskell himself put it in 1956:

> We regard as unjust a class structure in which a person's income, way of living, education, status, and opportunities in life depend upon the class into which he is born. We reject a society in which one man is regarded as superior or inferior to another, regardless of personal qualities again simply because of the section of society to which his parents happen to belong.[26]

The sort of society the Labour Party wished to create then was

> one in which there are no social classes, equal opportunity . . . a high degree of economic equality, full employment, rapidly rising productivity, democracy in industry and a general spirit of co-operation between its members.[27]

It will be evident at a glance that the Conservatives could agree with most of this; only the abolition of class and the reference to economic equality would be distasteful to Labour's opponents. Gaitskell's point was to question the value of nationalization in achieving these ends. It was for him a blunt instrument in ending abuses of power and waste, let alone in bringing about the redistribution of wealth and income (because of the need to pay compensation). Taxation and trade unions were far better instruments in achieving greater economic equality, especially when it was remembered that nationalization could actually confound some of Labour's other aims by creating unresponsive and gigantic units unable to motivate their employees and destructive of the competitive spirit in general.

Crosland used the journal *Encounter* to explore in more detail the meaning of equality for the Labour Party. His first point – which must have reassured the readership of this CIA-funded magazine – was that redistribution from the rich to the poor 'would make little difference to the standard of living of the British people . . . the main prop of traditional egalitarianism has been knocked away by its own success.' This alleged narrowing of the wealth and income differentials in British society meant that the case for equality must now rest on 'certain value or ethical judgements of a non-economic character'.[28] Indeed, for Crosland such was the progress on the economic front towards a better and wealthier society – one only had to remember full employment, rising incomes and 'a marked equality in the distribution of incomes' to see that this was so – that there was a real problem in explaining discontent, especially the depth of 'bitterness on the Left':

> so much resentment, so many unofficial strikes, so many touchy, prickly, indignant and frustrated citizens in politics and industry with grudges against society and grievances at work, sending telegrams and passing angry resolutions, flocking to meetings not with badges but with chips on their shoulders, peevishly waiting for someone to knock them off . . . [29]

Crosland belonged to that school of thought (with a pedigree stretching back to Sidney Webb) which found party activists, especially Labour Party activists, a nuisance; with the difference that by the mid-1950s this prejudice could be supported by the conventional wisdom in psephology which taught that activists were an expendable nuisance in an age of 'partisan identification' in which elections were won or lost by virtue of the whims of floating voters in a minority of marginal constituencies.

But the lesson drawn from this analysis of discontent in an age of affluence is that these problems arise from 'status anguish', which occurs when 'the income hierarchy gets out of alignment with the class or social hierarchy'.[30] The fact that it is the wealthy skilled working class which is 'now the main source of both industrial and political discontent' is attributable, according to Crosland, to the failure of a rigid class system to accord these people the enhanced status which 'corresponds' to their improved material standard of living. The conclusion to draw from this reasoning is that a sense of equality must derive for these people principally from changes in status rather than changes in income or wealth. But here Crosland discovered barriers within the working class where a sort of inverse snobbery regards changes in the income-status pattern with suspicion. In particular the feeling of 'class betrayal', a mentality 'absurdly irrational today', is directed at trade union officials who are well paid and, say, members of the board of a nationalized industry. In contrast we are invited to consider America and the case of the boss of the Teamsters' Union, who earns a salary of $50,000 and lives in a rent-free house worth $160,000 bought by the union without this causing any of the problems endemic in Britain.[31]

One might conclude from this ill-chosen example – the Teamsters were run by the Mafia – that Crosland's knowledge of America was not up to much. But this is beside the point. Crosland was persuaded that the USA was 'a fluid equal opportunity society' because its class system was relatively unencumbered by the contemptible status prejudices to be found in Britain. Indeed the perceived absence of such barriers was enough for Crosland to regard the USA as classless. He talked of 'the restless egalitarian ideology of contemporary America' and found it a truly equal opportunity society.[32] It was, he argued, living proof that equal opportunity did not lead to a hyper-competitive scramble as feared by its critics, for 'to push conspicuously ahead is no longer meritorious' and, to take another example, 'There are no schools in the world where less emphasis is laid on rivalry and competition and more on co-operation and adaptability.'[33] The conclusions to be drawn from this analysis are obvious: to achieve 'classlessness' the Labour Party must promote the one form of equality which everybody could identify with – equality of opportunity – and by steering Britain towards meritocracy rid the system of pernicious status barriers. Once the problem was defined in this way it was possible to identify educational reform as being 'of infinitely greater significance' in the pursuit of equality than the redistribution of wealth.[34]

In his search for the sources of anger and frustration which 'every Labour politician has observed . . . in his local party', Crosland need have looked no further than the party itself. For as Richard Crossman noted in 1956, the party was run with an internal discipline 'almost as harsh as Lenin's Democratic Centralism . . . any sustained criticism of official policy tends to be treated as an act of disloyalty.'[35] A 'law of increasing oligarchy' seemed to be at work in which the trade union leaders played a notable part. Between them the party and trade union leaders stifled and ignored dissent and contributed heavily to the demoralization of the membership. Until 1960 the leadership lost only a single vote at the carefully stage-managed party conference.[36] If the dynamic of change within the labour movement could only come from its socialist membership, as Crossman argued, the alliance between the Gaitskellites and the trade union bosses did much to freeze the organization in postures rooted in the recent past. The 'public ownership versus equality' controversy was an aspect of this freeze for those, like Crossman, who believed that 'the first task' of socialism was to expose the growth of irresponsible oligopolistic power protected by a vast bureaucratic state. And nowhere was this trade union alliance with the Gaitskellites more corrosive of the movement's idealism than in the matter of defence and foreign policy.

Labour's foreign policy under the Attlee governments was of course constructed at a time of rapidly changing events. However, as chapter 11 showed, Labour constructed a coherent picture of Soviet expansionism from the welter of contradictory signals emanating from the USSR and Eastern Europe. In creating this image the party leaders drew heavily on attitudes which they had acquired during years of conflict with British Communism—none more so than the Foreign Secretary, Ernest Bevin. Clearly a policy which enabled the Strategic Air Command of the USA to regard Britain as 'an expendable asset from which they could expect no more than six months use [in the event of war] and perhaps as little as thirty days'[37] required a powerful rationale if it was to hold sway in a party containing socialists suspicious of American post-war designs. Thus the Centre-Right of the party which directed British policy between 1945 and 1951 was also industrious in constructing an Atlanticist ideology which underpinned that policy. This held sway in the Labour Party for the next quarter century.

Denis Healey was at the forefront of this ideological drive from as early as 1947 when he wrote *Cards on the Table*, the first attempt to justify Bevin's policy systematically and reply to *Keep Left*. Here Healey asserted that 'the maintenance of Britain as a world power is the precondition of a socialist foreign policy.'[38] Moreover, in this view 'democratic socialism' would survive only if Britain's global power survived, because Soviet communism, the bitter enemy of democratic socialism, was bent on spreading its influence in Europe and the Middle East. Only if the Labour Party could make the USA an ally – strictly at Britain's convenience and *ad hoc*, according to Healey – would it be possible to meet this threat. On another occasion Healey explained the peculiar nature of the Communist challenge. He presented a picture of organized fanaticism impervious to reason and compromise:

> Parallel with this evolution of the Comintern there had been evolution in the structure, ideology and technique of the Communist Parties themselves. The nucleus of every party was now a small body of devoted men whose spiritual personality had been obliterated by automatic conformity over two decades. The inhuman character of the trained Communist impressed all observers. The Communist elite was a secret army of intelligent and courageous robots, a religious society without God in which rationalization replaced rationality, the organised replaced the organic.[39]

Healey's account of the evolution of the Comintern drew heavily on Trotsky's pre-war position. It took into account none of the momentous changes wrought by the war such as the spread of nationalism in Asia and the emergence of mass radicalism in some of the countries of Europe: Czechoslovakia, France, Greece, Yugoslavia, Italy and Bulgaria will serve as examples. In Healey's crude assessment, as in that of the party leadership, any country professing a Communist government was thereby simply 'adding' its people and resources to the USSR.

The old Trotskyist analysis of the communist parties purely as instruments of Soviet foreign policy was not even true of Europe, as Yugoslavia was to show in 1947. But this theory was especially wide of the mark in explaining the Communist insurgency actually faced by the British within the Empire-Commonwealth. Nevertheless it was useful to portray these nationalist movements as externally contrived affairs in order to legitimize Britain's own 'containment' strategy. Aneurin Bevan managed to persuade the Labour leadership by 1952 formally to acknowledge that these movements were popular and rooted in local conditions, but the old prejudices and allegiances survived, as Labour policy over Vietnam was to illustrate in the 1960s.

In Britain the CPGB was so tiny that it was impossible to depict it as a threat to the 'state machine' – though this did not prevent Labour from passing legislation to bar Communists from the Civil Service. Instead it was emphasized that the CPGB could only function effectively if it was able to exploit 'both the grievances and idealism' of those who accepted democracy and worked within its legal parameters. After 1951 this line of reasoning identified the Bevanites as the chief threat, since on many issues their concerns and policies overlapped with those of the CPGB. Healey, who was as he said himself 'very anti-Bevanite indeed',[40] had already played a notable part in the battle to drive socialists who were prepared to work with the Communists out of the Committee for an International Socialist Conference (COMISCO) which was set up in 1946 with a view to reconstituting the Socialist International. By 1948 those who were in favour of international unity with the Communists, such as Pietro Nenni of the Italian Socialist Party and several leaders of the French Socialists, had been driven out of COMISCO which was finally united on an anti-Communist basis. Its Executive statement, which was drafted by Healey in March 1948, said that 'Communists consider as enemies all those who do not surrender to their slightest whims: slave or enemy – there is no third way . . . Communists cannot achieve their aims without support from a minority within the camp of democratic socialism.'[41]

By the early 1950s the several strands of revisionism in the party – which included the Socialist Union group and *Socialist Commentary* as well as the parliamentary Gaitskellites – were united around three things: opposition to the Bevanites, support for NATO and its American leadership, and support for German rearmament. Even sympathizers with revisionism have been forced to acknowledge the 'strident and often authoritarian victimization of the Left [which was] a permanent feature of the early fifties'.[42] And yet, as we have seen, Bevan, Foot and the socialists around *Tribune* had been cured of any fellow-travelling propensities by 1948, while the tiny minority who had not were expelled from the party. It was not uncommon for the Labour Left to mount bitter attacks against the Soviet Union and the CPGB, but the very fact that it harboured doubts and gradually came to challenge the Atlanticist ideology was enough for many on the Right of the party to regard all such critics as the dupes of the Communists.

Gaitskell played a major part in setting the tone by his vitriolic attacks on the Bevanites in 1952. In a speech at Stalybridge in that year he alleged that one-sixth of the delegates at the annual conference held in Morecambe were Communists or their sympathizers. Yet this was at a time when Bevan and some of his supporters were the object of many Communist diatribes because of their admiration for Tito's Yugoslavia. Nevertheless Gaitskell's absurd allegations were music to the ears of many trade union anti-Communists, and Arthur Deakin, the leader of the TGWU, was from that time an enthusiastic

Gaitskellite. As Haseler says of the trade union leaders at this time, 'It was a commonly held belief among many of them that the Left in general and the "Bevanites" in particular were playing into Communist hands by splitting the Party.'[43] In fact the Left never threatened to 'split the Party'. But Gaitskell's anxiety about the Communists, as his diary shows, pre-dates the emergence of the Bevanites and stretched back to his time as Minister of Fuel and Power in 1947 when he was 'perfectly certain the unofficial elements are largely guided and controlled by the Communists', even though the CP-led Electricians' Trade Union (ETU) disavowed the unofficial strike in question.[44] By the mid-1950s the same source reveals Victor Tewson, TUC General Secretary advising Gaitskell – now party treasurer and hoping to increase the political levy – that the money could be raised if 'you make clear to them [the trade union Right] that the Labour Party would help in their internal troubles with the Communists – in other words that the Labour Party machine would be put into operation in favour of the Labour Party and against Communist candidates at Union elections.'[45]

No one would suspect from this that Communist Party membership had fallen considerably since the war and stood at a mere 32,681 by 1955. But Labour Party membership increased throughout the 1940s and early 1950s. It was the routine conflation of the Bevanites, who were a growing force within the Constituency Labour Parties until the mid-1950s, with the Communists which explains this anxiety among the trade union and Labour leadership and many of the deals struck between them. Thus in the context of a discussion about the struggle against Bevanism which Gaitskell had with George Brown in 1955, Gaitskell observed that his colleague 'was very firm and good about the things that ought to be done, about the need to resist the Communist infiltration, to do it by building up some organization between the Labour Party and the trade unions, the need to start a weekly paper.'[46] Tom Williamson and Arthur Deakin, two of the leading ideological heirs of Bevin, were mentioned as interested in this project. The following year at a small dinner party arranged to promote the Cold War journal *Forward*, Gaitskell once again identified the Bevanites with the Communists. As he recalled in his diary notes: 'At one point I had to come in rather vehemently to make it plain that we could not just stand aside and try to be above the battle all the time and that if we wanted to counter *Tribune* and the Communists generally, we must throw our weight behind the paper.'[47]

It made no difference that Bevan himself had castigated the Communist Party as 'the sworn inveterate enemy of the Socialist and Democratic Parties' which did not 'look upon a Socialist as an ally in a common cause' but 'as a dupe'.[48] The Gaitskellites were more impressed by the fact that the Communists and the Labour Left shared similar views on public ownership and that they could find common ground over the conduct of British foreign policy, whether by showing solidarity with nationalist movements in former colonies or in voicing similar criticisms of the American alliance. Another relevant consideration, and one which John Strachey belatedly warned against in

1956, was the 'anti-Communist obsession' which had become one of 'the basic impulses of some of the leaders . . . of such parties as the British Labour Party'.[49]

After the demise of the 'third force' idea which had dominated the Labour Left's thinking about foreign policy in the 1940s, Bevan and his followers did what they could to stop the polarization in world politics. They argued that the Soviet threat was grossly exaggerated and Britain's defence expenditure grossly inflated; they recognized the emergence of the technologically backward nations and saw Yugoslavia as a model of how a small socialist country could stay independent of both of the superpowers. After the death of Stalin in March 1953 and the first signs of internal reforms in the USSR Bevan, like Isaac Deutscher, the independent Marxist, expressed the view that the bureaucratic Communist dictatorship would be undermined by the very forces of modernization which Stalin had instigated back in 1928. There was hope then, in the Bevanite analysis, that the monolith would crack as an educated, urban proletariat rapidly replaced the illiterate peasantry as the bedrock of Soviet society. In 1954 Bevan denounced American and British pressure to assist the French against the Vietnamese. It was one of many occasions when the Labour Left objected to the holy war against Communism. It was also the Left which began to question the so-called 'independent nuclear deterrent' and which had the imagination to see the annihilation inscribed in this bogus strategy.

Despite these contributions from the Left of the party, foreign policy and defence issues were the domain of the Right just as social policy was an area in which the Left tended to specialize (though with less effect on actual policy). The spectre of a rapacious Soviet Union having been raised in the 1940s (contrasted with 'the scrupulous generosity shown by America to Western Europe'),[50] the party leadership persisted throughout the 1950s in justifying the policies which Labour had instigated in order to deal with it. Healey, who had scoffed at the Left's 'third force' as 'a dream for escapists', argued that

> The basic aim of Labour's foreign policy must be to create an organic unity throughout the world in every field – political, economic and social . . . Britain must limit [sic] her ambition to uniting those parts of the world which are outside Soviet control – Western Europe, the Americas, Southern Asia and Africa.[51]

If this grandiose plan meant anything it certainly meant the maintenance of the 'special relationship' with America on the assumption that Britain's status as a great power could survive by virtue of its influence through the Commonwealth. Both elements of this policy would be ruined if the British ever came to see their destiny integrated with that of Western Europe. Labour was accordingly in favour of European unity only insofar as it helped Britain to preserve its vital strategic interests. But the movement for European federation had to be dismissed as a 'psychological malaise' reflecting 'the continent's failure of nerve and loss of confidence', if such a federation meant that

'Europe could somehow contract out of a world struggle which they [the federators] see as primarily between America and Russia'.[52] Thus Churchill's notion of Britain's centrality in world affairs as the only power able to occupy a position within the three circles of strength in the non-Communist world – Europe, the Commonwealth and the 'special relationship' – also informed the perspective of Labour's 'realists' in the early 1950s and helped to keep Britain out of the movement for European unification when this chimera of the 1940s began to take shape during the following decade.

The rearmament of Germany was quite another matter. The Centre Right of the party – which believed that the USSR was intent on 'adding to its present resources the manpower and industrial potential of Western Europe' – were wholly committed to the idea of deterring the Soviet threat.[53] Once the USSR had obtained its own atom bomb, Labour strategists like Healey argued for greater expenditure on conventional weapons on the grounds that the USA would not risk atomic retaliation by intervening with A-bombs against Soviet conventional aggression.[54] Thus unless Western Europe could muster sufficient conventional forces it would no longer be defended in an age of rough atomic parity. But by 1955 both superpowers possessed hydrogen bombs – weapons of genocide which altered the nature of the problem again. Healey now argued that since it had proved practically impossible to match Soviet conventional forces and was obviously suicidal to use H-bombs, the only effective riposte to Soviet aggression on the borders of Central Europe was to retaliate with 'tactical' nuclear weapons. These, being not so 'dirty' as H-bombs and easy to fire in 'battlefield' conditions, were eminently usable.[55]

In the name of 'realism' the Labour leadership, with defence experts like Healey to the fore, entered the nuclear fantasy. In the name of defence, measures were accepted on the wholly unrealistic supposition that the USSR would not retaliate with its own 'tactical' weapons; that the surrounding society would not be wholly extinguished by these weapons; and indeed that both sides would recognize that a distinction between 'tactical' and 'strategic' nuclear weapons even existed. Thus it was that by the mid-1950s leading figures in the Labour Party actually advocated using nuclear weapons in reply to any large-scale attack by the Red Army. In addition, these same people reasoned that since the USSR's objective was to divide NATO, push the Americans out of Europe and finally persuade the West to abolish all nuclear weapons, these weapons were *ipso facto* a good thing.

It was from among the revisionists in the party that the argument was heard most often that the USSR would listen only in the face of superior force. This peculiarity of the Soviet Union derived, so it was argued, from the nature of the Communist regime. Other powers may be aggressive, duplicitous, expansionist and selfish but the USSR was *sui generis*. It was, in the first place, always in pursuit of goals fixed by dogma (according to Healey, who said, quoting Kruschev, that this dogma would be forgotten only 'when shrimps learn to whistle').[56] Indeed, the conviction that the USSR was a sort of 'mass society' where a totalitarian ideology set global utopian goals was continually expressed to justify the argument that it would not respond to ordinary diplomacy or compromise. These, it was argued, would be seen as evidence of weakness; only force or the threat of force would be efficacious. The corollary of this, of course, was that any gesture or sign of peaceful intent expressed by the Soviet leaders could never be taken at face value; such expressions had always to be regarded as tactical ploys subordinate to the same goal of world conquest. On this reasoning, then, the real business of establishing acceptable relations with the USSR was a matter of defence strategy based on the preparedness to use overwhelming force. Thus in 1957 Healey argued that the very difficulty in practice of actually limiting a nuclear war would work to the West's advantage, for:

> once the West is seen to believe in the general *possibility* of limiting nuclear warfare any residual uncertainty about the feasibility of maintaining the limitations in practice would simply add to the deterrent. If Russia once believes the West has both the capacity and the will to meet local aggression by limited nuclear war, she would avoid any risk of putting Western will-power to the test.[57]

With human lives depending on this kind of logic it is hardly surprising that 1957 was the year when the Campaign for Nuclear Disarmament emerged in Britain and the stultifying public consensus began to break. But already the previous year Kruschev's 'secret' speech to the 20th Congress of the CPSU had dealt a major blow to Stalinism by exposing some of the 'crimes' of the dictatorship under Stalin's leadership. The old monolith had already begun to disintegrate. In Italy Togliatti had renounced the one-party state as a model for Italian Communism as early as 1944; the Popular Front was revived after the war throughout Europe and Communists began to stress different national roads to socialism. Well before Togliatti invented the formula of 'polycentrism', with its implied denial of Moscow's leading role, the Western Communists were formally committed to democratic and parliamentary transitions to socialism. In 1951 the CPGB had adopted its own revisionist programme, *The British Road to Socialism*, which envisaged the creation of a broad anti-monopoly alliance embracing all the 'progressive' sections of the population. Behind the new language, of course, the old habits survived – particularly within the party leadership – but even these formal changes were real. Future debate within the Communist movement would centre on the meaning and application of the new democratic formulae where previously it had been rejected on principle.

Although the full text of Kruschev's speech was not available in the West until June 1956 and the Western Communist leaders were excluded from the meeting which Kruschev addressed the previous February, a debate, mainly subterranean, was provoked immediately within the movement. The obvious question which Communists asked themselves was why their own leaders had remained silent for so long. Within the CPGB the hope arose that the party could be reorganized so that genuine debate and democracy would flourish. The Kruschev revelations stirred doubts and misgivings on a host of fundamental questions. In *Tribune* Bevan observed that Kruschev had opened a Pandora's Box of pluralism. The leaders of the Italian and French Communists openly rejected Kruschev's analysis of the 'personality cult' as naive, but the main significance of the secret speech, in Bevan's opinion, was that the Communist monolith was finished: 'the first result will be much greater flexibility of political maneouvre by the Communists of the parliamentary democracies. It will no longer be possible to charge them with subservience to orders from Moscow.'[58]

In Britain a large section of the Communist membership was in open revolt against the party leadership, even though the latter had set up a Commission on Inner Party Democracy to placate its critics. Palme Dutt's complacent admission apropos Stalin that yes, 'there are spots on the sun', did not help matters. But by the end of June the Communist crisis had taken the form of rioting in Poland. This was succeeded in October by an uprising in Hungary which, though led by Communists, was aimed at ridding the regime of the Stalinist legacy and the dominance of Moscow. Bevan saw these events in Eastern Europe as evidence of an inevitable process of de-Stalinization which could not be checked – it was 'a gradual adaptation of Communist practice to the realities of modern society'.[59] But it was endangered, he said, by the gloating from Washington which talked of the disintegration of Soviet power. Even after Russian tanks rolled into Budapest to crush the revolution Bevan warned that the liberty of Eastern Europe also depended on reducing Western aggression towards the USSR, since the Soviets had only ever regarded those states as a buffer zone.[60]

Within the British Communist Party the crisis led to the departure of thousands of disillusioned members, including a number who helped to create the New Left such as E. P. Thompson and John Saville, the editors of the *New Reasoner*. In all, CPGB membership fell by 10,900 between June 1956 and March 1959, about 32 per cent of the party's total strength. The fact that so many of these socialists remained active on the Left has a great to do with the sharp reminder provided by the British and French governments at the beginning of November 1956 of the record of Western imperialism. For, together with the Israelis, these governments conspired to invade Egypt in order to topple Abdul Nasser who had had the temerity to nationalize the Suez Canal Company, an asset largely owned by the British and French states. The whole of the British Left was enraged by the Eden government's action. But whereas *Tribune* defended Nasser's right to nationalize the Canal Company, Gaitskell (who had succeeded Attlee as party leader after the 1955 general election defeat) argued that it was an act of banditry and denied any justice in Egyptian claims. Thus the Labour leadership argued that the Suez Canal was too important to belong to any single nation and should be controlled by an international agency.

It is perhaps not surprising that the committed Atlanticists should overlook the USA's control of the Panama Canal when making these suggestions. Gaitskell behaved as if he had been personally let down by Eden, who had jeopardized the 'special relationship' by acting without American consent. It is much more surprising that Bevan joined forces with Gaitskell and began to integrate with the Labour establishment. But within weeks of the start of the Suez crisis Bevan became Shadow Foreign Secretary, a position he had long sought. By December he was able to give vent to his own belief in Britain's moral superiority by denying, in a Commons speech, that Suez proved that Britain had become a 'second-class Power'; it was, he said, possible for Britain, with 'more concentrated experience and skill than any other country in the world', 'to seek . . . new ways of being great, new modes of pioneering, new fashions of thought, new means of inspiring and igniting the minds of mankind'.[61]

Ever since Britain developed the H-bomb in 1955 the Left had wrestled with the enormous moral questions posed by this weapon of genocide as it was commonly described. Bevan had thrown his weight behind disarmament talks, arguing that Soviet peace overtures should be taken seriously and that divisions within the Kremlin were more likely to be resolved in favour of the faction seeking peaceful co-existence with the West if the West recognized that the USSR was not ready for war and had no plans to make war.[62] The failure to make any progress towards significant disarmament, however, persuaded many on the Left that the USA in particular would not relax the assumptions about Soviet intentions which made war more not less likely. Barbara Castle drew these conclusions in the light of American objections to the agreements made with the Russian at Geneva in 1955.[63] Bevan also argued that Britain and France would have to 'break loose from the clamp in which we are held to the United States' if arms reductions were to go ahead. He demanded a ban on all nuclear tests in March 1957, but Gaitskell was opposed to unilateral action even on this question and would only talk of the need for international agreements. In May Bevan repeated the familiar Left-wing objections to the H-bomb, arguing that it was immoral, bound to proliferate and, far from acting as a deterrent, made war 'a certainty'.[64] Nevertheless, though his speeches often suggested otherwise, Bevan was not in favour of unilateral disarmament and disillusioned his supporters by saying so in a rambling speech at the party's annual conference in 1957. It was at the end of that year that the first moves were made towards a Campaign for Nuclear Disarmament (CND), which was launched in January 1958 with Bertrand Russell as President and Canon Collins as Chairman. The foundation of CND seemed to mark the end of a long period of apathy and the beginning of political initiatives on the Left which were independent of either Labour or Communist inspiration and patronage. Indeed, the Communists actually boycotted the first two Aldermaston marches in 1958 and 1959 in accordance with Soviet predilections for multilateral disarmament via summit conferences between the Powers. Not until 1960 did the CPGB line swing abruptly behind unilateralism. Meanwhile with CND as its best channel for public expression a New Left was finding its feet.

The group of Marxists around *New Reasoner*, formerly *The Reasoner* which began its life as the voice of CPGB dissidents in the summer of 1956, rejected Trotskyism as a form of Leninism and tried to articulate a position based on socialist humanism. E. P. Thompson argued that socialism was inconceivable 'unless we can fashion a new and humanized image of a socialist society within our reach which is clearly distinguished from both the Communist experience and the experience of over-centralised bureaucratic state monopoly'.[65] As far as the latter was concerned one of its major components, the Welfare State, was a contradictory phenomenon: to some members of the New Left it seemed a device to meet 'the requirements of industrial capitalism' in an age of highly productive labour, while others stressed the need to defend it as a 'profoundly anti-capitalist development' and the result of 'objective victories for working class values within capitalist society'.[66] All were agreed, however, in rejecting the argument that Britain was now a post-capitalist society in which socialists should focus on equality of opportunity. As E. P. Thompson put it:

> The socialist end has been the creation – *not* of equality of opportunity within an acquisitive society – but of a society of equals, a co-operative community. The pre-requisite for this is the replacement of production for profit by production for use. A socialist society might be under-developed or overdeveloped, poor or affluent. The distinction between socialist and capitalist societies is to be found, not in the level of productivity, but in the characteristic relations of production, in the ordering of social priorities, and in its whole way of life.[67]

Already there was evidence to dispute the claim that primary poverty had been overcome and that Labour's greatest achievement, the Welfare State, was characterized by petty meanness, the authoritarianism of the charity tradition, professional arrogance and practices which kept people ignorant of their rights. One influential study after another argued that the major beneficiaries of welfare services were the middle classes, who received more benefits and paid less in taxes than the working class who were kept on 'a Spartan minimum'.[68] But this evidence was largely ignored by the Labour leadership which was more impressed by the fact that it had lost a third consecutive general election in 1959, with the Conservatives boasting that the people had 'never had it so good'.

Only eight days after the 1959 defeat Douglas Jay wrote that 'we are in danger of fighting under the label of a class that no longer exists.' It seemed necessary in recognition of this apparent demise of the working class to change the party's name to indicate that it sought a broader base.[69] To almost everyone associated with Gaitskell, indeed, it seemed, to quote Rita Hinden – Gaitskell's friend and Secretary of the Fabian Colonial Bureau – , that the working class was 'objectively and subjectively on the wane'. Academic studies asked 'Must Labour Lose?' and implied an affirmative unless

Labour could change its image. The reason, as Gaitskell told the annual conference, was fundamentally because 'capitalism has changed largely as a result of our own efforts.'[70]

Under these circumstances nationalization was obsolete. The trade cycle, according to Gaitskell, was now a thing of the past so it was unnecessary to expand the public sector in order to control the economy; thus for all of the revisionists nationalization was now redundant for achieving the party's goals. It was simply a vote loser since even under the Tories effective planning could function without it. As living standards continued to rise and the consumer society cushioned by the Welfare State really got into its stride Gaitskell envisaged, as he told the conference, more leisure, more cars, more televisions. These changes represented not only the appearance of individuals defined by their consumption patterns but also shifts in the occupational structure of the workforce:

> Everywhere the balance is shifting away from heavy physical work and towards machine maintenance, distribution and staff jobs . . . it means that the typical worker of the future is more likely to be a skilled man in a white overall watching dials in a bright new modern factory.[71]

As party leader Gaitskell now sought to emulate the German social democrats, who had dispensed with their Marxist ideological legacy at Bad Godesberg earlier in the year. Jay and Crosland had argued for similar constitutional changes to remove Clause 4 from Labour's future commitments and reduce the power of both the unions and the constituency activists within the party. Gaitskell ignored most of this advice but decided to concentrate his fire on Clause 4, which ostensibly committed the party to a programme of comprehensive nationalization which few in the party actually wanted to see implemented. But he underestimated the sentimental attachment to this goal as well as the problems its excision would pose to particular unions with similar commitments in their own constitutions. He was thus compelled to abandon his plans and submit instead a new statement of principles which the 1960 conference accepted merely as a 'valuable expression of the aims of the Labour Party in the twentieth century'.

The new decade began, then, with a sort of stalemate between the party's ideological rivals. The Left had proved incapable of revitalizing its thinking about the nature of socialism and the way to achieve it while the revisionists, still in control of Labour's policy-making, were convinced that the affluent society had arrived and the embourgeoisement of the working class had undermined some of the old attachments to collectivism. Such collectivism as the revisionists remained attached to was to be achieved in areas of social policy by means of taxation and through the indirect hand of state management. Otherwise the private sector was to remain as it was under market forces.

Conclusion

Even before the Attlee governments came to an end the future purpose of the Labour Party had become an issue that divided the organization. The intellectual initiative was seized by the group around Gaitskell which argued that the public ownership question was secondary and subordinate to the goal of equality which could best be promoted by fiscal and social policy. The key assumption of these revisionists was that the Keynesian techniques of economic management would permit any reforming government to steer the economy for fast economic growth, thus providing the fiscal revenues required to finance a relatively painless abolition of poverty and enable Labour to introduce measures designed to achieve a more egalitarian, meritocratic and caring society. The Bevanite Left accepted these goals and subscribed to the concept of the mixed economy but believed that that Gaitskellites were far too complacent about the compatibility of Labour's ideals with the continued existence of a largely (80 per cent) private enterprise order. But while it was true that the revisionists completely ignored the problem of a private sector increasingly dominated by trans-national corporations there was no analysis of these giant companies forthcoming from the Bevanites which could force this issue into the centre of party economic debate and policy.

This may be connected to the fact that the Bevanites were almost as complacent about the British state and political system as the revisionists. After all, Bevan himself referred to Parliament as a sword pointed at the heart of property power as if, in other words, a socialist majority in the Commons would suffice to solve any problems presented by big capital. This bias may also help to explain the largely routine character of the Left's references to industrial democracy, verbiage which the revisionists were to prove equal to. With so much in common the ferocity of the conflict in the party, especially in the first half of the 1950s, requires an explanation which goes beyond the formal differences over policy which divided the two sides.

The Cold War and the nervous tensions generated by it provide the starting point for such an explanation. Since the 1930s a hatred of Marxism and Communism developed into a unifying factor on the Right of the party and the trade unions which after 1945 cemented the bond between the revisionists and the leaders of the biggets unions. This alliance kept critics of party policy in a state of permanent subordination and gave rise to a sense of frustration and anger on the Left which was further handicapped by the condition of apathy prevailing outside the party during the long boom of the 1950s. But the anti-Communist vigilance of the party and trade union bosses cannot be explained in terms of the influence of the CPGB, which was a declining force in this period despite a respectable presence in certain unions. As I have shown, the 'anti-Communist' effort in Britain was chiefly directed against the Bevanites for the simple reason that they were critical of aspects of the Cold

War orientation which the party took up after 1945. And in the constituency organizations, which experienced a rise in individual membership until 1952 when the figure stood at 1,014,524, the Left was a growing force and perceived as a potentially disruptive factor.

Faced with the concerted hostility of the revisionists and their friends, who were able to manipulate the party machine against them, the Bevanites might have concluded that the real priority of the party leadership was the destruction of the Left, not the creation of equality. The Communist threat, after all, brought the Right of the party into an international alliance with reactionaries of every stamp and when the occasion demanded, as in 1950–1, they were ready to compromise Labour's reforms in order to meet it. There was not much evidence of a commitment to freedom and equality about the USA's repeated interventions in Central and South America, for example, and yet the Gaitskellites turned a blind eye to them during the 1950s. When the Conservatives forcibly removed the elected government of British Guiana in 1953, formed by Cheddi Jagan's pro-Soviet, People's Progressive Party (PPP), the party leadership agreed with the repression. As Rita Hinden argued, the repression was necessary in order to prevent the spread of 'totalitarianism'.[72] It was after this episode that Fenner Brockway set up the Movement For Colonial Freedom with the support of 72 Labour MPs and about half a dozen trade unions to campaign for rapid withdrawal from colonialism, with target dates for every stage in the process.

But the Gaitskellites were fervent supporters of the British Commonwealth and continued to think of Britain as the occupant of a uniquely influential position ultimately because of this connection. There was a real basis to this belief in that as late as 1960 67 per cent of Britain's exports and 92 per cent of her foreign investments went to non-European destinies, while in the period 1955–9 47 per cent of British imports, 51 per cent of exports, and 60 per cent of capital exports were within the Commonwealth.[73] As Britain's grip over the colonies tightened in the first half of the 1950s, the Labour leadership echoed the official rationale that Britain's 'trusteeship' would only last until the colonies were ready for self-government since withdrawal would otherwise result, according to the revisionists, 'in chaos or a crueller subjection of the African'.[74] Only after Suez did they begin to relax the argument that one man one vote was inappropriate until the colonies were brought up to a level of economic and social development compatible with democracy on the Westminster model. This change was connected to the fact that by the late 1950s the movements for independence, unlike Jagan's PPP, were not led by Marxists and thus did not present the revisionists with the Cold War dilemma of 1953. Even so, Labour's greater receptiveness to decolonization did not come about much sooner than the actual withdrawal from empire instigated by the Conservative government, despite Labour having the luxury of Opposition.

All the evidence suggests that the revisionists blindly supported the Atlantic alliance against the Soviet Union and international Communism and continued to think of Britain as a Great Power by virtue of its Commonwealth connections throughout the 1950s. Once the Left of the party came to regard the European Economic Community as a capitalist club and an extension of NATO, it was even possible for Gaitskell to unite the party in a speech at the annual conference in 1962 by pouring scorn on the EEC as an inward-looking entity by contrast with the world-scope of the Commonwealth.[75] Yet these global pretensions were to play a part in scuppering Labour's next attempt to modernize Britain.

13

Pragmatism and Modernization

The success of a unilateralist motion at the Labour Party conference in October 1960 was dramatic evidence of a shift in the balance of forces within the movement against the bloc of parliamentarians and trade union leaders which had dominated during the 1950s. Ever since Britain had exploded its first H-bomb in May 1957 the challenge to the received wisdom on defence had grown apace. The small groups of MPs who launched Victory For Socialism in 1958 demanded unilateral nuclear disarmament and before the end of the year CND had held its first Aldermaston march, the *Daily Herald* had been converted to the cause and even the Liberal Assembly called for unilateral abandonment of the H-bomb. Bevan announced that the next Labour government would put a stop to nuclear tests, but within months of this declaration, in the summer of 1959, both the GMWU and the TWGU had voted to support unilateral disarmament. In May 1960 the AEU followed suit and that autumn the TUC supported unilateralist and multilateralist resolutions. The scene was set for Gaitskell's second major conference defeat, even though his great rival Nye Bevan died prematurely before the 1960 conference took place, only nine months after his unanimous election to the deputy leadership.

For a time Frank Cousins, who was elected General Secretary of the TGWU in 1956, looked the best candidate to replace Bevan as the leader of the Left. But even had Cousins been prepared to assume that role the locus of Left opposition could no longer be confined within the official structures of the Labour Party and its affiliated trade unions. By April 1963 CND was able to mobilize over 100,000 people to demonstrate against the British nuclear deterrent, and although this was the highpoint of its activity other unofficial movements continued to grow which could pose equally disturbing problems for the old bureaucratic alliance under the Gaitskellites. As early as September 1957 the TUC annual conference had rejected any form of wage restraint and the growth of shop steward power was reflected in the increase of unofficial strikes. Indeed, a TUC report in August 1960 denounced the emergence of what it saw as an attempt to bring a second shop stewards' movement into existence. In the short term Britain's economic difficulties, which began to displace affluence as an image of the country's condition in the light of the superior economic performance of its European neighbours, worked to the party's advantage. But the growth of industrial militancy, most of it unofficial, ultimately enabled the Left to break out of its isolation and upset the dominant Centre-Right bloc within the party.

The Notting Hill race riot in August/September 1958 in which a mob of around three thousand whites attacked black residents with petrol bombs was another sign of an emerging issue for which the Labour Party was unprepared and indisposed. Although the annual conference promised legislation against race discrimination in public places, many party and trade union leaders had ignored racism – including racism within their own organizations – and believed that positive action would actually be harmful by drawing attention to the problem and forcing it out into the open. For the obvious question arose of how trade union members and Labour voters would react if these organizations took an unequivocally anti-racist stand. It has to be said, too, the Labour's paternalism towards the colonial peoples hardly qualified it as the party of racial equality. It was therefore not entirely ironic that Patrick Gordon Walker, the Labour MP for Smethwick and a former Secretary of State for Commonwealth Relations, should be the first parliamentary victim of an overtly racist electoral campaign in 1964. Since the mid-1950s a number of public houses within his constituency had operated a colour bar without encountering any trouble from the sitting MP. Indeed, Walker had reflected the mood knowing that the branch of the Birmingham Immigration Control Association which was set up in Smethwick in 1961 contained Labour voters and even a former Labour councillor. This was one of many constituency Labour organizations which, to quote Paul Foot, 'had been rotting away for many years' under the benign indifference of its Member of Parliament. In 1962 Walker, no doubt seeking to placate the racists, had observed that 'This is a British country with British standards of behaviour. The British must come first.'[1]

This was precisely the sentiment which inspired the Conservatives' Commonwealth Immigration Act (1962), which Gaitskell denounced as a 'plain anti-colour measure in practice' and which Walker's racist opponent in the 1964 election, Peter Griffiths, employed to such useful effect; while Labour won nationally on a swing of 3.5 per cent against the Conservatives, Griffiths was elected on a swing of 7.2 per cent against Walker. The new Prime Minister, Harold Wilson, called on the Commons to treat Griffiths as a 'parliamentary leper' and for the moment the Labour Party held the initiative as the party of progress on this issue.

More than anyone else, Wilson had helped to identify Labour with modernity. It was at the 1960 annual conference that he first spoke of the need to 'harness Socialism to science and science to Socialism' later to become one of the main themes of *Signposts for the Sixties* (1961), which argued for planned industrial growth as the means of rejuvenating the British economy. Wilson had also challenged Gaitskell for the leadership after the latter's defeat over unilateralism, promising that he would observe the democratic decisions of the party. Although the attempt failed, Wilson's left-wing credentials – which originate with his resignation from the Board of Trade in 1951 to join Bevan in opposition to Gaitskell's rearmament Budget – were enhanced. After Gaitskell's sudden death in January 1963 Wilson took over as leader of the party at a time when the Conservative government was plagued by balance of payments problems, sluggish economic growth, the Profumo scandal and de Gaulle's recent rejection of Britain's attempt to join the European Economic Community (EEC). The circumstances could not have been more propitious.

Wilson also benefited from the strong impulse to unity which was felt on the Left after thirteen years of opposition. Moreover, the language he employed in expressing Labour's message was sufficiently vague to appeal to all factions of the party. In fact most detailed policy differed not at all from the revisionist agenda constructed during the 1950s. But the new awareness of Britain's economic failures enabled Wilson and his co-thinkers such as Tony Benn and Peter Shore to reject the affluent society image which the revisionists had largely embraced and castigate the old order with a radical rhetoric which appealed to the Labour Left. At the Scarborough annual conference in 1963 Wilson presented the policy statement *Labour and the Scientific Revolution* in a speech which contrasted the amateurism and nepotism of Conservative Britain with the rapid technological change which was needed unless the country was to 'become a stagnant backwater, pitied and condemned by the rest of the world'.[2] This was a challenge which only socialism could answer for:

> Since technological progress left to the mechanism of private industry and private property can lead only to high profits for a few and to mass redundancies for the many, if there had never been a case for Socialism before, automation would have created it.[3]

The vision Wilson put before the Labour conference was of a society in which the vast untapped potential of its members would be released by changes at every level of the education system – by the abolition of the Eleven Plus examination which maintained an educational apartheid; by the introduction of meritocratic and egalitarian comprehensive schools; through the creation of a Ministry of Higher Education which would preside over a massive extension in university and polytechnic provision designed to stop the 'brain drain' and furnish the skills required by a new Britain 'forged in the white heat of this revolution'. This new system would extend to every pocket of privilege and inefficiency in society. There was also the suggestion in Wilson's rhetoric that a Labour government would attack the power of the big corporations:

> For the commanding heights of British industry to be controlled today by men whose only claim is their aristocratic connections or the power

of inherited wealth or speculative finance is as irrelevant to the twentieth century as would be the continued purchase of commissions in the armed forces by lordly amateurs.[4]

This impression was strengthened by many other speeches in which Wilson talked of the need for 'socialist planning', 'structural changes', the development of new industries by the state and other measures of central control.

In fact Wilson's targets were much softer than the industrial and financial conglomerates which dominate the British economy. His first priority was 'the restoration of Britain's economic dynamic', not the redistribution of economic power. The Conservatives were chiefly lambasted for the 'pathetic economic performance' which had characterized the 1950s – 'the stagnant 'fifties' as Wilson called them.[5] Labour's diagnosis of these ills dwelt on the incompetence of the people concerned and the vested interests which obstructed economic progress:

> too many industries in the hands of the financiers . . . the technician and the expert in British industries are kept at a lower status than that of the well-born and well-connected amateurs in the company boardrooms.[6]

> Restrictive practices on both sides of industry, the hangover of the insecurity and unemployment of pre-war days are taking a generation to dissipate . . . the high command . . . is manned either dynastically or on the basis of a family school or social network.[7]

These were undoubtedly real problems in Britain, but Labour was saying much the same in the early 1960s as the leading revisionists had said in the mid-1950s. Most of Wilson's prescriptions were similarly drawn from the stock arguments associated with Crosland which Bevan had criticized as early as 1951.

Thus the structural changes and rationalization of industry which were required to enhance competiveness and strengthen the industrial base were to be achieved through 'tax incentives to stimulate types of investment', state-financed 'guaranteed orders' if commercial orders proved disappointing, 'tax incentives' to encourage firms to step up their own research and so on.[8] Nevertheless, the 1964 manifesto *The New Britain* set the party big targets. In spite of the fact that social research since the late 1950s had exposed the complacency of those who talked of poverty as a thing of the past, Labour promised to abolish it altogether. Economic privilege and the creation of real equality of opportunity were also identified as 'the immediate targets of political action', not remote ideals. These changes were to be achieved by a National Plan which would strike a 'wise balance' between public and private expenditure. Through 'Socialist planning' centred in a new Ministry of Economic Affairs each industry would discover 'what is expected of it and what help it can expect.' The government would also create new industries through a Ministry of Technology, and Regional Planning Boards would tackle the problem of depressed areas. Labour promised a national plan for transport; a major overhaul of the tax system so that it would be fair and seen to be fair; real power to the Monopolies Commission; the curbing of inflation; and – although the manifesto avoided a specific commitment – 400,000 new houses per year was mentioned as a reasonable target.

Certainly the manifesto addressed real and depressingly familiar problems. It referred to the 'selfish get-rich-quick mood' encouraged by the Conservatives; soaring land and house prices; transport chaos with the roads congested and the railways under-used; whole regions stagnant and neglected. At bottom the solution to all these problems was to be 'far more vigorous and sustained policies of economic growth', over which the proposed planning agencies would somehow keep sufficient control to enable the government to solve the specific problems highlighted. But the perceptive student of Wilson's speeches would also have noticed the recurring patriotic note which lamented 'a great nation unnecessarily accepting a rate of economic growth and a world status lower than its real abilities and qualities and needs would dictate'.[9] In 1964, as one study observes, the party 'largely ignored the European Community issue and its thinking about foreign policy was riveted to old doctrine which stressed the Atlantic and Commonwealth ties, with Britain having an important military role to play East of Suez'.[10] Its foreign economic policy was also firmly rooted in orthodoxy, for as Wilson assured his readers in 1964: 'Labour is determined to maintain the value of the pound and to take such steps, internal or external, monetary or physical, as are needed to achieve this end.'[11] Labour's position in 1964, therefore, amounted to a vague national socialist economic programme which was supposed to function alongside all the foreign commitments that had survived Britain's Imperial past: the Commonwealth and the special relationship with the USA; the primacy of the financial and commercial sectors of the economy together with their global orientations; NATO; the nuclear deterrent and military commitments overseas. But when the two halves of Labour's policy proved incompatible the promised national reconstruction was quickly jettisoned, and for most of his term as Prime Minister Wilson's nationalist rhetoric was no more than a device intended to relieve Labour of its identification with the working class and to transform it into the 'natural party of government'.

Wilson later argued that his first two governments had been 'dominated by an inherited balance of payments problem which was nearing a crisis at the moment we took office . . . It was a Government which had faced disappointment after disappointment and none greater than the economic restraints on our ability to carry through the social revolution to which we were committed.'[12] But this was to ignore the fact the 'social revolution' which Wilson alludes to was never more than an optimistic mood centred on the conviction that appropriate fiscal adjustments could encourage faster economic growth than that achieved under the Conservatives. Even had the inherited £800 million balance of payments deficit never existed, George Brown's National Plan would not have amounted to a radical restructuring of the British economy. The Plan was only ever based on the idea that private firms would achieve targets set by themselves; it was, as David Howell says, 'no more than a permissive incantation without instruments of implementation'.[13]

Though the government was re-elected in 1966 with a large majority, it promised no specific measures of public ownership. What it did seek to do, however, was to bolster the private sector by encouraging rationalization and merger through the business-dominated Industrial Reorganization Corporation which Wilson set up in January 1966 and by the injection of public expenditure and the incentive of tax concessions. Rather than devalue the pound, which would have annoyed the City, the USA and other monetary authorities, Wilson sought to correct the balance of payments deficit by dampening domestic demand at the expense of economic growth. Inevitably the government's social policies were affected adversely and large public expenditure cuts were announced in July 1966, together with tax increases (largely in the form of regressive indirect taxes) and a statutory wage freeze. Further public expenditure cuts followed the government's belated devaluation of sterling in November 1967. By the following year the rank and file rebellion against the government's prices and incomes policy had forced the TUC to take a stand against any statutory controls on free collective bargaining. The complete failure to achieve a more egalitarian tax system or to increase the social wage sufficiently to offset the deprivations of wage freezes and inflation set the government and the unions on a collision course. Many of the problems which the Labour government experienced stemmed from its determination to hang on to Britain's world role – military and financial – despite the absence of the resources required to reconcile these ambitions with its programme of domestic reforms. Wilson was committed to the maintenance of British forces East of Suez and as late as the Defence White Paper of February 1966 the government stressed Britain's continued role as a world power. The Prime Minister was equally concerned to protect the value of sterling and its role as a reserve currency, even though the pound was under enormous pressure from the first day of the Labour government because of the enormous balance of payments deficit left by the previous Conservative administration. Thus when President Johnson offered American support to maintain the value of the pound (in the hope, thereby, of securing the position of the dollar which was also under threat), in return for the maintenance of Britain's defence commitments and support for the Americans in Vietnam, Wilson was happy to oblige even though a further condition of this secret deal required Labour to pursue deflationary policies in Britain. Clive Ponting's research shows that this arrangement – concluded between Wilson and Johnson in the spring of 1965 – was kept secret from the Cabinet, and yet exercised a 'dominating influence' on policy during the first three years of the government's life.[14] Indeed, Ponting concludes that the 'new government . . . actively sought to increase British dependence on the United States and develop its relationship with the American administration into the central pillar of its policy in the strategic, foreign, defence, and economic fields'.[15]

In all important respects the government's deference to the Americans was consistent with the Atlanticist ideology which the Labour establishment propounded so enthusiastically at the height of the Cold War. Equally, Wilson's attempt to keep alive Britain's Great Power pretensions involved no new departure for the Labour leadership. But these policies were now destined to bring the government into massive disrepute with its own supporters. The Labour conference, for example, had voted in 1961 to reject the purchase of Polaris submarines, and in the same year Gaitskell and Healey were among those who had endorsed an NEC document which said that Britain should 'cease to attempt to remain an independent nuclear power'. Wilson had gone further by proposing that there should be no foreign nuclear bases in Britain, and during the general election of 1964 he added his voice to the movement's scornful dismissal of Polaris. But within three years of taking office the Labour government embarked on the Chevaline modernization of Polaris which, at a cost of one billion pounds, ensured the system's survival until the 1990s. By this time a pattern of broken promises and duplicity was well established.

For by the summer of 1965 the government had already borrowed one and half billion pounds from the International Monetary Fund (IMF), and had begun to implement the deflationary policies which effectively aborted the economic strategy it was elected to follow. George Brown's National Plan had aimed to achieve a 25 per cent growth in national output by 1970 – an ambitious 3.8 per cent per annum. This obviously had no chance of success, given the government's real priorities of correcting the balance of payments deficit and saving the pound by means of deflation. But it has to be said that the Plan was so easily brushed aside because it never represented anything more substantial than a pious hope from the outset. The much-vaunted Department of Economic Affairs (DEA), far from representing a real challenge to the dominance of the Treasury, was never given any real powers of action. The same is true of the Regional Economic Planning Councils which were in reality a mere public relations exercise. By the time of the deflationary package of July 1966 any residual confidence that the DEA could amount to something was gone and Brown was moved from the department, leaving it to wither away. It was finally scrapped in 1969.

Thus if the absence of a coherent strategy had been obscured by Wilson's radical rhetoric before October 1964, it very soon became apparent when such instruments of the 'white heat of technological revolution' as the new Ministry of Technology (Mintech) turned out to be little more than gatherers of statistical information. When, finally, Mintech was put to some use after Tony Benn took it over in 1966 it became associated with the formation of monopolies in the private sector – which the government encouraged – and continued the previous government's policy of supporting nuclear power as part of its enthusiasm for large-scale, high-tech industry. Such policies substituted for the broader modernization strategy which had figured prominently in Wilson's election promises and testified to the fact that when the government was re-elected in March 1966 it had no new ideas let alone any radical proposals to make.

Disappointment among the government's supporters was compounded by frustration leading to anger as the attempt to avoid devaluation inaugurated a long period of wage controls. The voluntary pay restraint which Labour had expected since December 1964 was succeeded by a six-month standstill on all wage rises in July 1966, as the government attempted to deal with another sterling crisis by dampening down domestic demand. Around £500 million was squeezed out of the economy during the following year at a time when Wilson was still bound by the deal which he had struck with President Johnson in 1965. The wage freeze introduced in July 1966 was succeeded by another six months of 'severe restraint' which in turn gave way to a 3–3½ per cent pay norm that lasted until the end of 1969. Conflict with the unions was inevitable and Wilson's attack on the National Union of Seamen when the latter took strike action soon after Labour was re-elected in 1966 was an early indication that the government needed scapegoats to explain away its poor record. On this occasion Wilson attempted to smear the union by alleging that the strike was the result of a Communist conspiracy. But by November 1967 the three-year battle to defend the pound was lost and Wilson – no longer bound by the agreement with President Johnson – was forced to devalue. The new Chancellor, Roy Jenkins, now calculated that public expenditure cuts of around £800 million were required to make devaluation work, although in the event the figure agreed was £712 million. All the government's efforts were henceforth focused on the elimination of the balance of payments deficit which began to improve from the spring of 1969 and was turned into a large surplus by the general election of 1970. By that time, however, unemployment had risen by 60 per cent (to 555,000) and inflation had almost doubled (to 6.4 per cent).

The government could, however, point to some positive achievements of social reform during its six years in office. It had made parliamentary time and had given encouragement to progressive backbench legislation on divorce, abortion, homosexuality and theatre censorship. Labour also introduced the Open University, legislation on race relations, and redundancy payments for workers with at least two years service in a firm. It also introduced a watered-down version of the Swedish Ombudsman but failed to make constitutional changes of real significance. The proposal to reform the House of Lords by eliminating its power of legislative delay was blocked both by the government's own dilatoriness on the matter and by an opportunistic alliance of proponents of complete abolition, led by Michael Foot, and opponents of any reform, led by Enoch Powell. Similarly the Fulton Report on reform of the civil service came to nothing. On most matters of social reform, such as housing and education, Labour was content to follow existing thinking and trends. Wilson was of the opinion that under his leadership Labour could be transformed into the 'natural party of government', and seems to have believed that this could be achieved by concentrating on administration and avoiding socialist ideology and vision. The one big initiative taken by the second Wilson government in the arena of domestic reforms succeeded in dividing the party from top to bottom when legislation was proposed in 1969 to reform the trade unions.

Wilson was normally so adept at balancing the party's various factions that the miscalculation involved in Barbara Castle's *In Place of Strife* proposals must be explained in terms of his desire to promote Labour as the custodian of national interests which the unruly elements within the unions were perceived to threaten. Given the government's real economic priorities this is not at all surprising; strikes, especially unofficial strikes, were coming to be seen as the major cause of Britain's economic rot. Wilson and Castle calculated that in return for measures designed to strengthen the national leaderships of the unions, organized labour would acquiesce in reforms designed to strengthen the state's ability to prevent many strikes from taking place by imposing secret ballots and 'cooling-off' periods of twenty-eight days. During the first six months of 1969 Wilson had to contend with opposition from within his own Cabinet, a majority of the NEC, and a large number of Labour MPs, as well as the unions themselves, until *In Place of Strife* was finally dropped. There is no doubt that the bitterness thus generated was a major factor in strengthening the Left of the party in the following decade, given that so many of Labour's central reforms had been ignominiously abandoned.

Looking back on these years in 1974, Anthony Crosland – who still believed in the revisionist emphasis on equality and the idea that that government could impose its will on the private firm – concluded that 'there was little sign of a coherent, overall egalitarian strategy', and admitted that by 1970 'unemployment was higher, inflation more rapid and economic growth slower than when the Conservatives left office in 1964.[16] Furthermore,

> For the first time the mass of manual workers found themselves caught in the net of progressive direct taxation. In the 1950s the typical manual worker paid virtually no income tax; even in 1960 his tax and insurance contributions took only 8 per cent of his earnings; but by 1970 they took nearly 20 per cent. The inevitable result was more inflation, strikes, and industrial unrest . . . extreme class inequalities remain, poverty is far from eliminated, the economy is in a state of semi-permanent crisis and inflation is rampant.[17]

Despite this negative post mortem Crosland retained his faith in the ability of social democratic governments to manage capitalism more equitably than their opponents and consoled himself with the thought that 'there are no clear signs of a new and fundamental crisis in the system.' It is a striking fact that the dismal performance of the Wilson governments produced no new socialist analyses from the leading revisionists, provoked no new understanding of the structure of the modern capitalist economy and the giant corporations which dominated it. Crosland had argued in 1962 that 'monopoly is in practice rather rare' and that modern corporations are 'slaves to their public relations departments', that is, 'apologetic where their predecessors were haughty'.[18] On this reasoning it was possible to conclude that 'a determined reforming government can now generally get its way without a change in ownership', by means of various fiscal inducements instead. Douglas Jay was if anything even more sanguine than Crosland at the start of the decade, concluding that it was 'almost true to say that progressive direct taxation can transform society'.[19] Neither of them changed their minds when six years of Labour government failed the expectations which they had helped to cultivate during thirteen years of Opposition.

But by 1968 the revisionist initiative was exhausted. Opposition to the Wilson government from within the party and the trade unions was demonstrated at the annual conference where the Executive lost the vote on thirteen occasions between 1966 and the end of 1969 on such key policy issues as prices and incomes, economic policy, the government's handling of the Rhodesia crisis and its attitude to the American war in Vietnam. Quite apart from the government's failure in respect of social policy and economic growth, almost from the start of Wilson's first term Labour rapidly surrendered the moral high ground and made a nonsense of the claims of many of its leaders that they stood for the 'unashamedly ethical' socialism of Tawney. In spite of the fact that Gaitskell had denounced the 1962 Commonwealth Immigration Act as a racist measure, for example, the Labour government introduced a White Paper on *Immigration from the Commonwealth* as early as August 1965, which was designed to strengthen the Conservative legislation. While it also introduced the promised Race Relations Act (1965) which made race discrimination illegal, housing and employment were exempt from its provisions; the government undid such useful work as it had begun by succumbing to the racist hysteria generated by Enoch Powell and the 1968 scare over the arrival of Kenyan Asians, and rushing through another Commonwealth Immigration Act even more explicitly racist than its predecessor.

This volte-face over immigration damaged Labour's standing with the immigrant community in Britain, as Wilson discovered when he was met by protestors representing a coalition of Indian and Pakistani organizations in Birmingham who advised their members in the Sparkbrook and All Saints constituencies to abstain in the next election.[20] This should have been an early warning to the Labour Party that it could not take the immigrant vote for granted, but the government was preoccupied with its competition with the Conservative Party

> over whether or not it really understood the feelings and interests of the 'British people' and . . . in the process . . . set up both the ideology and a large part of the structure of institutionalized racism which the subsequent Conservative government was able to rationalize in the form of the 1971 Immigration Act.[21]

The 'infamous debates'[22] on immigration and foreign policy which took place at the annual conference in 1965 were only the first of many which enraged and disillusioned thousands of party activists. By 1970 the party had lost around 240,000 individual members during the six years of Labour government and many constituency organizations were virtually defunct.[23] Coinciding as this did with an upsurge of socialist campaigning outside the party it is more than likely that the constituency parties shrivelled because of the government's policies. While opposition to the American war in Vietnam brought massive demonstrations on to the streets of London, for example, the Labour government (unlike de Gaulle's government in France) refused to criticize US policy. Even after the American government illegally extended the war to Cambodia Wilson made no public condemnation of its policy, while in the privacy of Cabinet the Chancellor, Roy Jenkins, apparently argued that Britain could not 'afford' to criticize Washington.[24] Crosland and Healey also argued that though Nixon had made a 'mistake' there should be no open criticism of it.[25]

We now know that Labour's ability to criticize American policy was severely compromised by the agreement between Wilson and Johnson in 1965 and that in economic terms Jenkins was right to suggest that the government could not 'afford' publicly to question US involvement in Vietnam. Nevertheless we must not underestimate the degree to which the leading figures in the Labour government were bound to the general sweep of American policy by conviction. Wilson resisted Johnson's attempts directly to involve British troops on the grounds that he would never be able to sell this policy to the British public, but he did offer facilities for jungle training and counter-insurgency advice as well as affirming his 'solid support' for US policy against 'communist infiltration'.[26] Britain also sold arms to the USA for use in Vietnam, but perhaps the most shameful episode in the obsequious 'special relationship' which the Labour government had with the Johnson administration was the forced removal of the 2000 inhabitants of the island of Diego Garcia in the Indian Ocean which was cleared to make way for an American military base between 1965 and 1970.

Once again a Labour government was involved in attempts to secure British interests abroad by supporting reactionaries. When Cheddi Jagan reappeared as a strong candidate in the British Guiana elections of 1965, Britain joined with America to conduct joint intelligence activities to prevent his election. Similarly British aid was dispensed to support the Right in Malta where Dom Mintoff's possible election threatened Britain's defence arrangements. Meanwhile aid to developing countries, which Labour had promised to increase to 1 per cent of Gross National Product in 1957, was actually cut from 0.53 per cent to 0.37 per cent between 1964 and 1970. Britain's balance of payments problems undoubtedly helped to reshape the Cabinet's conception of sensible economics – so much so, indeed, that a group led by Brown, Crosland and Healey wanted to lift the embargo on arms sales to South Africa at the end of 1967.[27] Wilson eventually blocked this move which would have further enraged the party – after all, in 1964 Labour had talked of a total embargo on trade with the racist regime. But the moral imperatives perceived in opposition had been so displaced by *realpolitik* while in office that it is easy to understand the reasoning of the group led by Brown; if we can sell arms to the Americans for use in Vietnam and allow British firms to trade with the illegal racist government of Rhodesia in defiance of our own sanctions, why can't we sell arms to South Africa? Such weapons sales would help with the balance of payments and the protection of British markets. When the Nigerian civil war began in May 1967 these were the considerations which brought Labour down on the side of the Federal government and boosted sales of armaments to Lagos.

Much of the seamy side of the government's foreign policy was kept secret, of course, but its broad thrust was clear enough to bring it into conflict with the annual conference. The government's defeat at the 1966 conference on the question of its support for the Americans in Vietnam and the level of British military expenditure was in fact the first time that a Labour government was defeated on defence and foreign policy issues by the annual conference. If anything, the gulf between the mass party and the leading ministers in the Wilson government was even bigger than such open conflicts suggested. For while the activists were increasingly questioning nuclear defence, the NATO alliance, and the special relationship with the USA, the minister of Defence, Denis Healey, was advising President Nixon and his Secretary of State Henry Kissinger, who visited London in February 1969, that the Americans should tell the Soviet Union of NATO's readiness to use nuclear weapons and thereby risk a full 'strategic' exchange in any future conflict between the two sides. Even Kissinger found in this advice evidence of backward thinking and remarked on the double-standards involved in advocating early resort to 'tactical' nuclear weapons by people who would never contemplate such a war if it was to be fought on their own soil.[28]

The government's corruption strengthened the case, powerfully expressed by Ralph Miliband as early as 1961 in *Parliamentary Socialism*, that Labour's only real commitment was to parliamentarism and that socialists who wanted socialist policies had better look elsewhere.[29] But where? That was the problem. The New Left to which Miliband belonged had no time for the CPGB, which had drifted since the Stalinist traumas of 1956 with a concoction of Russian Marxism and parliamentary socialism peculiar to the Western Communist parties. The CPGB still had a prominent presence in the leadership of many of the trade unions, though it had lost control of the ETU after the ballot-rigging scandal of 1961, but was without favour among the Marxist intellectuals, many of whom had deserted the party in 1956 and were associated with the *New Left Review* from 1960. Thus unlike its Italian and French counterparts, which remained mass parties supported by a significant element of the intelligentsia, the CPGB had neither electoral clout nor intellectual vigour. The dilemma of Marxists who rejected Stalinism was that either they belonged to the Labour Party as a dissident minority and operated like Sisyphus, with the added complication of risking expulsion (such as Ken Coates suffered in 1965 for his criticisms of government policy), or they attached themselves to radical campaigns when these arose.

A way out of this dilemma began to appear by the mid-1960s. The growing conflict between the Labour government and the trade unions, and between militant shop stewards and the TUC, combined with a more general disillusionment with the Labour Party, provided the basis for effective socialist activity outside these mass organizations. This was in complete contrast to the previous decade when the whole of the Left was compelled to operate inside these structures. The Cold War freeze and the unprecedented full employment boom had between them apparently squeezed out any spaces for independent radical activity until CND broke out of the containment at the decade's close. This was the reason why the fissiparous Trotskyist Left had kept an extremely low profile in such tiny entrist groups as The Club, the Revolutionary Socialist league and the International Group.[30] But by 1964 it was possible for the Socialist Labour League (SLL, formerly The Club) to destroy the Labour Party's Young Socialist organization by poaching 4000 of its members; Labour was forced to disband its youth section the following year. The SLL, under the authoritarian leadership of Gerry Healy, was the first of the entrist groups to leave the Labour Party in the hope of building an independent revolutionary party. While Healy was persuaded that a coming slump in the economy was the firm basis for these ambitions, a group around the non-sectarian Marxist journal *International Socialism* decided to pull out of the Labour Party in 1965 in order to establish itself among the shop stewards and connect with those factory struggles which promised to provide a real proletarian base for an independent party of the Left.

Only a year before the International Socialist group took this decision an Institute for Workers Control had been established by Ken Coates and others in Nottingham Labour Party which soon won the support of the Left in the unions. Two of the most important supporters of this initiative – Jack Jones and Hugh Scanlon – were to become leaders of the TGWU and AEU respectively. Jones had always favoured giving more power to the shop stewards and as socialists both he and Scanlon shared the Institute's vision of a decentralized trade union structure harnessing shop floor idealism and generating solidarity and political consciousness among the rank and file. Thus in the light of the growth in unofficial strikes, many of them concerned – as the Donovan Report of 1968 showed – with issues of control rather than simply pay, this evidence, even at the highest levels of the trade union movement, of a concern with the distribution of power in industry emboldened some Marxists to dream of a new Minority Movement. This was the perspective towards which the International Socialists moved after 1965.

But international events played a bigger part in inspiring the new radicalism than anything developed at home. In January 1966 Bertrand Russell helped to launch the Vietnamese Solidarity Campaign (VSC) which, after the decline of CND in the mid-1960s, became the main rallying point for forces opposed to US war-mongering. From the beginning the leadership of VSC included Trotskyists from a small entrist group based in Nottingham which publis ed *The Week* and initiated the Institute for Workers' Control. In 1969 this en ist organization emerged from the Labour Party as the International Marxist Group, the official British section of the Fourth International. By then its leaders such as Tariq Ali and Pat Jordan had played a notable part in the War Crimes Tribunal which with the support of Bertrand Russell, Jean-Paul Sartre, Isaac Deutscher and others had indicted the American war against Vietnam. The leaders of IMG had done a great deal to ensure that the VSC, which mobilized demonstrations of over 100,000 people by 1968, campaigned for 'Victory to the NLF' rather than the pacifist 'peace in Vietnam' slogan of the CP's British Council for Peace in Vietnam which VSC totally eclipsed. The IMG lost any connections it may have fostered with the trade unions, however, when its increasingly Leninist vanguard pretensions led to a break with Coates and the Institute for Workers Control in 1967.

Instead the IMG enthusiastically embraced the student radicalism which VSC drew on and helped to inspire. Student opposition to the war in Vietnam produced Students for a Democratic Society in the USA in 1966, the year when Mao Zedong launched the Cultural Revolution in China and student Red Guards took to the streets in their hundreds of thousands. In their different ways these events played a part in fuelling student radicalism in many other countries, including Britain. The first of many occupations and evidence of the mood for direct action in the British universities was provoked by the appointment of a new Director at the London School of Economics, a former senior academic figure in racist Rhodesia where the Smith government had operated unilateral independence from Britain since 1965. By 1968, a year in which students helped to topple de Gaulle's government in France and fought to resist Soviet intervention in Czechoslovakia, it was possible for the IMG to believe that universities could be turned into 'Red bases'. Assisted by an eclectic radical theorizing which included the recent works of Herbert Marcuse, Franz Fanon, R. D. Laing, the American proponents of Black Power, Europeanized 'Maoism' and various ultra-leftist tendencies in Italy, West Germany and France, it was possible to interpret these events as proof of the emergence of new vanguards which had displaced the proletariat as the future emancipators of mankind. The IMG went some of the way with this kind of reasoning while the International Socialists, who were also disproportionately dependent on student members, turned increasingly to traditional Leninist politics when the revolution, which May 1968 had promised in France, failed to materialize.

Because student radicalism faded and then disappeared almost entirely in the 1970s it is now easy to scoff at the mood of 1968. But many of the militants from these campaigns remained active in Left politics and re-emerged at the heart of the Labour Left when this was revitalized in the late 1970s. We shall see in chapter 14 that these socialists continued to think about politics in ways which first achieved prominence in the 1960s. It is ironic, given the retreat to Leninist vanguardism which the IMG, IS and SLL exhibited, that the events of 1968 gave rise to a 'great revival of interest in non-Leninist traditions on the left'.[31] This was nowhere more evident than in the new feminist movement which was initially inspired by libertarian traditions of direct action and direct democracy, the struggles of American blacks, the psycho-politics of R. D. Laing and David Cooper and socialist theories of many traditions. The first conference of the new women's movement set itself the task of developing 'an organization that in its form and content would eradicate the relevant faults of the other preceding radical groups'.[32] This entailed an emphasis on prefigurative politics. For it followed from the feminist slogan that 'the personal is political', that it was not enough to posit progressive goals if organizations and individuals behaved in ways which made these goals unattainable. Male-dominated, centralized and bureaucratic organizations were on this reasoning unlikely to develop participative politics, let alone genuine equality between the sexes. Thus the feminist movement championed autonomous and decentralized women's organizations which were anathema to the Leninist Left. Nevertheless the Labour Party was so patently uninterested in the issues which preoccupied the women's movement, so very far removed from its commitment to participatory democracy and its attempt to explain the subordination of women in terms of gender and patriarchy, that many socialist feminists at first gravitated to the Marxist Left where there were at least some organizations – the IMG and the CPGB for instance – receptive to their developing radicalism.

The Left had always complained about the Labour Party; even that portion of it wholly committed to parliamentarism had been on occasions 'heartily sickened' by its parliamentary wing, which Bevan had once described as 'rotten through and through: corrupt, full of patronage and seeking after patronage; unprincipled'.[33] But while the perspective of a 'fundamental transformation in the Parliamentary Party', which Bevan had set out, always had its advocates, the internal reform of the Labour organizations was not high on the agenda of the radicals in the late 1960s. The books that had inspired young socialists in the 1960s were written by critics of the party who belonged in many cases to the Marxist tradition. For this generation Deutscher was more influential than Crosland. Indeed, the Labour Party had ceased to be a source of socialist theory by 1968; it seemed increasingly to function merely as an electoral machine: 'No coherent analysis of capitalist power, no movement of socialist education and propaganda, no authentic ideology of social change, has emerged from the institutional Labour Party for two decades.'[34] As far as the New Left was concerned the Labour Party was not even a real coalition containing a socialist component capable of acting independently:

> it is certain that what has so far been thought of as the Labour Left has been a kind of shadow reproduction of the whole official Labour Party and its perspectives. Just as the Labour Party has been a compromise between working class objectives and the existing power structure, at the national level, so the traditional Labour Left has been a compromise between socialist objectives and the existing power structure at the party level.[35]

Since withdrawal from the party was anathema to this Labour Left it was compelled, on this view, to spend its days in impotence, directing the energies of socialists, moreover, into the very institutions and methods of action which socialists should fight.

It was the explosion of direct action in the form of mass protest and near-insurrection throughout the world which gave this negative assessment of the Labour Party an optimistic counterpoint at the end of the 1960s. Civil rights protesters in the USA and Northern Ireland were promoting social and political change outside the channels of mainstream politics, just as the French and Italian working-class movements were shaking their respective political systems. Labour's failure in office convinced some groups on the far Left that Parliament was now useless for obtaining 'direct, felt reforms' and that the two major parties presented a choice between Tweedledum and Tweedledee.[36] Strikes now seemed a better vehicle for acquiring private fringe benefits than improvements in the social wage acquired through Labour's reforms. By 1970 it seemed that 'the only principled course for revolutionary socialists during the coming election will be an active campaign to discredit both of Britain's large capitalist parties.[37]

This argument, briefly propounded by Robin Blackburn and Tariq Ali, was soon discredited even within the IMG when Labour lost the 1970 election and Edward Heath's Conservative government proceeded to introduce an Industrial Relations Bill designed to attack the rank and file trade union power which many on the Left saw as the potential base of a new socialist party. The Wilson government had been forced to abandon its own proposals for trade union reform in July 1969 when Barbara Castle's *In Place of Strife* was scrapped. But the Heath government was not as amenable to trade union protests and the prospect which the Conservatives held out was one of a major assault on the post-war consensus which would add up to a 'quiet revolution'.

In the years that followed, the belief that a powerful shop stewards' movement would help to break the mould in British politics was powerfully reinforced by a massive strike wave which ultimately engulfed the Heath government and precipitated the general elections of 1974 which the Conservatives lost. Trade union hostility to the Industrial Relations Bill enabled the Communist Party to revive the Liaison Committee for the Defence of Trade Unions (LCDTU), which it had originally set up in 1966 to co-ordinate opposition to Wilson's prices and incomes policy. The LCDTU campaigned for a general strike to oppose Heath's industrial relations legislation and managed to bring out around 600,000 workers as early as December 1970. The CPGB's industrial organizer, Bert Ramelson, was at the centre of this activity but the numbers of active opponents of the government's policies massively exceeded anything that the Communists were capable of mobilizing on their own.

Not that the government was averse to invoking the Communist conspiracy: even Wilson had played this card in order to discredit the seamen's strike of 1966 when he had called Ramelson 'the most powerful man in

Britain'. But this was even less credible in the early 1970s despite the imprison-
ment of Communists when dockers defied the Industrial Relations Act in July
1971 and building workers were charged with 'conspiracy' in 1972. By March
1971 three million strikers answered the call for a one-day general strike and
the number of political strikes was increasing. At Upper Clyde Shipbuilders
(UCS), Communist shop stewards led the opposition to the proposed closure
of the four yards in 1971 and transformed the dispute into a struggle for the
'right to work'. In the wake of the UCS 'work-in' something like 190 factory
occupations took place between July 1971 and December 1975.[38] This
innovative militancy was also apparent in the national miners' strike of
1972 – the first since 1926 – when the union deployed mobile or 'flying pick-
ets'. It was another successful miners' strike which provoked the general
election of 1974, but by that time the government had called no less than five
States of Emergency and had reduced industry to a three-day week.

Despite Heath's decision in 1972 to jettison the monetarist politics on which
his government had been elected, the strike wave continued throughout the
Conservative term of office as unemployment and inflation got worse. It was
this crisis which moved the Labour Party leftwards – a process which will be
described in chapter 14 – and spurred the whole of the Left to think about a
viable socialist strategy. The IMG, however, completely out of step with the
tide of industrial militancy, was informed by the positions adopted by the
ninth congress of the Fourth International in 1969. The armed struggles of
Third World nationalist movements as in Vietnam and the upsurge in guerilla
warfare in Latin America inspired the Fourth International to reason that
struggles in the capitalist 'periphery' would ultimately detonate the Western
working class. The IMG accordingly focused on solidarity campaigns and
identified Northern Ireland, where it wanted 'Victory to the IRA', as the weak
link in British politics. But the ninth congress also predicted a long period of
economic downturn in the advanced capitalist countries, taking place in the
context of a new balance in world forces opposed to capitalism. Thus on this
basis the socialist revolution was confidently predicted for Western Europe.[39]

Of course this was no strategy at all; IMG membership never exceeded 500
even though it posed as an independent party in embryo. The theorists of the
International Socialists saw the strike wave as more evidence of a militant
rank and file ready to burst the bonds of official trade unionism. It demonstrated 'that collective action represents a reaction against the economic
exploitation and deprivation of control inherent in the institution of wage-
labour and possesses a dimension of revolt which can never be wholly sup-
pressed'.[40] Roger Rosewell (later to become an enthusiastic Thatcherite)
argued that by mobilizing a national rank-and-file movement it would be
possible to convert the unions 'into organizations of real revolutionary struggle under a Marxist leadership'.[41] According to the IS analysis, the struggle
for reforms had shifted from Parliament to the trade unions in the 1950s. By
the time of the Donovan Commission's Report in 1968 an estimated 175,000
shop stewards existed – a figure which the Office of Manpower Economics

revised upwards to 300,000 in 1974. Faced with economic contraction, supine leaders and a moribund Labour Party, the shop stewards were becoming increasingly political, as the strikes against *In Place of Strife*, the Industrial Relations Bill and Phase 2 of Heath's policy of wage restraint were supposed to show. Strike action had also been taken to support old age pensioners, imprisoned trade unionists, greater control of the workplace and so on. But IS theorists believed that under the given conditions of crisis pure and simple wage militancy could lead to the emergence of socialist consciousness within the unions – especially if Marxists did their best to promote it by establishing factory branches in the relevant centres of industry. With perhaps as many as 4,000 members by 1974, the IS was in fact too small to make much of a difference and the organization effectively depended on spontaneous combustion to produce the necessary socialist movement in industry:

> when workers ask for a few shillings a week in a single shop, the ideological veil covering the system as a whole is not pulled aside, but when 100,000 workers demand a 20 per cent rise to keep up with rising prices the class struggle moves into the centre of the stage.[42]

But even as the IS elaborated this theory of economic militancy leading to socialist consciousness the incoming Labour government of 1974 produced a 'miracle' – as the Chancellor, Denis Healey, described it – by bringing the strike wave down to manageable proportions. By the time the IS launched itself as the Socialist Workers' Party (SWP) in January 1977 the prospects for establishing a national rank and file movement modelled on the Minority Movement were dismal indeed and the SWP was never able to construct the type of Leninist organization anchored in the factories which it favoured. At the same time, all the other vanguardist projects were reaching a stagnant denouement; student militancy had receded after the American withdrawal from Vietnam and all eyes were on the Labour Party, which had been elected with a programme more radical than anything it had adopted since the war.

Conclusion

The experience of the Wilson governments in the 1960s was the beginning of the end both for revisionism, which had always been dependent on sustained economic growth, and for those corporatist arrangements which had characterized British politics since the Second World War. As we have seen, Labour allowed the balance of payments crisis which it inherited from the previous Conservative administration to scupper its ambitious plans for economic modernization and faster growth. There was an element of choice here in that Wilson decided from the beginning to resist devaluation and to maintain Britain's unrealistic defence commitments around the globe. The last remnants of Britain's imperial legacy were finally abandoned, but not before Labour's programme of reforms was itself in tatters.

But the economic problems faced after 1964 also represented a conjunction of rising inflation, slower growth and increasing unemployment which traditional Keynesian policies were not designed to contend with. The government placed increasing emphasis on the control of wages, but in the given inflationary context no amount of 'beer and sandwiches' at Number Ten could enable the trade union leaders to deliver lasting wage restraint when they themselves were faced with an increasingly militant membership which was well organized at a local level. The idea that 'planning' wages was a necessary component of a socialist strategy was all well and good – the Labour Left had talked about it since the 1940s; the trouble was that nothing else was being planned. Moreover, after having entered office with promises of greatly increasing the social wage and of even abolishing poverty, the government actually embarked on a series of cuts in public expenditure which did nothing to compensate for wage controls. Labour further alienated its supporters by its obsequious posture in relation to the USA's war in Vietnam. On a range of foreign policy issues the government was profoundly reactionary at a time when a new generation of socialists was being formed around rejection of the Cold War, imperialism and racism. The Government's problems with an increasingly rebellious annual conference and Labour's bigger problem of a fast declining membership suggest that in this period party loyalists were beginning to be replaced by a more 'semi-detached', critical membership. Although no organization to the Left of Labour could even begin to challenge it electorally, thousands of young socialists passed through the Far Left groups. More importantly Labour had dried up as a source of ideas, vision and inspiration.

New social movements were to become much more significant in framing the radical agenda on issues such as defence and foreign policy, environmental protection, industrial democracy, race and gender. In some of these areas the Labour Party was completely out of touch with the new developments and in none of them did it hold the initiative. The New Left, which had first emerged after 1956, was far more important as a source of inspiration for the new generation of radicals. Its leading figures such as Raymond Williams, Edward Thompson and Stuart Hall had championed a Marxism more concerned with cultural critique and independent of both Labourist and Communist traditions, both in their different ways inclined to reduce the Left to a one-dimensional class analysis. In pointing to a much broader spectrum of moral, cultural, political, social and economic forms of domination, the New Left's analysis of how power operates in society was more relevant to radicals like the feminists of the 1960s who rejected the idea that all collective identity was encompassed in class. Both the New Left and the new social movements were interested in connecting with the humanitarian traditions of socialists such as William Morris and earlier concerns, blotted-out by Labourism and Leninism, with the politics of consumption, art, the environment, sexuality and so on. Labour's single-minded quest for governmental office, on the other hand, had served to narrow its conception of politics to questions of state action and corporatism supplemented by party committees and resolutions. One of the big questions for socialists in the immediate future, however, was whether the Labour Party could be recast sufficiently to bring all these diverse issues into a unified programme for social change.

14

The Rise and Fall of the Left

There had always been socialists who believed that Labour's failures in office (and, indeed, in Opposition) were intimately connected to the party's oligarchical structure which enabled the parliamentary and trade union leadership to dominate the mass party and insulate themselves from its more radical impulses. Harry Pollitt was wont to explain the rejection of Communist overtures for 'working-class unity' and the affiliation of the CPGB in this way.[1] By the 1950s the Bevanites saw the party machine in the vice-like grip of the Revisionists and their anti-Communist allies in the trade unions such as Will Lawther, Arthur Deakin and Tom Williamson. As we have seen, the permanent impotence of the Labour Left led the New Left to write it off in the 1960s as a mere classification devoid of organization, ideology and strategy, but functioning to legitimize the dominant power bloc in the party. Labour was coming to be seen as a graveyard for socialists, but this analysis was influential among activists only for as long as there seemed to be dynamic alternatives. But by the early 1970s it was pertinent to ask:

> 'If the Labour Party cannot be turned into a socialist party then the question which confronts us all is, how can we form a socialist party? If we are not ready to answer this question then we are not ready to dismiss the party that exists.'[2]

In fact the failure of the Wilson governments and the evident exhaustion of revisionism produced a Left backlash after 1970 which made the party a more congenial place for socialists. Undoubtedly Wilson's confrontation with the unions over prices and incomes and then over *In Place of Strife* had helped to alienate organized labour from the parliamentary leadership, and the leftward trend in the unions – as symbolized by the election of Hugh Scanlon as President of the AEU in 1967 and Jack Jones as General Secretary of the TGWU in 1969 – continued into the 1970s under the confrontationist Heath government. It was the fact that a large proportion of the trade union block votes were now sympathetic to the Left which enabled it to dominate the eighty or so policy committees and study groups which met between 1970 and

1974.[3] By 1973 Labour's programme reflected this change in the balance of party forces. For this was the period in which the elements of an Alternative Economic Strategy (AES) were assembled, featuring wide-ranging public ownership proposals and forms of planning inspired by European experience.

Once again Labour addressed the issue of how Britain's relative economic decline, and especially the decline of the country's manufacturing industries, could be reversed while taking larger steps towards a more just society. The formulation of a national-socialist economic programme also preoccupied the Communist Party and the Conference of Socialist Economists which met annually from 1970. Variants of the AES were thus common currency on the Labour and Communist Left by the early 1970s. The most creative thinking, however, was done by Stuart Holland, who tried to bring Labour's analysis of capitalism up to date by acknowledging the central role in the national economy played by multinational companies and other groups of oligopolists. These had been ignored by the revisionists and yet the British economy had a higher proportion of multinationals than any other economy in the world. Keynesian macro-economic policies had virtually no effect on this sector, which was largely self-financing. Thus Holland proposed that around twenty-five of these companies, one from twenty-five different branches of industry, be nationalized while statutory planning agreements enforced by fiscal measures and the threat of public ownership would be imposed on the rest of this 'meso-sector'. It was reasoned that the nationalization of the leading firm in each of twenty-five industries would allow the state indirectly to influence the investment, location and labour policies of this loss-leader's competitors and thus achieve standards for entire industries without recourse to the bureaucratic and inefficient nationalization measures of old. The dynamic of competition would remain; in fact it would be enhanced by virtue of the state's direct control of some of these firms in the national interest. Furthermore, each of these firm's competitors would be set targets by the state, and failure to comply would result in punitive taxation, success in tax incentives.[4]

The planning effort, then, in this analysis, would be concentrated on about a hundred companies in the manufacturing sector aimed at improving their investment strategies and their strategies for training, location and so on. The Left reasoned that proper control over these strategies could not be achieved bureaucratically. Trade union expertise would have to be harnessed in partnership with government. Hence, if for no other reason, industrial democracy – long championed by influential trade union leaders like Jack Jones and Hugh Scanlon – was firmly on the Left's agenda. But of course the idea of workers' control – 'the aggressive encroachment of trade unions on management powers in a capitalist framework' – was also championed by some of the Labour Left because it was seen as a genuinely transitional measure to the sort of society they wanted; a democratically administered socialized economy.[5] The new planning proposals would take the so-called commanding heights of the economy – which in Holland's words had come to represent 'a dead weight on the backs of the working class people'[6] – and subject it to both encroaching control from below and state ownership and co-ordination from above. According to Holland's reckoning, the state would own a sector representing 33 per cent of total turnover, 40 per cent of profits and 50 per cent of employment in manufacturing simply by the nationalization of these twenty-five companies.

It cannot be said that industrial democracy and planning proposals were always discussed side by side or that the centralist and decentralist elements in this thinking were brought into harmony. There are always tensions and contradictions between statist and decentralist elements in any complex society; nevertheless the AES was evolved without much attention to the issue of industrial democracy. The main centre for thinking about industrial democracy in the development of *Labour's Programme 1973* was the TUC/Labour Party Liaison Committee which concerned itself with the abolition of the Industrial Relations Act and the formulation of new legislation designed to enhance workers' rights and trade union representation in industry. In February 1973 the committee published a *Statement on Economic Policy and the Cost of Living* which committed the next Labour government to price controls, a major programme of public housing, better public transport, taxes on wealth and gifts, steeply progressive direct taxation, increased pensions, the end of prescription charges, policies of public ownership, capital controls, state-directed investment and industrial democracy. In the view of Jack Jones, who was a leading participant in the committee's work, this Social Contract, as it became known 'above all . . . placed Industrial Democracy . . . into the centre of Party thinking and policy.'[7] The unions' part in this bargain was to exercise voluntary wage restraint.

Some of the more radical proposals which found favour with the policy committees were either watered down or quashed altogether before they had a chance to get into the party's election manifestos in 1974. Stuart Holland's proposal to nationalize the leading banks, building societies and insurance companies was rejected by the party leadership and his idea of planning agreements was completely transformed by 1974 into a purely voluntary arrangement. The 1973 annual conference was dominated by the demand to nationalize the twenty-five largest companies, but Wilson personally vetoed its inclusion in the 1974 manifesto. Nevertheless the party did vote to nationalize North Sea oil and gas, ports, shipbuilding, aircraft production and parts of the pharmaceutical, machine tool and construction industries, together with a proportion of the road haulage industry and development land. These measures were to be taken by a National Enterprise Board (NEB) based at a new Department of Industry. With promises to establish sex equality at work and to renegotiate the terms of Britain's entry into the EEC (which Heath accomplished in 1973), it all added up to 'the finest Socialist Programme I have seen in my lifetime', according to Michael Foot.

Certainly the party now wanted 'a fundamental and irreversible shift in the balance of power and wealth in favour of working people and their families'. It had apparently moved beyond the Keynesian economic management thinking of the revisionists because:

> The experience of Labour Government has made it increasingly evident
> that even the most comprehensive measures of social and fiscal reform
> can only succeed in masking the unacceptable and unpleasant face of a
> capitalist economy and cannot achieve any fundamental changes in the
> power relationships which dominate our society.[8]

This kind of talk suggested that Labour was interested in the question of
power and its distribution. Tony Benn was certainly concerned with this issue
and by 1970 had rejected the technocratic corporatism which he and Wilson
had earlier championed. In that year he wrote of the need to go 'beyond
parliamentary democracy' and invoked many of the movements concerned to
increase democratic participation which had developed in the 1960s as sources
of socialist renewal.[9] The Labour constituencies undoubtedly had need of
new recruits. Many of them had reached a state of terminal decay by the end
of the 1960s and one influential study of Labour's grassroots was able to talk
plausibly of 'the decline of working class politics'. For in the constituencies
studied the meagre membership was found to lapse into chronic inactivity
between elections and the few who did attend meetings could 'go for months
without hearing anything authoritative about the party's problems and
actions; for years without ever discussing "socialism".'[10] This situation had
come about partly by design, in that for years past the parliamentary leadership had been inclined to view activists with distaste unless they fell into the
category of deferential work-horses. According to Barry Hindess it was the
view of the Labour Right that: 'precisely because strictly political activity is
no longer necessary . . . anyone who tries to stir up political activity must be a
trouble-maker however much he or she may claim to represent the local
membership or the working-class.'[11]

The Labour strongholds were often the worst afflicted by this stultifying
attitude because entrenched officials and elected representatives seemed to be
guaranteed re-election with or without a thriving party membership. This is
why the disastrous municipal election results of 1968–9 opened up spaces for a
younger, more vigorous cohort in the 1970s. Many of the old practitioners of
boss-politics were undermined when the entrenched councillors were uncere-
moniously dumped.[12] It is from this time that the way was opened for a generation influenced by the politics of the new social movements in the 1960s. By
the mid-1970s this new Labour Left was a force in a number of cities including
London, where it managed to gain a majority on the Executive of the party
in 1977. Even in the 1960s it had not been possible to manage the party with
the authoritarianism of the 1950s. But Wilson and his colleagues frequently
ignored decisions taken at the annual conference. This was something which
the less deferential recruits of the 1970s were not prepared to tolerate. Aided
by the growing power of the Left on the party's committee structure – which
in 1973 used its influence to abolish the list of proscribed organizations – a
more tolerant attitude to factions of the Left developed. In 1973 a Campaign

for Labour Party Democracy (CLPD) was established by some party activists determined to make the parliamentary wing more accountable to the mass party. Wilson's last-minute personal veto of the proposal to nationalize twenty-five companies in 1974 was just the sort of thing that the CLPD wanted to put an end to.

It was reasoned that the parliamentary party's contempt for conference decisions and its neglect of manifesto commitments when in office would only be prevented if MPs were subject to regular reselection procedures and the franchise for both leadership elections and the determination of the manifesto were extended. The Left's conviction was that any democratization of the party would promote radicalism at the expense of the timid constitutionalism of the parliamentarians:

> any struggle for radical policies within the Labour Party is bound up with a more difficult but nonetheless absolutely crucial struggle to change the structure and functioning of the Party itself. This points to the . . . issue of reselection of sitting MPs by their Constituency General Management Committees . . . GMC control over MPs represents the crucial nexus between constituency politics, local struggles, strikes, community action etc. and Parliament. The reselection issue . . . could mean, if it is won by the left, that Parliament is more directly and immediately responsive to the pressures of the class struggle.[13]

But the prospects for achieving these constitutional reforms looked slim indeed in 1973 when the CLPD was founded. While the Left in the unions had always worked hard to get dissenting resolutions brought before annual conference, in the entire period 1956–70 only six resolutions concerning party administration and only eleven constitutional amendments were submitted by the unions and none were successful.[14] It would take years of conflict between the parliamentary party and the unions before the latter could be brought

General Election	Share of the electorate		Turn-Out %
	Conservative %	Labour %	
1950	37.6	39.9	86.5
1951	39.6	40.3	82.5
1955	38.1	35.6	76.7
1959	38.8	34.5	78.8
1964	33.4	34.0	77.1
1966	31.7	36.3	75.8
1970	33.2	31.5	72.0
1974 (Feb.)	29.5	29.0	78.1
1974 (Oct.)	26.1	28.6	72.8

Source: I. Budge and I. Crewe (eds), *Party Identification and Beyond* (Wiley, 1976), p. 35.

behind constitutional reform; but Wilson had begun this process in the mid-1960s.

The two general elections of 1974 gave Labour an overall majority of only three seats. The victory could not disguise Labour's waning electoral support which, with the exception of 1966, had fallen in every year since 1951.[15]

The figures seemed to show that both parties were losing support, to the extent that a quarter of the electorate had deserted them in the space of only twenty-three years. It was possible to argue persuasively that the statistics revealed a weakening public allegiance to the political system and growing alienation from ideologically similar organizations which had repeatedly failed to arrest the country's economic decline.[16] None of this was unpalatable to the Labour Left, which wanted the party to move away from the middle ground and deal radically with the stagnant economy. But the evidence also suggested that the degree of strong identification with the Labour Party had declined among Labour supporters; automatic working-class loyalty was being displaced by a more conditional, critical support.

If the Labour Party had taken seriously its role in mass campaigning, debate and the education of its members, the new type of supporter would have been an unalloyed blessing. But these party functions were always neglected and by the mid-1960s it was painfully obvious that the Conservatives were a far better mass party than Labour, with three times as many individual members (40 per cent of whom were working class), about twice as many activists, and a more intimate bond with their core supporters in every way.[17] By the time of the defeat of the Wilson–Callaghan government in 1979 Labour membership had declined to one-third of the figure for 1951, the number of full-time agents had fallen by three-quarters, and the proportion of the electorate voting Labour had dropped by almost one-third.[18] One estimate of the number of party activists in 1980 put the figure as low as 55,000 and reported that 65 per cent of CLPs had less than a hundred active members.[19] Party membership stood at 659,058 in 1976 when the minimum affiliation figure was one thousand and CLPs inflated their membership figures accordingly. When this was revised down to 256 in 1980 individual membership shrank to 348,156; when minimum affiliation for CLPs was again lowered in 1981 membership fell to 276,692. But within this shrinking membership the proportion of critical, articulate and militant socialists was growing. These would have to work very hard indeed to establish or even maintain Labour's links with the working-class electorate.

The best propaganda for any party is that which a successful government affords – something which even an inevitably hostile anti-socialist press cannot disguise. But when the Labour government was formed in 1974 the economy was still operating on the three day week which the previous Heath administration had established and inflation and wage increases were running at something between 15 and 20 per cent. On the day Labour took office the Organisation for Economic Co-operation and Development (OECD) estimated a balance of payments deficit for 1974 of £3,350 million. Nevertheless the government started its work positively. A Ministry of Prices, Consumer Protection and Fair Trading was established, the Conciliation and Arbitration Service was set up and Tony Benn and Eric Heffer were put at the head of a new Industry Department where many of the party's manifesto commitments were expected to be enacted. As early as Benn's White Paper of 1974, however, the much-vaunted planning agreements, which Stuart Holland had presented as compulsory 'programme contracts' to an NEC sub-committee in 1972, were mentioned as voluntary arrangements with none of the sanctions originally attached to them.

The big turn-around in government policy came after the referendum in 1975 which Wilson had promised on Britain's membership of the EEC. The vast majority of the Left in all the socialist organizations campaigned for Britain's withdrawal on the grounds that the EEC was a capitalist club whose rules would prevent the reconstruction of the British economy along the lines of the AES – specifically by means of import controls. A 2:1 majority was recorded in favour of staying in the EEC, and Wilson used the defeat of the Left on this issue as an excuse for moving Benn to the Department of Energy. During Benn's short tenure at the Department of Industry workers' co-operatives had been helped at Meriden Triumph Motorcycles, Glasgow's *Scottish Daily News* and the KME factory at Kirkby. It was at Benn's suggestion that the Lucas Aerospace shop stewards produced an alternative corporate plan, but by the time their report on 'socially useful' production was presented Benn had been removed and the government was allowing workers' co-operatives to sink.

1975 was a year of growing unemployment, rising prices (inflation was 30 per cent) and continuous balance of payments crises. The government was a victim of forces over which it could exercise little or no control, such as the oil price rises which helped to worsen the economic situation it had inherited. But once again manifesto commitments were openly flouted on issues relatively independent of the general economic situation. The 1973 annual conference, for example, had passed a resolution in favour of industrial democracy moved by Ken Fleet, secretary of the Institute for Workers' Control, without the need for a card vote, and the October 1974 election manifesto was explicitly pledged to honour it. Instead, Wilson set up a Commission of Inquiry under Lord Bullock which did not report until January 1977. It was predictable that this committee, which was stacked against the trade unions, would produce only tepid proposals which the TUC nevertheless approved the following September. But by the time a Cabinet sub-committee chaired by Shirley Williams (author of *Politics is for People* in 1981) had finished with Bullock's recommendations nothing was left of them and no legislation on industrial democracy ever appeared.[20]

In this way an issue which leading members from all sides of the party had discussed since the early 1950s was tossed into the dustbin at the first sign of business opposition. The emasculation of the National Enterprise Board was in even less doubt as the government focused on the short-run problem of solving the massive balance of payments deficit, which involved raising an IMF loan at the end of 1976 financed by cuts in public expenditure. There was no possibility under these circumstances of effecting the 'fundamental and irreversible shift in the balance of power and wealth to working people and their families' which Labour had promised. No wealth tax was introduced and no progress was made in the redistribution of incomes. Indeed a Fabian study of the government's social policy observed that the recession of 1975 was allowed to turn

> the short term imperative of restraint into a permanent philosophy for public expenditure. The government seemed to have no belief in public services. It put much weight on the element of waste in the public sector. For years we had anecdotes about the surplus bureaucrats of the National Health Service and falling standards in the schools. These tales often turned out on close examination to have little substance or to be fairly minor issues but they had a major impact on opinion. The Labour government itself contributed greatly to the crisis of opinion about public spending.[21]

After decades of discussion of fiscal reform, Labour left office in 1979 with 'the tax system no longer progressive except for very low incomes',[22] and the evidence showed that 'In net terms the corporate sector hardly pays any tax at all and Britain has the reputation of being a corporate tax haven.'[23]

What the government did achieve during its first four years was a major reduction in the numbers of days lost in strikes and a remarkable degree of wage restraint from the unions. No doubt the union leaders' co-operation was won by virtue of measures such as the Employment Protection Act which contributed to the strengthening of workers' rights and helped the unions to reach a peak membership by 1979, when for the first time just over half of the workforce was organized. But wage controls did nothing to assist the lower paid and it is significant that it was from this quarter that irresistible opposition to pay restraint came when James Callaghan – against all the relevant indicators – tried to force through another period of controls.[24] Thus is was that after years of lingering on with the aid of the Liberals and even the Ulster Unionists, the government collapsed in the so-called 'winter of discontent' of 1978–9.

During this period of Labour government the Left of the party – excluded by Wilson from any real say over government policy as early as 1975 – continued to grow. This is reflected both in voting for the constituency section of the NEC and in the membership of the Tribune Group which from only 41 members between 1966 and 1970 rose to 86 by 1978. The package of measures associated with the AES – public ownership, planning agreements, import controls, withdrawal from the EEC and vastly increased public expenditure – gained in popularity within the party. In 1978 two of Benn's former colleagues at the Industry Department, Frances Morrell and Michael Meacher, set up the Labour Co-ordinating Committee (LCC) in order to champion the AES, open the party's policy-making to left pressure groups and transform Labour into a mass campaigning organization. The LCC published *Labour Activist* and organized conferences as part of its project to inform and mobilize party opinion. It is a measure of how far the party had travelled since the 1950s that this endeavour received financial assistance from unions such as NUPE and the TGWU. By the time the party published its lacklustre manifesto for the 1979 election the LCC was able to present a detailed alternative of its own. One of the emphases of this new Labour Left which marked it off from old Tribunites such as Michael Foot was that it wanted reforms throughout the state as well as in the Labour Party, and it was dissatisfied with the traditional and singular parliamentarism which had prevented the Bevanites from mobilizing an extra-parliamentary movement in the 1950s. Using a quasi-Marxist language, the LCC argued that

> Britain is not as democratic a country as is often assumed. Our society is dominated by the class system: it has a ruling class who run financial and big business enterprises, the civil service and the media. They have common interests in keeping elected government weak so that it does not interfere in their financial and industrial operations. So we must redistribute power as well as wealth and income.[25]

For Tony Benn, too, 'Parliamentarism is the disease that has infected the Labour Party.'[26] It was a disease which Benn diagnosed as an elitist disposition to exclude all those who were outside the parliamentary club from participation in decision-making. His remedy was to encourage a host of left pressure groups and factions in their bid to change the party constitution. Benn also advocated measures to end the patronage of Prime Ministers and state secrecy. The broad Bennite Left was also the strongest advocate of industrial democracy and opponent of corporatism. From this quarter came support for workers' co-operatives, shop steward initiatives and stronger local democracy. It amounted to a rejection of Labour's paternalist traditions. Some of Benn's supporters believed that the old statist strategies had to be replaced by participatory alternatives with an extra-parliamentary dimension. A regenerated Labour Party was to emerge from the radical movements of the 1960s which could be seen as the political nuclei of a decentralized, democratic socialism.[27] On this view even the most successful of Labour's parliamentary achievements, such as the National Health Service, had helped to undermine the capacity for solidarity and collective action of the working class.

These arguments certainly chimed in with the thinking which motivated a new Labour Left in local politics. By 1982 this Left had emerged victorious in the Greater London Council, the Inner London Education Authority, the Merseyside County Council and the councils of Manchester, Sheffield, Stirling, Walsall, South Yorkshire and half a dozen London boroughs. Its appearance represented 'a series of initiatives which have largely developed from the bottom up rather than from the top down'.[28] In part the growth of this new Labour Left was attributable to the prior appearance of militant trade unionism, socialist feminism, anti-racist groups, movements for peace and unilateral disarmament (which began to grow again from the late 1970s), community politics, sexual politics and environmentalism. Naturally the younger Labour councillors gave greater priority to these issues. But they also rejected the style of local politics associated with the Labour Party in the 1960s, for

> An analysis of local authority proceedings in the 1960s had shown that the existence of a Labour majority was associated with short council meetings, few questions, few items referred back for reconsideration, low attendance of the public, less ready availability for council documents to the press and restricted admission of the public to council meetings.[29]

The new style of local democracy was revealed in attempts to involve community groups in council business and in the establishment of committees and monitoring groups with personnel drawn from the new social movements. These councils were not only centres of resistance to Conservative government policy after May 1979 but also centres of innovation where an effort was made to use the local authority as a resource to foster and encourage the activities of radical organizations by devolving power to them and financing their endeavours. Thus in the financial years 1983–4 and 1984–5 the Greater London Council (GLC) administered grants to a total of £42 million and £47 million respectively to over a thousand organizations. When these councils also established women's committees, police monitoring groups, nuclear free zones and the rest their opponents (including a good proportion of the Labour establishment) went to considerable lengths to depict them as a 'looney Left' out of touch with ordinary people.

There was undoubtedly an important element of truth in the argument that the Left was out of step with the party's traditional supporters, if only because the Labour Party was not a mass movement in the old working-class communities and drew more of its activist base from white collar occupations. An authentic socialist strategy could only emerge from within a mass movement and this simply did not exist. A number of vanguardist organizations armed with ready-made socialist programmes nevertheless saw the new Labour Left as a congenial milieu for their own ideas. The growth of the Militant tendency, which until 1978 was the only entrist group of any size active in the Labour Party, seemed to prove this. With around 2,000 members by 1979, Militant campaigned for the nationalization of the 'top 200 monopolies' as the high road to socialism and scornfully rejected the AES as inadequate. Since 1970 Militant had dominated the Labour Party Young Socialists (LPYS) largely because its Trotskyist rivals had already left the Labour Party. From 1972, when it was decided to allot a place on the NEC to represent the youth section of the party, a Militant member was regularly elected to the Labour executive. But Militant was quite incapable of working on equal terms with other factions on the left of the party. It saw itself as the embryo of a

mass Leninist vanguard and as such needed no allies in the job of transforming the Labour Party:

> What guarantees the superiority of our tendency – the tendency of
> Marxism – from all others inside and outside the labour movement is
> our understanding of all the myriad factors which determine the atti-
> tudes and moods of the workers at each stage. Not only the objective
> but the subjective ones too.[30]

Thus enfeebled by its own delusions, Militant played no part in initiating
the CLPD or the elaboration of left policy; it was simply a minor beneficiary
of the left turn in the party since 1970. But this was only possible because the
low-profile persistency of the tendency stretched back to 1957. The group
eschewed all the fads and fancies of the other Trotskyist organizations in
favour of a narrow theory of class struggle refracted through the unions and
the Labour Party. Its long-standing presence in the Walton CLP enabled
Militant to emerge as an influence in the Liverpool Labour Party by 1979.
Other Trotskyist groups were drawn back to the Labour Party in the late
1970s by Militant's relative success. The Socialist Organiser Alliance, for
example, was formed in 1979 from a fusion of the International-Communist
League and Workers' Fight. Likewise, the International Marxist Group
(IMG), after failing to promote 'socialist unity' on the revolutionary Left,
moved increasingly towards total immersion in CND and the Bennite Left.
Well before 1983, when it re-named itself the Socialist League, it was oriented
to entrist activity. Another group of Trotskyists, the Chartist Group, established the *London Labour Briefing* in 1980, the only one of these initiatives to
make much of an impact on the wider Labour Left, and then largely because
the *Briefing* was open to the entire spectrum of London socialists and its
Trotskyist origins were left behind.

Ever since it had joined with the other Western Communist Parties in
denouncing the Soviet invasion of Czechoslovakia in 1968, the CPGB had
also been ideologically divided. The party's accustomed oppositional role had
centred its activities around support for trade union militancy but this came
under question during the 1970s when the great upsurge in wage militancy
failed to strengthen socialism within the unions. The rediscovery of Antonio
Gramsci's writings gave theoretical support to those in the party who believed
that a genuinely 'counter-hegemonic' strategy was required which would
involve the construction of socialist alternatives across a broad range of
cultural, political and economic issues.[31] Instead,

> What above all characterised the decade from 1966–75 was that the
> ruling class was unable decisively to impose a new strategic course on
> the working class whilst the working class . . . failed to advance beyond
> the bounds of corporate defencism to mount an offensive political
> struggle around a credible alternative economic programme of its
> own.[32]

This was not only a criticism of the party's support for the 'corporate defencism' of the unions but the beginning of an attack on the AES, whose incoherence and implausibility rested, according to this Communist minority, on its desire to plan everything except wages and to promote statist and bureaucratic reforms which could not produce the sort of socialist democracy which its advocates wanted.

As elsewhere on the Left the CPGB was now composed of a confused mixture of ideological currents which ranged from the advocates of decentralism and participatory democracy to old-fashioned Stalinists who looked to the socialist state as the provider of truth. The apparent successes of the Italian Communist Party in the 1970s strengthened the party's innovators, however, because of its obvious remove from the politics of 'Marxism-Leninism'. The rise of Thatcherism – even before the election of May 1979 – also illustrated the potency of a strategy which attached party ideology to popular beliefs and values in the construction of a new common sense.[33] It also seemed that Thatcherism was succeeding in this enterprise precisely because it was possible to exploit the deficiencies of centralism, bureaucracy, the lack of choice and popular control and so on in the old social democratic consensus; but these were deficiencies which, according to some theorists associated with the party, were set to be reproduced and magnified in the AES.

With the success of the Conservatives in May 1979 all these convictions on the Left were strengthened. The doubters were now confirmed in their suspicion that Thatcherism represented a new 'authoritarian populism' which drew strength from the defects of mainstream Labourist and socialist thought. But most of the Left saw Thatcher's victory as the result of five barren years of Labour government and the betrayal of the 1974 manifesto. From this vantage point even Callaghan's conduct of the campaign indicated where the real fault lay; for while the unpopular Conservative leader had achieved a resounding victory by the promise of radicalism, the Labour leader's moderate posturing had resulted in defeat. The election statistics themselves, of course, could prove neither of these analyses, but they did show Labour's lowest share of the poll for 48 years – 36.9 per cent of the vote and only 28 per cent of the electorate. Only the unevenness of constituency electorates and the below-average swing in Labour marginals prevented a landslide Conservative victory. But this did not prevent Labour from being virtually eliminated as a parliamentary force in the South of England and in much of rural and small-town Britain.[34]

Labour's biggest problem was the desertion of manual workers, especially among the young and skilled, and the further decline which the election recorded, of strong identifiers with the party. The British Election Survey found, furthermore, 'that on 6 of the 8 contentious issues of the 1979 election the Conservative Party was more representative than the Labour Party of the views of the electorate.'[35] Thus on social issues such as unemployment, race relations, incomes policy, industrial relations, law and order, social welfare benefits and nationalization the Tories were closer to the positions of the electorate than Labour. Even among Labour supporters only one-third were in favour of further nationalization and increased public expenditure on social services; and whereas opinion polls found that nearly 60 per cent of Labour supporters rejected the myth of excessive trade union power in 1964, by 1979 only one-third did so. Other studies also found an increased volatility within the electorate, a corresponding attention to issues and an erosion of deference. All this seemed to suggest that 'Today neither class, party or trade union membership have such pervasive influence that a community of interests and views among members can be assumed.'[36] Socialists could draw the conclusion that the missing consciousness had to be forged by increasing Labour's campaigning effort, promoting party education, launching a socialist newspaper and theoretical journal, and extending the opportunities for meaningful participation in decision-making across a whole range of institutions, including the party itself and the unions. Benn talked, for example, of how 'The substitution of Lord Robens for a bunch of private coal owners is not the same as socialism . . . The central question that remains to be settled is therefore the democratisation of public enterprise from the bottom up.'[37] But the basic assumption on the Left was that no new thinking about socialist policies was required – most of that had been done in the late 1960s/early 1970s; the point now was to change Britain with the AES.

Accordingly the annual conference of 1980 voted for withdrawal from the EEC, selective import controls, a 35-hour week with no loss of pay, a non-nuclear defence policy, cuts in arms expenditure, abolition of private education and health care, a wealth tax, industrial democracy and the extension of public ownership and public expenditure. The previous year had witnessed how far the CLPD had progressed when conference agreed to institute the regular re-selection of MPs: this was followed up with a majority for extending the franchise in leadership elections at the 1980 conference. Immediately afterwards, James Callaghan resigned the leadership in order to force a leadership contest under the old system; but this manoeuvre backfired and Michael Foot was elected by the parliamentary party. A special conference was convened at Wembley in January 1981 to decide on a new electoral college for determining leadership elections. In March the Social Democratic Party (SDP) was formed when opponents of these reforms, led by David Owen, Bill Rodgers and Shirley Williams, left the party in the belief that the revisionist tradition now had no future in the Labour movement.

In December 1980 the Gallup Poll showed that Labour enjoyed the support of 47.5 per cent of the electorate but by December 1981 after a year of internal conflict this support was down to 23.5 per cent.[38] Foot was now put under considerable pressure to take action against the 'infiltrators and extremists' who had allegedly taken over the party. When Tony Benn decided to campaign for the deputy leadership, shortly after joining the Tribune Group, he did so against the advice of close colleagues such as Eric Heffer as well as against the publicly expressed wishes of Michael Foot. During the months of campaign between April and October 1981 the amorphous Tribune Left began to break up into warring factions over the question of how Labour should regard groups like the Militant tendency as well as Benn's candidature for deputy leader. When it came to the actual vote for the deputy leadership, enough of the Tribune Group either abstained or voted against Benn for Denis Healey to win by a very slender margin. Foot meanwhile supported the idea of an investigation into the activities of Militant which resulted in the Hayward–Hughes report and the establishment of a register of all non-affiliated groups, from which Militant was excluded. When conference endorsed these arrangements in 1982 divisions emerged in the CLPD, which was torn between its long-standing commitments to internal democracy and its tolerance of party factions. When the Tribune Group registered under the new arrangements it too was split, and in December 1982 a Campaign Group was formed around Tony Benn which was opposed to all party purges. These ideological divisions also affected *Tribune* when Foot's former paper turned against him after Chris Mullin a Bennite, became editor in May 1982; a legal wrangle organized by John Silkin to remove Mullin lasted until November 1985.

Mullin told the Trotskyist newspaper *Socialist Challenge* that he regarded the Parliamentary Labour Party as the biggest single obstacle to the achievement of socialism in Britain.[39] It was this kind of talk and the advocacy of 'extra-parliamentary' action which did most to antagonize the old Tribunites and which fuelled the gathering purge against Militant. The level of panic in the leadership was revealed in 1981 when Foot told the Commons that the adopted Labour candidate for Bermondsey – Peter Tatchell, an advocate of extra-parliamentary action with no ties to any of the Trotskyist groups – would never be endorsed by the Labour Party. But internecine conflict dragged on until 1983 before five members of the *Militant* editorial board were expelled from the party. As the 1983 general election approached, four Militant supporters looked set to be adopted by Liverpool constituencies alone; but in the event only Terry Fields (Kirkdale) was adopted and together with Dave Nellist (Coventry South East) was elected to Parliament.

Labour fought the 1983 general election on a thoroughly Bennite platform – the manifesto entitled *The New Hope for Britain* – which promised withdrawal from the EEC; a non-nuclear defence policy; a huge programme of public expenditure in part designed to reduce unemployment by two million inside five years; import controls; a National Investment Bank and a 5-year plan centred in a new and powerful Department of Economics and Industrial Planning; industrial democracy; the extension of public ownership and the return to public ownership of assets privatized by Mrs Thatcher's government: open government and increased powers for local government. In short, the aim once again, as *New Hope for Britain* pointed out, was 'nothing less than . . . a fundamental and irreversible shift in the balance of power and wealth in favour of working people and their families'. The Conservative leader denounced Labour's manifesto as 'the most extreme manifesto that has ever yet been put before the British people'. Labour also had to contend with sabotage from some of its own elder statesmen who made no secret of their disdain for the 1983 package of policies.

But the result of the 1983 election was a disaster for the party, which registered its lowest share of the popular vote since 1918 and the worst parliamentary return since 1935. Labour's 8,437,120 votes represented a share only 2 per cent higher than that received by the SDP and Liberal Alliance. It meant that the divided anti-Conservative vote had enabled Mrs Thatcher to form a second government – this time with a majority of 144 seats – even though her first term of office had helped to produce an economic catastrophe in whole sectors of industry and society. This reversal for the Left deepened the divisions which already existed within it. With the election of a new leadership at the party conference in October 1983 the Left was divided between those who supported the Kinnock–Hattersley project of formulating a new revisionism and those who believed that the policies of 1983 were basically sound. This division into 'soft' and 'hard' Lefts seemed to show a realignment of forces throughout the whole spectrum of left organizations.

Within the CPGB, for example, ideological divisions were so deep that the 38th congress in November 1983 was presented with an alternative recommended list of candidates for election to the Executive Committee. This challenge was defeated, but the proponents of traditional class struggle policies, centred on the industrial working class and support for the socialist bloc of countries, defied the party's decisions and used their control of its newspaper the *Morning Star* to organize factions against the leadership. Within a year of these events opposition majorities were elected to the district leaderships in London and the North-West of England. By now the *Morning Star* was more closely associated with non-party socialists such as Tony Benn, Arthur Scargill – the leader of the National Union of Miners – and other proponents of the policies of 1983. The CPGB leadership by contrast supported the positions taken by the party's theoretical journal *Marxism Today*, which was engaged in a thoroughgoing revisionism. *Marxism Today* became the voice for a democratic pluralistic socialism partly inspired by the new social movements and the innovative local socialists such as Ken Livingstone but also repelled by vanguardism as practised by groups such as Militant, as well as the bureaucratic paternalism with which the Labour Party and the trade unions were riddled. In January 1985 the CPGB began to expel or lose thousands of members opposed to the new thinking.

The election defeat of 1983 brought to the fore differences not only over the assessment of specific policies canvassed by the broadly Bennite Left but also fundamental divergences over the various visions of socialism which the enlarged and amorphous Left contained. Such ideological conflict ranged from the issue of social agency – the industrial working class, the new social movements, the growing intermediate class, which all had their advocates – to differing emphases on strategy and tactics. In Liverpool, for example, Labour won its first majority for ten years in 1983. Among the 51 councillors, 16 Militant supporters were elected. The entire council was committed to an urban regeneration strategy designed to build houses and create jobs. This was an entirely centralist affair which alienated independent tenants' groups and housing co-operatives and also led to a head-on collision with the government's rate-capping policy. Militant's caucusing and control over key council committees as well as the executive committee of the district party showed its intention to run the whole of local politics on its own terms, to the extent that by November 1986 it was accused of 'wrecking race relations' in the city. Its exclusion of local black organizations was only one instance of Militant's centralist style of politics – a style completely at variance with that of the new Labour Left councils in other cities. It was also consonant with Militant's disparagement of any socialist approach which departed from its own narrow economistic definition of working-class interests. When sixteen Labour councils, also in defiance of government policy, set a legal rate in 1985 the Liverpool Labour Group failed to comply and the city was faced with bankruptcy. By September 1985 this policy led the council to announce 31,000 impending redundancies which divided the local workforce and resulted in the need to raise a costly loan of £30 million from Swiss bankers.

This strategy of confrontation failed to galvanize the local workforce as Militant expected, just as the conduct of the miner's strike in 1984–5 failed, despite heroic sacrifices on the part of the striking miners, to galvanize the union. Both of these struggles further embittered the various components of the old Bennite Left. But Militant was by now sufficiently discredited to allow the Labour leadership to investigate its activities on Merseyside with a clear intention of expelling the leading personalities concerned. By the time the NEC inquiry reported back in February 1986 nearly forty constituency parties had already taken action to expel Militant supporters, and by June seven of the leaders of Militant in Liverpool were also purged. In the short run the only ones to gain by the internecine conflict on the Left – apart from anti-socialists, of course – were those in the Labour Party who believed that these differences could be settled by expulsions. Certainly there was nothing ideologically neat and tidy about the realignments which occurred after 1983: the spectrum on the 'soft Left' ranged from Marxists to social democrats, while the 'hard Left' contained Stalinists, Trotskyists, Bennites and radicals from various Labour pressure groups. When the much reduced Bennites regrouped in Labour Left Liaison in 1986 the new umbrella organization comprised the Campaign Group, the CLPD, the Labour Party Black Sections, *Socialist Action, Socialist Organiser*, the Labour Campaign for Lesbian and Gay Rights, Labour CND, the Labour Committee on Ireland and the Labour Women's Action Committee. But other groups that have been called 'fundamentalist' – such as Militant, the Socialist Workers' Party and a host of others – are not involved.

All this shows, of course, is that the Thatcherite offensive could not produce a coherent, unified response from a disunited, incoherent Left. At a time when Atlanticism was in retreat and the permanence of the EEC was finally beginning to sink in, the old Labour Left had to contend with complex changes in the British social structure and the realization that the British economy was more than ever integrated into a global division of labour. By the time that revisionism was finally discredited, some of the certainties of state-centred planning were also in decay as the problems of the socialist bloc of countries became better known. Now that elements on the Left began to have grave doubts about the feasibility of a national-socialist economic programme, no over-arching socialist alternative was on hand to bring the fragmented radical groups together, let alone to convince the electorate.

Before the Conservatives were elected in Many 1979 with the self-avowed intention of dismantling the post-war consensus, Labour had been in office for eleven of the previous fifteen years. It is not surprising then that most socialist analyses of the Left's problems since 1979 begin with the failures of these Labour governments as the starting point for understanding the subsequent success of Thatcherism. Indeed elements on the Left of the labour movement had formulated their own critique of corporatism and the bureaucratic features of the post-war 'Butskellite' consensus long before the Conservative Party was reoriented around the programme of monetarism and the reintroduction of 'market forces'. One of the problems for the Left, however, was that as the Callaghan government itself turned to monetarist policies as a way of dealing with rising inflation and the fiscal crisis of the welfare state, the only attractive alternative to hand was the revamped Keynesianism of the AES, the product of Left thinking since the late 1960s which was being overtaken by events at the very time when the Labour Party was finally converted to it. Thus after 1979, and especially after the crushing electoral defeat of 1983, a growing proportion of the erstwhile proponents of the AES argued that the economic policies contained in the 1983 manifesto were obsolete.

As it became clearer that Britain was increasingly integrated into the world economy and that the latter was itself subject to a radical restructuring involving a new international division of labour, the prospect for dealing with the local structural crisis behind the 'closed walls' of import controls seemed extremely unlikely. This analysis was given extra conviction by the retreat of the Mitterand government in France after 1981, which started out with radical, state-led policies to nationalize five of the country's largest industrial groups, thirty-five banks and major insurance companies, while increasing wages and numerous benefits, only to find that the world recession together with the opposition of French business left the country with rising inflation, a balance of payments problem and mass unemployment.

Withdrawal from the EEC also lost its appeal for large sections of the former Bennite Left and this proposal was quietly dropped from the manifesto Labour put before the electorate in 1987. The leader of the Labour group in the European Parliament could now argue that 'important democratic socialist objectives can no longer be accomplished within the boundaries of a single country.'[40] The Labour Left had long opposed

Britain's membership of the EEC which it had originally seen as an arm of NATO and an obstacle to détente as well as a capitalist club which encouraged multinational companies whilst obstructing national socialist measures.[41] But even though it was the Left, through such publications as Michael Barratt Brown's *From Labourism to Socialism* (1972) and Stuart Holland's *The Socialist Challenge* (1975), which drew attention to the role of multinational companies in undermining traditional Keynesian policies, it was assumed that the problem they posed could be overcome on a national level provided a socialist government took sufficiently tough measures. By 1987, however, the proposal to withdraw from the EEC was pronounced 'politically romantic and economically self-defeating' by Neil Kinnock, the Labour leader.[42] For if transnational corporations, as Ken Coates has argued, have 'largely neutralised the macro-economic controls of medium-sized nation states', only socialist action across national frontiers would suffice to bring about fundamental socialist change in national economies.[43] Britain's deepening integration into the European economy underlined this point. But the volte-face over the EEC was also connected to the perception that as the Conservative government set about dismantling 'the ancient role of the British state', the Community represented a way of bypassing Thatcherism altogether.[44] In terms of state intervention to maintain and improve environmental protection, health and safety at work, standards of food hygiene and a host of other issues the EEC was now seen as more active than the British government with its obsession with 'market forces'. The prospect of European political federation held out in 1988 by Jacques Delors, the French socialist President of the Commission, seemed only slightly more repellent to Thatcherism than the idea of a common social charter embodying rights and benefits currently denied to British workers. Undoubtedly a growing proportion of the Left, formerly preoccupied with the loss of parliamentary sovereignty which membership of the EEC allegedly entailed, thus turned towards Europe; but the old policy of withdrawal continued to find advocates in leaders such as Tony Benn and Arthur Scargill.

Doubts about purely national solutions to fundamental economic problems also led to rethinking about socialist planning. For how effective could planning be if it was confined to the national economy as envisaged by the AES? The ecological lobby had long argued that only international action could begin to tackle such problems as the depletion of the ozone layer and the destructive effects of acid rain; the Chernobyl nuclear disaster brought these arguments home by demonstrating in practice the international repercussions of policies pursued by nation states. The measures formerly advocated by the Left entailed such a growth in state power that they also conflicted with the aspirations for decentralization variously propounded by advocates of regional, local and community politics. Nor did the Bennite Left really address the question of Scottish and Welsh nationalisms with their demands for autonomous assemblies. New Right thinking challenged the very principle of planning, of course, maintaining that only the market could cope with the mass of complex information about consumer preferences which large-scale economies produced. The fact that the Eastern European countries began to reintroduce the market in the 1980s in order to deal with problems generated by their own command economies underlined the limitations of planning at a time when advocates of free enterprise were riding high in Britain. The questions which had to be addressed now, according to some socialists, concerned the relationships between the goals of freedom and greater democracy and the coexistence of planning, regulation and the market at both the international and the national level.[45]

It can be seen, therefore, that disagreements on the Left were not simply reducible to a question of those who were open to doubts about the AES and those who were not. The Left as a whole was having to come to terms with radical demands from feminists, the Green movement and a range of calls for greater democracy at a time when the old class loyalties were breaking down and a new, popular, modernizing programme capable of galvanizing these disparate trends did not exist. For those actually engaged in struggle, such as the miners, the new thinking had little that was tangible to offer. Indeed many sections of the Labour movement were put into a largely defensive posture as the Conservative government set about reducing trade union power, privatizing the public corporations, and introducing stringent economies which helped to produce millions of unemployed and poverty-stricken people. To make matters worse, the Thatcher government justified its policies with a critique of the public sector which made it synonymous with bureaucracy, queues, inefficiency, impersonality, uniformity, compulsion and an insupportable fiscal burden – arguments which socialists had also employed against the old social democratic consensus. A certain ambivalence was thus bound to arise in so far as socialists opposed Thatcher's transparent class war policies but could not wholly support the *status quo ante*.

While the Labour Party changed its policies from one election to another in a desparate bid to regain governmental office, the CPGB – free from such concerns and small enough to adapt quickly to the new situation – built on the theoretical writings of the Italian Marxist Antonio Gramsci, whose work was rediscovered after the publication of the *Prison Notebooks* in English in 1971, to elaborate a theory of Thatcherism. As we have already observed, Communist intellectuals had begun to express their doubts about the Left's ability to resolve the economic crisis in the 1970s and even though there was still a Labour government, a rising Left and a larger trade union membership than ever before, the CP historian Eric Hobsbawm was asking as early as 1978 if 'the forward march of Labour' had been halted. Hobsbawm referred to a thirty-year crisis of the labour movement characterized by a decline of the manual working class, a growth of sectionalism at the expense of solidarity, and a long term fall in the Labour vote and membership of socialist organizations. While Hobsbawm specifically drew attention to the largely sterile economistic militancy of the period 1970–4, his opponents in the debate which followed, such as the Communist trade union leader Ken Gill, asserted that the labour movement had never been stronger and that 'wage battles . . . will through militancy challenge contemporary capitalism'.[46]

Coupled with these weaknesses of labour, the group around *Marxism Today* perceived a new and dangerous 'authoritarian populism' in Thatcherism which was able to exploit the deficiencies and contradictions in the old social democratic consensus in order to make a fundamental break with it. After 1979, while mounting unemployment and a massive slump in manufacturing industry gave every appearance that it was capitalism that was in crisis, the CPGB continued to stress the potency of Thatcherism and concluded that its defeat was 'the most crucial task' before any progress could be made towards socialism; so much so, in fact, that 'the broadest possible set of alliances' was required if it was to be accomplished.[47] One of the key emphases in this CP analysis concerned the extent to which Thatcherism was able to exploit and articulate a range of anxieties about the erosion of standards, rising crime, the disintegration of the family, social security 'scroungers', trade union bullies, a nation 'swamped' by alien cultures and so on. It played on popular consciousness, so the argument ran, in order to construct a new reactionary settlement. In so doing it exposed the neglect and weaknesses of the Left which was so easily routed on this plane of ideology.

The authoritarian side of Thatcherism was apparent to all shades of opinion on the Left. Police powers were increased by legislation such as the Criminal Evidence Act, the Public Order Act and the Criminal Justice Act. Legislation also enforced secret ballots, restrictions on picketing, a ban on sympathetic strikes, and the threat of sequestration of trade union assets in order to emasculate the unions. Local authorities were less and less able to act independently of central government and the metropolitan county councils were abolished altogether. Government became even more obsessed with secrecy; there were repeated attempts to censor and intimidate broadcasters, educators and Thatcher's critics in the Church of England. The list of authoritarian developments could be extended indefinitely – not least those connected with the Prime Minister's personal domination of the institutions of government. But if Thatcherism could be understood in terms of the formula 'free economy, strong state',[48] there were still socialist critics of the CPGB's analysis who doubted both the extent of the changes brought about by Thatcher in the economy and in the state's relationship to it as well as the degree to which a real shift to the Right had occurred in popular consciousness.

The monetarist policies pursued in the 1980s were, after all, begun by Labour. After a decade of Thatcherism there had been no great reduction in the scale of public expenditure in part because of the high costs of unemployment, poverty, defence and policing. Taxation also remained very high and actually increased as a proportion of GDP from 33.1 to 37.6 per cent in the period 1979–88, showing an increasing government reliance on regressive indirect taxes. Although a massive privatization programme took place in the 1980s, there is no obvious sense in which market forces were re-established by the policy of creating private monopolies whose pricing policies were to be supervised by government regulatory bodies where there had formerly been a public monopoly. As for the 'sound money' policy of Thatcherism, it is relevant to observe that the boom of 1988 left £40 billion outstanding in consumer credit. The economic miracle which was by then being heralded actually involved rising interest rates, rising inflation, mass unemployment, and a worsening balance of payments deficit standing around £18 billion by 1989.

It can also be argued that even after ten years of Thatcherism the unions were still remarkably strong and had lost members principally because of unemployment rather than because of a sea-change in attitudes which had rendered them less relevant. The strength of the labour movement, according to some accounts, can also be gauged from the fact that average wages had not declined and the population remained overwhelmingly composed of wage and salary earners who could be regarded as working class.[49] Surveys such as those carried out in *British Social Attitudes* (1987) did not show a shift to the Right in popular values, nor did those conducted on the tenth anniversary of Mrs Thatcher's premiership.[50]

Thus the fundamentalist Left argued that what really changed, especially after the 1983 election when Thatcher's victory could be attributed to the wave of chauvinism generated by the Falklands War, were the policies, values and ideas of the Left around Neil Kinnock and the Labour leadership, which was shifting to the Right with the CPGB providing a rationale for this retreat. Certainly the 1987 Labour manifesto, *Britain Will Win*, jettisoned such elements of the AES as import controls, withdrawal from the EEC, and the public ownership proposals of 1983. Gone also was the commitment to an early return to full employment. Instead Labour scaled down its ambitions for economic restructuring to familiar proposals, redolent of the Wilson era, such as an Industrial Investment Bank, state-sponsored new industries and a Ministry of Science and Technology. In an obvious and half-hearted attempt to capture the electoral support of the new social movements Labour also put forward policies for energy conservation, environmental protection, devolution, improved local democracy, worker's co-operatives, freedom of information and sex equality. When these proposals failed to deliver a Labour government the party embarked on a full-scale policy review which inaugurated yet another attempt to fashion a new revisionism.

There is no doubt that after this third consecutive defeat in a general election the parliamentary leadership of the party talked and behaved as if Labour would be permanently marginalized unless it could steal some of Mrs Thatcher's clothes. The first phase of the policy review vaguely referred to the 'intrusive state', which was now rejected, and with equal imprecision favoured a 'positive and enabling role' for the state on the grounds that this would enable a future Labour government to champion freedom where this was understood as a condition in which individual rights are given meaning because people have the economic and political power to exercise them. Since these objectives were said to 'clearly require a greater sector of the economy to be socially owned', it was by no means obvious what the distinction between the two types of state actually entailed.[51] It was clear, however, that the language of Thatcherism had been adopted. Thus the role of government was defined in terms of how it could help companies, entrepreneurs, risk-takers, scientists, trainers and technologists to create 'an opportunity economy'.[52] The policy review specifically rejected 'pre-1979 policies of economic management' as inadequate unless supported by changes that 'ensure a modern supply response from those who make industry responsive'. The 'Morrisonian form of public ownership' was also found defective in relation to consumer interests and workforce participation, but this was just as well since apart from the obvious truth in this belated recognition it was apparent by the end of the 1980s that Labour had no intention of restoring all the privatized industries to public ownership, since such a project would cost around £40 billion.

On defence there was considerable backtracking after 1983. Although Labour stuck to the unilateralist position and the demand for the withdrawal of all American nuclear bases from Britain, which had dominated annual conferences since 1981, it fought the 1987 election promising compensatory expenditures on conventional forces to allay fears that its policies would leave the country defenceless. One reason for these fears was that Labour had never confronted the myth of the Soviet threat which the Tories under Mrs Thatcher played up to the full after 1979. In 1987, however, Labour's unilateralist policy came to be seen as less relevant than it had been at the start of the decade, when President Reagan and Mrs Thatcher had turned up the volume of Cold War rhetoric, because of the agreement to reduce 3 per cent of the nuclear stockpile in the deal over intermediate nuclear forces which was struck by Reagan and Mikhail Gorbachev before the British general election took place. By 1989 it was clear that the unilateralist policy was to be ditched in favour of some sort of multilateralist approach. It cannot be said, however, that Labour had used the opportunity of the Gorbachev initiative to rethink British foreign policy, although any progressive defence policy requires such a rethink. Thus while the party leadership responded to the argument that unilateralism was a vote loser, the apparent disintegration of the Cold War was not used as an occasion for establishing a new agenda in this more fundamental area.

By 1989 the second phase of Labour's policy review produced many valuable reform proposals. In response to growing concerns over the environment and related issues such as food hygiene, Labour proposed to establish a Minister of Environmental Protection, a Food Standards Agency and a policy of energy conservation. It also aimed to establish a national minimum wage, a major housing programme, and enhanced nursery and childcare facilities. British Telecom and the provision of water would be brought back into public ownership and a new body, British Technology Enterprise, would be set up to fund long-term investments in advanced technologies. A revamped

Department of Trade and Industry was to become the centre for shifting industry, with the co-operation of organized labour and business groups, towards greater investment, but the mechanisms for achieving this goal were not spelled out in the policy documents. These documents also contained proposals for an elected Second Chamber, a Scottish and possibly a Welsh Assembly, a Freedom of Information Act, state funding for political parties, and modernization of Commons procedure. As for the trade unions, these would be able to engage in sympathetic strikes and would be freed from the risk of sequestration of their funds.

The radical extension of industrial democracy that was proposed in 1986, however, was now dropped and there was no commitment to full employment, only the rather fatalistic assertion that 'there is no reason to believe that unemployment will fall'. Compulsory ballots, as introduced by Mrs Thatcher, would remain and on picketing and the closed shop the documents are silent. In the area of constitutional reform no special democratic vision emerged from the policy review. Labour seems not to have reconsidered the way it governs and uses power. On the contrary all the signs are that despite the references to an 'enabling state' Labour is heading back to the corporatist approach of old, though perhaps with less conviction than Wilson had in 1964. It has apparently been forgotten that this is the approach which brought failure, the Thatcher 'revolution', and ten years or more of internecine strife.[53]

A much more comprehensive *Manifesto for New Times* has been produced by the CPGB in response to the decision of its fortieth National Congress to prepare a new draft of the *British Road to Socialism*. According to the CPGB's analysis, 'society is in the midst of an epochal shift' characterized by fundamental changes in the structure of industry, the occupational composition of the workforce, and the configuration of class. The system allegedly in decay was based on large-scale units of production, employing highly supervised and regimented semi-skilled workers geared to the production of standardized products for mass consumption. This system, pioneered by Ford in the US automobile industry, reached its zenith in Britain during the 1950s. On this basis the big unions established their power base in the sprawling conurbations which developed around certain regional concentrations of industry. The Fordist arrangements thus described flourished during the full employment boom of the post-war years when the 'Butskellite' consensus existed and both major parties pursued Keynesian and corporatist policies. Just as minor parties were excluded from Parliament during this period, corporatist institutions excluded all but the centralized organizations of the unions and big business from any real say in policy. Similarly women were largely excluded from the institutions of the labour movement, racism went unnoticed, and there was no inclination on the part of these institutions to shift power away from the central state.[54]

By 1979 the decay of the old Fordist system had produced, according to the CPGB, a major 'structural crisis' in Britain coinciding with a international wave of capitalist restructuring based on new technologies and a new international division of labour. Thatcherism was able to set about its 'regressive modernization' of Britain in this context partly because the Left was associated with a discredited past and had no modern vision of its own to offer. The unions were also caught out by these changes which, on the basis of a shift to information technology and microelectronics, promoted flexible, automated and integrated production, the rapid decline in the numbers of people employed in manufacturing and a growth in the numbers of part-time, low-skill, low-wage, low-tech employees. Old centres of industry and trade union power fell into decline, new centres of growth based on the most competitive, modernizing companies were able to keep the unions out altogether or force them to accept new terms such as 'no-strike' agreements. This new employment mix, so the argument runs, encourages greater social fragmentation, diversity and polarization between the core, full-time employees whose skill and remuneration will increase in certain key sectors of employment, and the much larger numbers of badly paid workers. Thatcherism is seen as having exploited this new segmentation politically by 'investing its values in the fabric of everyday life' while restructuring, renovating and internationalizing the British ruling class.[55] Unlike the Labour Party it is described as having 'a driving ideological vision and clear moral values' which have enabled it to win wide class support and 'transform' the state.[56]

If socialists are to work with the grain of 'new times', as the CPGB's analysis insists, they have to recognize the new aspirations generated since the 1960s by the new social movements and realize that 'the poles of the political map of the 1990s will be the politics of race and the underclass in the inner city and the growth of new industrial regions' where the labour movement 'is not central to the spirit emerging in them'.[57] The new segmentation of the workforce allegedly creates an underclass representing about one-third of the working class while the rest live in 'relative material prosperity'. This recompositioning of the working class is held to have fractured traditional class identities and cultures at the same time as the new social movements began to emerge, with their stress on common identities other than those based on class. So while the CPGB continues to hold that 'class remains central to British politics', it has emphasized that a new class politics is required which can match the present diversity of the working class. Indeed the emphasis of *Marxism Today* has actually been on the second part of the equation created by 'new times' – that is, the need for a new relationship between class politics and the social movements concerned with ecology, feminism, race, peace and various forms of decentralized democracy. It was the CPGB's apparent retreat from class politics which contributed to the splits within the party which have already been discussed and which is regarded by its critics as all of a piece with the 'new revisionist spectrum' emerging after 1983.[58]

In fact the CPGB talks about 'an historic change in the range and character of political forces' which has been produced since the 1960s and of how, in the new circumstances, 'gender, race, and class provide three connected vantage points for understanding how power in society operates'. Although Britain is regarded as no less of a class society than ever before, the CPGB's argument is that the issues raised by the new social movements cannot be subsumed within class and that even those issues which can be organized best by a class analysis have to contend with the fact that the working class is internally divided along new lines. In particular a new class politics has to find a way of overcoming the increasing gap between the underclass and the relatively prosperous workers. It also has to recognize, or so it is said, the fact that women will be at the core of the working class in the 1990s and that their oppression, like that of ethnic minorities, springs in part from factors other than class.

The Communists have also struck a controversial note by arguing that 'progressive change' is required 'before socialism can be put back on the agenda'. This chimes in with the argument that the most urgent task for progressive politics is to defeat Thatcherism and that Labour should join in an electoral pact with the other opposition parties in order to bring this about. It is argued, however, that such a pact should be created around 'a vision of how the defeat of Thatcherism could usher in a new phase of popular social progress' and that a new political settlement is one of the essential elements of any such development. Clearly one of the main obstacles here is the Labour Party itself which 'retains a conservative commitment to the central state and the British union'. This bias, however, also disqualifies Labour from drawing together the disparate forces for radical change since the common threads linking many of the new social movements are precisely the critique of power and state in British society coupled with the aspiration for more self-management and democracy. Yet the British political system operates in such a way that these radical pressures are marginalized and Labour's refusal to countenance sweeping changes in the constitution benefits only its Conservative opponents in the short run. Indeed the ability of the Conservative governments to chip away at civil liberties in Britain since 1979 owes much to the 'peculiarly undeveloped nature of our democracy', according to the CPGB's analysis.

The Communists accordingly advocate a new conception of popular sovereignty to replace that of the Crown in Parliament and want appropriate changes in the institutions of British politics, including a written constitution, that would give this new conception real force. Some form of proportional representation is needed to open up Parliament to a much wider spectrum of political viewpoints than the present electoral system permits. Parliamentary reforms, such as powerful select committees, an elected second chamber, fixed-term parliaments, and a stricter separation of powers between the different branches of government, are also urgently required so that the executive can be properly controlled and scrutinized by the opposition and public opinion. The Communists also want stronger local government and separate assemblies for Scotland and Wales with some form of regional government in England. They call for democratic control of the police, reform of the judiciary, disestablishment of the Church of England, a Bill of Rights and (taking a longer view of it) abolition of the monarchy. Many of these reforms have already been taken up by the minor parties from the Greens to the Social and Liberal Democrats and the Social Democratic Party, as well as pressure groups such as Charter 88. More important, they meet the needs of a socialism defined as 'popular, democratic control of production, work, and consumption' in which the individual is able to develop capacities for 'creativity, thought, and pleasure'. The Communists now reject 'the models of Eastern European socialist states which are riven with inefficiency, corruption, inequality, centralized control, repression, and environmental despoliation'.[59] They argue that 'socialism will be created by myriad movements through a long uneven struggle to change society'. This political pluralism takes account of the fact that although the Labour Party can still have its uses – since parties can unify the demands of fragmented social movements and form governments – the party, as this study has shown, is slow to adapt to changing values and ideas and can easily lose touch with its constituency. Labour's fixation with parliament and government has always functioned to the neglect of social struggles which form popular consciousness and in the last twenty years in particular it has ceased to be the major source of the socialist, or indeed any other, radical vision. The contribution of groups outside the Labour Party is thus vital in producing a dynamic for social change.

In the CPGB's analysis flexibility, diversity and dynamism are also encouraged by the market, which has a place in the socialist future alongside democratic planning so long as the latter sets the strategic aims of economic development. Key sectors of the economy would be taken into social ownership, and though the form this could take would be varied decentralized democratic control is envisaged. Here too a long view is taken on the grounds that there is no political coalition in favour of socialization, this still needs to be built. The same is true of the Communists' preference for a new economic mix involving efficiency and sustainable development, although it is clearly expected that the Green question will force itself more and more onto the political and economic agenda. Similarly the problem of unaccountable concentrations of economic power, a problem for which the merger boom of the 1980s was a constant reminder, is not something which can realistically be solved in the near future and the best that is offered in *Manifesto for New Times* is the prospect of its long-term erosion.

But then this is true of all the great problems of the last quarter of the twentieth century and helps to explain much of the gloom and pessimism which has descended on the socialist movement during the last decade or so. The ecological crisis, the internationalization of production, power and politics, the growing, disastrous gap between the rich capitalist countries and most of the world's population, are some of the issues which seem to dwarf the efforts of socialists, confined as they are, largely, to purely national organizations. In Britain the experience of Labour governments since 1964 has added to the frustration. Apart from failing on the big economic issues and therefore achieving much less in social policy than had been promised, these governments adhered rigidly to conservative precepts in foreign and defence policy and showed no inclination to reform a backward political system at home. It would be difficult to take seriously now, after this experience, the promises to 'eliminate' poverty, to bring about a fundamental and irreversible shift in the balance of power and wealth, to create a classless society and so on which have featured in Labour propaganda since the 1950s.

If this means socialists are much more sceptical of such rhetoric then so much the better. The electorate, the vast majority of whom do not support Thatcherism, has also become less uncritical about its allegiances. It is not a socialist electorate but it does appear to be concerned with issues which socialists can champion. Labour can only rely on a diminishing proportion of the voters for automatic loyalty and now has to compete with other parties for the anti-Conservative vote as well as a range of organizations which want radical change. If it is serious about the creation of an 'enabling state' it will have to reform the present disabling state. When that task has begun it will at least be possible for more radical forces to break into the political system and then the task of creating a democratic socialist society can commence.

Notes

Chapter 1   Introduction

1   A. Gramsci, *Selections From The Prison Notebooks* (Lawrence and Wishart, 1971), pp. 160–1.
2   N. Kirk, *The Growth of Working Class Reformism in Mid-Victorian Britain* (Croom Helm, 1985), pp. 341–2.
3   H. Perkin, *Origins of Modern English Society* (Routledge and Kegan Paul, 1985), p. 227.
4   T. Tholfsen, *Working Class Radicalism in Mid-Victorian England* (Croom Helm, 1976), pp. 203 and 201.
5   R. Gray, 'Bourgeois hegemony in Victorian Britain,' in J. Bloomfield (ed.), *Class, Hegemony, and Party* (Lawrence and Wishart, 1977), p. 85.
6   K. Marx and F. Engels, *Marx – Engels Selected Correspondence* (Progress, Moscow, 3rd edn, 1975), pp. 295 and 300–1.
7   J. Hinton, *Labour and Socialism* (Wheatsheaf, 1983) p. 7.
8   J. Saville, *The Labour Movement in Britain* (Faber and Faber, 1988), p. 24.
9   H. Pelling, *Popular Politics and Society in Late Victorian Britain* (Macmillan, 1968), pp. 2–5.
10   B. Webb, *The Diary of Beatrice Webb*, vol. 1, *1873–92*, ed. N. and J. Mackenzie (Virago, 1982), pp. 173–4.
11   Quoted in W. H. Greenleaf, *The British Political Tradition*, vol. 1, *The Ideological Inheritance* (Methuen, 1983), p. 113.
12   P. Weiler, *The New Liberalism: Liberal Social Theory in Great Britain 1889–1914* (Garland, 1982), pp. 19–20.
13   M. Richter, *The Politics of Conscience: T. H. Green and His Age* (Weidenfeld and Nicolson, 1964), p. 290.
14   R. Jay, *Joseph Chamberlain: A Political Study* (Oxford University Press, 1981), p. 7.
15   G. Stedman Jones, *Outcast London* (Peregrine, 1971), pp. 320–1.
16   Quoted by B. Semmel, *Imperialism and Social Reform* (Allen and Unwin, 1960), p. 62.
17   D. Winch, *Economics and Policy* (Hodder and Stoughton, 1969), pp. 41 and 32.
18   A. F. Mummery and J. A. Hobson, *The Physiology of Industry* (1889).
19   T. Rothstein, *From Chartism to Labourism* (Martin Lawrence, 1929), pp. 196–7.

Chapter 2   The Marxists

1 G. D. H. Cole, *A History of Socialist Thought*, vol. 2: *Marxism and Anarchism 1850–1890* (Macmillan, 1954), p. 381.

2 D. Geary, *European Labour Protest 1948–1939* (Croom Helm, 1981), p. 20.

3 M. Beer, *History of British Socialism,* vol. 2 (Bell, 1929), p. 239.

4 ibid., p. 245.

5 Quoted by C. Tsuzuki, *H. M. Hyndman and British Socialism* (Oxford University Press, 1961), p. 35.

6 Marx to Hyndman, 8 December 1880, K. Marx and F. Engels, *Marx–Engels Selected Correspondence* (Progress, Moscow, 1975), pp. 313–14.

7 Engels to Bebel, 30 August 1883, ibid., p. 343.

8 H. M. Hyndman, *England For All* (1881; Harvester, 1973), pp. 109–10.

9 ibid., pp. 88–9.

10 Democratic Federation, 'Socialism made plain', in H. Pelling (ed.), *The Challenge of Socialism* (Black, 1954), p. 131.

11 Cole, *A History of Socialist Thought*, vol. 2, p. 400.

12 G. Stedman Jones, *Outcast London* (Peregrine, 1964), p. 29.

13 P. Thompson, 'Liberals, Radicals and Labour in London 1880–90', *Past and Present*, no. 27 (1964), pp. 74–80.

14 H. M. Hyndman, *The Historical Basis of Socialism in England* (Kegan Paul, 1883), p. 232.

15 ibid., pp. 287–8.

16 ibid., p. 289.

17 ibid., p. 291.

18 K. Marx, 'Critique of the Gotha Programme', in *Marx–Engels Selected Works* (Progress, Moscow, 1968), pp. 310–32.

19 H. Collins, 'The Marxism of the Social Democratic Federation', in A. Briggs and J. Saville, *Essays in Labour History 1886–1923* (Macmillan, 1971), pp. 52–5.

20 H. M. Hyndman, *A Commune For Britain* (1887).

21 G. B. Shaw, 'Morris As I Knew Him', in M. Morris, *William Morris*, vol. 2: *Artist, Writer, Socialist* (Blackwell, 1936), pp. xiii–xiv.

22 Morris to J. L. Joynes, 25 December 1884, in M. Morris, *William Morris*, vol. 2, p. 590.

23 For example, H. M. Hyndman, 'Something better than emigration', *Nineteenth Century*, vol. 16 (1884), p. 998.

24 Quoted by C. Tsuzuki, *Hyndman and British Socialism*, p. 71.

25 Quoted in C. Tsuzuki's introduction to Hyndman, *England For All*, p. xxi.

26 T. Mann, *Tom Mann's Memoirs* (Labour Publishing Company, 1923), p. 57.

27 ibid., p. 61.

28 D. Torr, *Tom Mann and His Times*, vol. 1 (Lawrence and Wishart, 1956), p. 218.

29 T. Rothstein, *From Chartism to Labourism* (Martin Lawrence, 1929), pp. 269–71.

30 Y. Kapp, *Eleanor Marx*, vol. 2: *The Crowded Years 1884–98* (Virago, 1979), pp. 262 and 263.

31 ibid., pp. 333–4.
32 *Justice*, 3 May 1890.
33 See J. Joll, *The Second International 1889–1914* (Routledge, 1955), pp. 30–5.
34 See Engels to Sorge, 7 December 1889, and his letter to Schlüter, 11 January 1890, *Marx–Engels Selected Correspondence*, pp. 385–6 and 388.
35 ibid., p. 448.
36 T. A. Jackson, *Solo Trumpet* (Lawrence and Wishart, 1953), pp. 55–6.
37 Quoted in J. D. Young, *Socialism Since 1889: A Biographical History* (Pinter, 1988), p. 45.
38 ibid., pp. 37–59.
39 E. P. Thompson, *William Morris: Romantic to Revolutionary* (Merlin, 1977) pp. 413–14.
40 Kapp, *Eleanor Marx*, p. 63.
41 ibid., p. 197.
42 F. Boos (ed.), *William Morris' Socialist Diary* (Journey man Press, 1985), p. 7.
43 W. Morris, 'The Policy of Abstention' (1887), in M. Morris, *William Morris*, vol. 2, pp. 437–8.
44 W. Morris, 'The Deeper Meaning of the Struggle', in William Morris, *News From Nowhere and Selected Writings and Designs*, introduced by A. Briggs (Penguin, 1986), pp. 44–5.
45 W. Morris, 'The Policy of Abstention', p. 444.
46 W. Morris, 'The Society of the Future' (1887), in A. L. Morton (ed.), *Political Writings of William Morris* (Lawrence and Wishart, 1973), p. 189.
47 W. Morris, 'How I Became A Socialist', in *News From Nowhere and Selected Writings and Designs*, p. 36.
48 Quoted by R. Page Arnot, *William Morris: The Man and The Myth* (Greenwood, Conn., 1964), p. 17.
49 W. Morris, 'The Workers' Share of Art' (*Commonweal*, 1885), ibid., pp. 140 and 141.
50 W. Morris, 'Art and Socialism' (1884), in Morton, *Political Writings of William Morris*, p. 123.
51 W. Morris, 'The Society of the Future', ibid., p. 194.
52 W. Morris, 'News From Nowhere', in *News From Nowhere and Selected Writings and Designs*, pp. 221, 241 and 251.
53 W. Morris, 'The Policy of Abstention', p. 436.
54 Shaw, 'Morris As I Knew Him', p. xi.
55 W. Morris, 'Communism' (1893), in Morton, *Political Writings of William Morris*, p. 230.
56 Kapp, *Eleanor Marx*, vol. 2, p. 52.
57 *Justice*, 14 January 1893.
58 Quoted by R. Page Arnot, *William Morris: The Man and The Myth*, p. 108.
59. Quoted by E. P. Thompson, review of C. Tsuzuki's biography of H. M. Hyndman, *Bulletin for the Study of Labour History*, no. 3 (1961), pp. 66–71.
60 See G. Foote, *The Labour Party's Political Thought* (Croom Helm, 1985), pp. 19–24.
61. Jackson, *Solo Trumpet*, p. 51.

62 ibid., p. 52.
63. R. McKibbin, 'Why was there no Marxism in Britain?', *English Historical Review*, 99 (1984), p. 324.
64 T. Nairn, *The Break-Up of Britain* (New Left Books, 1977), p. 33.
65 Engels to Sorge, 7 December 1889 in *Marx-Engels Selected Correpondence*, pp. 385-6.

Chapter 3   Fabianism

1 E. Pease, *History of the Fabian Society* (Allen and Unwin, 1916), pp. 32-7.
2 S. Webb, *Facts for Socialists* (Fabian tract no. 5, 1887).
3 G. B. Shaw, 'The Transition', in *Fabian Essays in Socialism* (Fabian Society, 1889), p. 171.
4 B. Webb, *My Apprenticeship* (Cambridge University Press, 1979), p. 410.
5 S. Webb, 'Socialism historic', in *Fabian Essays*, p. 28.
6 ibid., p. 29.
7 ibid., p. 57.
8 B. Webb, *The Diary of Beatrice Webb*, vol. 1: *1873-92* ed. N. and J. McKenzie (Virago, 1982), p. 327.
9 B. Webb, *My Apprenticeship*, p. 395.
10 ibid., p. 184.
11 S. Webb, *Socialism in England* (Swan Sonnenschein, 1890), p. 7.
12 ibid., pp. 118-22.
13 ibid., p. 25.
14 ibid., p. 83.
15 S. Webb, 'Socialism Historic', p. 54.
16 G. B. Shaw, *Report on Fabian Policy and Resolutions* (Fabian track no. 70, 1896), p. 5.
17 ibid., p. 5.
18 ibid., p. 14.
19 ibid., p. 5.
20 ibid., p. 5.
21 ibid., p. 3.
22 S. Webb, *Socialism: True and False* (Fabian tract no. 51, 1895), p. 8.
23 S. Webb, *The Difficulties of Individualism* (Fabian tract no. 69, 1896), p. 4.
24 ibid., p. 16.
25 S. Webb, *English Progress Towards Social Democracy* (Fabian tract no. 15, 1890), p. 8.
26 G. B. Shaw, *The Fabian Society: Its Early History* (Fabian tract no. 41, 1892), p. 10.
27 Fabian Society, *A Democratic Budget* (Fabian tract no. 39, 1892), p. 3.
28 B. Webb, *My Apprenticeship*, pp. 42-4.
29 ibid., pp. 51-2.
30 B. Webb, *Our Partnership* (Longmans, 1948), p. 7.
31 B. Webb, *My Apprenticeship*, p. 96.

32 ibid., p. 120.
33 B. Webb, *Our Partnership*, p. 108.
34 ibid., p. 120.
35 W. Magnusson, 'Bourgeois theories of local government', *Political Studies*, 34.1 (March 1986), p. 2:
36 Fabian Society, *The Workers' Political Programme* (Fabian tract no. 11, 1891).
37 Fabian Society, *A Democratic Budget*, p. 10.
38 S. Webb, *The Difficulties of Individualism* (Fabian tract no. 69, 1896), p. 11.
39 G. B. Shaw and S. Webb, *A Plan of Campaign For Labour* (Fabian tract no. 49, 1894), p. 22.
40 B. Webb, *Our Partnership*, pp. 125, 132, 134.
41 ibid., p. 122.
42 ibid., pp. 61–2.
43 S. Webb, *The Difficulties of Individualism*, p. 12.
44 S. Ball, *The Moral Aspects of Socialism* (Fabian tract no. 72, 1896), p. 5.
45 ibid., p. 19.
46 S. Webb, *Labour in the Longest Reign 1837–97* (Fabian tract no. 75, 1897), p. 18.
47 B. Webb, *Our Partnership*, pp. 83–4.
48 ibid., pp. 256–7.
49 Cited in *The Diary of Beatrice Webb*, vol. 2, p. 10.
50 See M. Cole (ed.), *The Webbs and Their Work* (Muller, 1949), p. 255.
51 S. Webb, *Socialism: True and False*, p. 12.
52 B. Webb, *Our Partnership*, p. 210.
53 ibid., p. 92.
54 Shaw, *Report on Fabian Policy and Resolutions*, p. 3.
55 B. Webb, *Our Partnership*, p. 7.
56 ibid., p. 202.
57 ibid., pp. 228–9.
58 S. Webb, 'Lord Rosebery's escape from Houndsditch', *Nineteenth Century*, 50 (1901), p. 375.
59 ibid., p. 376.
60 ibid., p. 384.
61 H. G. Wells, *Anticipations of the Reaction of Mechanical and Scientific Progress Upon Human Life and Thought* (Tauchnitz, Leipzig, 1902), p. 76.
62 B. Webb, *Our Partnership*, p. 226.
63 Wells, *Anticipations*, pp. 77–8.
64 ibid., p. 133.
65 N. Mackenzie (ed.), *The Letters of Sidney and Beatrice Webb*, vol. 2: *Partnership 1892–1912* (Cambridge University Press, 1978), p. 144.
66 ibid., p. 144.
67 ibid., p. 264.
68 B. Webb, *Our Partnership*, p. 231.
69 G. B. Shaw, *The Impossibilities of Anarchism* (Fabian tract no. 45, 1895), p. 17.
70 Quoted in M. Cole, *The Story of Fabian Socialism* (Mercury, 1963) pp. 196–7.

71 H. G. Wells, *Experiment in Autobiography*, vol. 2 (Gollancz, 1934), pp. 661 and 663.
72 G. B. Shaw *Fabianism and the Empire* (Grant Richards, 1900), p. 17, p. 15, p. 23.
73 J. M. Winter, 'The Webbs and the non-white world: a case of socialist racialism', *Journal of Contemporary History*, 9.1 (1974), p. 182.
74 The character and extent of imperialist propaganda and its popular appeal are explored in J. M. Mackenzie (ed.), *Imperialism and Popular Culture* (Manchester University Press, 1986).

Chapter 4   Independent Labour Representation

1 H. Pelling, *Origins of the Labour Party* (Oxford University Press, 2nd edn 1965), p. 45.
2 E. J. Hobsbawm, 'Hyndman and the SDF', in *Labouring Men* (Weidenfeld and Nicolson, 2nd edn 1968).
3 Quoted by H. M. Hyndman, 'The Radicals and socialism', *Nineteenth Century* 18 (1889), p. 836.
4 Quoted by P. Adelman, *Victorian Radicalism: The Middle-Class Experience 1830–1914* (Longman, 1984), p. 115.
5 H. M. Hyndman, 'The Radicals and socialism', p. 838.
6 See Pelling, *Origins of the Labour Party*, p. 54.
7 H. Pelling, 'H. H. Champion: Pioneer of labour Representation', *Cambridge Journal* 6 (1953), p. 226.
8 H. H. Champion, 'The new Labour Party', *Nineteenth Century*, 24 (1888), pp. 85–6.
9 ibid., p. 82.
10 ibid., p. 85.
11 H. H. Champion, 'An eight-hour law', *Nineteenth Century*, 26 (1889), p. 521.
12 ibid., pp. 514–15.
13 Quoted in S. Pierson, *Marxism and the Origins of British Socialism* (Ithaca, NY: Cornell University Press, 1973), p. 183.
14 The account which follows depends on F. Reid, 'Keir Hardie's conversion to socialism', in A. Briggs and J. Saville (eds), *Essays in Labour History*, vol. 2; *1886–1923* (Macmillan, 1971), pp. 17–46.
15 ibid., p. 40.
16 T. Mann, 'The Development of the labour movement', *Nineteenth Century*, vol. 27 (1890), p. 714.
17 E. Hobsbawm, 'General labour unions in Britain 1889–1914', in Hobsbawm, *Labouring Men*, p. 187.
18 Pelling, *Origins of the Labour Party*, p. 90.
19 H. H. Champion, 'The Labour platform at the next election', *Nineteenth Century*, 30 (1891), pp. 1037 and 1042.
20 See E. P. Thompson, 'Homage to Tom Maguire,' in A. Briggs and J. Saville (eds), *Essays in Labour History*, vol. 1 (Macmillan, 1960), p. 285.

21 C. Tsuzuki, H. M. *Hyndman and British Socialism* (Oxford University Press, 1961), p. 97.
22 D. Howell, *British Workers and the Independent Labour Party 1888–1906* (Manchester University Press, 1983), pp. 293–4.
23 ibid., p. 124.
24 S. Yeo, 'A new life: the religion of socialism in Britain 1883–96', *History Workshop Journal*, no. 4 (Autumn 1977), p. 11.
25 Quoted in R. Blatchford, *The New Religion* (Clarion Press, nd), p. 2.
26 *Clarion*, 11 February 1893.
27 *Clarion*, 5 March 1892.
28 W. Morris, 'Makeshift', in M. Morris (ed.), *William Morris*, vol. 2, *Artist, Writer, Socialist* (Blackwell, 1936) p. 482.
29 *Clarion*, 11 February 1893.
30 *Clarion*, 13 April 1896.
31 See L. J. W. Barrow, 'The socialism of Robert Blatchford and the Clarion 1889–1918' (unpublished PhD thesis, London University, 1975).
32 Blatchford, *The New Religion*, pp. 3–4.
33 J. Keir Hardie, 'The Independent Labour Party', *Nineteenth Century*, 37 (1895), pp. 2, 7, 12–13.
34 ibid., p. 9.
35 ibid., p. 10.
36 Hardie and R.J. MacDonald, 'The Independent Labour Party programme', *Nineteenth Century*, 45 (1899), pp. 20, 23, 25.
37 ibid., p. 27.
38 ibid., p. 37.

Chapter 5   Forming the Labour Party

1 J. Lovell, 'Trade unions and the development of independent labour politics, 1889–1906', in B. Pimlott and C. Cook (eds), *Trade Unions in British Politics* (Longman, 1982), pp. 53–4.
2 D. Marquand, *Ramsay MaDonald* (Cape, 1977), p. 79.
3 C. J. Wrigley, *David Lloyd George and the British Labour Movement* (Harvester, 1976), p. 18.
4 H. Pelling, *Origins of the Labour Party* (Oxford University Press, 2nd edn, 1965) p. 158.
5 J. Hinton, *Labour and Socialism* (Wheatsheaf, 1983), p. 77.
6 Marquand, *Ramsay and MacDonald*, pp. 86–7.
7 N. and J. MacKenzie (eds), *The Diary of Beatrice Webb*, vol. 3, 1905–24 (Virago, 1984), p. 149.
8 ibid., p. 118.
9 ibid., p. 159.
10 F. Brockway, *Inside the Left* (Allen and Unwin, 1942), p. 22.
11 ibid., p. 24.
12 J. Bruce Glasier, *The Meaning of Socialism* (ILP, 2nd edn 1925), p. vii.
13 Quoted in L. Thompson, *The Enthusiasts* (Gollancz, 1971), p. 88.

14 Bruce Glasier, *The Meaning of Socialism*, p. 13.
15 ibid.
16 See H. Pelling (ed.), *The Challenge of Socialism* (Black, 1954), p. 201.
17 J. Keir Hardie, 'From serfdom to socialism', in R. E. Dowse (ed.), *From Serfdom to Socialism* (Harvester, 1974), pp. 87–8.
18 P. Snowden, *Labour and the New World* (Waverley, 1921), p. 266 and pp. 288–9.
19 ibid., p. 289.
20 J. R MacDonald, *Socialism* (Jack, 1907), p. 3.
21 ibid., p. 55.
22 ibid., pp. 60 and 64.
23 ibid., p. 79.
24 ibid., p. 73.
25 ibid.
26 ibid., p. 122.
27 B. Barker (ed.), *Ramsay MacDonald's Political Writings* (Allen Lane, 1972). See *Socialism and Society* in this volume, first published in 1905, and especially p. 84.
28 ibid., p. 93.
29 J. Ramsay MacDonald, *The Socialist Movement* (Williams and Norgate, 1911), p. 90.
30 J. Ramsay MacDonald, *Socialism and Government*, vol. 1 (ILP, 1909), pp. 3–4.
31 ibid., p. 10.
32 ibid., p. 107.
33 ibid., pp. xxv and 116.
34 ibid., p. xxv.
35 H. A. Clegg, *A History of British Trade Unions*, vol. 2: *1911–1933* (Clarendon Press, 1985), pp. 19–20 and 15.
36 Quoted in B. Holton, *British Syndicalism 1900–1914* (Pluto Press, 1976), p. 36.
37 Quoted in R. Page Arnot, *The Impact of the Russian Revolution in Britain* (Lawrence and Wishart, 1967), p. 59.
38 See R. Challinor, *The Origins of British Bolshevism* (Croom Helm, 1977), pp. 30–2.
39 Reprinted in R. Blatchford, *Germany and England: The War That Was Foretold* (Clarion pamphlet, 1914), pp. 3–4.
40 Brockway, *Inside the Left*, p. 47; see also K. Laybourn, *Philip Snowden* (Temple Smith, 1988), p. 64.
41 Challinor, *Origins of British Bolshevism*, p. 125.
42 See M. Ceadal, 'The Peace Movement between the wars', in R. Taylor and N. Young (eds), *Campaigns for Peace* (Manchester University Press, 1987), p. 79.
43 G. D. H. Cole, *History of the Labour party from 1914* (Routledge and Kegan Paul, 1948), p. 48.

Chapter 6   The Democratic Challenge

1 H. A. Clegg, *A History of British Trade Unions since 1889*, vol. 2: *1911-1933* (Clarendon Press, 1985), p. 1.

2 This argument is put most eloquently by G. Dangerfield, *The Strange Death of Liberal England* (1935; Paladin, 1970).

3 B. Pribićević, *The Shop Stewards' Movement and Workers' Control 1910-22* (Blackwell, 1959), p. 2.

4 Quoted by B. Holton, *British Syndicalism 1900-1914* (Pluto Press, 1976), pp. 86-7.

5 James Connolly, 'Socialism Made Easy' (1909), in *Selected Political Writings*, and introduced by Owen Dudley Edwards and Bernard Ransom (Cape, 1973), p. 264.

6 ibid., p. 271.

7 ibid., pp. 273-4.

8 See S. T. Glass, *The Responsible Society: The Ideas of Guild Socialism* (Longmans, 1966); R. Barker, *Political Ideas in Modern Britain* (Routledge and Kegan Paul, 1978); W. H. Greenleaf, *The The British Political Tradition*, vol. 2 (Methuen, 1983); A. W. Wright, G. D. H. Cole and Socialist Democracy (Clarendon Press, 1979).

9 These articles were collected in S. G. Hobson, *National Guilds: An Inquiry into the Wage System and the Way Out* (1914).

10 J. T. Murphy, *The Workers' Committee: An Outline of its Principles and Structures* (1917; Pluto Press, 1972), p. 15.

11 ibid., p. 18.

12 ibid., p. 26.

13 J. T. Murphy, *Preparing for Power* (1934; Pluto Press, 1972), p. 152.

14 G. D. H. Cole, *Self-Government in Industry* 1917; Hutchinson, 1972), pp. 2-6.

15 ibid., p. 1; see also H. J. Laski, *A Grammar of Politics* (Allen and Unwin, 1925), p. 28.

16 G. D. H. Cole, *Labour in Wartime* (1915), p. 3.

17 G. D. H. Cole, *Guild Socialism Re-stated* (1920), p. 22.

18 See A. Briggs and J. Saville, *Essays in Labour History*, vol. 2: *1886-1923*. (Macmillan, 1971), where the Storrington Document is set out in full.

19 G. D. H. Cole, *Guild Socialism Re-stated*, p. 46.

20 Introduction to Pribićević, *The Shop Stewards' Movement*, p. v.

21 M. Dobb, 'The Webbs, the state and the workers', *Plebs*, 15.4 (April 1923), pp. 169-71.

22 R. H. Tawney, *Equality* (Allen and Unwin, 1931), p. 30.

23 R. H. Tawney, 'The conditions of economic liberty', in *The Radical Tradition* (Allen and Unwin, 1964), p. 120.

24 R. H. Tawney, *The Acquisitive Society* (1921; Wheatsheaf, 1983), p. 119 and pp. 140-55.

25 R. H. Tawney, *Equality*, p. 179.

26 *The Syndicalist*, no. 9 (October 1912), p. 2.

27 *The Syndicalist*, no. 1 (January 1912), p. 1.
28 Quoted in C. Wrigley, *Government and Industrial Relations in Britain 1910–21* (Department of Economics, Loughborough University, 1979), p. 9.
29 J. M. Winter, 'R. H. Tawney's early political thought', *Past and Present*, no. 47 (1970), p. 78.

Chapter 7   The Impact of the Bolshevik Revolution

 1 *The Diary of Beatrice Webb*, vol. 3: *1905–24*, ed. N. and J. McKenzie (Virago, 1984), p. 278.
 2 See Tom Quelch's report in *The Call*, 7 June 1917.
 3 B. Webb, *The Diary of Beatrice Webb*, vol. 3, pp. 280–1.
 4 ibid., pp. 289–90.
 5 *The Call*, 29 November and 6 December 1917.
 6 *LPACR*, January 1918, p. 94.
 7 *LPACR* June 1918, p. 60.
 8 *LPACR* June 1919, p. 10.
 9 M. Cowden, *Russian Bolshevism and British Labour 1917–21* (New York: Columbia University Press, 1984), p. 26.
10 Lloyd George quoted by R. Palme Dutt, *World Politics 1918–36* (Gollancz, 1936), pp. 43–4.
11 *The Call*, 23 January 1919.
12 S. White, *Britain and the Bolshevik Revolution* (Macmillan, 1979), pp. 39–40.
13 Ramsay MacDonald's contribution to the debate. See J. Riddell (ed.), *The Communist International in Lenin's Time: The German Revolution and the Debate in Soviet Power, Documents 1918–19* (New York: Pathfinder, 1986), p. 412.
14 *The Call*, 17 July 1919.
15 From the defeated resolution put by Frossard, Faure and Loriot at the Berne Conference 1919. See Riddell, *The Communist International in Lenin's Time*, p. 421.
16 G. Brown, *Maxton* (Mainstream, 1986), pp. 100 and 98.
17 The Council of Action, *Report of the Special Conference on Labour and the Russian-Polish War*, 13 August 1920, Central Hall Westminster (Labour party, 1920) p. 3.
18 W. P. and Zelda K. Coates, *History of Anglo-Soviet Relations* (Lawrence and Wishart, 1944), p. 42.
19 ibid., p. 149.
20 *British Labour Delegation to Russia 1920 Report* (Labour Party, 1920) p. 8.
21 J. T. Murphy, *New Horizons* (John Lane, Bodley Head, 1941), p. 115.
22 H. Pollitt, *Looking Ahead* (CPGB, 1947), pp. 41–2.
23 J. Hinton, *The First Shop Steward's Movement* (Allen and Unwin, 1973), p. 336.
24 F. Claudin, *The Communist Movement: From Comintern to Cominform* (Penguin 1975), p. 107.
25 Murphy, *New Horizons*, pp. 150–1.
26 See V. I. Lenin, 'Imperialism and the Split in Socialism', October 1916, in

Collected Works, vol. 23; 'Imperialism, The Highest Stage of Capitalism', *Collected Works*, vol. 22 (Progress, Moscow, 1961).

27 See V. I. Lenin, 'Left Wing Communism: An Infantile Disorder', April–May 1920, *Collected Works*, vol. 31 (Progress, Moscow, 1961), pp. 41–2; L. Trotsky, *Terrorism and Communism* (University of Michigan Press, 1961) p. 109.

28 M. Dobb, 'The Webbs, the state, and the workers', *Plebs*, 15.4 (April 1923), pp. 170–1.

29 S. McIntyre, *A Proletarian Science: Marxism in Britain 1917–33* (Cambridge University Press, 1980), p. 220.

30 *Second Congress of the Communist International: Minutes of the Proceedings*, vol. 2 (New Park, 1977), pp. 183–4; see also 'Fundamental Tasks of the Communist International' (written by Trotsky), in B. Hessel (ed.) *Theses, Resolutions and Manifestos of the First Four Congresses of Comintern* (Ink Links, 1980), p. 141.

31 *LPACR*, June 1921, p. 7.

32 See *Communist Review*, 2.2 (December 1921) and 3.3 (July 1922), pp. 117–18.

33 J. T. Murphy, *Preparing for Power* (1934; Pluto Press, 1972), p. 18.

34 R. Palme Dutt, 'Notes of the month', *Labour Monthly*, January 1924.

35 S. R. Graubard, *British Labour and the Russian Revolution 1917–24* (Oxford University Press, 1956), p. 246.

36 K. Radek, 'The British Labour government', *Communist International*, 5.3 (1924), p. 101.

37 G. Zinoviev, 'Fifth World Congress of the Communist International, Report to the Third Session', *Inprecorr*, 4.41 (1924), p. 402.

38 See P. Kingsford, *The Hunger Marches in Britain 1920–40* (Lawrence and Wishart, 1982).

Chapter 8   Labour in Power?

1 *Report on Organisation*: Presented by the Party Commission to the 5th Annual Conference of the CPGB, 7 October 1922 (CPGB, 1922), pp. 22–3.

2 ibid., p. 36.

3 ibid., p. 38.

4 R. P. Dutt, 'The general election and British foreign policy', *Labour Monthly*, 6.1 (January 1924), pp. 23–5.

5 R. P. Dutt, 'Notes of the month', ibid., p. 4.

6 C. A. Cline, *Recruits to Labour: The British Labour Party 1914–31* (Syracuse, 1963), p. 66.

7 R. C. Reinders, 'Racialism on the Left: E. D. Morel and the 'Black Horror on the Rhine', *International Review of Social History* 13, (1968), p. 1.

8 E. J. Hobsbawm, *The Age of Empire* (Weidenfeld and Nicolson, 1987), p. 72.

9 S. MacIntyre, *Imperialism and the British Labour Movement in the 1920s* (Our History pamphlet number 64, CPGB, 1975), p. 12.

10 B. Jones and M. Keating, *Labour and the British State* (Oxford University Press, 1985), p. 167.

11 R. Palme Dutt, 'Notes of the month', *Labour Monthly*, 6.5 (May 1924), p. 264.

12 G. Lansbury, 'Empire Day', *Lansbury's Labour Weekly*, 23 May 1925.

13 D. Howell, *A Lost Left* (Manchester University Press, 1986), pp. 261–2.

14 R. Palme Dutt, 'Notes of the month', *Labour Monthly*, 6.5 (May 1924), p. 266.

15 *LPACR*, 1924, p. 109.

16 J. Saville, *The Labour Movement in Britain* (Faber and Faber, 1988), pp. 50–1.

17 J. Pepper, 'Britain's balance sheet for 1926', *Communist International*, 3.5 (15 December 1926), p. 13.

18 See, for example, R. Palme Dutt, 'The British working class after the election', *Communist International*, 5.8 (1924).

19 See S. and B. Webb, *A Constitution For the Socialist Commonwealth of Great Britain* (1920); for Margaret Cole's remark see M. I. Cole (ed.) *The Webbs and Their Work* (1949).

20 S. and B. Webb, *A Constitution For the Socialist Commonwealth*, p. 92.

21 T. Smith, *The Politics of the Corporate Economy* (Martin Robertson, 1979), pp. 18–19.

22 M. Cole, *Beatrice Webb* (London, 1945), p. 146.

23 S. and B. Webb, *A Constitution For the Socialist Commonwealth*, pp. 196–8.

24 B. Russell, *The Autobiography of Bertrand Russell* (Allen and Unwin, 1975), p. 75.

25 S. and B. Webb, *The Decay of Capitalist Civilisation* (3rd edn, 1923), pp. 144–6.

26 ibid., p. 57.

27 ibid., p. 84.

28 ibid., pp. 124–5.

29 R. H. Tawney, *Acquisitive Society* (1921; Wheatsheaf, 1983), p. 10.

30 R. H. Tawney, *Religion and The Rise of Capitalism* (1922; Pelican Books, 1938), pp. 17–27.

31 Tawney, *The Acquisitive Society*, pp. 106–7.

32 G. D. H. Cole, *Chaos and Order in Industry* (1920).

33 G. D. H. Cole, *The Intelligent Man's Guide Through World Chaos* (Gollancz, 1932), pp. 576–8.

34 G. D. H. Cole, 'Marxism and the world situation today', in J. Midddleton Murry (ed.), *Marxism* (Chapman and Hall, 1935).

35 H. J. Laski, *Democracy in Crisis* (Allen and Unwin, 1933), p. 30.

36 H. J. Laski, *Political Thought in England From Locke to Bentham* (1920).

37 H. J. Laski, *Authority in the Modern State* (Yale University Press, New Haven, 1919), p. 38.

38 ibid., p. 87.

39 ibid., p. 81.

40 H. J. Laski, *A Grammar of Politics* (Allen and Unwin, 1925), pp. 444–53. Compare p. 91 of *Authority in the Modern State* with p. 439 of *A Grammar of Politics*.

41 ibid., p. 53.,

42 ibid., p. 16.
43 H. J. Laski, *Communism* (1927), p. 182.
44 G. D. H. Cole, *The Next Ten Years in British Social and Economic Policy* (Macmillan, 1929).
45 J. T. Murphy, Socialism by kind permission', *Communist Internationa*, 3.1 (15 October 1926), p. 18.
46 A. Marwick, *The Deluge: British Society and the First World War* (Macmillan, 1973), pp. 252–3.
47 G. D. H. Cole, *The Next Ten Years* p. 7.
48 ibid., p. 63.
49 ibid., p. 139.
50 J. M. Keynes, 'Can Lloyd George do it?', *Essays in Persuasion, Collected Writings* vol. 9 (Macmillan, 1972), p. 91.
51 D. Winch, *Economics and Policy* (Hodder and Stoughton, 1969), p. 124.
52 R. Skidelsky, *Politicians and the Slump* (Pelican Books, 1970).
53 Editorial: 'The Labour party and social democracy', *History Workshop Journal*, no. 2 (Autumn 1981), pp. 1–7.
54 ibid., p. 7.
55 See, e.g., J. Reynolds and K. Laybourn, *Labour Heartland: A History of the Labour Party in West Yorkshire During the Inter-War Years 1918–1939* (Bradford University Press, 1987).

Chapter 9   The 1930s

1 F. Brockway, *Inside the Left* (Allen and Unwin, 1942), pp. 238–9.
2 S. Cripps, 'Can socialism come by constitutional methods?', in C. Addison et al., *Politics of a Socialist Government* (Gollancz, 1933), p. 38.
3 H. J. Laski, preface to the 3rd edn of *A Grammar of Politics* (Allen and Unwin, 1925; 3rd edn, 1934).
4 H. J. Laski, *Democracy in Crisis* (Allen and Unwin, 1933), p. 233.
5 Quoted by P. Williams, *Hugh Gaitskell* (Oxford University Press, 1982), p. 65.
6 E. Durbin, *The Politics of Democratic Socialism* (Routledge, 1940; Routledge, 1957), pp. 240–4.
7 ibid., pp. 288–9.
8 ibid., p. 289.
9 ibid., p. 71.
10 ibid., p. 305.
11 ibid., p. 91.
12 M. Dobb, *Soviet Russia and the World* (Sidgwick and Jackson, 1932), p. 12.
13 ibid., pp. 50–1.
14 ibid., p. 78.
15 ibid., p. 81.
16 H. L. Beales, 'The political system', in M. I. Cole (ed.), *Twelve Studies in Soviet Russia* (Gollancz, 1933), p. 137.
17 ibid., p. 136.
18 S. Webb, 'The future of Soviet Communism', in G. D. H. Cole, *What is*

Ahead of Us? (Macmillan, 1937), pp. 127–8.

19 G. R. Mitchison, 'The Russian worker', in M. I. Cole, *Twelve Studies in Soviet Russia.*

20 H. L. Beales, 'The political system', p. 136.

21 Quoted in D. Caute, *The Fellow-Travellers: A Postscript to the Enlightenment* (Weidenfeld and Nicolson, 1973), p. 102.

22 B. Wooton, *Plan or No Plan* (Gollancz, 1934), pp. 308–9.

23 ibid., pp. 310–11.

24 ibid., p. 311.

25 See *Britain Without Capitalists: A Study of What Industry in a Soviet Britain Could Achieve by a Group of Economists, Scientists and Technicians* (Lawrence and Wishart, 1936), pp. 7–8 and 15.

26 ibid., pp. 414–15, 417–18.

27 Quoted by G. Werskey, *The Visible College* (Allen Lane, 1978), p. 194.

28 See I. Deutscher, *Stalin* (Pelican, 1966), p. 367.

29 See Werskey, *The Visible College*, pp. 187, 199, 176 and 169–70.

30 B. Pimlott, *Hugh Dalton* (Cape, 1985), p. 160.

31 ibid., p. 213.

32 Durbin, *The Politics of Democratic Socialism*, pp. 103–4.

33 E. Durbin, *New Jerusalems: The Labour Party and the Economics of Democratic Socialism* (Routledge and Kegan Paul 1985), p. 165.

34 See for example, E. A. Radice, 'The state and investment, in G. D. H. Cole (ed.), *Studies in Capital and Investment* (Gollancz, 1935), p. 310.

35 E. F. Wise, 'The control of finance and the financiers', in C. Addison et al., *Problems of a Socialist Government*, pp. 83–4.

36 G. D. H. Cole, *Principles of Economic Planning* (Macmillan, 1935), pp. 114–15 and 165–79.

37 Pimlott, *Hugh Dalton*, p. 224.

38 N. Branson, *History of the Communist Party of Great Britain 1927–41* (Lawrence and Wishart, 1985), p. 5.

39 See K. Newton, *The Sociology of British Communism* (Allen Lane, 1969), pp. 159–60.

40 P. Kingsford, *The Hunger Marches in Britain 1920–40* (Lawrence and Wishart, 1982) p. 22.

41 *Daily Worker*, 31 January 1933.

42 L. Trotsky, 'For New Communist Parties and the New International', 27 July 1933, in *Writings of Leon Trotsky 1933–34* (Pathfinder, New York, 1972), pp. 26–8.

43 See J. Callaghan, 'The background to "Entrism": Leninism and the British Labour Party', *Journal of Communist Studies*, 2.4 (December 1986), pp. 380–404.

44 *Democracy versus Dictatorship*, National Joint Council, March 1933.

45 R. Palme Dutt, *Democracy and Fascism: A Reply to the Labour Manifesto on Democracy versus Dictatorship* (CPGB, 1933), pp. 7–8.

46 *Communist and Other Organisations*, National Joint Council, June 1933.

47 P. Weiler, *British Labour and the Cold War* (Stanford University Press, 1988) p. 18.

48 ibid., p. 39.
49 ibid., p. 40.
50 J. F. Naylor, *Labour's International Policy* (Weidenfeld and Nicolson, 1969), p. 43.
51 A. Davidson, *The Theory and Practice of Italian Communism* (Merlin, 1932), p. 3.
52 J. Fyrth (ed.), *Britain, Fascism and the Popular Front* (Lawrence and Wishart, 1985), pp. 13–14.
53 ibid., p. 41.
54 ibid., pp. 62 and 71.
55 J. Jupp, 'The Left in Britain 1931–41' (MSc dissertation, London University, 1956), p. 182.
56 Brockway, *Inside the Left*, pp. 268–9.
57 J. Wood, *The Labour Left and the Constituency Labour Parties 1931–51* (unpublished PhD thesis, University of Warwick, 1982), p. 67.
58 Branson, *History of the Communist Party of Great Britain*, p. 191.
59 Caute, *The Fellow-Travellers*, p. 162.
60 S. Samuels, 'The Left Book Club', *Journal of Contemporary History* 1.2, p. 68; J. Symons, *The Thirties: A Dream Revolved* (Faber and Faber, 1975), p. 94.
61 J. Strachey, 'The Soviet trials', *Left News*, no. 15 (July 1938), p. 885.
62 K. Martin, 'Trotsky in Mexico', *New Statesman*, 10 April 1937.
63 Quoted by P. Deli, 'The image of the Russian purges in the *Daily Herald* and *New Statesman*, *Journal of Contemporary History*, 20.2 (April 1985), pp. 263–4.

Chapter 10   The Second World War

1 *Tribune* 25 August 1939.
2 J. Attfield and S. Williams (eds), *1939: The Communist Party and the War* (Lawrence and Wishart, 1984), p. 26.
3 D. Childs, 'The British Communist Party and the war 1939–41: old slogans revived', *Journal of Contemporary History*, 12 (1977), pp. 237–53, 240.
4 'The Man of Steel, *New Statesman*, 9 December 1939, p. 811.
5 G. Orwell, *Collected Essays, Journalism and Letters*, vol. 3 (Penguin 1970), p. 178.
6 B. Crick, *George Orwell: A Life* (Secker and Warburg, 1980), p. 318.
7 'The Man of Steel', p. 811.
8 ibid., p. 812.
9 J. Strachey, 'The war', *Left News*, December 1939, pp. 1410–11.
10 V. Gollancz, 'Show down', *Left News*, January 1940, pp. 1416–17.
11 H. Pollitt, *The War and the Labour Movement* (CPGB, June 1940); R. Palme Dutt, *We Fight For Life* (CPGB, November 1940).
12 *Daily Worker* 1 February 1940.
13 Quoted by V. Gollancz, *Russia and Ourselves* (Gollancz, 1941), p. 97.
14 Attfield and Williams (eds), *1939: The Communist Party and the War*, p. 32.

15　V. Gollancz, 'The lessons of France', *Left News*, July 1940, p. 1495; see also V. Gollancz (ed.) *The Betrayal of the Left* (Gollancz, 1941).
16　J. Strachey, 'The Communist party line now', *Left News*, July 1940.
17　Quoted by B. Jones, *The Russia Complex* (Manchester University Press, 1977), p. 35.
18　*Daily Herald*, 1 December 1939.
19　J. Hinton, 'Coventry Communism': a study of factory politics in the Second World War', *History Workshop Journal*, 10 (Autumn 1980). The figure for Metro-Vickers was given to me by Edmund Frow.
20　P. Addison, *The Road to 1945* (Quartet, 1977), p. 163.
21　ibid., p. 143.
22　A. Calder, *The People's War* (Cape, 1969), p. 18.
23　Addison, *The Road to 1945*, p. 143.
24　D. Winch, *Economics and Policy* (Hodder and Stoughton, 1969), p. 273.
25　B. Pimlott, *Hugh Dalton* (Cape, 1985), p. 397.
26　ibid., p. 398.
27　H. J. Laski, 'The Party and the future', 4 April 1942, *Laski/Labour Party Papers*, Labour Party archive, Walworth Road, London.
28　C. R. Attlee, *The Labour Party in Perspective* (Gollancz, 1937), pp. 157–8.
29　*LPACR*, 1942, pp. 95–6.
30　*LPACR*, 1943, p. 166.
31　G. D. H. Cole, *Europe, Russia and the Future* (Gollancz, 1941), p. 27.
32　ibid., p. 31.
33　ibid., p. 29.
34　ibid., pp. 31–2.
35　ibid., p. 31.
36　ibid., p. 34.
37　H. J. Laski, *Faith, Reason, and Civilisation* (Gollancz, 1944), pp. 45–6.
38　ibid., pp. 57–8.
39　ibid., p. 62.
40　H. J. Laski, *The Secret Battalion: An Examination of the Communist Attitude to the Labour Party* (Labour Party, 1946), p. 15.
41　'Are we bolshevising Europe?', *New Statesman and Nation*, 8 January 1944, p. 17.
42　*Tribune*, 7 April 1944.
43　*New Statesman*, editorial, 29 September 1945.
44　J. Schneer, *Labour's Conscience* (Unwin Hyman, 1988), p. 44.
45　Quoted ibid., p. 44.
46　G. Orwell, *Collected Essays, Journalism and Letters*, vol. 1: *1920–40* (Penguin, 1970), pp. 434–8.
47　S. E. Ambrose, *Rise to Globalism: American Foreign Policy Since 1938* (Penguin, 1985), p. 30.
48　P. Spriano, *Stalin and the European Communists* (Verso, 1985), p. 208.
49　D. Mayers, 'Soviet war aims and the Grand Alliance: George Kennan's views 1944–46', *Journal of Contemporary History*, 21.1 (January 1986), p. 57.
50　Quoted by Schneer, *Labour's Conscience*, pp. 18–19.
51　Ambrose, *Rise to Globalism*, p. 26.

52 H. Richter, *British Intervention in Greece* (Merlin, 1985), p. vii.
53 See J. T. Grantham, 'Hugh Dalton and the international post-war settlement: Labour party foreign policy formulation 1943–44', *Journal of Contemporary History*, 14.4 (1978).
54 E. Wertheimer, *Portrait of the Labour Party* (1929), p. 91.
55 T. D. Burridge *British Labour and Hitler's War* (Deutsch, 1976), p. 167.
56 ibid., p. 167.
57 J. Leruez, *Economic Planning and Politics in Britain* (Martin Robertson, 1975), p. 19.

Chapter 11   Welfare and Cold War

1 M. Foot, *Aneurin Bevan 1945–60* (Paladin, 1975), p. 13.
2 R. Palme Dutt, 'Notes of the month', *Labour Monthly*, April 1945.
3 See for example M. Djilas, *Conversations with Stalin* (Penguin, 1969).
4 H. Pollitt, *Looking Ahead* (CPGB, 1947), p. 88.
5 ibid., p. 90.
6 Quoted by J. Schneer, *Labour's Conscience* (Unwin Hyman, 1988), pp. 21–2.
7 K. O. Morgan, *Labour in Power 1945–51* (Oxford University Press, 1985), p. 39.
8 H. Dalton, *Practical Socialism For Britain* (Routledge, 1935), pp. 26–7, 247.
9 H. Dalton, B. Thomas, J. N. Reedman, T. J. Hughes, W. J. Leening, *Unbalanced Budgets* (Routledge, 1934), p. 457.
10 See D. Bryan, 'The Development of Revisionist Thought among Labour Intellectuals and Politicians 1931–64' (unpublished D. Phil, University of Oxford, 1984), p. 70.
11 K. Harris, *Attlee* (Weidenfeld and Nicolson, 1982), p. 326.
12 P. Armstrong, A. Glyn and J. Harrison, *Capitalism Since World War 2* (Fontana, 1984), p. 51.
13 R. M. Hathaway, *Ambiguous Partnership: Britain and America 1944–47* (Columbia University Press, 1981), pp. 28–9.
14 H. Pelling, *The Labour Governments 1945–51* (Macmillan, 1984), p. 56.
15 C. Barnett, *The Audit of War* (Macmillan, 1986), p. 159.
16 J. C. R. Dow, *The Management of the British Economy* (Cambridge University Press, 1964), p. 172; Morgan, *Labour in Power 1945–51*, p. 130.
17 A. Shonfield, *Modern Capitalism* (Oxford University Press, 1976), p. 90.
18 A. Oldfield, 'The Labour Party and planning 1934 or 1918?', *Bulletin of The Society for the Study of Labour History*, no. 25 (Autumn 1972), pp. 45–6.
19 R. H. S. Crossman, M. Foot and I. Mikardo, *Keep Left* (*New Statesman* pamphlet, May 1947), p. 11.
20 ibid., p. 11.
21 ibid., p. 25.
22 R. Ovendale (ed.), *The Foreign Policy of the British Labour Governments 1945–1951* (Leicester University Press, 1984), p. 11.
23 Crossman et al., *Keep Left*, p. 31.
24 ibid., p. 32.

25 Ovendale, *The Foreign Policy of the British Labour Governments* p. 4.
26 D. Cameron Watt, 'Britain, the United States and the opening of the Cold War', in Ovendale, *The Foreign Policy of the British Labour Governments*, p. 52.
27 See L. Freedman, *The Evolution of Nuclear Strategy* (Macmillan, 1981), p. 57.
28 S. E. Ambrose, *Rise to Globalism: American Foreign Policy Since 1938* (Penguin, 1985), p. 53.
29 A. Bullock, *Ernest Bevin: Foreign Secretary* (Oxford University Press, 1985), pp. 31 and 33.
30 D. K. Fieldhouse, 'The Labour Governments and the Empire-Commonwealth 1945-51', in Ovendale, *The Foreign Policy of the British Labour Governments*, p. 86.
31 Quoted in Pelling *The Labour Governments 1945-51* p. 150.
32 Fieldhouse, 'The Labour Governments and the Empire-Commonwealth', p. 88.
33 ibid., p. 89.
34 ibid., p. 95.
35 ibid., p. 98.
36 ibid., p. 98.
37 Pelling, *The Labour Governments*, p. 159.
38 I. Deutscher, *Stalin* (Pelican, 1966), p. 521.
39 Quoted by D. Horowitz, *From Yalta to Vietnam* (Penguin, 1967), p. 23.
40 Freedman, *The Evolution of Nuclear Strategy*, p. 57.
41 Pelling, *The Labour Governments*, p. 60.
42 D. Carlton, *Anthony Eden* (Allen and Unwin, 1981), pp. 280-1.
43 ibid., p. 186.
44 Pelling, *The Labour Governments* p. 49.
45 A. Foster, 'The politicians, public opinion and the press: the storm over British military intervention in Greece in December 1944', *Journal of Contemporary History*, 19.3 (1983) p. 488.
46 See *Labour Research* between 1945 and 1950 for reports on the saga of the World Federation of Trade Union.
47 See *Tribune*, 12 January 1945 and 24 August 1945, p. 1.
48 Crossman et al., *Keep Left*, p. 34.
49 *Socialist Commentary*, September 1945, p. 165.
50 Crossman et al., *Keep Left*, pp. 40-1.
51 Quoted in Schneer, *Labour's Conscience*, p. 44.
52 ibid., p. 44.
53 ibid., p. 45.
54 *Tribune*, 17 October 1947, p. 3.
55 M. Hudson, 'The Marshall standard of life', *Labour Monthly*, 3.12 (December 1948).
56 See K. Jeffrey and P. Hennessey, *States of Emergency: British Governments and Strikebreaking Since 1919* (Routledge and Kegan Paul, 1983), pp. 196 and 220-1.
57 *Tribune*, 30 January 1948, p. 3.

58 *Tribune*, 5 March 1948, p. 8.
59 *Tribune*, March 12 1948, p. 11.
60 *Tribune*, 19 March 1948, editorial.
61 *Tribune*, 26 March 1948, editorial.
62 *Tribune*, 23 April 1948, editorial.
63 Crossman et al., *Keep Left*, p. 35.
64 Schneer, *Labour's Conscience*, p. 72.
65 *Tribune*, 7 July 1950, editorial and p. 4.
66 A. Marwick, 'Middle opinion in the thirties: planning, progress, and 'political agreement', *English Historical Review* 79 (1964), pp. 287–94.
67 C. Benn, 'Comprehensive school reform and the 1945 Labour government', *History Workshop Journal*, no. 10 (Autumn 1980), pp. 197–203.
68 See R. Palme Dutt, *The Crisis of Britain and the British Empire* (Lawrence and Wishart, 1953), pp. 215–71.
69 See, e.g., the editorial 'Let's Stay in Africa', *Tribune*, 20 August 1948.
70 See M. Jenkins, *Bevanism: Labour's High Tide* (Spokesman, 1979), p. 70.

Chapter 12 Revisionism

1 G. D. H. Cole, *Socialist Economics* (Gollancz, 1950), p. 7.
2 ibid., p. 8.
3 C. A. R. Crosland, 'The transition from capitalism', in R. H. S. Crossman (ed.), *New Fabian Essays* (Turnstile Press, 1952), p. 35.
4 ibid., p. 37.
5 J. Burnham, *The Managerial Revolution* (1941; Bloomington, Ind. 1960).
6 See D. Bryan, 'The Development of Revisionist Thought Among Labour Intellectuals and Politicians 1931–64' (unpublished D. Phil., University of Oxford, 1984).
7 Crosland, 'The transition from capitalism', p. 39.
8 ibid., p. 43.
9 ibid., p. 40.
10 ibid., p. 44.
11 ibid., pp. 50–6.
12 J. Strachey, 'Tasks and achievement of British Labour', in Crossman, *New Fabian Essays*, pp. 207 and 208.
13 D. Healey, 'Power politics and the Labour Party', in Crossman, *New Fabian Essays*, p. 178.
14 ibid., p. 169.
15 R. H. S. Crossman, 'Towards a philosophy of socialism,' in *New Fabian Essays*, p. 27.
16 R. H. Tawney, 'British socialism today', *Socialist Commentary*, June 1952, p. 126.
17 A. Bevan, *In Place of Fear* (Quartet, 1978), p. 23.
18 ibid., p. 26.
19 ibid., p. 49.
20 ibid., pp. 133–42.

21 *LPACR*, 1955, pp. 111–19.
22 C. A. R. Crosland, *The Future of Socialism* (Cape, 1956), p. 29.
23 ibid., p. 39.
24 ibid., p. 61.
25 ibid., pp. 498 and 515.
26 H. Gaitskell, *Socialism and Nationalisation* (Fabian tract no. 300, July 1956), p. 3.
27 ibid., p. 5.
28 C. A. R. Crosland, 'About equality I', *Encounter*, 7 (July 1956), p. 5.
29 ibid., p. 7.
30 ibid., p. 7.
31 ibid., p. 9.
32 C. A. R. Crosland, 'About equality II: Is equal opportunity enough?', *Encounter*, 7 (August 1956), p. 39 and pp. 43–4.
33 ibid., pp. 42 and 43.
34 C. A. R. Crosland, 'About equality III: Education and the class systesm *Encounter*, 7 (September 1956), p. 27.
35 R. H. S. Crosman, *Socialism and the New Despotism* (Fabian tract no. 298, February 1958), p. 23.
36 L. Minkin, *The Labour Party Conference* (Allen and Unwin, 1978).
37 D. Campbell, *The Unsinkable Aircraft Carrier: American Military Power in Britain* (Paladin, 1986), p. 18.
38 D. Healey, *Cards on the Table: An Interpretation of Labour's Foreign Policy* (Labour Party, 1947), p. 4.
39 D. Healey, 'The Cominform and world communism', *International Affairs*, 24 (1948), p. 341.
40 Quoted in B. Reed and G. Williams, *Denis Healey* (Sidgwick and Jackson, 1971), p. 100.
41 ibid., p. 68.
42 S. Haseler, *The Gaitskellites* (Macmillan, 1969), p. 6.
43 ibid., pp. 26–7.
44 P. M. Williams (ed.), *The Diary of Hugh Gaitskell 1945–56* (Cape, 1983), p. 42 and p. 159.
45 ibid., p. 345.
46 ibid., p. 393.
47 ibid., pp. 545–6.
48 D. Healey (ed.), *The Curtain Falls: The Story of the Socialists in Eastern Europe*, foreword by Aneurin Bevan (Lincoln-Prager, 1951), p. 6.
49 J. Strachey, *Contemporary Capitalism* (Gollancz, 1956), pp. 273–6.
50 D. Healey, 'The new Russian empire', in *The Curtain Falls*, p. 22.
51 D. Healey, 'Britain and Europe', *Socialist Commentary*, May 1951, p. 111.
52 ibid., p. 113.
53 D. Healey, 'The defence of Western Europe', *Socialist Commentary*, October 1951, p. 234.
54 ibid., p. 235.
55 D. Healey, 'The Bomb that didn't go off', *Encounter*, 6 (July 1955).
56 D. Healey, 'When shrimps learn to whistle: Thoughts after Geneva',

International Affairs, 32.1 (January 1956). See also Socialist Union, *Socialism and Foreign Policy* (Brook House, 1953).

57 D. Healey, 'Prometheus bound', *Encounter*, 9 (December 1957), p. 75.
58 A. Bevan, 'What next for the Western communists?', *Tribune*, 22 June 1956.
59 *Tribune*, 26 October 1956.
60 *Tribune*, 16 November 1956.
61 Quoted in J. Campbell, *Nye Bevan and the Mirage of British Socialism* (Weidenfeld and Nicolson, 1987), pp. 332–3.
62 *Tribune*, 23 November 1956.
63 B. Castle, 'West does not want to disarm!', *Tribune*, 20 July 1956.
64 *Tribune*, 24 May 1957.
65 E. P. Thompson, 'At the point of decay', in E. P. Thompson (ed.), *Out of Apathy* (Stevens and Sons, 1960), p. 13.
66 See J. Saville, 'The Welfare State, *New Reasoner*, no. 3 (Winter 1957–8), and the reply by D. Thompson in *New Reasoner*, no. 4 (Spring 1958).
67 Thompson (ed.), *Out of Apathy*, pp. 3–4.
68 See for example B. Abel-Smith, 'Whose Welfare State?', in N. J. MacKenzie (ed.), *Conviction* (MacGibbon and Kee, 1958), pp. 55–6.
69 See *Forward*, 16 October 1959.
70 *LPACR*, 1959, p. 107.
71 ibid., p. 107.
72 P. S. Gupta, *Imperialism and the British Labour Movement* (Macmillan, 1975) p. 360.
73 B. Porter, *The Lion's Share: A Short History of British Imperialism 1850–1983* (Longman, 2nd edn 1983), p. 320.
74 *Socialist Union, Socialism and Foreign Policy* (Penguin, 1953), pp. 47–8.
75 LPACR, 1962, pp. 159–65.

Chapter 13 Pragmatism and Modernization

1 P. Foot, *Immigration and Race in British Politics* (Penguin, 1965), pp. 61 and 58.
2 *LPACR*, 1963, p. 134.
3 ibid., p. 135.
4 ibid., p. 140.
5 H. Wilson, *The Relevance of British Socialism* (Weidenfeld and Nicolson, 1964), pp. 11 and 16.
6 ibid., pp. 22–3.
7 ibid., p. 24.
8 ibid., pp. 35–7 and 52.
9 ibid., p. 28.
10 L. J. Robins, *The Reluctant Party: Labour and the EEC 1961–75* (Hesketh, 1979), p. 45.
11 H. Wilson, *The Relevance of British Socialism*, p. 56.
12 H. Wilson, *The Labour Government 1964–70: A Personal Memoir* (Weidenfeld and Nicolson 1971), p. xvii.

13 D. Howell, *British Social Democracy* (Croom Helm 1976), p. 253.
14 C. Ponting, *Breach of Promise* (Hamish Hamilton, 1989), p. 48.
15 ibid., p. 49.
16 C. A. R. Crosland, *Socialism Now* (Cape, 1974), pp. 21 and 18.
17 ibid., pp. 25–6. See also P. Townsend, *Labour and Inequality* (Fabian Society, 1972), for an equally damning indictment of the Labour government's performance.
18 C. A. R. Crosland, *The Conservative Enemy: A Programme of Radical Reform for the 1960s* (Cape, 1962), pp. 58 and 55.
19 D. Jay, *Socialism in the New Society* (Longmans, 1962), p. 181.
20 S. Patterson, *Immigration and Race in Britain 1960–67* (Oxford University Press, 1969), pp. 412–13.
21 R. Miles and A. Phizacklea, *White Man's Country: Racism in British Politics* (Pluto Press, 1984), p. vii.
22 K. Coates, *The Crisis of British Socialism* (Spokesman, 1972), p. 77.
23 L. Minkin, *The Labour Party Conference* (Allen and Unwin, 1978), pp. 86–7.
24 B. Castle, *The Castle Diaries 1964–70* (Weidenfeld, 1984), p. 794.
25 Coates, *Crisis of British Socialism*, p. 77.
26 Ponting, *Breach of Promise*, p. 29.
27 ibid., p. 339.
28 H. Kissinger, *The White House Years* (Weidenfeld and Nicolson, 1979), p. 219.
29 R. Miliband, *Parliamentary Socialism*, (Merlin, 1961).
30 See J. Callaghan, *British Trotskyism* (Blackwell, 1984) and *The Far Left in British Politics* (Blackwell, 1987).
31 S. Rowbotham, Lyn Segal and Hilary Wainwright, *Beyond the Fragments: Feminism and the Making of Socialism* (Merlin, 1979), p. 95.
32 J. Mitchell, *Women's Estate* (Penguin, 1971), p. 54.
33 Bevan warned that 'the problem of democracy in the Party must be solved if we are to make further substantial advance. Unless we can give the membership of the Party a greater sense of participation in the formulation of the policies of the Re Party. We shall go into decline.' *Tribune*, 2 March 1956.
34 R. Williams (ed.), *May Day Manifesto 1968* (Penguin, 1968), p. 156.
35 ibid., p. 173.
36 M. Kidron, *Western Capitalism Since the War* (Penguin, 1968), p. 104.
37 R. Blackburn, *Red Mole*, 1.3 (15 April 1970).
38 J. Foster and C. Woolfson, *The Politics of the UCS Work-in* (Lawrence and Wishart, 1986), p. 3.
39 See *International*, 2.1 (1973), and E. Mandel, *Late Capitalism* (New Left Books, 1972).
40 R. Hyman, 'Industrial conflict and the political economy', *Socialist Register*, 1973 (Merlin, 1973), p. 125.
41 R. Rosewall, *The Struggle for Workers' Power* (International Socialism pamphlet, n.d.), p. 26.
42 T. Cliff, *The Crisis: Social Contract or Socialism?* (Pluto Press, 1975), p. 111.

Chapter 14 The Rise and Fall of the Left

1 H. Pollitt, 'What Margate means' (1926), in *Selected Articles and Speeches* vol. 1: *1919–36* (Lawrence and Wishart, 1953), pp. 32–4.
2 K. Coates, 'Socialists and the Labour Party', *Socialist Register*, 1973 (Merlin, 1973), p. 155.
3 For a detailed account see M. Hatfield, *The House the Left Built* (Gollancz, 1978).
4 S. Holland, *The Socialist Challenge* (Quartet, 1975).
5 K. Coates, *Essays on Industrial Democracy* (Spokesman, 1971), pp. 10–11.
6 Holland, *The Socialist Challenge*, p. 69.
7 Quoted by D. Coates, *Labour in Power?* (Longman, 1980), p. 5.
8 *Labour's Programme 1973* (Labour Party, 1973), p. 3.
9 T. Benn, *The New Politics: A Socialist Reconnaissance* (Fabian tract no. 402., September 1970), p. 23.
10 B. Hindess, *The Decline of Working Class Politics* (Paladin, 1971), pp. 98–100.
11 ibid., p. 108.
12 See H. Elcock, 'Tradition and change in Labour Party politics: the decline and fall of the City Boss', *Political Studies*, 40.3 (September 1981).
13 P. Jenkins, 'The Labour Party and the politics of transition', *Socialist Register*, 1977 (Merlin, 1977), p. 26.
14 L. Minkin, *The Labour Party Conference* (Allen Lane, 1978), p. 40.
15 I. Budge and I. Crewe (eds), *Party Identification and Beyond* (Wiley, 1976), p. 35.
16 ibid., pp. 35 and 39.
17 P. Anderson, 'Problems of socialist strategy', in P. Anderson (ed.), *Towards Socialism* (Fontana, 1965), pp. 251–2.
18 New Statesman, 28 September 1979.
19 Paul Whiteley and Ian Gordon, *New Statesman*, 11 January 1980, p. 41.
20 See K. Coates, *The Social Democrats* (Spokesman, 1983).
21 N. Bosanquet and P. Townsend (eds), *Labour and Equality* (Heinemann, 1980), p. 39.
22 ibid., p. 40.
23 ibid., p. 41.
24 See *Contemporary Record*, 1.3 (Autumn 1987), Symposium on the Winter of Discontent, pp. 34–44.
25 Quoted by P. Seyd, *The Rise and Fall of the Labour Left* (Macmillan, 1987), p. 93.
26 T. Benn, *Parliament, People and Power* (New Left Books, 1982).
27 See P. Hain, *The Democratic Alternative: A Socialist Response to Britain's Crisis* (Penguin, 1983).
28 J. Gyford, *The Politics of Local Socialism* (Allen and Unwin, 1985), p. ix.
29 ibid., p. 8.
30 *British Perspectives 1977*, internal document, September 1977, p. 15.
31 See J. Callaghan, 'The British road to Eurocommunism', in M. Waller and M. Fennema, *Communist Parties in Western Europe: Decline or Adaptation* (Blackwell, 1988).

32 D. Purdy, 'British capitalism since the war', part 2, in *Marxism Today*, October 1976, p. 316.

33 See S. Hall, 'The Great Moving Right Show', *Marxism Today*, January 1979.

34 I. Crewe, 'The Labour Party and the electorate', in D. Kavanagh (ed.), *The Politics of the Labour Party* (Allen and Unwin, 1982), p. 10.

35 ibid., p. 28.

36 See, for example, H. Himmelweit, P. Humphreys, Marianne Jaefer and Michael Katz, *How Voters Decide* (Academic Press, 1981), p. 197.

37 J. Bodington (ed.), *Speeches by Tony Benn* (Spokesman, 1974), p. 31.

38 P. Whiteley, *The Labour Party in Crisis* (Methuen, 1983), pp. 4–5.

39 Quoted by P. J. Hubert, 'Party and propaganda in the newspapers of the Left' (unpublished PhD thesis, University of Leeds, 1988), p. 119.

40 D. Martin, *Bringing Common Sense to the Common Market: A Left Agenda For Europe* (Fabian tract 525, March 1988), p. 3.

41 M. Newman, *Socialism and European Unity* (Junction Books, 1983), p. 170.

42 N. Kinnock, preface to Martin, *Bringing Common Sense to the Common Market*.

43 K. Coates, 'Europe Without Frontiers', *New Socialist*, no. 59 (February/March 1989), p. 36.

44 K. Coates, review of 'Thatcherism', ibid., p. 51.

45 Re-thinking about the role of planning was stimulated by A. Nove, *The Economics of Feasible Socialism* (Allen and Unwin, 1983) especially chapters 1 and 2.

46 M. Jacques and F. Mulhearn (eds), *The Forward March of Labour Halted?* (Verso, 1981). See Ken Gill's essay, especially p. 21. See also E. J. Hobsbawm, 'Syndicalism and the working class', *New Society*, 5 April 1979, pp. 8–10.

47 S. Hall and M. Jacques (eds), *The Politics of Thatcherism* (Lawrence and Wishart, 1983), p. 16.

48 See A. Gamble. *The Free Economy and the Strong State: The Politics of Thatcherism* (Macmillan, 1988).

49 See T. Cliff and D. Gluckstein. *The Labour Party: A Marxist History* (Bookmarks, 1988), pp. 378–9.

50 ibid., pp. 379–81.

51 Labour Party, *Statement of Democratic Socialist Aims and Values* (Labour Party, 1988), p. 11.

50 Labour Party, *Social Justice and Economic Efficiency: First Report of Labour's Policy Review for the 1990s* (Labour Party, 1988), pp. 3, 5 and 10.

53 See *New Statesman and Society*, 19 may 1989, for a number of surveys of the policy review, second stage.

54 CPGB, *Manifesto For New Times: A Communist Party Strategy for the 1990s* (CPGB, June 1989), pp. 6–7.

55 ibid., p. 9.

56 ibid., p. 10.

57 ibid., p. 7.

58 See Ellen Meiksins Wood, *The Retreat From Class: A New 'True' Socialism* (Verso, 1986), and R. Miliband, 'The New Revisionism in Britain', *New Left Review*, no. 150 (March/April 1985).

59 CPGB, *Manifesto For New Times*, p. 3.

Select Bibliography

Useful collections of British socialist thought can be found in H. Pelling, *The Challenge of Socialism* (Black, 1954) and A. Wright, *British Socialism* (Longman, 1983). Of the many histories of the Labour Party, see G. D. H. Cole, *History of the Labour Party From 1914* (Routledge and Kegan Paul, 1948), R. Miliband, *Parliamentary Socialism* (Merlin, 1961), D. Howell, *British Social Democracy* (Croom Helm, 1976), J. Hinton, *Labour and Socialism* (Wheatsheaf, 1983), T. Cliff and D. Gluckstein, *The Labour Party: A Marxist History* (Bookmarks, 1988) and J. Saville, *The Labour Movement in Britain* (Faber and Faber, 1988).

M. Beer, *History of British Socialism* (Bell, 1929), is still one of the best accounts of early socialist thought in Britain, while for a recent commentary on ideological developments in the Labour Party see G. Foote, *The Labour Party's Political Thought* (Croom Helm, 1985). The internal politics of the party is also covered in quite different ways by L. Minkin, *The Labour Party Conference* (Allen Lane, 1978); E. Shaw, *Discipline and Discord in the Labour Party* (Manchester University Press, 1987), and H. Wainwright, *Labour: A Tale of Two Parties* (Hogarth Press, 1987). The Marxist and Trotskyist Left is covered in J. Callaghan, *The Far Left in British Politics* (Blackwell, 1987), and a good account of the Communist Party of Great Britain can be found in N. Branson, *History of the Communist Party of Great Britain 1927–1941* (Lawrence and Wishart, 1985).

Primary Sources

A. Bevan, *In Place of Fear* (1952; Quartet, 1978)

G. D. H. Cole, *Self-Government in Industry* (1917; Hutchinson, 1972)

G. D. H. Cole, *Guild Socialism Re-stated* (Macmillan, 1920)

G. D. H. Cole, *The Next Ten Years in British Social and Economic Policy* (Macmillan, 1929)

Communist Party of Great Britain, *Manifesto For New Times: A Communist Party Strategy For the 1990s* (CPGB, 1989)

J. Connolly, *Selected Political Writings*, ed. and introduced by O. Dudley Edwards and B. Ransom (Cape, 1973)

C. A. R. Crosland, *The Future of Socialism* (Cape, 1956)

C. A. R. Crosland, *The Conservative Enemy* (Cape, 1962)

R. H. S. Crossman (ed.), *New Fabian Essays* (Turnstile Press, 1952)

H. Dalton, *Practical Socialism for Britain* (Routledge, 1935)

E. Durbin, *The Politics of Democratic Socialism* (Routledge, 1940)

Fabian Society, *Fabian Essays in Socialism* (Swan Sonnenschein, 1889)

J. Bruce Glasier, *The Meaning of Socialism* (Independent Labour Party, 2nd edn 1925)

S. Holland, *The Socialist Challenge* (Quartet, 1975)

H. M. Hyndman, *The Historical Basis of Socialism in England* (Kegan Paul, 1883)

H. J. Laski, *Authority in the Modern State* (Yale University Press, 1919)

H. J. Laski, *Democracy in Crisis* (Allen and Unwin, 1933)

J. R. MacDonald, *Socialism and Government* (Independent Labour Party, 1909)

T. Mann, *Tom Mann's Memoirs* (Labour Publishing Company, 1923)

R. Miliband, *Parliamentary Socialism* (Merlin, 1961)

M. Morris (ed.), *William Morris: Artist, Writer, Socialist* (Blackwell, 1936)

A. L. Morton (ed.), *Political Writings of William Morris* (Lawrence and Wishart, 1973)

R. Palme Dutt, *The Crisis of Britain and the British Empire* (Lawrence and Wishart, 1953)

G. B. Shaw, *Fabianism and the Empire* (Grant Richards, 1900)

J. Strachey, *The Coming Struggle For Power* (The Modern Library, New York, 1935)

J. Strachey, *Contemporary Capitalism* (Gollancz, 1956)

S. Rowbotham, Lyn Segal and Hilary Wainwright, *Beyond the Fragments: Feminism and the Making of Socialism* (Merlin, 1979)

R. H. Tawney, *Equality* (Allen and Unwin, 1931)

R. H. Tawney, *The Acquisitive Society* (1921; Wheatsheaf, 1983)

B. Webb, *My Apprenticeship* (Cambridge University Press, 1979)

B. Webb and S. Webb, *A Constitution for the Socialist Commonwealth* (1920)

R. Williams (ed.), *May Day Manifesto 1968* (Penguin, 1968)

B. Wooton, *Plan or No Plan* (Gollancz, 1934)

Secondary Sources

1880–1900

H. Collins, *The Marxism of the Social Democratic Federation*, in A. Briggs and J. Saville (eds), *Essays in Labour History 1886–1923* (Macmillan, 1971)

D. Howell, *British Workers and the Independent Labour Party 1888–1906* (Manchester University Press, 1983)

Y. Kapp, *Eleanor Marx*, vol. 2: *The Crowded Years 1884–98* (Virago, 1979)

H. Pelling, *Origins of the Labour Party* (Oxford University Press, 2nd edn, 1965)

S. Pierson, *Marxism and the Origins of British Socialism* (Cornell University Press, 1973)

E. P. Thompson, *William Morris: Romantic to Revolutionary* (Merlin, 1977)

C. Tsuzuki, *H. M. Hyndman and British Socialism* (Oxford University Press, 1961)

S. Yeo, 'A new life: the religion of Socialism in Britain 1883-96, in *History Workshop Journal*, no. 4 (Autumn 1977)

1900-1920

R. Challinor, *The Origins of British Bolshevism* (Croom Helm, 1977)

S. T. Glass, *The Responsible Society: The Ideas of Guild Socialism* (Longmans, 1966)

J. Hinton, *The First Shop Stewards Movement* (Allen and Unwin, 1973)

B. Holton, *British Syndicalism 1900–1914* (Pluto Press, 1976)

D. Marquand, *Ramsay MacDonald* (Cape, 1977)

R. Page Arnot, *The Impact of the Russian Revolution in Britain* (Lawrence and Wishart, 1967)

B. Pribićević, *The Shop Stewards Movement and Workers Control 1910–22* (Blackwell, 1959)

L. Thompson, *The Enthusiasts* (Gollancz, 1971)

A. W. Wright, *G. D. H. Cole and Socialist Democracy* (Clarendon Press, 1979)

1920-1940

N. Branson, *History of the Communist Party of Great Britain 1927–41* (Lawrence and Wishart, 1985)

F. Brockway, *Inside the Left* (Allen and Unwin, 1942)

D. Caute, *The Fellow-Travellers* (Weidenfeld and Nicolson, 1973)

E. Durbin, *New Jerusalems: The Labour Party and the Economics of Democratic Socialism* (Routledge and Kegan Paul, 1985)

D. Howell, *A Lost Left* (Manchester University Press, 1986)

P. Kingsford, *The Hunger Marches in Britain 1920–40* (Lawrence and Wishart, 1982)

S. McIntyre, *A Proletarian Science: Marxism in Britain 1917–33* (Cambridge University Press, 1980)

J. T. Murphy, *Preparing For Power* (Pluto Press, 1972)

J. T. Murphy, *New Horizons* (John Lane, Bodley Head, 1941)

R. Skidelsky, *Politicians and the Slump* (Pelican Books, 1970)

1940-1960

P. Addison, *The Road to 1945* (Quartet, 1977)

A. Bullock, *Ernest Bevin: Foreign Secretary* (Oxford University Press, 1985)

T. D. Burridge, *British Labour and Hitler's War* (Deutsch, 1976)

A. Calder, *The People's War* (Cape, 1969)

J. Campbell, *Nye Bevan and the Mirage of British Socialism* (Weidenfeld and Nicolson, 1987)

M. Foot, *Aneurin Bevan 1945–60* (Paladin, 1975)

S. Haseler, *The Gaistskellites* (Macmillan, 1969)

M. Jenkins, *Bevanism: Labour's High Tide* (Spokesman, 1979)

J. Leruez, *Economic Planning and Politics in Britain* (Martin Robertson, 1975)

K. O. Morgan, *Labour in Power 1945–51* (Oxford University Press, 1985)

G. Orwell, *The Lion and the Unicorn* (Penguin Books, 1982)

R. Ovendale (ed.), *The Foreign Policy of the British Labour Governments 1945–1951* (Leicester University Press, 1984)

B. Pimlott, *Hugh Dalton* (Cape, 1985)

J. Schneer, *Labour's Conscience* (Unwin Hyman, 1988)

A. Warde, *Consensus and Beyond* (Manchester University Press, 1982)

E. P. Thompson (ed.), *Out of Apathy* (Stevens, 1960)

P. Weiler, *British Labour and the Cold War* (Stanford University Press, 1988)

P. M. Williams, *Hugh Gaitskell* (Oxford University Press, 1982)

1960–1980

P. Anderson (ed.), *Towards Socialism* (Fontana, 1965)

T. Benn, *The New Politics: A Socialist Reconnaissance* (Fabian Tract no. 402, September 1970)

T. Benn, *Arguments For Socialism* (Cape, 1979)

T. Benn, *Parliament, People, and Power* (New Left Books, 1982)

D. Coates, *Labour in Power?* (Longman, 1980)

K. Coates, *The Crisis of British Socialism* (Spokesman, 1972)

A. Gamble, *The Free Economy and the Strong State: the Politics of Thatcherism* (Macmillan, 1988)

J. Gyford, *The Politics of Local Socialism* (Allen and Unwin, 1985)

P. Hain, *The Democratic Alternative: A Socialist Response to Britain's Crisis* (Penguin, 1983)

S. Hall and M. Jacques (eds), *The Politics of Thatcherism* (Lawrence and Wishart, 1983)

R. Hattersley, *Choose Freedom: The Future For Democratic Socialism* (Penguin, 1987)

G. Hodgson, *Labour at the Crossroads* (Martin Robertson, 1981)

M. Jacques and F. Mulhearn (eds), *The Forward March of Labour Halted?* (Verso, 1981)

A. Nove, *The Economics of Feasible Socialism* (Allen and Unwin, 1983)

C. Ponting, *Breach of Promise* (Hamish Hamilton, 1989)

P. Seyd, *The Rise and Fall of the Labour Left* (Macmillan, 1987)

P. Foot, *Immigration and Race in British Politics* (Penguin, 1965)

P. Townsend, *Labour and Inequality* (Fabian Society, 1972)

Index

Index by Keith Seddon